HIGH LIGHTS ON HYMNISTS
AND THEIR HYMNS

AMS PRESS
NEW YORK

HIGH LIGHTS ON HYMNISTS AND THEIR HYMNS

"Hymns are the exponents of the inmost piety of the church; they are crystalline tears, or blossoms of joy, or holy prayers, or incarnated raptures. They are jewels which the church has worn, the pearls, the diamonds, and the precious stones, formed into amulets, more potent against sorrow and sadness than the most famous charms of wizard or magician. Angels sat at the grave's mouth, and so hymns are the angels—that rise up out of our griefs and darkness and dismay."

Henry Ward Beecher.

PUBLISHED BY THE AUTHOR

CAROLINE LEONARD GOODENOUGH

ROCHESTER, MASSACHUSETTS

1931

Library of Congress Cataloging in Publication Data

Goodenough, Caroline Louisa (Leonard) 1856–
    High lights on hymnists and their hymns.

    1. Hymns—History and criticism. 2. Hymn
writers. 3. Hymns—Indexes. I. Title.
BV310.G6 1974   245   72-1626
ISBN 0-404-08310-2

Reprinted from the edition of 1931, Rochester
First AMS edition published in 1974
Manufactured in the United States of America

AMS PRESS INC.
NEW YORK, N. Y.   10003

1821900

TABLE OF CONTENTS

CHAPTER I

INTRODUCTORY

"Work thou for pleasure, paint or sing or carve
The thing thou lovest, though the body starve.
Who works for glory, misses oft the goal.
Who works for money, coins his very soul.
Work for work's sake then, and it may be
That these things shall be added unto thee."
—from Good Stories, April 1931.

EVERY action in life has both a cause and an occasion. The underlying cause of the writing of the following chapters is my lifelong interest in hymns, which I can truly say "have been my songs in the house of my pilgrimage." This transcendent interest in hymns doubtless began when, an unconscious babe on my mother's breast, I was lulled to sleep by her singing to me, as to all her children, Watts' cradle hymn, "Hush, my dear, lie still and slumber." Later this love of hymns was fostered by the family custom, still preserved, of singing hymns in the twilight of each Sunday evening. This was the supremely sacred hour of the week in my childhood's home in the old farmhouse by Lake Nipinickett. Something soft and deep struck home to the heart in those solemn and hallowed evenings.

So much for the cause of these chapters; now to speak of the occasion of writing them.

I had returned to our ancestral home in Massachusetts from my missionary life in Africa, and found waiting my attention many notes left by my literary sister, Mary Hall Leonard. Some of these were upon the margins of an old hymn book and related to the various hymns contained therein and their composers.

I did not at first discover this mine of spiritual wealth. I chanced upon it in the following way: The old hymn book was not with my sister's papers, but was stacked up with similar books in a secluded part of the house. I went to this pile to obtain material for my solace when attacking the never empty mending basket. I have a lifelong custom of making household tasks easier by singing hymns when my hands are busy. Among these books the old hymn book with my sister's notations was discovered. I read the notes with fascination, and mentally resolved that, when the requisite leisure was available, I would use them as the basis of a magazine article on hymnists. Such an opportunity seemed to present itself in the summer of 1928, when I was for the most part alone for several weeks. I began writing with the idea that one magazine article could contain all I had to say on the subject of hymns. I soon discovered that I was launched on a vast sea of exploration in the lives of the wonderful people who have enriched our literature in what I believe is the most valuable part of it, with the exception of the sacred scriptures. I hope that others may enjoy the little snapshots of these characters which are here furnished. For convenience of reference I have arranged them in each chapter in alphabetical rather than in chronological order.

CHILDHOOD'S SUNDAY NIGHT

We used to sit on Sunday nights and sing
   Until the daylight faded into gloom
That blotted out the objects in the room;
   I could recount each well-remembered thing,
And tell the sweet old songs that used to ring
   Out on the summer dusk, hymn after hymn,
Until our hearts were soft and eyes were dim.
   I never hear those songs except they bring
Vision of faces I shall see no more
   Until they greet me on a heavenly shore.
O household band, now sundered wide and far!
   O fair young brows, now lined with care and pain!
O tender tones we ne'er shall hear again
   Till we with them have joined the angels' song.

CHAPTER II

THE PATRISTIC HYMNISTS.

"The Beautiful Book makes the Christian Era to begin with a burst of song. In Acts and the Epistles there occur what seem to be snatches from early hymns."—*From Matt. 26:30 we infer that Jesus himself was accustomed to sing hymns with His disciples.*

EMPEROR ADRIAN
76-138 A. D.

"Animula vagula blandula
  Hospes comesque corporis" *

These are the opening lines of Adrian's death-bed address to his soul. He of course was a heathen and not at all a Christian hymnist, and he would have no place in this category, were it not that the above lines were in the mind of Alexander Pope when he wrote the old hymn which begins:

"Vital spark of heavenly flame,
  Quit, oh quit this mortal frame."

Adrian was the successor of the Emperor Trajan. He was absent from Rome when Trajan died, but the army in Syria, of which he was in command, proclaimed him Emperor, and the Senate ratified the appointment. Adrian was in general a conciliatory ruler with a comprehensive view of his office, yet he was at times jealous and cruel. He was a man of ability, fond of poetry and philosophy and the cultus of Greece. He took a celebrated journey, mostly on foot, to Gaul, Germany, and Britain, where he built a wall extending from the Solway to the Tyne. He also visited Spain, Egypt, Asia Minor, and Greece. His mournful address to his soul is in strong contrast to the note of Christian triumph in Pope's hymn above quoted.

---

* Pope thus translates Adrian's dying address to his soul: "Alas, my soul! Thou pleasing companion to this body, thou fleeting thing that art now deserting it, whither art thou flying? To what unknown region? Thou art ·all trembling, fearful, and pensive. Now what has become of thy former wit and humor? Thou shall jest and be gay no more."

Saint Ambrose of Milan

340-397 A. D.

"We praise Thee, O God;
  We acknowledge Thee to be the Lord;"
All the earth doth worship Thee, the Father Everlasting."
The opening lines of the great "Te Deum"* are attributed
to St. Ambrose and were doubtless sung in his cathedral at
Milan, but it is believed that they represent a still more
ancient hymn. Ambrose was born in Gaul, probably near
Treves where his father was Prefect. When he was in the
cradle his astonished nurse noted that a swarm of bees
clustered about his mouth without harming him. His father,
who recalled that a similar incident was related about Plato,
regarded this as a good omen for his son, who was sent early
to Milan for education as a lawyer. The boy distinguished
himself and was appointed Prefect of Upper Italy and later
consecrated as a Bishop. His anniversary is cherished as a
fête in the Romish church. He was gentle, but could be
stern toward wrong doers, even repulsing the Emperor
Theodosius from his church door on account of his cruelty. St.
Ambrose was himself persecuted through Justina, the mother
of the Emperor. This is referred to by Augustine, who was
baptized by Ambrose and regarded him with great affection
as his spiritual father.

The Te Deum is perhaps the most stately hymn or chant
of the ages. It has accompanied martyrs to the stake. It
was sung by the crew of Columbus as they fell weeping into
each others' arms when they sighted the first gray outlines
of the shores of the New World.

---

* In an address by Sir John Pease Fry, broadcasted from New Castle
on Tyne and printed in the Friends' Intelligencer of Sept. 3, 1927, are
the following remarks: "Perhaps the most wonderful verse of the most
magnificent of all hymns of praise and thanksgiving, the Te Deum, is
that which concludes the glorification of Christ—
  'When Thou hadst overcome the sharpness of death
  Thou didst open the Kingdom of Heaven to all believers.'
  The Kingdom is an everlasting Kingdom based on perfect law, order,
and harmony, and those seeking to enter must obey its laws. Instead
of this, what do we see around us? Want, strife, bitterness, sorrow,
and suffering beyond belief, evils that don't bear thinking of, nothing
approaching a Kingdom of God; and why? Because millions of people
in so-called Christian countries know nothing about the Kingdom. Some
can't see it; others deliberately turn their backs on their Creator."

Ambrose has written other hymns which have been translated into English and are in use. One of these begins:

> "O Christ, with each returning morn
> Thine image to my heart is borne."

This was translated by John Chandler an English translator 1806-1876. There are also a number of Latin hymns of unknown authorship which are called Ambrosian.

SAINT ANATOLIUS

d. 458 A. D.

> "Fierce was the wild billow,*
> Dark was the night,
> Oars labored heavily,
> Foam glimmered white;
> Trembled the mariners,
> Peril was nigh;
> Then said the God of God,
> 'Peace! It is I!'

> Ridge of the mountain wave,
> Lower thy crest!
> Wail of Euroclydon,
> Be thou at rest!
> Peril can never be,
> Sorrow must fly,
> Where saith the Light of Light—
> 'Peace! It is I!'

---

* The first line of Neale's translation sings much better if the last two words are transposed thus: "Fierce was the billow wild." This avoids putting the accent on the last syllable of billow, instead of on the first where it properly belongs.
This hymn is a special favorite with me.
Anatolius wrote another beautiful hymn, Neale's translation of which begins "The day is past and over."

> Jesus, Deliverer,
> Come Thou to me;
> Soothe Thou my voyaging
> Over life's sea.
> Then, when the storm of death
> Roars sweeping by,
> Whisper, O Truth of Truth,
> 'Peace! It is I!'

This vivid hymn was written by a Greek ecclesiastical poet of Constantinople, who was an ambassador to the Byzantine court, and later Pontiff of Ephesus, and later still, Patriarch of Constantinople. He lived in a stormy period of religious persecution, during which he exerted a peaceful influence. The splendid translation of it is by John Mason Neale, written in 1862.

SAINT ANDREW OF CRETE

660-732 A. D.

> "Whence shall my tears begin?
> What first fruits shall I bear
> Of sorrow for my sin?
> Or how my woes declare?
> O Thou, the merciful and gracious one,
> Forgive the foul transgression I have done."

This fine penitential hymn was written first in Greek by a Jerusalem monk, who was born at Damascus and died near Mytelene in Crete. His hymns have been translated into English by John Mason Neale.

Here is the closing stanza of another of Saint Andrew's hymns called "Triumph in Christ."

> "Well I know thy trouble,
> O my servant true!
> Thou art very weary,
> I was weary too!
> But that toil shall make thee
> Some day all my own,
> And the end of sorrow
> Shall be near my throne."

AURELIUS AUGUSTINUS

d. 430 A. D. at Hippo

It is impossible to omit St. Augustine from the catalogue of patristic hymnists, although I am unable to attribute any familiar hymns to his authorship. "His story is one of the immortal adventures of the soul of man." The modern story of personality may be said to begin with his Confessions. He likened himself to a derelict ship. "And Thou wast at the helm, but very secretly." No man in Latin Christianity had so deep an influence on the church. He is a dynamic being who speaks with the power of a burning experience. There are some of his pages on which men will always shed tears. He said, "The most deadly sin of man is pride."

CLEMENT OF ALEXANDRIA

170-220 A. D.

'Shepherd of tender youth
Guiding in love and truth
Through devious ways—"

These are the opening lines of Dr. Henry Dexter's translation of what is called the earliest Christian hymn. However, there were earlier Christian hymns, doubtless, only they are not seemingly preserved, at least not in entirety. Pliny the younger refers to Christians as "singing hymns when they met before daylight on a fixed day." Pliny was born in the north of Italy in 61 A. D., so he antedated Clement by 100 years.

Clement was born in Athens of heathen parents. He travelled extensively when young in Italy, Syria, Assyria, and Tiberias, in search of knowledge. It may be that at that period of his life he answered to a supposable description of him given by Christophers in his book on hymnists as "A human form dressed in wash leather, with a sallow face expressive of quiet earnestness and high purpose, the lustrous depths of his upturned eyes revealing the joy of his communion with heaven." This figure is occupying an oasis near the desert pass of Mt. Kallel, where were a few palms, three springs, a little garden where were growing pot herbs—onions and dourah—from here issued streams of hymns and songs which helped to preserve the spiritual life of a cloistered church.

After Clement's conversion to Christianity, he settled in Alexandria, which was at that time a place of palaces, libraries, and lecture halls. It was "like a great centre of telegraphic communication, mysteriously linking itself with all the outstanding points in the world of thought." Clement was connected with the Alexandrian church, where he held a music school in which he and his pupils used to sing hymns. One of these pupils deserves special mention, and at the risk of seeming discursive, I must digress to tell of him. His name was Origen, (186-254 A.D.) and he is perhaps more celebrated than is Clement himself. I am not aware that Origen wrote hymns, but he is called the father of biblical criticism and exegesis. He was the son of Leonidas, who died a martyr in the persecution of the churches when Origen was seventeen years of age. Had it not been for his impoverished mother and her children, Origen would have been a voluntary martyr at that time. He was a man of fiery religious zeal which led him to mutilate himself in accordance with his interpretation of Matthew 19:12, an act he afterward deeply regretted. The amount of writing that went through the busy brain and hands of Origen was simply enormous. He had at one time fourteen secretaries and copyists writing for him. One wonders how he managed to pay this force of helpers, as the church paid him no salary for his services as a catechist, and he was forced to part with his dearly loved collection of classical authors for a daily stipend of 4 oboli (two pence a day) in order to supply his extremely limited needs.

Both Clement and Origen were considered heretical in doctrine, and for that reason Clement has never been canonized as a saint, and as for Origen, who did not believe either in the plenary inspiration of the Bible or in eternal damnation—his writings so displeased both the Roman and Greek Church authorities that an interdict was laid on even the copying of them and only fragments are preserved. Thus are linked together two pioneers in independent thought. As such they should be held in honor all the more because their contemporaries were too short sighted and bigoted to appreciate their splendid courage and advanced thinking. Origen was finally tortured by the Roman political authorities in Tyre and died in consequence of his sufferings. His tomb was shown there for many centuries near the high altar of the cathedral until it was destroyed during the Crusades. Clement held the doctrine of Christian perfection.

SAINT COSMAS THE MELODIST

d. about 760 A.D.

"The holy children boldly stand
Against the tyrant's dread command.
The kindled furnace they defy.
No doom can shake their constancy;
They in the midmost flame confessed
God of our fathers,* Thou art blessed."

This is the translation by John Mason Neale of the first stanza of a hymn written by St. Cosmas, a monk in the convent of St. Sabas, between Jerusalem and the Dead Sea, as was his foster brother, St. John of Damascus. He was in later life a bishop near Gaza, and died after a life of holiness in the performance of his episcopal duties.

He must not be confused with another Cosmas who lived two centuries earlier and was a merchant of Alexandria, and a great traveller in India and other countries. He spent the evening of his life in monastic retirement and wrote a "Topography of Many Lands" in twelve volumes.

---

* St. Cosmas seems to have first coined the expression "God of our fathers" used by so many hymnists since,—notably Rudyard Kipling in the opening of his great Recessional.

Saint Ephraem Syrus

d. 378 A. D.

"Child, by God's sweet mercy given
To thy mother and to me,"

These are the opening lines of an elegiac hymn written by
a Syrian monk, who of course had no children of his own,
but puts his tender lament into the mouth of a father who
has lost his boy. Ephraem was probably born at Nisibis,
between the Tigris and the Euphrates, on that plain which
was the early home of Abraham. Ephraem's parents are
said to have been heathen, and the boy, when converted to
Christianity, had to leave home, but his education was directed by Jacob, the Bishop of Nisibis. Political upheavals
drove Ephraem to Edessa on the banks of a lake surrounded
by mulberry groves. Here he lived to the end of his days as
a hermit, except for a memorable visit to Basil the Great in
Cappadocian Caesarea. The two men, who had each previously known only his childhood's language, began (so the story
goes) from that time on, fluently to speak each the language
of the other; that is, Basil could then speak Syrian and
Ephraem could speak Greek. However that may be, it is
known that Ephraem wrote some commentaries in Greek.
His death is attributed to his exertions for the relief of sufferers in an epidemic. His memory is celebrated in some
churches.

Venantius Fortunatus

530-609 A. D.

"Vexilla regis prodeunt."
"The royal banners forward go;
The cross shines forth with mystic glow;"

These lines, translated from the Latin by John M. Neale,
were written and sung as a processional hymn when a great
company carrying banners went out from the town of

Poictiers in France to receive what purported to be a fragment of the true cross. The author, Fortunatus, was an
Italian by birth, who, under the influence of Queen Rhadegunda, left a life of pleasure for the priesthood. Educated
at Ravenna and trained in oratory and poetry, he wrote fine
hymns of which several have been translated. He did not,
however, confine his literary efforts to the writing of hymns,
but wrote secular rather than sacred poetry for the most part,
and was considered the chief Latin poet of his time. He
also presided over a monastic institution in France and harmonized his monastic vows with cheerful laughs with saintly
ladies. He was a friend of St. Gregory of Tours, and of
Queen Rhadegunda, who was his patroness. His work marks
the transition from ancient to medieval hymnology. A passion hymn of his has found a place in the Roman breviary.

Pope Gregory the Great

544-604 A. D.

"Ecce jam noctis tenuatur umbra—"
"Lo, fainter now lie spread the shades of night,
And upward shoot the trembling gleams of morn."

These are the first two lines of a translation by Edward
Caswall of a beautiful Latin morning hymn written by that
Pope whose name is one of the landmarks of history.
Gregory the Great (although physically small) was born in
France of a patrician family. While still a youth he lavished
on the poor his gold and jewels and robes of silk and began
to perform the lowest duties in a monastery. He was forced,
however, by his ability and character, to take his place in
charge of the Roman church "where nothing seemed too
great or too insignificant for his earnest personal solicitude."
He is best known by the oft repeated incident of his meeting
some Anglo Saxon youths in the slave market and being so
impressed with their beauty that he undertook the conversion
of England, with a still greater result even than that which

grew out of Lincoln's viewing a slave market in New Orleans, which resulted in the emancipation of the negro slaves in the United States. Gregory not only evangelized England, sending St. Augustine and forty other monks there for the purpose, but he used his influence to mitigate and suppress slavery. From the work of Gregory in the evangelization of England has grown up the legend of "St. George and the Dragon", Saint George being Gregory, and the dragon being the paganism of England.

Gregory introduced what is known as the Gregorian chant, through which the eight tones of the octave have come down to us. These were fixed a hundred years later by the royal mandate of Charlemagne.

Gregory was at one time shut up in Rome with savage hordes of Gauls without, and pestilence, flood, and famine within. He met every demand, was prompt, resourceful, and generally successful in his efforts, modest, simple in dress, severe with himself and ceaselessly kind to others, of passionate eloquence in the pulpit, of wide correspondence with kings, queens, and scholars, keeping the monks to their discipline in the cloisters, devoting himself when possible to the study of the scriptures and music. He is the crowning character of his generation.

Gregory of Nazianzus in Cappadocia

325-389 A. D.

"Where are the winged words? Lost in the air!
The fresh flower of youth and glory? Gone!
The strength of well-knit limbs? Brought low by care!
Wealth? Plundered! None possess but God alone!
* * * * * * * * *
But Thou, O Christ my King, art fatherland to me!"

This is a partial translation of a Greek sonnet written by another and earlier Gregory than Gregory the Great. He was the son of a fire-worshiper like the Persians, who, however, was later converted to Christianity through the influence of his wife Nonna. The father became a bishop and lived to see his son Gregory associated with him in this office. Gregory was trained in piety by his mother. He went to schools of eloquence at Alexandria˙ and Athens, where he formed a friendship with Basil, (afterward Basil the Great) another student. The apostate Julian was also a student at Athens at the same period. Gregory and Basil retired to a desert to pursue a life of solitude and devotion, having an innate repugnance to public life, but Gregory was later so sought for that he became an archbishop of great eloquence.

There is another Church Father called Gregory of Nyassa (331-396) who was a younger brother of Basil the Great. This last Gregory was one of the writers of the Nicene Creed. He believed, like Origen, in final restoration.

Thus there are three Gregorys, all fathers in the early Christian Church.

St. Hilary of Arles

401-449 A. D.

"This hope inspires us as we pray,
That this, our holy matin light
May guide us through the busy day."

This is the translation of the closing lines of a beautiful hymn composed in Latin by the above named French Bishop of the Monastic School. Hilary led a little, saintly band of worshipers who were wont to gather in the morning shadows to sing their hymns of praise. Hymns sung in the early morning sanctify and inspire the entire day. Hilary had a serious controversy with Pope Leo as to the exercise of authority in the church, but in the end he sought and obtained reconciliation with his pontiff.

John of Damascus

d. after 754 and before 787 A. D.

"From my lips in their defilement,
From my heart in its beguilement,
From my tongue which speaks not fair,
O my Jesus, take my prayer."

The lines translated from the Greek by Elizabeth Barrett Browning give us a glimpse right into the glowing heart of this last of the Eastern Church fathers but one, and the greatest of her poets. John was born in Damascus and is said to have obtained his education from an Italian named Cosmas, who was redeemed from a band of slaves by John's father, Sergius, who held a high office under the Caliph. Later in life John retired to the monastery of St. Sabas, where he spent his last days. He was a theologian and priest, but he wrote in defense of image worship, which Pope Leo was trying to suppress. John's hymns are great. There is one splendid "Hymn of Victory" used by him in the Eastern Church on Easter morning accompanied by the lighting of tapers, also he probably wrote the stichera of the "Last Kiss" sung at funerals. John should be associated with his nephew, St. Stephen of Sabas.

St. Joseph the Hymnographer

d. 883 A. D.

"O happy band of pilgrims,
If onward ye will tread,
With Jesus as your Fellow
To Jesus as your Head,"

This paraphrase of an ancient Greek hymn was made by John M. Neale, but the original writer was a native of Sicily who went to Thessalonica in 830 A. D. and became a monk.

On a journey to Rome he was taken prisoner by pirates and spent some years as a slave in Crete. Later he went into exile with St. Ignatius and devoted himself to hymnology. The above translation is said to be so free that it is almost original with the translator. It is very frequently sung in England and her colonies. Joseph was a voluminous writer. One beautiful hymn of his translated by Neale begins:

> "Safe home, safe home in port!
> Rent cordage—shattered deck,
> Torn sails—provisions short,
> And only not a wreck.
> But oh! the joy upon the shore
> To tell our voyage perils o'er."

AURELIUS CLEMENS PRUDENTIUS

348-413 (?)

> "Corde natus ex parentis,"
> "Of the father's love begotten
> E'er the world began to be—"

These are the opening lines of a translation by John Neale of an old Latin hymn written by a Spanish lawyer and judge born at Saragossa. In his youth he was dissipated, but at the age of fifty-six he became convinced of the unsatisfying nature of earthly pleasures and honors and spent the remaining years of his life in religious pursuits, including the writing of twelve hymns for daily use and verses of praise for the martyrs. Here is an extract from a funeral hymn of his:

> "Mother Earth, in thy soft bosom cherish
> Whom we lay to repose in thy dust,
> For precious these relics we yield thee;
> Be faithful, O Earth, to thy trust."

St. Stephen the Sabaite
725-794 A. D.

"Art thou weary, art thou languid,
Art thou sore distrest?
'Come to me' saith One, 'and coming,
Be at rest'."

The is the opening stanza of the beautiful translation by
John M. Neale of a Greek hymn written by a monk who lived
at the monastery of St. Sabas. He was the contemporary
of his uncle, John of Damascus, and of St. Cosmas, both of
whom lived in the same monastery at the same period. This
monastery was between Jerusalem and the Dead Sea. Little
otherwise is known of this Stephen. He is to be remembered
by this lovely hymn, a great favorite among English people,
which deserves to be sung more often than it is. This hymn
I associate with another also written by an Eastern Church
Father which begins, "Fierce was the wild billow." Neale
has done a great service in making these two transcendent
hymns available in the church.

Synesius of Cyrene
392-430 A. D.

"Mine be the low portal, paths in silence trod,
Knowing not things mortal, knowing things of God,
While still at my side Wisdom holds her rod.
Wisdom, youth adorning, wisdom cheering age,
Wisdom, wealth's best warning, want's best heritage,
Poverty herself shall with smiles engage."

These lines are translated from a hymn by a Greek poet
who had been a pupil of Hypatia at Alexandria. He was
born at Cyrene in Africa and was converted from paganism
through the influence of his Christian wife. He was eventually
made Bishop of Ptolemais, but he was too deeply impregnated
with Platonic philosophy to be considered orthodox. One
writer calls him the finest of the Greek Christian hymnists,
but Dr. Schaff reserved that honor for St. John of Damascus.
Synesius died at the age of thirty-eight.

Theodore of Constantinople

d. in banishment 826 A. D.

"Enter Thou not in judgment with each deed,
Nor each intent and thought in strictness read!
Forgive and save me then,
O Thou that lovest men!"

These lines are translated by John M. Neale from the Greek poem entitled "The Judgment," written by Theodore, who was at the head of the Great Abbey of the Studium, called the most influential abbey that ever existed anywhere. Theodore's hymns are ranked very high by Dr. Neale.

St. Theophanes, the Confessor

758-817

"Who will venture on the strife?
Blest who first begin it!
Who will grasp the land of life?
Warriors, up and win it!"

These lines are translated from a hymn written by a Greek ascetic who was canonized after his death by the church. He was born into a noble and wealthy family and was at first in political life, but later founded a monastery, the ruins of which may still be seen in Greece. However, he was a worshiper of images, and two years before his death was summoned to Constantinople and ordered to renounce his principles, which he refused to do. He was therefore imprisoned and then banished to the island of Samothrace, where he died. He wrote a historical chronicle of value, which has been used by later historians. I have wondered whether it was for standing up for the right to worship images that he endured banishment!

CHAPTER III

MEDIEVAL HYMNISTS OF THE WESTERN CHURCH

"The church has sung its way down through the centuries. How would our faith languish without its great sweet hymns? When we are cast down, these hymns lift us as on wings. When we are wayward, they recall us to memories of better days. They express our joy, they comfort our sorrow."

—From the Fellowship of Prayer.

Webster's Collegiate Dictionary gives the Middle Ages as the period between the fall of Rome, 476 A. D., and the revival of letters, about 1400 A. D. I am, with less exactness, using the term as reaching to the beginning of the 16th century, and in some cases still longer, as the hymnists I enumerate usually belong partly in one century and partly in another. The Middle Ages are also the dark ages, and were in general a time of moral defection, but the lives of truly devout Christians run through these dreary centuries like golden threads in a dark fabric.

ADAM OF ST. VICTOR

d. between 1173 and 1194 A. D.

"Pone luctum, Magdalena,"
"Still thy sorrow, Magdalena,
Wipe the tear-drops from thine eyes;"

Adam* of St. Victor, a cloister which was destroyed in the French Revolution, is believed to be of French birth, France being the great seat of Latin poetry in the 12th

---

* His matin hymn beginning:
"Now the sun is gleaming bright—"
was sung by full choir in the hearing of William the Conqueror at Rouen in 1087 A. D. Before the song had ceased William had passed on. Where? To what? A few days before that, he was engaged in burning down the city of Mantes, putting the inhabitants to the sword. This was done in reprisal for a ribald jest made by King Phillipe I of France on the size of William's enormous stomach. The death of William grew directly out of this act of vengeance. His horse stepped on a hot coal among the burning ruins of Mantes, and stumbling, threw William against the pommel of the saddle, with such force that the injury thus caused, resulted in his gloomy death, away from all his family.

century. This Adam wrote 36 Latin hymns, and was the most fertile, and, in the estimation of Trench and Neale, the greatest of Latin hymnologists of the Middle Ages. He was the contemporary of the two Bernards mentioned later in this chapter.

St. Thomas Aquinas
1227-1274

"O bread to pilgrims given,"

This is the first line of Ray Palmer's translation of a beautiful and well known hymn, ascribed, yet with some doubt, to the above named "angelic doctor," as he was called. Aquinas is regarded as the greatest divine of the Romish church. He was a Neapolitan of noble family, and was kept in his ancestral castle as a prisoner for two years in his youth to keep him from going into a monastery. He contrived to escape to Cologne, where his fellow students in the university called him "the dumb ox," for his reticence. His teachers predicted that "this ox would one day fill the world with his bellowing." He became a great writer and teacher. He wrote a glowing communion hymn beginning "Pange lingua gloriosi," of which Neale's translation begins, "Of the glorious body telling." He died suddenly at the age of fifty, and some believed that he was maliciously poisoned.

Ludovico Ariosto
1474-1533

"To spare offenders, being penitent,
Is even ours; to drag them from the pit,
Themselves resisting, Lord, is thine alone."

These lines are translated from a poem by the eminent Italian named above. He had to support a large family left on his hands by his father's decease. He early developed his literary talent, and obtained a position in the service of the duke, which gave him leisure to write. His chief work was an epic poem describing the wars of Charlemagne with the Saracens. He was taken ill with a distressing internal disease and died at the age of fifty-nine. He was buried at Ferrara where there is a magnificent monument to his memory. He was a man of noble appearance and amiable character.

The Venerable Bede

672-735 A. D.

"Hymnum canamus gloriae."
"A hymn of glory let us sing,
* * * * * * * * *
And as the countless ages flee,
Let all our glory be in Thee!"

These lines, translated from the Latin by Elizabeth Charles, were written by the Anglo-Saxon monk of Yarrow, the most distinguished scholar of his age, the historian of England in five volumes, and the first translator of portions of the New Testament into our language, finished by dictation to pupils just before his death. He entered the monastery in his seventh year, and was educated in music and literature. Violence and slaughter filled England in these days, but Bede's gentle spirit and holy life were a light in a dark place. His disciple Cuthbert relates his dying testimony, "I go to my Creator. I have lived long enough." (He was only 63) "I long to depart and be with Christ." In his last hours a pupil told him that the last thought he had given them had been written down. He replied, "Thou hast well said. Raise my head in thy hand. It will do me good to sit where I was wont to kneel down and pray." So sitting on the ground in his cell, he sang, "Glory to Thee, Father, Son. and Holy Ghost," and when he had named the Holy Ghost he drew his last breath. What a wonderful departure twelve hundred years ago! His remains were placed under the altar of Durham cathedral. His dying song was the "Gloria Patria" believed by many to have came down from the Apostolic Age.

JACOBUS DE BENEDICTIS

d. about 1303 A. D.

"Stabat Mater Dolorosa"
"Stood the mournful mother weeping,
By the cross her vigil keeping,
While her Jesus hung thereon."

These are the opening lines of J. S. B. Monsell's* translation of the most pathetic hymn of the Middle Ages, which has furnished the inspiration for some of the finest musical compositions of Hayden and others. Benedictis belonged to a noble Italian family. After the death of his pious wife he entered the order of St. Francis, and so zealously attacked the abuses of the church that he was imprisoned therefor, but was released on the death of Pope Boniface. His last hours were solaced by his own songs. There is doubt about the authorship of the "Stabat Mater." Julian puts the probability with Pope Innocent III, but also acknowledges the possibility of Benedictis having written it.

ST. BERNARD OF CLAIRVAUX

1091-1153

"Jesus, the very thought of Thee
With sweetness fills my breast,"

This hymn, translated into German by Count Zinzendorf, and later into English by Caswall, was first written in Latin by the "mellifluous doctor" above named, that mystic called by Luther "the best monk that ever lived."† Bernard was

---

* The "Stabat Mater" has also a good translation by Lord Lyndsay. It is much like Monsell's, but transforms the opening lines thus:
"By the cross sad vigil keeping
Stood the mournful mother, weeping."

† There seems to have been another side altogether of the character of St. Bernard of Clairvaux. He is called in Dr. Julian's Dictionary of Hymnology, p. 891, "fiery", and "domineering". Sad to say, most of us have such a seamy side to our characters that
"There is so much bad in the best of us,
And so much good in the worst of us,
That it hardly behooves any of us,
To talk about the rest of us."

born of a knightly family at Fontaine, Burgundy. He was
of great physical beauty. He had five brothers and they
were all monks together. The influence of their mother,
Aletta, followed them through life. Bernard wrote and sang
his hymns, which were called "a river of Paradise", in a
woodland bower. Another of Bernard's well known hymns
translated by Ray Palmer begins:

"Jesus, thou joy of loving hearts,"

Another still, which shows its imperishable vitality by passing through three communions, Catholic, Lutheran, and Reformed, and in three languages, Latin, German, and English,
begins:

"O sacred head, now wounded,"

Bernard taught his neighborhood to be industrious and to
be the model farmers of Europe, and breathed the spirit of
holy song into the work of his helpers. His religious community was on the banks of the Saone in eastern France,
begun in a pathless forest infested with robbers and originally called the Valley of Wormwood. It became Clairvaux
(the bright). Two errors marred his life; one was his in-
tolerant treatment of Abelard,* the other his exciting the
disastrous crusade of 1146, from which nine tenths of the
multitude who went to the East never returned.

The death of St. Bernard at the age of 62 was in this
wise: his monks were gathered around him weeping as he
counseled them to abound more and more in every good
work. His own eyes filled with tears and he said, "I am in a
strait betwixt two, having a desire to depart and to be with
Christ, but the love of my children urgeth me to remain."

---

* St. Bernard's opponent, Abelard, was the first avowed rationalist,
as he laid down the principle that nothing should be believed except
what is understood. Bernard, on the other hand, was for banishing
enquiry altogether from the sphere of religion. Abelard had wonderful
power in public disputation, but his colorful romance with Heloise, the
lovely seventeen year old niece of Canon Fulbert, who engaged Abelard
as her tutor, is most arresting. When Fulbert understood that the girl
and her teacher were lovers, he tried to separate them, but they fled
to the country, where Heloise bore Abelard a son. Fulbert in rage, had
Abelard emasculated, and Heloise took the veil. The lovers were buried
in one grave in Paris.

BERNARD OF CLUNY

d. about 1156

"Hora novissima"
"The world is very evil!
The times are waxing late!
Be watchful and keep vigil;
The Judge is at the gate."

These opening lines of Neale's translation of what he considered the loveliest of medieval hymns was written by another Bernard, often confused with St. Bernard of Clairvaux. It seems strange that two Bernards should both be living in Burgundy at the same time and both be authors of immortal Latin hymns. Bernard of Cluny was of English stock. He came from near old Brittany, and found his way to the cloister of Cluny, where he spent his life in song and worship. He, like the other Bernard, was a mystic, and used to say to his brother monks when walking with them in the cloister, "Brethren, I must go. There is some one waiting for me in my cell." Thus he referred to his intimacy with the unseen Christ, of whom he said, "The name of Jesus is honey in the mouth, melody in the ear, joy in the heart, medicine in the soul, and there is no charm in any discourse where his name is not heard." The teacher of Bernard of Cluny was Peter the Venerable, a master of spiritual song, then at the summit of his reputation. Bernard's great hymn contains the glowing lines.

"Jerusalem, the golden,
With milk and honey blest."

and also

"Exult, O dust and ashes,
The Lord shall be thy part;
His only, his forever,
Thou shalt be and thou art."

THE EMPEROR CHARLEMAGNE

742-814

"Veni, Creator Spiritus,"
"Creator Spirit, by whose aid
The world's foundations first were laid,"

These are the opening lines of Dryden's translation of this great Latin hymn of the ages. I am diffident about inserting Charlemagne as the author, although Schaff and Gilman attribute it (along with doubts) to that mighty monarch, for Dr. Julian says in connection with four and a half pages of learned discussion on the subject, that neither Charlemagne nor Gregory could possibly have written it. I give it up as a too difficult problem for me, but will just say of the hymn itself that it has been used extensively for hundreds of years at the creation of popes, the coronation of kings, and the ordination of bishops. Those who advocate Charlemagne* point to the fact that he could speak Latin as well as his native German, and that he was musical and literary, and fostered all learning and the fine arts, studying rhetoric and astronomy. He was more than that. He fostered the advancement of his people in all lines, encouraging them in practical matters like the planting of fruit trees, etc. He was tall, of a commanding appearance. He reigned over France, half of Germany, and four fifths of Italy. He was amorous, and is said to have had nine wives and fourteen children, and would not let his daughters marry because he wanted them with him.

---

* Possibly my readers will consider me unduly partial to the idea that Charlemagne wrote "Veni, Creator Spiritus" when I confess that I happen to be myself descended from him, but this fact carries with it the somewhat disconcerting corollary that I am also descended from his chief wife, Hildegarde, "who roared at him with a loud voice." I must say that I have some sympathy with Hildegarde in this. Believing as I do, that young love should have its scope, I think Hildegarde had some occasion to roar at Charlemagne if he was preventing one of her daughters from a happy marriage which she desired. (See p. 322, Memoirs of the Leonard Thompson, and Haskell Families.)

GEOFFREY CHAUCER

1340-1400

"Trust not to fortune,
Be not o'er meddling;
Thankful receive thou
Good which God gave.
Truth to thine own heart
Thy soul shall save."

The above lines are only a paraphase by another writer of Chaucer's last song which might be used as a hymn. Chaucer's own poems as he wrote them are too archaic to be used as hymns. His earlier poems also, which reflect the gaily appareled time in which he lived, do not touch the heart, but those he wrote in retirement and the disgrace which overtook him for alleged abuses, and those on the sorrow attendant on the death of his wife, deal with that which is elemental and eternal. Chaucer was the son of a London vintner, and we learn that one day in his youth he thrashed in the street a Franciscan friar, and the next day was fined two pounds for it. He wrote books while at the university, was made a prisoner in the French campaign, married Catherine, a sister of the wife of John of Gaunt, went on an embassy to Genoa where he met Petrarch and is supposed to have got from him the story of Griselda, was granted by the king a pitcher of wine daily for life, lost his position, died in reduced circumstances, and was the first poet to be buried in Westminster Abbey.

Dante Allighieri

1265-1321

"O thou Almighty Father, who dost make
The heavens thy dwelling, not in bounds confined,
* * * * * * * *
This last petition, dearest Lord! is made
Not for ourselves, since that is needless now,
But for their sakes who after us remain."

This is a translation by Henry Francis Carey of a few
lines from the 11th canto of the Divine Comedy by the
Florentine poet of the ages. Dante was born of an ancient
family and, until the age of twenty-five, was engaged in
study under the direction of his mother, Bella. His youth
was clouded by the losing of his childhood's friend, Beatrice,
who had been the source of his poetical inspiration from the
age of nine. Both Dante and Beatrice married others, but
Dante did not marry until after the early death of Beatrice.
He was a political exile at the age of thirty-seven. His
property was confiscated and he was threatened with death
at the stake. He spent his closing years at Ravenna and
died at the age of fifty-six. T. W. Parsons, b. Boston 1819,
wrote a poem on the bust of Dante, from which we cull
these lines:

"Faithful, if this wan image be,
No dream his life was,—but a fight!
Could any Beatrice see
A lover, in that anchorite?

Peace dwells not here—this rugged face
Betrays no spirit of repose,
The sullen warrior sole we trace,
The marble man of many woes.

O Time, whose verdicts mock our own,
The only righteous judge art thou;
That poor old exile, sad and lone,
Is Latium's other Virgil now."

St. Francis of Assisi

1182-1226

"Set love in order, thou that lovest me.
Never was virtue out of order found.
  * * * * * * * *
When to my love thou dost bring charity,
Even she must come with order girt and gowned.
  * * * * * * * *
Charity, most of all, when known enough,
Is of her very nature orderly."

These lines, (severe on some of us who find order an extremely difficult virtue to practice) are a translation by Dante Gabriel Rossetti of a poem by Francis of Assisi, considered the most gentle and blameless of saints. He was a gay and prodigal youth who was for a year a political prisoner, but his trouble and sickness conspired to turn his thoughts to God, and he dedicated himself to Poverty, which he called his bride. Henceforth he would not touch money. When it was offered to him he said, "Let it be given to those who cannot smile." His smile was wonderful. It gave him access to the homes where he begged for crusts of bread. Everyone loved the smiling beggar and fed him gladly. His love for all took in the beasts, and many stories are told of his love for them and power over them; how he rescued two lambs from the slaughter, paying for them, since he had no money, by parting with his cloak, and carried the lambs home; how, when a live fish and live hare were brought him for food, he set them at liberty and would not suffer them to be killed and eaten; how he tamed a savage wolf that had been the terror of the country side; how the birds flocked around him, lighting on his head and shoulders; and how he addressed a little sermon to the birds, exhorting them to praise God. He called the birds and animals his little sisters and brothers. His father was angry that he wore mean clothes and shut him up in a dark room of the house. At one time he took refuge in a cave. Others gradually joined him and a house was assigned to them by a church. He died at the age of forty-four, and, at his own request, was laid on the bare floor of the church to die. He is the founder of the Franciscan order, and has been called the most extraordinary man of the ages. His memory goes down the years like sweet incense.

St. Fulbert

d. 1028 or 1029

"Ye choirs of New Jerusalem"

This hymn, translated from the Latin by J. Neale and found in most English collections, was written by Fulbert of Chartres who was a contemporary and intimate friend of Robert II of France. He was a Bishop and was connected with the theological college at Chartres, the ancient capital of Celtic Gaul.

Michael Angelo (Buonarrotti)

1474-1564

"The prayers I make will then be sweet indeed,
  If Thou the spirit give by which I pray."

These are the opening lines of a sonnet translated by William Wordsworth, composed by the unsurpassed Italian painter and sculptor of the ages. Angelo was of noble origin, and was trained in a seminary for the study of ancient art, where he developed his marvelous skill in executing human figures. No name in art shines with a more unsullied lustre than his. His Sistine Madonna, Mater Dolorosa, and picture of the Last Judgment, have immortalized him. He also planned the reconstruction of St. Peter's at Rome. His poetry was only a side issue, but in that he was fine also. He was beloved as a man of piety and liberality. He is buried in Florence.

Peter the Venerable

1092-1156

"Mortis, portis fractis, fortis"
"Lo, the gates of death are broken, and the strong
man armed is spoiled."

This line is quoted from Mrs. Charles' translation of a
hymn written by the gentle Abbot of Cluny, a past master
of song, and the teacher of Bernard of Cluny. Peter's rule
was so mild in the monastery that it was a matter of criticism with St. Bernard of Clairvaux, whose monks sometimes
found the discipline at Clairvaux too galling, and one, at
least, Robert, Bernard's cousin, went away to Cluny for that
reason. This and other things led to sharp controversy
between Peter the Venerable and Bernard of Clairvaux,
who seems to be Dr. Jekyl to some writers and Mr. Hyde
to others, such contrary characters are ascribed to him.
Another matter of controversy between the two abbots was
Abelard, who came to Cluny, silenced and broken after the
persecution he had endured through the attack upon him by
Bernard of Clairvaux. Peter took Abelard's part and let
him stay in the refuge of Cluny until his death two years
later. Peter's forbearance and love of peace are conspicuous
in that age of fiery denunciations by ecclesiastics of all who
disagreed with them. A soft halo seems to linger around
the figure of Peter the Venerable.

Francesco Petrarch

1302-1374

"And my last hour, oh, be Thou there to aid!
On Thee, Thou knowest, my only hope is stayed."

These lines are culled from a translation of "Future
Blessedness", written by Petrarch, the great lyric poet of
Italy. He was the son of a Florentine notary and himself
studied law, but devoted himself to literature and to his ro-

mantic love for Laura, a French golden-haired beauty,* who
was the wife of another. Once only he made to her an
avowal of his love, but was sternly reproved by her for it.
However, Petrarch lived for ten years in her city in order
to be near her. At last be removed to a sequestered place
and wrote to a friend, "My life has been uniform since age
extinguished that fatal passion which so long tormented me."
His lyrics in honor of Laura, many of them written after
her death, are the summit of his writing. At one time he
was crowned with a laurel wreath at Rome. In his closing
years annoyed by visitors, not over-rich, and subject to
epileptic fits he still worked hard at his writing. He was
found dead at last, sitting with his head resting in a book.

Robert II of France, "The Pious"

996-1031

"Veni, Sancte Spiritus,"
"Come, Holy Ghost, in love,
    Shed on us from above,
    Thine own bright ray."

These are the opening lines of a translation by Ray Palmer
of a renowned Latin hymn, called the most beautiful in the
whole range of Latin sacred poetry, which was written by
the royal musical composer, chorister, and poet, named
above. Some of his musical compositions are still in use in
churches. Robert the Pious might have ruled in Italy, but
he preferred that his palace should be his cloister, where he
lived "in the sacred spells of melody and song." He used
to conduct the matins and vespers at church in his royal
robes. He was a truly devout man who is called "meek and
afflicted", and his hymns imply this. He was married twice,
first to Constance and then to Bertha. His last days were
embittered by the opposition of his sons.

---

* Laura's beauty was such that Emperor Charles IV begged to be
introduced to her and to be allowed to kiss her forehead.

Jerome Savonarola

1452-1498

"Ah, vanish each unworthy trace of earthly care and pride,
Leave only graven on my heart, the cross, the crucified."

These lines are from a translation by Harriet Beecher Stowe of a hymn by the great reformer and martyr of Italy named above. Savonarola was born at Florence of a noble family, and highly educated in Greek philosophy. He entered a convent where his zeal and genius attracted notice, and he preached with a prophetic earnestness which attracted to him many penitents who were called "weepers." He tried to found a Christian commonwealth in Florence where there should be no ruler but God. This drew down upon him the papal wrath, and he was tried for heresy for which he and two others were put to death and their bodies burned by the executioner. He died at the age of forty-six, professing his adherence to the Catholic church and humbly accepting the last absolution from the papal commissary. He wrote several treatises in either Latin or Italian, of a deep spiritual nature. Some of his writing was done in prison and at the request of his jailer. His works exemplify the lofty and even fierce enthusiasm of this genius who exerted a tremendous influence in an age both cultivated and corrupt.

St. Theodulph, Bishop of Orleans

d. 821 A. D.

"Gloria, laus et honor,"
"Glory and honor and praise
To Thee, our Redeemer and King."

These lines are from a translation of a Latin medieval processional hymn by St. Theodulph, who is supposed to have been born in Italy but brought to France by Charlemagne, perhaps in 781. He was imprisoned on a false charge in 818, after the death of Charlemagne. This story is told

of the origin of the above hymn, but whether truly or not I
cannot say. It is said that the then Emperor, Louis the
Debonaire, was on his way to the cathedral at Metz on Palm
Sunday, and that, as he passed the grated window of the
dungeon where Theodulph was confined, he heard the
prisoner singing this hymn of his own composition. The
story goes that the good Theodulph was immediately released; however, Dr. Julian seems to think that Theodulpl
died at the place of his confinement on Sept. 1, 821.

THOMAS OF CELANO

d. 1255

"Dies irae, dies illa,
Solvet saeclum in favilla."

This great "Sequence of the Western Church" was probably written about 1208 by the above named obscure Franciscan monk for his own private devotion. He was born in
a Neapolitan village and doubtless died without knowing
that he had written what some consider the greatest of all
hymns, or that it would echo and re-echo to the end of
time. Mozart made it the basis of his Requiem, and is said
to have become so excited over its theme as to hasten his
death. Neither Walter Scott nor Doctor Johnson could re-
cite it without tears. Scott made a translation of it which
he incorporated into "The Lay of the Last Minstrel." Dean
Stanley also translated it into English. Goethe in Faust
describes the effect of this hymn on a guilty conscience in
the following words. "The trump sounds; the grave
trembles; and thy heart from the repose of its ashes, for
fiery torment brought to life again, trembles up." Thomas
of Celano was a contemporary of Francis of Assisi and was
his biographer.

1821900

T<small>HOMAS</small> Á K<small>EMPIS</small>
1380-1471

"See the happy dwellers there
Shine in robes of purity,
Keep the laws of charity,
Bound in firmest unity."

These lines are a translation from a poem on heaven by
the celebrated monk of the order of St. Augustine named
above. They were written in the long, calm evening of his
life when he waited for the coming of the Lord. He took
his name from the little village of Kempen, near Cologne,
in which he was born of poor parents whose name was
Hemmerken. He had a silent, assiduous mother and a hard-
working father. He was placed at the age of six in a society
that had held property in common, but the members made
no vows and could withdraw if they pleased. Thomas a
Kempis speaks of the devout consecration, the irreproachable
manners, and the humility of these people. His youth was
spent in copying useful books. At nineteen he entered a
monastery. The life of a monk is thus described: "his
prayers must be incessant, his fasts frequent, his sleep short,
and the whole of his spare time given to manual labor."
It is said that when singing, the face of Thomas á Kempis
was so lit up with holy rapture that the beholders were filled
with awe, but he said himself, "I have sought for peace
everywhere, but have found it nowhere except in a corner
with a little book." It is said that no other book but the
Bible has been translated into so many languages as his
"Imitation of Christ."* The King of Morocco prized his
copy in Arabic above all other books.

---

* I prize a copy given me by my husband the year after my marriage,
with his words of love on the fly leaf.

I have been much interested recently to learn that the writings of
Thomas a Kempis contributed much to the spiritual development of
Madame Guyon, and also to the formulation of the doctrines she held
and taught. She imbibed these teachings as she studied in convents in
her girlhood.

Thomas a Kempis wrote a pretty Christmas carol, of which I give
a few verses in its English translation form:

"O sweetest Jesus, come from heaven
That life might to the world be given,
Thou pardonest much to lovers that
Once loving Thee, forsake Thee not.

'Tis soul's delight, 'tis all our glory,
Jesus, to read thine humble story.
Let's now rejoice! Lo, Christ is here!
Let captive souls put off their fear."

St. Francis Xavier

1506-1552

"O Deus, ego amo te,"
"My God, I love Thee, not because
I hope for heaven thereby,"

These are the opening lines from a translation by Edward
Caswall of a much admired Latin Hymn attributed to the
"Great Apostle of the Indies," but of which Dr. Julian thinks
that it may not have been written by him. However, Xavier
did write Latin hymns and must be classed anyway among
the Latin hymnists. He was born of a noble family near
Navarre in Spain, and educated at Paris, where he met
Ignatius de Loyola,* and both these friends helped to found
the Jesuit Society at Rome. Xavier was sent by King John
of Portugal as a missionary to the East. He established
a mission in Japan which lasted over one hundred years
until the expulsion of Christianity from the Empire. He
attempted to establish a mission on the mainland of China,
but was disappointed in this, and died at the age of forty-six
on the island of Saucian, belonging to China, but his remains
were sent to Goa, on the coast of Hindostan. Xavier was a
missionary of burning zeal, and many miracles are attributed
to him, among others the gift of tongues. He was canonized
as a saint. His saint's day is December third.

---

* Xavier's friend, Ignatius Loyola, 1491-1556, was fifteen years older
than he and outlived him by four years. He was born in a castle in
the Basque province, and was in youth a page in the court of Ferdinand.
Later he became a soldier and one of his legs was fractured by a cannon
ball. This accident was the turning point in his career. His leg was
set wrong and rebroken, which involved great suffering. During his
convalescence he read the lives of the saints and then threw himself
with the ardor of his temperament into a barefooted pilgrimage to
Jerusalem. Finding his lack of education was an impediment, he went
to Paris to study, where he met Xavier, who became his friend and
comrade in the establishment of the Jesuit Society, of which Loyola
became the first general. He died at the age of sixty-five and has been
canonized as a saint.

CHAPTER IV

LATER CONTINENTAL HYMNISTS

1500-1900

As France was the centre of Medieval hymnology, so Germany was similarly the centre of hymnology during the period of the Reformation and the century that followed it. Therefore the larger number of Continental hymnists here recorded are Germans, but other nationalities are represented.

GUSTAVUS ADOLPHUS

1594-1632

"Fear not, oh little flock, the foe
That madly seeks your overthrow;"

This hymn, connected with the battle in which the gallant king of Sweden lost his life, has been called "a little feather from the eagle wing" of the great Adolphus himself—which, however, has probably been a mistake, as the evidence seems to be that it was written by Altenburg. However, it was certainly sung by the army of Adolphus on the eve of that victorious battle where the leader showed "the spirit of a king, and fervor of a hero, and the heart of a Christian." He had left his infant daughter Christina in the hands of his Chancellor, and, with three thousand soldiers, landed in Germany to defend the Reformation and religious liberty. Before going into that battle of Lutzen he knelt beside his horse in the presence of his soldiers, prayed God to bless his army, and said, "I seal with my blood the liberty of religion." Then, swinging his sword above his head, he led his soldiers into battle, giving them as a watchword for the fight, "God with us." The fatal bullet struck him at eleven A. M. His horse with the empty saddle came flying into the camp. The battle raged until twilight, leaving the victory with the Evangelicals.

GOTTFRIED ARNOLD

1666-1714

"With downcast eyes we seek Thy face again;
Thou kissest us; we promise fair amends;
Once more Thy spirit rest and pardon sends,
And curbs our passions with a stronger rein."

This vivid description of one of the humbling seasons of contrition before God, experienced by all true Christians, is translated from the German, written by the above named teacher of a town school. This particular hymn was a favorite of the celebrated philosopher. Friedrich Schelling, 1775-1854. Arnold has an eventful history, not especially connected with his hymn writing. He became a disciple of the mystic Spener, and formed a society called the New Angel Brotherhood, which represented Wisdom as a pure virgin, and taught that union with her precluded earthly marriage. These views were so denounced that Arnold came near banishment. He afterward was himself married to Anna Maria Spragel, which caused his expulsion from the New Angel Brotherhood and gained for him the ridicule of his enemies. About the time of his marriage he became a preacher, and when he was recovering from a severe illness brought on by over study, a recruiting party burst into his church and carried off a number of his followers from the communion rail where he was administering the communion. The outrage so distressed him as to hasten his death. Arnold's fame really rests on a great work in prose in which he shows the beautiful lives of the early Christians.

JOHANN MICHAEL ALTENBURG

1584-1640

This German pastor is probably the true author of the hymn beginning "Fear not, oh little flock, the foe", as explained in the notes about the reputed author, Gustavus

Adolphus. His spirited hymn has been finely translated into English by Catherine Winkworth. Altenburg had to flee to Erfurt during the troublous war times in which he lived, and while there composed his immortal hymn. He was a good musician and composed melodies for hymns also.

ERNST MORITZ ARNDT

1789-1860

"I know in whom I put my trust.
I know what standeth fast."

These are the opening lines of a translation by Catherine Winkworth of a beautiful hymn by the above named German patriot who was once suspended from his professorship of history at Bonn as a "demagogue." Later he was restored, and later still elected a member of the German National Assembly. In his early life he attacked Napoleon in his writings with such vehemence that he had to fly in 1807 to Stockholm for his life, but returned to Germany in 1810 under an assumed name. His popular song entitled "Was ist des Deutchen Vaterland?" is sung wherever German is spoken.

PEDRO CALDERON

1600-1681

"Thou art of all created things,
O Lord, the essence and the cause."

This Spanish dramatist was the author of various hymns. As far as I know none of them are familiarly sung in English translations, but Archbishop Trench has finely translated some of these remarkable productions. Calderon is second in rank of the dramatic poets of Spain. He was born at Madrid and belonged to a military order, but later in life was ordained a priest. He was a man of religious spirit, and Schlegel says that his poetry is an incessant hymn of joy on the majesty of creation.

MATTHIAS CLAUDIUS

1740-1815

"We plow the fields and scatter."

This is a translation of one of the hymns written by the son of a German clergyman who studied theology at the University of Jena but turned his attention to law and literature and business. He was constantly harassed by both ill health and poverty and had a life of struggle. For a while he was associated with Goethe at Darmstadt among a circle of free thinking philosophers, but realizing the emptiness of that life he returned to the faith of his childhood.

SIMON DACH

1605-1659

"O how blest are ye whose toils are ended."

This is the opening line of a translation by H. W. Longfellow of a poem called "Blessed are the Dead" written by a professor of poetry at Königsberg. He wrote simple, devout lyrics which betoken the quiet studiousness of his nature. After his education in theology and philosophy at the university he was for a time a private tutor where hard work for poor pay so injured his health that he was always something of an invalid, and died at last of a lingering consumption. He wrote about 165 hymns, profound in thought and elagant in expression, but only about five have found their way into English use,—partly because they are so personal, and so largely deal with preparation for death. He seems to have taken a somewhat melancholy view of life, which may be accounted for partly by his ill health, and partly by the trials of his times owing to the effects of the Thirty Years War in Germany—depression of trade, famine and pestilence which carried off many of his fellow professors at Königsberg.

GABRIEL ROMANOVITCH DERZHAVIN

1743-1816

"O Thou eternal one, whose presence bright
All space doth occupy, all motion guide,"
* * * * * * * * *
And when the tongue is eloquent no more,
The soul shall speak in tears of gratitude."

These are the opening and closing lines of an ode to God
translated by Bowring from the Russian, by the above named
brilliant poet and statesman of Russia. It is a remarkable
production which has been translated into various languages.
After Derzhavin had retired from political life he devoted
himself to poetry and published five volumes of verse. His
writings are marked by sublimity and originality, but his
oriental imagery is scarcely appreciated by the colder fancy
of the West.

WILHELM MARTIN LEBERECHT DEWETTE

1780-1849

"Love the Lord, and thou shalt see Him;
Do His will, and thou shalt know
How the spirit lights the letter,
How a little child may go
Where the wise and prudent stumble."

These lines are quoted from a translation of a poem called
"The Way and the Life" written by the above named German
preacher and professor at Heidelberg, where he lost his
position on account of a letter he wrote to the mother of an
assassin. (Very probably he showed too much sympathy for
her and perhaps expressed himself in favor of the abolition
of capital punishment.) However, he obtained another leading
position soon where he acquired much fame. He was broad
minded, a philosopher of moderate rationalistic opinions,
liberal views, and great individuality. Such persons are bound
to get into hot water from the conservatism of the "best
people." What a world to live in!

Francis de la Motte Fenelon
1651-1715

"Living or dying, Lord, I would be Thine."

This is the first line of the translation by Sarah Adams of a hymn written in French by the celebrated French Archbishop named above. He had a fine education and preached his first sermon at the age of fifteen. He became the preceptor of the Duke of Burgundy, grandson of Louis XIV, who had a great affection for his teacher. Fenelon was a man of consecrated life and beautiful personal character. However, this did not save him from bitter persecution on account of his defense of Madame Guyon and her quietist principles. He was cut to the heart by a pamphlet published against him by Bosuet. A copy of this with Fenelon's delicate and beautiful handwriting on the margins is preserved in the British Museum. With wonderful submission he accepted the condemnation of Rome and even published it from his own pulpit. Louis XIV also was angry with him. He endured all this with patience, but it was a bitter chapter in his life. We honor him for his defense of that noble woman of suffering, Madame Guyon.

Friedrich Ferdinand Fleming
1778-1813

"Oh Holy Savior, Friend unseen,"

This hymn, translated from the German in 1834 by Charlotte Elliott was written in 1810 by the above named author who also composed the tune for it. Some other tunes in our hymn collections were composed by him. One of these is called "Integer Vitae" to which is set the beautiful hymn of Whittier's called "At Last."* which deserves to be sung more often than it is.

---

* It may seem out of place to quote here a stanza from Whittier's hymn, but since Fleming's music is so closely connected with the words, I venture to do so:

> "Suffice it if—my good and ill unreckoned,
> And both forgiven through thy abounding grace—
> I find myself by hands familiar beckoned
> Unto my fitting place."

PAUL FLEMING

1609-1640

"Where'er I go, whate'er my task,
The counsel of my God I ask."

These lines from the translation of the German by
Catherine Winkworth, are the opening ones of a beautiful
poem entitled "On a Long and Perilous Journey," written
by a brilliant young doctor who died at the age of thirty-one,
and was married just a year before he died. He is considered the finest of the German lyrists of the seventeenth
century. He wrote not only hymns but exquisite love songs
also, unequaled in sweetness and finish in Germany for a
hundred years. At the age of twenty-four he was attached
to a splendid embassy which was sent to Persia. It may be
that the distractions of the Thirty Years War hastened his
death, which deprived the world of a writer of originality,
force and vigor.

JOHANN FRANCK

1618-1677

"Deck thyself, my soul, with gladness,"

This is the opening line of the translation of the best
eucharistic hymn of the Lutheran church. It was written by
the great German hymn writer named above. He was born
at Guben and educated at the university of Königsberg
where Simon Dach, his professor in poetry, encouraged his
verse writing. This was the only German university left un-
disturbed by the Thirty Years War. In 1640 he returned
to his mother in Guben, as she was timid because hostile
troops were frequently in the town. This tender care of his
mother gives a sweet human interest to his character, which
was a very fine one. His hymns disclose his firm faith,
earnestness, and longing for mystic fellowship with Christ,
as well as the literary quality of fine finish. He ranks very
high as a hymn writer. He was a lawyer and in political
life, but his fame rests upon his hymns, of which he left a
number of excellent ones.

August Hermann Francke

1663-1727

"Bless God that toward eternity
Another step is won."*

These are the opening lines in the translation by Catherine
Winkworth of a New Year's hymn written by a noted
teacher, preacher, and philanthropist of Germany. He in-
stituted a remarkable educational movement for neglected
poor children. In 1714 he had 1075 boys and 700 girls and
108 teachers under his direction. His orphan asylum at
Halle still exists. He was a spiritual disciple under Spener
and a leader in the pietist movement. For this he suffered
persecution as a heretic. The above mentioned hymn was
written when under this stress of affliction. He died at the
age of sixty-four "in the full experience of the unspeakable
consolations of the Holy Spirit."

Christian F. Gellert

1715-1769

"Jesus lives; no longer now
Can thy terrors, Death, appal me."

These opening lines from a translation by an English lady
named Frances Cox, are from an original German hymn
written by the Leipsic professor who was a teacher of the
poet Goethe, who later paid a high tribute to him in his
writings. Gellert's lecture-room was crowded with admiring
young men who reverently drank in admonitions and warn-
ings which poured from his beautiful soul into their own.

*Francke seems to have been in a hurry to get through with life, a
natural feeling when life is very hard.
"So pray we oftentimes, mourning our lot,
God in his mercy answereth not."
* * * * * * * *
So pray we afterward, low on our knees,
Pardon those erring prayers, Father, hear these."
Once in my youth I was wishing a long, dreary winter to be over.
My mother, smiling, said, "Are you in such a hurry to be done with
life?"

Princes and celebrated people visited him. Even Frederick the Great had an interview with him, and his death at the age of fifty-four was considered a national calamity. His biographer says of him "Perhaps no grave has been watered by so many and such sincere tears. Yet this talented writer of poetry, fables, and stories, has a pathetic side to his life. During seven years of war he was a poor student at Leipsic, the son of a minister in Saxony. He suffered from sickness, and (like Cowper, whom he resembled) from attacks of melancholy. He was so generous that he sometimes suffered for the necessities of life. In his little student room among his heaped up books was his worn Bible, opened at the second chapter of Job, which says, "Shall we receive good at the hand of God and shall we not receive evil?"

PAUL GERHARDT

1606-1696

"Give to the winds thy fears!
Hope, and be undismayed!
God hears thy sighs and counts thy tears,
God shall lift up thy head."

This hymn which no Christian can sing without fresh inspiration, is translated by John Wesley from the German of Gerhardt, who stands next to Luther as the beloved sacred poet of Germany. There is a beautiful story connected with its composition. Gerhardt married the daughter of a Berlin advocate named Berthold in whose home he had spent several years as a tutor after completing his ecclesiastical studies. Later he held a pastorate in Berlin, but was deposed because of his sympathy with the Reformation, and obliged to flee with his family toward Saxony to save his life. On the way the refugees stopped for the night at a little inn, and in the garden, to comfort his distressed wife, he wrote the hymn mentioned above. He was then called to meet two strangers who were seeking him; whereupon his wife turned pale with

fear of fresh calamity. Instead, they brought the message
from a Duke saying that a pension was bestowed upon him
to atone for the injustice he had suffered. Then Gerhardt
presented to his wife the hymn he had just written, saying,
"See how God provides." Gerhardt wrote other familiar
hymns,* one of which begins, "Since Jesus is my friend."

Gerhardt was twelve years old when the Thirty Years War
broke out. He was later a soldier under Gustavus Adolphus.

JOHANN WOLFGANG VON GOETHE

1749-1832

"Rest is not quitting this busy career;
Rest is the fitting of self to one's sphere."

These lines are translated from the German of the acknowledged prince of German poets, of whom Carlyle says, "No
nobler or grander intellect has lived in the world since
Shakespeare left it."

Goethe, the son of an imperial counsellor, was born at
Franfort-on-the-Main and educated at Leipsic. Like
Burns, he was of an amorous nature and it was said of him,
"The female sex will never forgive a man who is so light to
lend his heart, and so fearful to give his hand." He shrank
from legal marriage as from a conventional shackle. He
lived with the mother of his oldest son eighteen years before
he married her. His fame, of course, does not rest with his
hymns,† but with his supremest effort, Faust.

---

* One hymn of Gerhardt's which has been a personal comfort to me
begins:
    "Here I can firmly rest;
    I dare to boast in this,—
    That God, the highest and the best,
    My friend and father is."
This was printed in the Andover Sabbath Hymnbook in 1858.

† Another familiar hymn of Goethe's begins:
    "Without haste, without rest!
    Bind the motto to thy breast."
Here are also four lines I like exceedingly:
    "Up then, my soul, and never flag!
    Soaring the mark of error past,
    Through clouds of doubt, o'er trial's crag,
    Struggle to home in Truth at last."

MADAME JEANNE DE LA MOTTE GUYON

1648-1717

"While place we seek, or place we shun,
The soul finds happiness in none;
But with our God to guide our way
'Tis equal joy to go or stay."

These lines are translated from the French of the remarkable woman named above. They were perhaps written in the Bastille* where she was imprisoned four years, having suffered two previous imprisonments in other places. Her cell in the Bastille was next to that of the "man with the iron mask." The walls of the Bastille were nine feet thick and light entered only by narrow slits. The cells were dirty with the mould of ages, bitterly cold in winter, suffocating in summer. The captives were deprived of employments, books or recreation. Madame Guyon expected to be released only to martyrdom, but she said. "I have no anxiety of what my enemies may do to me. So long as God is with me, neither death nor imprisonment will have any terror." She had displeased the Roman Church to which she belonged by her views† and teachings as to Quietism and spiritual marriage with Christ. Fenelon was persecuted for defending her views. She was finally banished to Diziers and died at Blois at a very advanced age. Her last

---

* Years ago I heard these lines quoted as from Madame Guyon in imprisonment, translated by Thomas Upham.
"A little bird I am, shut in from fields of air,
And in my cell I sit and sing, to Him who placed me there."
Here is one of her sayings: "It is pride that dies last in the soul."
Here is a stanza of hers which seems to me to express the modern scientific explanation of God as an "over-self."
"Soul of our soul, whom yet no sense of ours
Discerns, eluding our most active powers,
Unknown, though dwelling in our inmost part,
Lord of the thoughts, and sovereign of the heart."
An accredited text book in sociology by Park and Rogers says: "Prayer is submission to an over-self", the precise idea of Madame Guyon. She called herself "A Bride of Christ."

† Her quietist views were formulated during her girlish studies at the convents. Reading Thomas a Kempis contributed to this end. One of her hymns which was written in French during the first year of her banishment and translated by William Cowper begins: "O Lord, how full of sweet content." Another which was translated by Upham begins: "I would love thee, God and Father."

years were devoted to charity. She seemed to dwell in
Immanuel's land, enjoying unbroken communion with God.
She was born at Montargis, fifty miles south of Paris, of
gentle blood. She seemed for several hours to have been
born dead. Her father was distressed, as he believed she
was lost without baptism. Her mother did not love her.
She was educated in convents and developed into a tall,
beautiful girl, of delicate constitution. At the age of seventeen she was forced by her tyrannical mother into a marriage
with a man twenty-two years her senior. At the age of
twenty-eight she was a widow with three children. The
boys were placed with tutors. The little daughter was torn
from her in the convent where she was first imprisoned.*
She lived in the reign of Louis XIV. Her opponent was
Bossuet. Dr. Thomas Upham wrote of her. The hymn
"Thou sweet beloved will of God" is sometimes ascribed to
her, but Julian says that Tersteegen wrote it.

KARL RUDOLPH HAGENBACH

1801-1874

"Since thy Father's arm sustains thee
Peaceful be."

This hymn which is found in the Gilman-Schaff "Library
of Religious Poetry" was written by a German Professor of
medicine and church history. He was a writer of distinction
and Catholic temper.

---

* Always a pure and moral woman, yet her reputaton was assailed
because of her intimacy with a priest named Father le Combe, who at
one period escorted her through a dangerous journey crossing the Alps.
The cruel tongues of slander misrepresented this innocent action, as it
is wont to do in the case of those who transgress the conventional rules
of society.

Many persons have been profoundly influenced by her writings;
among these was that great missionary Adoniram Judson.

GEORGE FRIEDRICH LEOPOLD VON HARDENBERGH

1772-1801

"Where only I have Thee, there is my fatherland;
For everywhere the gifts I share
From Thy wide-spreading hand.
"And in all human kind, long-lost brothers dear I find."

This is the closing stanza of the translation of a German hymn written by the above named poetic genius who died of consumption at the early age of twenty-nine. He was born in Saxony where his father was a director of salt works. He was a member of the Herrnhut Commune. His mother was full of Christian mildness. Friedrich studied at Leipsic. He is classed as belonging to the romantic school of poetry. He published his verses under the nom-de-plume Novalis. Carlyle calls him "the most ideal of idealists." His hymns are characterized by profound and beautiful aspiration. His young life ended at his home in Weissenfels in the arms of his friend Schlegel. His death was hastened by a hemorrhage brought on by the sudden death of a younger brother.

JOHANN HEERMANN

1585-1647

"Yet this shall please Thee, if devoutly trying
To keep Thy laws, mine own wrong will denying,
I watch my heart, lest sin again ensnare it,
And from Thee tear it."*

These lines are from the translation by Frances E. Cox of a German hymn written by a native of Silesia, who wrote his beautiful hymn during the horrors of war. The sentiment of the lines above are an admonition to us all, and in accord with the exhortation of Scripture, "Keep thy heart with all diligence, for out of it are the issues of life."

---

* Here are two more of Heermann's choice lines:
"All that I ever undertake I would begin in Thee,
Thee first, Thee last, Thee midst, O Christ!
And evermore to be."

There was another German hymnist with a similar name, Johann Gottfried Herrmann, 1707-1791. This pastor lived in Saxony, and one of his fine hymns beginning, "On wings of faith, ye thoughts, fly home," was translated into English by Catherine Winkworth.

There was also a later writer of the same name, whose dates were 1772-1848. This last one was a distinguished professor of philosophy and poetry at Kiel. Whether these various writers are connected by ties of kinship, I have not discovered.

ERHART HEGENWALT

fl. 1523

"Shew pity, Lord, O Lord, forgive"

This is the first line of a translation made in 1722 by J. C. Jacobi of a powerful German hymn written by a graduate of Wittenberg. (See Julian p. 506.) This penitential hymn sung to the wailing tune Windham is unforgettable.

MRS. META HEUSSER-SCHWEIZER

1797-1876

"The seed before it flourish
Must low in darkness lie,
And love, to live forever,
Must for a season die."

These lines, from a hymn called "Christ the Comforter", were written in the original German by a talented Swiss lady who is called by Dr. Julian "the most important of the modern female German sacred poets." Dr. Schaff calls her "the most gifted poetess in the German tongue." She was the wife of a doctor who lived in a lovely home in the Alps,

It is said of her that "she was trained in the school of affliction."* She did not have much education except as she gained her poetic inspiration from the Bible and the sublime scenery with which she was surrounded. She had a Scottish friend named Jane Borthwick who translated her beautiful poems into English and they were published in a book called "Alpine Lyrics." Her husband died in 1859 and she continued to live at her home at Hirzel near Zurich, Switzerland until her death.

VICTOR HUGO

1802-1885

"Pray thou for all who living tread
Upon this earth of graves,
For all whose weary pathway leads
Among the winds and waves."

These lines, culled from the translation by some unknown writer, were written originally in French by the famous novelist named above. They are taken from a beautiful poem entitled "Prayer for All Men." While his chief writ-

---

* I have been curious to find out in what this lady's special "school of affliction" consisted. The only explanation I can find is that she had seven children and wrote her hymns in the middle of her household cares. I know something about the distraction under which she did her writing. If her seven children were of the venturesome type (as mine were when out among the poisonous serpents of Africa) they may have supplied their mother with a "school of affliction" by getting on the edge of precipices in the Alps, thus reducing the poetess to a state of nervous prostration; or possibly her doctor husband might have been "no better than he should be!.. Who knows what is behind Dr. Julian's dark hint about Mrs. Meta's "school of affliction?" However, many of us are graduates of that school, as my father used often in his prayers to remind the Almighty that "Man is born to trouble as the sparks fly upward."

I am interested in the hyphenized name of the poetess. As a maiden her name was Meta Schweizer—(daughter of a Reformed Church pastor at Hirzel.) When she married, instead of retaining her maiden surname as an unostentatious middle name, as we Americans are wont to do, (and as I did) she flaunted it as an appendage to her husband's name, (he being Dr. Johann Jacob Heusser.) This may be entirely customary among Swiss ladies when they marry, but to my unsophisticated eyes it looks like a conspicuous way of voicing Mrs. Meta's share in the modern revolt of married women against being submerged in their husband's identity.

ings were novels* and lyrics, he wrote a few beautiful hymns. Here are some lines of his on wisdom:

" 'O man, I've not deceived thee; Wisdom cries.
'My first denials end in generous light;
As winter yields to spring, hate yields to love'."

Hugo imbibed royalist principles from his mother, but later swung off to the extreme left, and was banished for life by Louis Napoleon. He went to reside in the island of Jersey, but after the fall of the empire he returned to France and then went to Brussels, but the Belgians expelled him from the country. In Paris in 1871 he pleaded without effect for the lives of the Communists. His writings have great excellence but are much criticised. He formed with others the School of Romanticists, who brought into prominence disagreeable things in order to conform to Nature—which Nature herself is displeased with.

BERNHARDT SEVERIN INGEMANN

1789-1862

"Through the night of doubt and sorrow,
Onward goes the pilgrim band."

These are the opening lines of a beautiful Danish hymn by the above named distinguished poet and professor of literature in Zealand, Denmark. The translator is Sabine Baring-Gould.

Ingemann was born in the island of Falster. His earlier writings were largely lyrics. Later he wrote tragedies for the stage. Later still he wrote historical novels modelled on those of Walter Scott, in which he endeavored to portray the life of his own country in the Middle Ages. He did considerable also in the line of religious poetry and anthems. He is regarded as one of the best Danish authors.

---

* I read when a child Hugo's story "The Toilers of the Sea." It greatly took hold of my imagination, particularly a description of the fight of a diver with a sea monster—which was, I believe an octopus or devil-fish, about as horrible a story as I ever read. What a book for a child!

Edward Christian von Kleist

1715-1759

"Starry hosts exalt by thousands
My Creator's pomp and might."

The writer of the original of this hymn was a Prussian officer who devoted his leisure to poetry. He was fatally wounded at the battle of Kunersdorf where he defended a narrow defile and probably saved a whole army by his gallantry. He died at Frankfort-on-the-Oder at the age of forty-four. One of his hymns beginning, "Great is the Lord! The heavens proclaim afar—" was a great favorite with the Prussian army.

Friedrich Gottlieb Klopstock

1724-1803

"Thou shalt arise! My dust, thou shalt arise."

This is the translation of the first line of a hymn on the Resurrection by "the German Homer", as Klopstock is called. He was the oldest of seventeen children, the son of an advocate. When he was only sixteen he conceived the ambition to write an epic poem, getting the idea from reading Tasso and Milton. At the age of twenty-four he published the first three books of his Messiah, which attracted the attention of a high official who introduced him to the King whom he accompanied on his travels. He also obtained a pension to give him opportunity to write. His future wife, Margaretta Moller, fell in love with him through his poetry, and he made her acquaintance and married her. Their married life was like a dream of felicity. Margaretta wrote a friend, "I am the happiest wife in the world." She died soon after the birth of her son. At her deathbed Klopstock asked her to be his guardian angel, and she replied, "Who would not be so?" and added, "Thou wilt follow me." Klopstock had a remarkable spiritual elevation after his

Meta's death, of which he said, "I was never before with such certainty convinced of my salvation." He was buried at Ottensen with civic honors under a lime tree in the church yard. His Messiah is his greatest work and was greeted with much enthusiasm, but although suggested by Milton's Paradise Lost, it lacks the calm majesty of Milton's style, Klopstock's genius being rather lyric than epic. It is, however, a noble work.

KARL THEODOR KÖRNER

1791-1813

"Father, I call on Thee!
Roaring, the cannons hurl round me their clouds."

These are the opening lines from the German of the "Prayer During Battle" of the glowing young patriot who lost his life at the age of twenty-two to free his country from Napoleon. His countrymen regard him with such impassioned affection as to preclude any adverse criticism either of his literary work or of his college irregularities, which necessitated his leaving Leipsic University. He gave his young life for his country; all else is forgiven. Mrs. Hemans wrote a beautiful tribute to his memory. His songs had a most inspiring influence on his countrymen, of whom he became an idol.

JOHANN PETER LANGE

1802-1885

"My father is the mighty Lord whose arm—
* * * * * * * * *
My grave, so long a deep and dark abyss,
Is now scarce noticed on my way to bliss."

These lines, translated from the German by Mrs. Eric Findlater, (b. 1823) wife of a Presbyterian minister in the

Highlands of Scotland, were written originally by a distinguished professor of theology at Bonn. The lines are a clear statement of how the prospect of death is changed, for a sincere believer in Christ. Lange was the son of an Eberfeld farmer and was educated at Bonn, where he became a teacher, and continued to lecture up to five days before his death at the advanced age of eighty- three. He is noted rather as a thinker than as a poet. He wrote an able commentary on the whole Bible, which has been largely used and translated into English. He lectured on hymnology, but his religious poems, although spiritual and useful for private reading, are not well adapted for social worship and lack the popular style required for church services, He is called, however, the most important hymn-writer of the modern German reformed church.

LUIS PONCE DE LEON

1527-1591

"There, without crook or sling,
Walks the Good Shepherd. Blossoms white and red
Round his meek temples cling,
And to sweet pastures led
His own loved flock beneath his eye is fed."

These lines translated by Wm. Cullen Bryant from the Spanish, were written by the above named gifted poet of Granada, whose personal history is peculiarly touching. He was a lecturer in a university, a hymn writer and a lyric poet. He was brought fifty times before the Inquisition on the charge of Lutheranism and of translating the sacred writings. He was condemned to the rack and only rescued from that horror by the intervention of powerful friends. After being imprisoned five years, he returned to his lecture room and, without mentioning his long absence, began his lecture by saying, "As we observed in our last discourse—"! His lyrics are considered the finest in the Spanish language.

MIKHAIL W. LOMONOZOFF

1711-1766

"Man! Let thy towering wisdom say
Where wert thou when the stars new-born
Sprang into light at my command."

These lines from a paraphrase of a passage in Job were written originally in Russian by "the father of modern Russian literature" named above. Lomonozoff was the son of a poor fisherman, who, in the midst of want, showed such a hunger for knowledge and an instinct for poetry that a priest obtained for him entrance to the University of Kiev. He became a professor of chemistry and director of the mineralogical cabinets of the University of St. Petersburg, and was sent by that university to Germany to investigate minerals. The range of his authorship is remarkable. He wrote on chemistry, mineralogy, grammar and rhetoric, annals of the Russian sovereigns, and also poetry. He died at the age of fifty-five, much admired and esteemed.

MATTHAUS APELLES VON LOWENSTERN

1594-1648

"And give us peace; peace in the church and school;
Peace to the powers that o'er our country rule;
Peace to the conscience; peace within the heart,
Do Thou impart!"*

The author of the original of these lines was the son of a saddler, and was born in Silesia. He was distinguished by his musical abilities and occupied honored positions in the service of emperors. He wrote thirty hymns and accompanied them to melodies of his own composition.

---

* These lines, written during the Thirty Years War, were particularly admired by the German historian Barthold Georg Niebuhr, 1776-1831, who used to refresh his sensitive soul with them in times of mental depression and physical debility. Niebuhr was a juvenile prodigy in learning and became a great lecturer and writer on history. He was also a political opponent of Napoleon in his early manhood. The lines of Lowenstern are indeed noble ones and such that we might all with profit learn them and quote them in times of personal or political turmoil.

Martin Luther*

1483-1546

"Ein' feste Burg ist unser Gott,"

This famous German hymn was written by the inaugurator of the Reformation and became the national hymn of the German Lutherans. It was written in 1529 on the occasion of the evangelical princes delivering the "Protest" which resulted in Luther's followers being known as Protestants. It was chanted over Luther's grave with sobs and tears. It was sung by the soldiers of Gustavus Adolphus as they went into the battle of Lutzen. Luther wrote other hymns. One charming Christmas hymn was written for his son Hans. It begins:

"Away in a manger, no crib for his bed,
The little Lord Jesus laid down his sweet head."

Luther's home life with his children and his wife Catherine, an emancipated nun, is full of touching evidence of the affectionate side of his nature. His life as a reformer and a religious zealot is full of dramatic incidents like his throwing his ink stand at the devil, and his courage at the diet at Worms where he uttered his immortal words, "Here I stand! I cannot do otherwise! God help me—Amen!"

Luther as a poor little boy used to sing in the streets of Magdeburg for his bread. This interested a good woman named Ursula in him. She helped educate him in music. At eighteen he entered the University of Erfurt and found and read the Bible, which eventually he gave to the people in the vernacular.

---

* With the name of Martin Luther should always be associated that of his friend Philip Melancthon, 1497-1560, who was fourteen years Luther's senior, but also outlived him by fourteen years. He was born at Bretten and graduated at the University of Heidelberg. He became a great scholar in Greek language and philosophies. He espoused the cause of Protestantism, but with a gentleness and moderation which contrasted strongly with Luther's vehemence. The conciliatory attitude he showed toward the Romanists caused displeasure among the Protestants. (It would seem that in his desire to please everybody, he pleased nobody.) His very desire for peace brought him into controversies which filled his gentle spirit with disquietude, as he was emotional and excitable. He was much admired by his students who flocked from all parts of Europe to his lecture room. He published many learned books. The tercentenary of his death was greatly celebrated in 1860 in Germany.

Dr. Henri Cesar Malan

1787-1864

"No, no, it is not dying to go unto our God"

The original Latin of this hymn was translated into French by a native of Geneva, Switzerland, who died there also. The English translation was by Robinson Porter Dunn b. 1825. Another translation which begins "It is not death to die" is by Bethune. Malan was a Calvinistic preacher who founded a theological school to combat Rationalism. He wrote eighty-three hymns which were translated by Jane Arnold and published in London under the title of "Lyra Evangelica." Malan composed his own melodies, and had a workshop with forge, carpenter's bench, and printing press. He left a numerous family. He was a man with burning zeal for souls.

Marguerite de Valois, Queen of Navarre

1492-1549

"Who would be a Christian true,
Must his Lord's example follow;"
* * * * * * * *
He must hold death beautiful, and over it in triumph sing;
Love it with a warmer heart than he loveth mortal thing;"

The original of the above lines was written in French by the celebrated Queen of Navarre. She was a sister of Francis I of France. Before her marriage she had as a valet the renowned poet Clement Marot who was passionately attached to her. After her marriage to Henri d'Albret, King of Navarre, (her second marriage) she protected Marot from his enemies who had twice imprisoned him for sympathy with the Huguenot doctrines which also interested her. Other Protestants also found shelter in the territory of her husband. Marguerite was highly educated. She

could speak Latin, Spanish, and Italian, and understood
Greek and Hebrew. D'Aubigne says of her. "The goodness
of her heart, the purity of her life, and the abundance of her
works, spoke eloquently to those about her of the beauty of
the gospel." One of her books (she wrote much) was condemned as Protestant in its teachings. She is best known
as the author of "The Heptameron", a collection of tales.
Some of the nobility of France owed their first religious im-
pressions to her verses and ballads. She wrote a remarkable
poem on the death of her brother, Francis I. It is inserted
in the "Library of Religious Poetry."

QUEEN MARIA OF HUNGARY

fl. 1526

> "The Eternal God I rather choose,
> And fearless, all for this I lose.
> God help me thus to conquer."

These lines from a poem called "The Song of the Cross"*
were probably written when the above named persecuted
Queen was obliged to flee from Buda on account of her adherence to the Reformed doctrine. Her husband had been
recently killed, along with the flower of the Hungarian
nobility, in trying to defend his country from the invading
Turkish hordes. What brave souls both he and Maria were!

CLEMENT MAROT

1497-1544

> "Is Christ dead? Yes, certainly!
> What caused his death? Perfect charity!
> For whom? For us sinners who have offended him."

This is a prose rendering of a few lines of a French poem
written by the friend of Calvin named above. He made a
metrical version of fifty of David's psalms which were sung
in the churches of Paris and Geneva and by the persecuted

---

* This song and its story are given in a book called "Evenings with
the Sacred Poets", p. 214, published by the press of John Wilson and
Son, of Cambridge, Mass., in 1869.

Huguenot exiles who worshipped in the shelter of the woods. He composed lyrics also which were chanted by children in the streets of Paris. Marot's father was valet de chambre to Francis I of France and the son became at the age of twenty-one valet de chambre to Marguerite de Valois whom he passionately loved. (She married someone else and so did he.) Her interest in the Huguenot doctrines turned his thoughts to them, and his confession of simple faith and his biting ridicule of the vices of the monks brought upon him eventually persecution and twice imprisonment. On release he sought refuge with the before mentioned Marguerite, then the Queen of Navarre. Later Marot took refuge with the Reformers at Geneva, but they were cold to him because he played backgammon,* also called tric-trac, which these stern people regarded as frivolity. He had a gay, mercurial nature, but that he was ever prosecuted for adultery is stated to be a malicious invention of his enemies, who probably also are responsible for the report that he recanted his Huguenot principles. He had charming manners with a many-sided nature. Many different estimates are given of his character.

REV. JOSEPH MOHR
1792-1848
"Silent night! Holy night!"

The original of this beautiful Christmas carol found in so many of our hymnals, was written in German by the above named Roman priest who was born in Austria. It is the only hymn of his translated into English. It was written when the author was twenty-six years old, and was set to music by the school master of a neighboring village. It is a great favorite among our well-loved Christmas hymns.* There have been many translations of it into English.

---

* I am much pleased with learning the antiquity of the game of backgammon, to which I am also addicted. The fact that Marot played it makes him a pal of my own.

* A few days ago there came among my Christmas greetings one from Chicago, written by a college classmate of over fifty years ago. She said in her letter. "Almost Christmas again! I can almost hear voices singing Christmas carols in parks and everywhere.
'Holy night! Silent night!'
I love it—so beautiful."

THEODORE MONOD

1836--

"O the bitter shame and sorrow"
This well-known hymn was written by a native of Paris
who became a pastor in the French Reformed Church in
Paris where Moody later held meetings. Monod was edu-
cated for the ministry at Western Theological Seminary at
Allegheny, Pa. The above named hymn was set to music by
James McGranahan.

JOACHIM NEANDER†

1650-1680

"Hear the broken, scarcely spoken
Utterance of my heart to Thee!
Let me find Thee! Let me find Thee!
Thus I pray vehemently."

These penitential lines were written in the original by the
remarkable young German named above, who died at the
age of thirty, the son of a Bremen school master. Ten years
before his death he was wild and careless, and went with
two equally wild young men to the church on Sunday for
the purpose of ridicule. The earnest words of the preacher,
Theodore Under-Eyck became the turning point of his life.
He later became the pastor of that very church which he
had once entered in mockery. He, however, introduced into
a school at Dusseldorf belonging to the Reformed Church
some prayer meetings which caused offense and was deposed
from his position and banished from the town. He went to
live in a cave which is still called Neander's Cave. Here, in
the consolation of God and Nature's beautiful scenery, he
wrote some of his excellent hymns of lofty power. He is
called the greatest hymn writer of the German Reformed
Church. Dr. Julian's Dictionary of Hymnology gives about
two pages to him and his hymns.

---

† This Neander must not be confounded with the great church historian Neander of a century later, who seems to have been a name-sake
of this early writer, whose record is remarkable as he died at the age
of thirty.

GEORGE NEUMARK

b. 1621 at Thuringen

"Leave God to order all thy ways,
And trust in him whate'er betide."

These are the opening lines of a translation by Catherine Winkworth of a beautiful hymn by the above-named German author that has a pretty story connected with it. Neumark was a poor young man in Hamburg who got a slender living by means of his violincello which, in a time of sickness, he had to pawn, and on recovery had not the means to redeem from the pawn shop. In tears he asked the Jewish pawn-broker if he might play one more tune on the beloved instrument before surrendering it entirely. Then he sang to his own melody one of his own hymns, and going out into the darkness he stumbled against a person who had been listening to the song, and asked Neumark for a copy of it, offering him a florin. This person was John Gutig, valet to a Baron, the Swedish Ambassador, and through him Neumark obtained first a secretaryship with the Baron, and later the post of Librarian of Weimar. The above hymn was Neumark's expression of gratitude for the good Providence which had rescued him. He studied at the University of Königsberg when Simon Dach was President there, and like his teacher, was both poet and musician.

ERDMANN NEUMEISTER

1671-1756

"Sinners Jesus will receive"

This is the first line of a German hymn translated by Mrs. Emma Bevan. Neumeister was an eloquent court preacher of Germany who wrote hymns on Sunday and was an ardent upholder of Lutheranism. He was a controversialist against the Moravians and Pietists of the period.

JOHANN FRIEDRICH OBERLIN

1740-1826

"O Lord, Thy heavenly grace impart"

This is the first line of the translation of a French hymn attributed to the celebrated Alsatian Protestant pastor above named. Oberlin used the hymn as a compiler of French hymns, but may not have been the original author. He was born at Strasburg and his church was at Waldbach. He searched with the minuteness of an inquisitor into the most insignificant details of the private life of his parishioners and kept a register of their moral character in which obnoxious practice he was ably assisted by a housekeeper of like meddle-some propensities. He was a philanthropist who introduced better methods of cultivating the soil and a man of great piety.

KING OSCAR OF SWEDEN

1799-1872

"Is there thy home,—those unknown realms Elysian,
Which shine beyond the stars, a heavenly vision?
Then first my heart made answer, Yes!"

The original poem on "Where is thy home?" was written by the above- named King of Norway and Sweden who was also a sacred poet and musical composer. He was French by birth and married a granddaughter of the Empress Josephine, by whom he had five children. He was a just and liberal ruler and immensely popular with his subjects. The above mentioned poem was translated into English by Mary Howitt.

SANDOR PETOFI

"When I look upon the sky in its blue immensity,
Fancy fashions out a road
Fading to the distance far, where from smiling star to star
We are welcomed up to God."

The original of these lines was written by the young man called "the Burns of Hungary." Petofi, the son of a butcher of Slavonic origin, was born in the county of Pesth on New Year's Day. The family was reduced to poverty by the overflowing of the Danube, but a relative sent Sandor to a lyceum where he began to write verses, but ran away from school with some German strollers. His father brought him back and kept him awhile in quasi custody. Again he ran away, and joined some comedians, but at the age of twenty-one he went to Pesth and showed his manuscript verses to Vorosmarty the foremost of the Magyar poets of the time. At first the shabby young stranger was coldly received, but after his lyrics were read, Vorosmarty said, "Hungary never had such lyrics. You must be cared for," and thereafter treated Petofi as a son and never rested until his countrymen acknowledged his protege's genius. Petofi soon had a host of friends and never rose in the morning or went to bed at night without hearing his own songs sung on the street, so popular did they become. Finally Petofi joined the army of the patriot Bem and was killed in the memorable retreat after the defeat at Segesvar. His body was not found, probably because it was so trampled as not to be recognized. For years the Magyars hoped he would still return from some Austrian prison. So he died at the age of twenty-six leaving a widow and a son.

EUGENE POTTIER
fl. 19th century

"Arise, ye prisoners of starvation!
Arise, ye wretched of the earth."

The original of the great "Internationale" was written by a Russian and translated into English by Charles H. Kerr.

JEAN RACINE

1639-1699

"Naught can exceed the joy, the calm and holy rest
Of hearts, pure hearts that love—"

The author of the original of these lines written in French
was an orphan at the age of four. He was brought up
religiously by his grand-parents and went to an ultra religious school where his fondness for Greek plays and stories
so distressed his teacher that, to punish him for reading a
Greek love story, they burned the book, at which the brilliant
boy laughed, as he had already absorbed the story. Later
he broke away from this training and became a celebrated
French dramatist of irregular life. At the age of thirty-
eight, in full vigor and very famous, he returned to religion
and purposed to become a monk, but instead married a
religious lady by whom he had seven children. Thereafter
he pursued his life with great regularity in civic office. He
gave one-third of his day to God, one-third to his family,
and one-third to the king. He died after a brief illness at
the age of sixty.

MARTIN RINKART

1586-1649

"Now thank we all our God"

This is the opening line of a translation by Catherine
Winkworth of a German hymn written by a brave clergyman
who went through the horrors of the Thirty Years War. He
was at one time shut up in Ellenburg with many hundreds
of refugees. Pestilence broke out and there were deaths by
the hundreds. All the other clergymen in the place were
dead with the plague. Rinkart used to read the burial service
over the blackened bodies of forty or fifty victims each day
until he too fell, exhausted. One victim at this time was his

first wife. The hymn of praise he wrote at that terrible epoch has survived 250 years in Germany and has been sung on all important public occasions. It may be called the German Te Deum.

Rinkart was the son of a cooper and was born and died at Ellenburg where a tablet has been placed on the house where he lived. He was a voluminous writer and a good musician.

SAMUEL RODIGAST

1649-1708

"Whate'er my God ordains is right,
His will is ever just.
Howe'er he orders now my cause,
I will be still and trust."

This is the translation by Catherine Winkworth of the first stanza of a famous German hymn written by the above-named rector of a gymnasium in Berlin. He was born near Jena and educated at Jena University. The hymn above quoted was the favorite of Friedrich Wilhelm III of Prussia and was by his command sung at his funeral in 1840. The hymn was written by Rodigast for a sick friend at Jena.

FRIEDRICH RÜCKERT

1788-1866

"I shall not in the grave remain,
Since Thou death's bonds hast severed;"

These lines are from the grand choral which was a favorite of Prince Albert, and which, set to music by him, was sung at his funeral. The original was written by the Bavarian poet Rückert who was born at Schweinfurt and was educated at the University of Wurtzburg. He became Professor of Oriental Languages at Berlin in 1841, but during the revolutionary period in 1848 he left Berlin and never returned, though he received a pension. His last days were spent in retirement upon his own estate at Coburg. He had a wonderful mastery of the German language and also made translations from the Arabic, Sanskrit, and Persian languages into German. He was one of the greatest lyric writers that Germany has produced, but most of his poems are not hymns. His literary work preserves a high level of thought and expression. I find no mention of his having any domestic life.

Hans Sachs

1494-1576

"Laugh as ye will, I hold
This one thing fact that he hath taught:
Who trusts in God shall want for naught."

The original of these confident lines was written by a German shoemaker who was called by Luther "the Wittenburg nightingale." This hymn of trust was written during the siege of Nuremburg in 1561. Sachs made shoes and poetry, both,—visiting various cities in the pursuance of his trade, and calling on the guilds of his craft, where verse making was encouraged and taught. Goethe was the first to discover that Sachs possessed real literary merit. A few of his hymns came into common use, and he was the most prolific German poet of his time. He lived a merry life was married twice and had nine children. His grave is still to be seen in St. John's churchyard, Nuremburg.

HEINRICH THEOBOLD SCHENK

1656-1727.

"Who are these like stars appearing?
These before God's throne who stand?"

These are the opening lines of the translation by Frances
E. Cox of a German hymn which has been sung in Germany
for about 200 years. The original was by a pastor at
Heidelbach. It is a beautiful hymn on the Church Triumphant. It has been repeatedly translated and has come into
wide use in other countries beside Germany. It is not known
that Schenk wrote any other hymns than this one.

JOHANN FRIEDRICH VON SCHILLER

1759-1805

"Thou must believe and thou must venture!
In fearless faith thy safety dwells.
By miracles alone men enter
The glorious land of miracles."*

These are from the translation by Bulwer Lytton of a
poem called "The Longing," the original of which was
written by Schiller, the second greatest tragic poet of Germany, the friend of Goethe and the one who has the strongest
hold on the German heart. His father was a gardener on
a great estate. A duke offered to educate the boy free of
expense. He studied medicine but abandoned his profession
for literature. The duke who educated him was scandalized
by Schiller's drama "The Robbers" which aroused such
criticism that Schiller had to fly and live under an assumed
name. After a while he went to Dresden and did his composing in the night, a practice which shortened his life.

---

* The sentiments in these lines are a fine tonic to the soul in many
a severe crisis of life. I have lately had occasion to use them in giving
advice to one of my adult children in a time of stress. They may well
be graven on the soul of us all. Nothing else but that daring spirit will
take us through!.

He began the study of philosophy, married a high-born lady, and the emperor raised him to the rank of nobility. He lived in great seclusion. The last ten years of his life were the most fruitful in composition. His success in drama is supposed to be due to his study of Shakespeare. His over application was partly responsible for his death at the age of only forty-six. His fame has ever since been on the increase. His sentiments were pure and lofty, and Carlyle says he was a fine example of German character.

Benjamin Schmolke
(also written Schmolch)

1672-1737

"My Jesus, as Thou wilt!
Oh may Thy will be mine."

These are the opening lines from a translation by Jane Borthwick of a precious and well-known hymn written in the original by the above named German Lutheran pastor who was born in Silesia and who wrote more than a thousand hymns. During his last year of study at the University of Leipsic he was crowned as a poet, but returned after graduation to help his father in the ministry. He married Anna Rosina, the daughter of a merchant. By the Peace of West-phalia the Lutheran churches were greatly hampered, allowed only one church building for the whole district, and that without tower or bells and built only of timber and clay. Three ministers, of which Schmolke was one, had to care for a people scattered through 36 villages. His arduous labors brought on repeated strokes of paralysis from which he never recovered the use of his right hand. This affliction was followed by cateract which made him blind. The last months of his life he was confined to his bed. He was a diligent pastor, of great tact and discretion. His hymns express his sufferings, conflicts, and consolations. One of his hymns was written when a great part of his town was destroyed by fire. He resembles Gerhardt in style.

CARL JOHANN SPITTA

1801-1859

"A gentle angel, walketh through a world of woe;"
The original German of this hymn entitled "The Angel
of Patience" was written by the above named poet, born in
Hanover but descended from a family of French Huguenot
refugees. His father, who was a teacher of the French
language, died when Carl was four years old. His mother
apprenticed him to a watchmaker when he was fourteen,
but this was an uncongenial employment, and when he was
seventeen he began to prepare for the ministry, completing
his theological course at the University of Göttingen. Later
he would have been appointed permanent chaplain of the
prison at Hameln, but the authorities were alarmed at a
report that he was a "mystic and a pietist." (What a terrible
character!) So he became a pastor and Lutheran superintendent and married in 1837, just before settling down to
these duties. In July, 1859, he had gastric fever and seemed
to have recovered, but in September, when sitting at his
writing table, he was seized with cramp of the heart and
died in a quarter of an hour, at the age of fifty-eight. So in
the midst of life we are in death. Spitta began to write
verse at the age of eight. During his university course he
wrote songs and secular poems. A spiritual change came to
him about the end of his university course, after which his
hymn writing proper began. Spitta had been an intimate
friend of Heinrich Heine until one day when Heine visited
him he so jested before Spitta's pupils at things sacred that
the friendship came to an end. Spitta's hymns were mostly
composed in the evenings in his own room, often after fast-
ing. He wrote the hymn "I know no life divided" translated
into English by Richard Massie, an English rector.

GERHARD TERSTEEGEN

1697-1769

"Thou hidden love of God, whose height,
Whose depth unfathomed no man knows,"

These are the opening lines of a spirited translation by
John Wesley of a German hymn by the important hymn
writer named above. Tersteegen was the son of a merchant
at Mors in Prussia. His father died when he, a delicate
and thoughtful child, was six years old. His mother gave
him an elementary education and then apprenticed him to a
merchant at Mulheim. At this period he was one day
attacked with violent spasms when alone in a forest. He
prayed for deliverance which came, and he dedicated himself
to God, but found his peace under the instruction of a mystic
at Mulheim. He used to spend whole nights in prayer, even
when earning the living for himself and family as a weaver
of ribbons. The family did not like his peculiar habits of
devotion and forsook him; even when he was sick they
would not come near him. For five years he was in a state of
spiritual darkness—even doubting whether there was a God
at all. Finally he received such an inward manifestation
of the goodness of God that all doubts vanished in a moment.
Thenceforth for thirty years he ministered with great power
to the spiritual needs of others. He gave up his handicraft
and lived where he provided the poor with food and simple
medicines. He did public speaking also, in which his over
exertion produced dropsy in 1767 and after patient endurance
for two years he died. At the age of twenty-eight he had
signed with his own blood a covenant with God. He wrote
many hymns. The one I learned to love when in South
Africa begins "Thou sweet beloved will of God." It was
translated into English by Mrs. Bevan in 1858. The English
translation by Mrs. Findlater of one of his fine hymns begins
"God calling yet—shall I not hear?"

Johann Ludwig Uhland

1787-1862

"There is a land where beauty will not fade
  Nor sorrow dim the eye,
  Where true hearts will not sink nor be dismayed
  And love will never die."

The original writer of these lines was a German lyrist who
was born and died at Tubingen. He wrote popular songs
as well as hymns. His poetry, which is full of spirit and
imagination, has run through about a dozen editions. His
ballads are especially fine. He was a politician as well as a
poet, and a man of patriotism and truth. Germany has
reason to be grateful to him for his services to constitutional
liberty, yet it is as a poet that he will be chiefly remembered.
He is the acknowledged head of the "Suabian School" of
German poets. There is a romantic sweetness and purity of
style about his poetry. Longfellow in his Hyperion has
translated some of Uhland's beautiful ballads into English.

Anton Ulrich, Duke of Brunswick

1633-1714

"Leave all to God, forsaken one, and stay thy tears,"*

This hymn entitled "God's sure help in sorrow" and translated into English from the German by Catherine Winkworth
was written in the original by the above-named Duke. His
father (also a Duke) was married three times. Anton was
the only son of the second marriage. His mother died when
Anton was an infant and two years later his father, who was
pious and fond of music, married a lady of like tastes and

---

* There is one stanza of the above hymn which has become so dear
to me in the past months that I have copied it and put it on my study
wall where my eyes often fall on it. Here it is:
  "O teach Him not
  When and how to hear thy prayers;
  Never doth our God forget!
  He the cross who longest bears
  Finds his sorrow's bounds are set;
  Then teach Him not!"

the children were trained in simple evangelical piety. Anton wrote a number of beautiful hymns before he was twenty-two, showing a deep sense of sin, a longing for grace, and love of the Savior. After his father's death a desire for fame and power became his ruling passion and he did not fulfil the promise of his youth as to spiritual things. He joined the Roman Catholic Church, indulged in lavish expenditure for magnificence, and lost the love of his subjects and the respect of his former friends. When he was taken with a fatal illness he sent for an evangelical clergyman to prepare him for death and then received the sacrament by the Romish rite, gave his blessing to his surviving children, and died at the age of eighty-one. His granddaughter married Charles of Spain who was Emperor in 1711. Anton died without male issue and the dukedom passed to a son of his younger brother by his father's third marriage.

LOPE FELIX DE LA VEGA

1562-1635

"Shepherd, that with thine amorous sylvan song
Hast broken the slumber that encompassed me,
Who madst Thy crook from the accursed tree
On which Thy powerful arms were stretched so long,
Lead me to mercy's ever-flowing fountains!"

These lines, translated from the Spanish by H. W. Longfellow, were written in the original by the wonderful poet of Spain above named. Vega was born and died in Madrid. He read Latin at the age of five, and composed poetry before he could use a pen. He used to bribe his schoolmates with part of his breakfast to take his poems down from dictation. He had an adventurous life; once was arrested as a thief; was in the Armada; had a difference with another gentleman and ran him through, for which he was imprisoned and exiled; lost two wives and a son by death', after which he had a mistress who bore him two children. Later he became a priest and helped to burn a heretical brother of his order. (What inconsistencies we discover in other good people besides ourselves!) He scourged himself so terribly that his chamber was spattered with blood, and he died from the effects of his own scourging. Few writers in any age have surpassed this poetic genius in style or productiveness.

Joost van den Vondel

1587-1679

"Who sits above heaven's height sublime
Yet fills the grave's profoundest place
Beyond eternity or time
Or the vast round of viewless space."

The lines are translated from the epic poem "Lucifer" written by the above named Dutch poet. Vondel was a hosier by trade, but left the management of his business to his capable wife, Maria de Wolf, while he devoted himself to writing poetry. "Lucifer" was published thirteen years before "Paradise Lost" and some suppose that Milton got his ideas from it. Vondel's parents were exiles from persecution, both religious and political. He wrote scathing political satires as well as religious poetry. Finally, through poverty, he became a pawn-broker. He had an eagle eye and could read without glasses until very late in life. He died at the age of ninety-one. It is said that fourteen poets acted as his pall bearers.

"Take Thou my part against myself,
Nor share in that just hate."
—*Credit lost.*

HENRIETTE LUISE VON HAYN

1724-1782

"I am Jesus' little lamb"

This pretty child's hymn was written in German by a
Moravian lady, a teacher in the Girls' School at Herrnhut,
where she also died. She was a gifted hymn writer and her
hymns are marked by a fervent love to Christ. This translation is by Dr. W. F. Stevenson. It was a great favorite
in my own home when I had my little ones around me in
South Africa. I sang it to the babies as I rocked them in
my arms at bed time as we sat in an old rocking chair.

REV. GEORG WEISSEL

1590-1635

"O miracle of love and might,"

This is the opening line of the translation of what Dr.
Julian considers the best hymn of Weissel, called one of the
most important early hymn writers of Prussia. He wrote
about twenty hymns in all; several of them have been translated into English. One fine one translated by Catherine
Winkworth is a metrical version of the twenty-fourth psalm
and begins, "Lift up your heads, ye mighty gates." Weissel
was the son of a judge and burgomaster. He studied for the
ministry in various universities and became pastor of a
church at Königsburg. He died at the age of forty-five.
He lived during the period of the Thirty Years War when
many of the splendid hymns of Germany were written. It
was a time of terrible suffering which proved that "The
blood of the martyrs is" not only "the seed of the church"
but also the seed of her imperishable songs. The sufferers
die and their songs live on from age to age.

Daniel Wülffer

1617-1685

"Eternity! Eternity! How long art thou, Eternity?
* * * * * * * *
Ponder, O man, eternity!"

These are the opening and closing lines of each stanza of an old hymn* called by Dr. Julian anonymous, but which was so improved and added to by original verses written by the above-named minister of Nurnburg that he should always be associated with this solemn and powerful hymn.

Count Nicolaus Ludwig Zinzendorf

1700-1760

"Jesus, Thy blood and righteousness
My beauty are, my glorious dress;
Midst flaming worlds, with these arrayed,
With joy shall I lift up my head."

These lines, translated from the German by John Wesley and often quoted at deathbeds, were written in the original by one of the most remarkable Christians of all history. Zinzendorf was born at Dresden, and his early education was directed by his maternal grandmother, the widow of Baron Gersdorf, whose chief friend Spener was the leader

---

* Wulffer found the hymn in an old hymn book, perhaps that of Cologne.
Here is one of the stanzas:
    "Eternity! Eternity! How long art thou, Eternity?
    A little bird with fretting beak
    Might wear to naught the mightiest peak
    Though once each thousand years it came,
    Yet thou wert then as now the same.
    Ponder, O man, Eternity!"
The whole poem is given on p. 934 in the "Library of Religious Poetry."
The translator is Catherine Winkworth.

of the Pietist movement which preceded and was largely the cause of the Methodist revival under the Wesleys. The Pietists as a sect originated in Germany and sought to revive a sincere and emotional type of religion rather than follow an intellectual ideal of Christianity. As a child Zinzendorf used to gather other children about him and talk to them of Christ and pray with them. He used also in childhood to write letters to Jesus.* He went to school at Halle where the Pietist Franke was his teacher. Trained in this spiritual atmosphere he was at the age of twenty-two prepared in heart† to receive the persecuted followers of John Huss who arrived at his estate in Bethelsdorf, Saxony, as refugees from Moravia. By his permission they settled on his land and became the nucleus for the village of Herrnhut, where other refugees from Moravia and Bohemia joined them. Zinzendorf was recognized as their leader and they were called "The United Bethren." They became a center for missionary activity and their enterprises extended to many lands. Through them Greenland became a Christian country, and colonies were formed wherever practicable in their various mission fields, which included Labrador, Russia, Cape of Good Hope, and the West Indies. Zinzendorf himself labored more than a year in Pennsylvania. He wrote two thousand hymns. One of these beginning "Jesus, still lead on" was translated by Jane Borthwick. It is a favorite with children. His work for the world has been of untold value. The impulse his work gave to the Methodist movement is incalculable. Julian attributes to him the wonderful hymn "Glory to God whose witness train."

---

* I knew two little girls in the missionary home in Oberlin who used each to write a letter to Jesus every day, keeping the letters in a little book. Stimulated by the example of these children, I myself found the practice of great help for a limited period of my own life when going through a time of great stress. There is no better stimulus to a holy life.

† Zinzendorf in youth loved Theodosia, daughter of a countess, but although she loved him, he felt he must give her up to marry another. (Was this right? Is not true love too sacred to be thus put aside? What about Theodosia's happiness?) Zinzendorf told Wesley that after that act of sacrifice he was freed from all self seeking, and said, "My own will is hell to me."

ULRICH ZWINGLI

1464-1531

"Father, I live! healed of my pain,
Myself I give to Thee again."

These lines were written in German by the above-named reformer of Switzerland on recovery from the plague, during an attack of which he had believed himself dying. Zwingli was a contemporary of Luther and had a pathetic end to life. He perished in a battle which he had vainly tried to prevent between the papal and the protestant cantons of Switzerland. He was not a combatant, but accompanied his flock to the combat as their pastor. While bending over a fallen comrade, he was struck by a hostile spear with fatal force to the ground. His body was quartered by a hangman and his ashes mingled with those of swine so that his friends could not distinguish his remains. So died this gentle reformer, than whom none is more worthy of love and respect. It was the abuse of the Romish church in the sale of indulgences which aroused his determined opposition and enlisted him like Luther in the cause of the Reformation.

Sleep baby sleep!
Thy father is tending the sheep,
Thy mother is shaking the dreamland tree
And down comes a little dream on thee,
Sleep baby sleep!

Sleep baby sleep!
The large stars are the sheep,
The little stars are the lambs I guess,
And the fair moon is the shepherdess,
Sleep baby sleep!

Sleep baby sleep!
Dear Jesus loves the sheep
And you His little lamb may be,
And in His arms He'll carry thee,
Sleep baby sleep!

—From the German

CHAPTER V

EARLY BRITISH HYMNISTS

"A singing faith is secure; it has the victory that overcomes the world."—*From the Fellowship of Prayer.*

RICHARD BAXTER

1615-1691

"Lord, it belongs not to my care
Whether I die or live."*

This hymn was written by the author of "The Saints' Rest"† when an old man. He was the son of a Shropshire yeoman and became first a school-master and later a clergyman of the Church of England at Kidderminster, where he toiled and labored until from every home in his pastorate there were almost ceaseless songs of praise to God. Baxter was an opponent of Cromwell but got into trouble under Judge Jeffries for writing a paraphrase of the New Testament, and when Jeffries said to him, "Richard, I see the rogue in thy face,‡ Baxter replied, "I had not known before that my face was a mirror." He went through perils and trials,§ kept out of his pulpit by a military guard, his goods

---

* The title of this hymn was "The Covenant and Confidence of Faith." Of it he said, "This covenant my dear wife in her former sickness subscribed unto with an heroic will." The hymn was a favorite with his wife who used to sing it to him in his last illness. It contains these well-known lines:
"Christ leads me through no darker rooms
Than He went through before."
The hymn was written shortly after Baxter's release from prison.

† It is said that 20,000 copies of Baxter's "Saints' Rest" were sold in the space of twelve months. I am not able to speak with confidence as to the reason for this extraordinary interest in an old book which was a familiar object in my childhood's home. I was attracted by its pretty red cover, but its contents held no appeal to me at that time, so I have never read it.

‡ I have seen a picture of Richard Baxter. It is in an English book called Famous Hymns, by F. A. Jones. Baxter had a remarkable face, long, decided, even hard, but evincing a brave soul.

§ Among Baxter's trials that of a sickly body should not be omitted. We cannot wonder, however, at his having bad health when we read that he was given by doctors "over-doses of scurvy-grass, wormwood beer, horse radish and mustard." Poor man! It would have been better for him to have taken Nature only as his physician.

and books were sold to pay a fine for preaching five sermons, which caused offense. He was driven from place to place and was imprisoned on the false charge of sedition. His end was peaceful, after a life of wonderful patience and resignation. During his last sickness a friend asked him how he did and he replied, "Almost well."

ROBERT BLAIR

1699-1746

"How shocking must thy summons be, O Death,
    To him that is at ease in his possession,
    Who, counting on long years of pleasure here,
    Is quite unfurnished for that world to come."

These lines are taken from a forcible poem on "The Grave" written by a Scotch Presbyterian minister (second cousin of the Rev. Hugh Blair who revised the Scottish Hymnody). Robert Blair himself died at the age of forty-seven. Was it to him a sudden and "shocking summons"? How we ought all, in the sure prospect of death soon or late, to remember the solemn injunction of Christ, "What I say unto you I say unto all,—watch!"

REV. SIMON BROWNE

1680-1732

"Come, Holy Spirit, Heavenly Dove,
    With light and comfort from above."

These opening lines of a well-known old hymn were written by an Independent English minister, a contemporary of Isaac Watts, whose book of hymns he supplemented in an appendix.

This hymnist is now nearly forgotten, and most of his many hymns are now disused. He was in later life afflicted with a strange mental malady, supposed to be the result of his having killed in self defense a highwayman after a severe struggle, this tragedy being followed soon by the death of his wife and son. Browne imagined thereafter that God had annihilated in him the thinking substance and divested him of consciousness. While contending that such was his condition, he yet "produced a work in defense of Christianity, another in defense of the Trinity, a third as an exposition of the First Epistle to the Corinthians, and a fourth in the form of a dictionary." His publications number over twenty. What strange things are mental maladies! How good that our Christ included them all in his power to heal!

SIR THOMAS BROWNE

1605-1692

"While I do rest, my soul advance!
Let me sleep a holy trance."

These lines from a poem in "Religio Medici" called "A Colloquy with God" were written by an English doctor of fame and erudition. He said of this poem, "It is the dormative I take to bedward. I need no other laudanum than this to make me sleep,* after which I close mine eyes in security, content to take my leave of the sun and sleep until the resurrection."

Browne was born in Cheapside, London, educated at Oxford, practised as a physician in Yorkshire and at Norwich, was knighted by Charles II, wrote numerous scientific and other works, and traveled extensively. He wrote a fine hymn beginning, "The night is come, like to the day." His literary style is quaint and pleasing. He died on his seventy-ninth birthday.

---

* It would be interesting to collect the kinds of mental "laudanum" that different persons use to obtain desired sleep. I am finding that the mental repetition of one or more sections of the 119th Psalm is usually a very effective sedative. I have fairly well mastered the memorizing of the psalm since I was seventy years old. It was difficult to do, but is a help about inducing sleep and in other ways.

JOHN BUNYAN

1628-1688

"He that is down need fear no fall."

This line from Pilgrim's Progress begins a hymn (if so it may be called) which is included in some hymnals. The writer of the immortal "Pilgrim's Progress", written during twelve years' imprisonment in Bedford jail, during which time he supported his family by making tagged boot-laces, can scarcely be accounted a hymnist, though he wrote much religious doggerel. But the splendid contribution to our English literature made by this illiterate tinker forbids us to leave him out in the category, since he at least tried to write hymns, and he was essentially a poet in his make-up. "Pilgrim's Progress", born in the horrors of captivity, is supposed to have gone through more editions than any other English book. When, released from prison, Bunyan resumed his itinerant preaching, it might be said of him in his own words, "'Tis e'en as though an angel shook his wings." It should be mentioned that such an authority as Louis F. Benson has written a paper on "The hymns of John Bunyan" which is published by the Hymn Society of N. Y.

JOHN BYROM

1691-1763

"Christians, awake! Salute the happy morn
Whereon the Savior of the world was born!"

These opening lines of a famous old hymn were written by a celebrated English poet as a Christmas gift to his favorite little daughter Dolly, and were entitled "Christmas Day for Dolly," the original battered manuscript being preserved in the archives of Cheetham's Hospital, Manchester. John embarassed his financial prospects in youth by marrying his cousin Elizabeth Byrom against the wishes of both families. Thereupon the impecunious pair went to London and Byrom earned their living by teaching a system of shorthand which he had invented and which was the best then known. In his thirties and after the death of his eldest brother he succeeded to the family estate at Manchester where he spent the rest of his life. He was a member of the Royal Society, an associate of John Wesley and of William Law, the great mystic. A man of joyous religious temperament, he was also witty and wrote for the Spectator, as well as composing sacred poetry.†

RICHARD CRASHAW

1610-1650

"Great Little One, whose glorious birth
Lifts earth to heaven, stoops heaven to earth,"

These are lines from a Christmas hymn by the above poet, who, as supposed, died in the year of Shakespeare's death and has been compared to Shelley and Keats for the music and delicacy of his verse. He was ejected from his fellowship at Cambridge because he refused in 1644 to sign the Covenant, after which he went to France, became a Romanist and was made canon of the church of Loreto in Italy, where he died at the age of about forty.

† Here are two stanzas of a quaint little hymn of his:
  "My spirit longeth for Thee
  Within my troubled breast,
  Though I unworthy be-
  Of so Divine a Guest.
  Of so Divine a Guest
  Unworthy though I be,
  Yet has my heart no rest
  Unless I come to Thee."
  In all the four verses which are found on p. 63 of F. A. Jones' book on " Famous Hymns" the last line of each stanza is repeated in the next one, an original and striking arrangement. In the same book is given the reproduction of a drawing from life by a friend of Byrom in his old age. It shows him with a cane and a long, flowing white wig, a curious hat with a long, pointed brim in front, a straight figure (except for a bent head) in a long coat buttoned to the chin, and unornamented with even a button, and a smile on his profiled face. The picture, while not handsome, is exceedingly arresting, and I am grateful to F A Jones for this and other pictures of these interesting hymnists. John Byrom is to me a vivid and delightful figure that stands out from the past.

SIR JOHN DAVIES

1570-1626

"God has raised man, since God a man became,
The angels do admire this mystery."

These lines are culled from a sacred poem on "The Divinity of Man" by the writer of elegant verse above named. Davies was the son of a lawyer and was himself an exceptionally able lawyer. He was educated at Oxford and was for a short time Chief Justice of England. He died suddenly at the height of his career when fifty-six years old. He is chiefly remembered as a talented writer of flowing verse. His chief poem is entitled "Know Thyself."*

DAVID DICKSON

1583-1662

"Jerusalem, my happy home, name ever dear to me,"

The reputed author of this hymn which seems to be a part of a longer hymn which begins, "O mother dear, Jerusalem."† was the above named Presbyterian minister of Glasgow and later of Edinburgh who was deprived of his office for refusing to take the Oath of Supremacy. Dr. Julian, however, gives nearly three pages of learned discussion to the authorship of the above and says it is older than Dickson's time, that the author is unknown and was very likely a priest. There is a legend that it was written in London Tower by a prisoner there toward the close of Elizabeth's reign. It has been in use and a favorite a long time. It has been also attributed to Francis Baker on insufficient evidence.

---

* The opening lines of this poem are these:
"O ignorant, poor man! What dost thou bear
Locked up within the casket of thy breast?
What jewels and what riches hast thou there?
What heavenly treasure in so weak a chest?"
Davies was at one time expelled from the bar on account of certain indiscretions. It is of interest that for once Mrs. Grundy got after a man, it seems! Usually women are her victims.

† The long hymn of thirty-one verses which contains both "O Mother dear, Jerusalem" and "Jerusalem, my happy home," was a favorite of the Cameronian martyrs in the glens and mountains of Scotland. It was written first in Latin.

JOHN DONNE, D. D.

1573-1631

"Seal thou this bill of my divorce from all
On whom those fainter beams of love did fall;"

These lines taken from a "Hymn to Christ" were written by a famous preacher of the time of King James. He was born in London of Roman Catholic parentage, his father being an eminent merchant. He was educated at Cambridge but could not at first get a degree because he was a Romanist. However, he became an Episcopalian at the age of nineteen. He became the Secretary of a nobleman and was imprisoned for secretly marrying the niece of his employer. After his liberation he recovered his wife by legal process. He became Dean of St. Paul's, had a small salary and a large family. His life was one of vicissitudes. He was buried in St. Paul's and his poems* were later edited in a charming manner by Izaak Walton. He was the leader of the so-called metaphysical poets of England. He is known as a poet of strange conceits. It was of him that Sir Henry Wotton quaintly said, "That body which was once a temple of the Holy Ghost and is now become a small quantity of Christian dust, I shall see re-animated."

---

* Here are more lines "from a heavenly hymn" written on a sick bed near the close of his life:
"Wilt Thou forgive that sin through which I run,
And do run still, though still I do deplore?
When Thou has done, Thou has not done, for I have more.
Wilt Thou forgive that sin which I have won
Others to sin, and made my sin their door?
Wilt Thou forgive that sin which I did shun
A year or two, but wallowed in, a score?
When Thou hast done, Thou hast not done, for I have more.
        *   *   *   *   *   *   *   *
I have a sin of fear that when I've spun
My last thread, I shall perish on the shore;
But swear by Thyself, that at my death, Thy Son
Shall shine as He shines now and heretofore;
And having done that, Thou hast done; I fear no more."
Dr. Donne had this hymn set to solemn music and used at St. Paul's services.
Dr. Donne once writing to his spouse signed himself, "John Donne, undone."

WILLIAM DRUMMOND

1585-1649

"One cup of healing oil or wine,
One tear-drop shed on mercy's shrine
Is thrice more grateful, Lord, to Thee
Than lifted eye, or bended knee."

These lines culled from Fox's "Hymns and Anthems" were written by a Scotch poet of noble family who lived in a beautiful estate called Hawthornden. Drummond was educated at Edinburgh and later studied law on the continent, returning to Scotland in 1609 when he was twenty-four years of age. His father died the following year and William spent the rest of his life, except for an interval of travel, in the "sweet and solitary seat" of the family estate where he was visited by his literary contemporaries including Ben Jonson. His verses show a mind inclined to melancholy.* It is said that his death was hastened by his grief over the fate of Charles I, son of the Scottish James I.

JOHN DRYDEN

1631-1701

"Make us eternal truths receive,
And practise all that we believe."

These lines from his fine translation of Gregory's "Veni Creator Spiritus" have come to us from the pen of the

* Milton was a great admirer of Drummond's sonnets. One of these on John the Baptist closes with these striking lines:
"Who listened to his voice, obeyed his cry?
Only the echoes which he made relent,
Rung from their flinty caves, Repent! Repent!"
One of Drummond's exquisite sonnets is entitled "To His Lute." It carries with it a suggestion that he lost his love by death. These are the closing lines:
"Or if that any hand to touch thee deign,
Like widowed turtle, still her loss complain."
Mourning a lost love and brooding on the inequalities of life, no wonder Drummond's verse betrays a melancholy mood.

above-named dramatist and satirist (rather than hymnist).
He was the third son of Sir Erasmus Dryden and of Puritan
blood on both his father's and mother's side. However, in
1660, like most other English people, he turned Royalist and
in 1685 he joined the Roman church. For this change of
faith Macaulay calls him "an illustrious renegade." That
he was conscientious in religion is however indicated by his
remaining steadfast to the Roman Church at the fall of
James II, when it straightened his means and compelled him
to great literary exertion in his closing years. He was
educated at Cambridge and married Lady Elizabeth Howard.
The marriage did not turn out happily and there seems to
be proof of Dryden's unfaithfulness. In 1670 he was made
Poet Laureate and Historiographer Royal and retained these
positions until the accession of William in 1688. He is
famous not only for his verse, but for what he so finely
called "that other harmony of prose." He is estimated very
highly by literary critics—was at one time the leader of the
English stage. He is buried in Westminster Abbey.

GILES FLETCHER, JR.

1580-1623

"He is a path, if any be misled;
    He is a robe, if naked be;
If any chance to hunger, He is bread;
    If any be a bondsman, He is free;
    If any be but weak, how strong is He!"

These lines from a poem called "The Excellency of Christ"
were written by a son of Dr. Giles Fletcher who was the
ambassador of Queen Elizabeth to Russia. Giles Fletcher
Jr. was a poet and a follower of Spenser. It is believed that
his poetry in some measure molded Milton's majestic muse.

PHINEAS FLETCHER

1582-1660

"From the deeps of grief and fear,
    O Lord! to Thee my soul repairs."

These lines from a metrical version of Psalm CXXX were written by a brother of Giles Fletcher Jr. and a cousin of John Fletcher, the dramatist who wrote with Beaumont. He was educated at Cambridge and became a rector at Norfolk where he held the position for about twenty-nine years. His work called "Apollyonists", a satire against the Jesuits, is said to have suggested some ideas to Milton for his "Paradise Lost." Fletcher's principal poem is called "The Purple Island." Here is one of his fine lines:

"Thrice noble is the man who of himself is king."

GEORGE GASCOIGNE

d. 1577

"From depth of dole wherein my soul doth dwell"

This remarkable poem entitled "De Profundis" was composed while the author was riding in a shower of rain toward London. He was educated at Cambridge, became distinguished as a dramatist, and devised a masque performed for Queen Elizabeth's entertainment. He also distinguished himself in service with William of Orange in the Low Countries. Julian lists him as the author of a morning hymn beginning, "Ye that have passed in slumber sweet." This poem is found in "A Library of Religious Poetry" p. 533.

WILLIAM HABINGTON

1605-1645

"What claim have I to memory?
God, be Thou only praised!"

The writer of these lines was the son of Thomas

Habington, a godson of Queen Elizabeth. His mother, Mary Habington, is said to have been the author of the celebrated letter received by Lord Mounteagle the day before the meeting of Parliament which led to the discovery of the gunpowder plot. William was born in Worcestershire, England, but educated in Paris under the eye of his father. He married Lucia, daughter of Lord Powis, and his principal poem* is a series of verses addressed to her before their marriage, in which he calls her Castara. The lines above occur in that poem. He has been called "the choicest of the royal lyrists." He was only forty when he died.

George Herbert

1593-1632

"Teach me, my Lord and King, in all things Thee to see;
And what I do in anything, to do it as for Thee."†

The writer of these lines was born in Montgomery Castle in Wales, had a witty and pious mother, and was educated at Cambridge. He was favored by James I and was intimate with Lord Bacon, but his bright political hopes clouded

---

* He also wrote a fine poem on "The Firmament." These are its opening lines:
> "When I survey the bright celestial sphere
> So rich with jewels hung that night
> Doth like an Ethiop bride appear,
> My soul her wings doth spread and heavenward flies."

Habington was a Roman Catholic, but is said during the Commonwealth to have "run with the time, and was not unknown to Oliver, the Usurper." He doubtless had the faults of his age except its licentiousness.

† This hymn has in it these quaint lines:
> "Who sweeps a room as for Thy laws
> Makes that and the action fine."

Two of Herbert's hymns (or poems) have been dear to me for years. One is called "The Pulley." It closes with these lines:
> "Let him be rich and weary, that at least
> If goodness lead him not, yet weariness
> May toss him to my breast."

The other little gem beginning—
> "Sweet day, so cool, so calm, so bright,
> The bridal of the earth and sky,"

was so loved that I myself composed a melody for it. Here are a few lines on the advent by George Herbert:
> "The shepherds sing, and shall I silent be?
> My God no hymn for Thee?
> My soul's a shepherd too; a flock it feeds
> Of thoughts and words and deeds;
> The pasture is Thy word; the streams Thy grace,
> Enriching all the place."

and he turned to Holy Orders and became an English Church Rector at Bemerton. He had a wife named Jane who (somehow) fell in love with him before she ever saw him. They married three days after their first interview and had a happy union. Izaak Walton says of them, "There was never any opposition between them, unless there was a contest which should most incline to a compliance with the other's wishes." Herbert was a faithful pastor. He was on the ground before the altar on the day of entrance to his charge. Twice a day he went with his wife and household to prayers in the church. Twice a week he went to Salisbury Cathedral "to find heaven on earth." He was a great lover of music. He died at the age of forty-one, full of peace and love. On the last Sunday night he took his favorite instrument and played and sang, "My God, my God, my music shall find Thee." Worn to a shadow, his life ended with the hymn.

ROBERT HERRICK

1591-1674

"Sweet Spirit, comfort me."

This is the closing line of each of twelve stanzas of a "Litany to the Holy Spirit"* written by a vicar who was born in London and was one of the best English song writers, his poems† ranging all the way from amatory verse, sometimes indelicately expressed, to hymns showing deep religious feeling. He was at the age of fifty-seven ejected

---

* This Litany has some curious stanzas, viz:
    "When the artless doctor sees
    No one hope, but of his fees,
    And his skill runs on the lees,
    Sweet Spirit, comfort me.
    When his potion and his pill,
    His, or none, or little skill
    Meet for nothing but to kill,
    Sweet Spirit, comfort me."
Herrick seems to be somewhat sarcastic as to doctors.

† One of his poems is called "A Thanksgiving to God for a Home in the Green Parish of Devonshire." His lady's name was Julia, as disclosed in the poem beginning "When as in silks my Julia goes." His love lyrics are simply delightful.

from his parish by the Long Parliament, but reinstated on the restoration of Charles II. He published two volumes of graceful and melodious lyrics. His death occurred in his old parish in Devonshire at the age of eighty-three.

BEN JONSON

1574-1637

"Good men are the stars of the world."

These words were written by the above named friend of Shakespeare and of Sir Walter Raleigh. Ben Jonson's father died before his birth, but in his early life he is said to have assisted his step-father as a brick-layer. Later he studied at Cambridge and was for a time a soldier, and then an actor on the stage. He became a successful playwright and poet laureate. However, he was a drinking man and died at last in poverty. He wrote a few hymns.*

THOMAS KEN

1637-1711

"Praise God from whom all blessings flow;
Praise Him all creatures here below;
Praise Him above, ye heavenly host;
Praise, Father, Son, and Holy Ghost!"

This great Trinitarian Doxology, which has probably been sung more often than any other stanza in the English language, was written by "good Bishop Ken" of whose saintliness of character Macauley said it "approached as near, as human infirmity admits, to the ideal perfection of

---

* His "Hymn to God the Father" is a true lyric. Here are its opening lines:
"Hear me, O God!
A broken heart
Is my best part;
Use still Thy rod
That I may prove
Therein Thy love."

Christian virtue." His combination of boldness,* gentleness, modesty, and love, has been universally recognized. He was an orphan, but under the guardianship of Izaak Walton, the husband of his elder sister Ann. He went to school at Winchester College, where the school custom of singing a Latin hymn every morning may have given Ken his inspriation for his beautiful morning† and evening hymns which have appeared in nearly every English collection for 150 years and of which the great Doxology is the closing stanza of both. It is said of these hymns that "they will only perish with the religion that inspired them. Montgomery says of the Doxology that "it is a masterpiece of amplification and compression; of amplification in that 'Praise Him' is repeated in every line; of compression, for it exhibits God as the object of praise in every view in which we can imagine praise due to Him,—all blessings, every creature, here below, heaven above, and in each of his characters, Father, Son, and Holy Ghost."

Bishop Ken endured many trials and afflictions for conscience' sake. He was persecuted alternately by each of the political parties,—was at one time imprisoned in the Tower, and at another was deprived of his see and reduced to poverty in his declining years, yet he was able to sing to

---

* Ken was uncompromising in matters where his conscience was concerned He was dismissed from being chaplain to Queen Mary because of his faithful remonstrance against a case of immorality at court, and later he refused the use of his house at Winchester to Nell Gwynne, mistress to King Charles II. The easy-going king, however, from humor or respect for Ken's honesty, gave him, not long after, the bishopric of Bath and Wells. King Charles said he "would go and hear Ken tell him of his faults," and Ken spoke noble words of faithfulness to Charles on his death-bed. Ken attended the terrible execution of the Duke of Monmouth on Tower Hill and interceded for the prisoners after the fateful battle of Sedgmoor, retrenching his own estate to assist them.

† The morning and evening hymns were first printed on sheets of paper sent to each student's room in Winchester College. Ken was accustomed to sing his own morning hymn at the beginning of each day, accompanying his song by the lute, which he played. (Julian calls his instrument a viol or spinet.) After Ken's death his mourning assistants used to carry on the practice of singing Ken's morning hymn. Late in life he refused what might have been a position to gratify personal ambition, and spent his last years in contemplation, praise, and prayer, in retirement.

the end of his life with unabated cheerfulness, which
Emerson calls the last test of character. He died at the age
of seventy-four* and is buried† in Somersetshire.

WILLIAM KETHE

d. about 1593

"All people that on earth do dwell"

This splendid old metrical version of the 100th Psalm
published in England in 1563, which is generally ascribed
to the above-named rector of the parish of Okeford in
Dorset, England, may have been written to the tune Old
Hundred‡ which appeared first in a French Genevan Psalter
issued by Marot and Beza (?) about 1543. Kethe was an
exile with John Knox in Geneva in 1555. It is believed
that Kethe was a Scotchman by birth, and his name should
be associated with that of the Scotch reformer, John Knox,
as fellow sufferers in persecution. This hymn of Kethe's
is known everywhere and has been sung on important occasions, such as the opening of the Pan-Presbyterian Council
in Edinboro in 1876. Kethe also wrote metrical versions of
other psalms.

---

* F. A. Jones in his book entitled "Famous Hymns" gives us a
picture of Bishop Ken in his old age. The face is long, but with a kind
and gentle expression under a close cap, beneath which peep soft, half
curling locks of hair, arranged very much like those seen on coquettish
school girls of today.

† Lord Houghton has a beautiful poem on the grave of Bishop Ken,
from which I cull these lines:
"Yet laid he to the sacred wall
    As close as he was able;
The blessed crumbs might almost fall
    Upon him from God's table.

But preciously tradition keeps
    The fame of holy men;
So there the Christian smiles or weeps
    For love of Bishop Ken,

That dared with royal power to cope,
    In peaceful faith persisting,
A braver Becket, who could hope
    To conquer, unresisting."

‡ When, as a child, I attended a New England singing school, our
teacher, a Mr. Winch of Taunton, Mass., was teaching us to sing Old
Dundee, which he characterized as "the greatest tune in the world
except Old Hundred" which he thus placed first in excellence.

Richard Langhorn

Unjustly hung 1679

"It is told me I must die.
O happy news!"*

These touching lines are part of an irregular poem penned just before his execution by a noble lawyer of England who was condemned on the charge of high treason and complicity in the "Polish plot" by the infamous Titus Oates. On a calm July day a great concourse of people came together to see the judicial murder of this pure-minded man. Langhorn ascended the scaffold with calm dignity and made a little address declaring his innocence of the crimes of which he was accused, and then prayed with deep sincerity for his murderers and that God would bring them to repentance. He committed his soul unto Jesus, forgave the sheriff after the rope was adjusted, and added, "I am desirous of being with my Jesus. I am ready and you need stop no longer for me."

---

*The title of this irregular but exquisite poem is "Affection of My Soul." The quarterly Review said of it "perhaps there is not in this or any other language a poem that appears to have flowed so entirely from the heart." That of course seems to me to be an over-statement, as being the heart's true expression is the criterion of all lyrics. I append a few more lines from the dying Langhorn's undying contribution to our literature:

"Be glad, O my soul,
And rejoice in Jesus thy Savior.
If he intended Thy perdition
Would He have laid down His life for thee?
    *   *   *   *   *   *   *   *   *   *
O my Father,
O Thou Best of all fathers,
Have pity on the most wretched of all Thy children.
    *   *   *   *   *   *   *   *   *   *
Give him Thy kiss of peace,
Remit unto him all his sins,
Permit him to have a place at Thy feast,
And forgive all those who are guilty of his death."

"When I survey the heavens, with all their shining forms,
Lord, what is man, that feeble thing, akin to dust and worms?
Lord, what is worthless man, that Thou shouldst love him so?
Next to the angels he is placed, and lord of all below."
                                                —*Credit Lost*

ANDREW MARVELL

1620-1698

"What should we do but sing His praise
That led us through the watery maze?"*

These lines were written by Milton's friend, Cromwell's
private secretary, who had such a notable parliamentary
career that he has been called the "British Aristides." The
patriot Marvell was often in pecuniary straits, and lived in
extreme simplicity that he might carry out his ideals of life
in showing his sympathy with the suffering and persecuted
for conscience' sake. His lodgings in London were off a
little court and up two flights of stairs. He was faithful to
principle although tempted by royal bribes in his hours of
need. His genius and art were always employed for goodness. One of his exquisite poems is entitled, "A Drop of
Dew" and another "The Death of the White Fawn." Some
people attribute to him the hymn which begins "The spacious
firmament on high," but this seems on the whole evidence
to be the composition of Addison. It was published originally in the Spectator, and Dr. Julian is very sure that
Addison wrote it, not Marvell.

---

* The above quoted lines are taken from "The Emigrants' Sacred
Song." In 1621, the year after the Pilgrims sailed for America, the
Bermuda company granted the privileges of religious liberty to emigrants
to the islands, and many went thither from England. This poem was
written to celebrate their enterprise. It contains these curious lines:

"Where the huge sea monster wracks
That lift the deep upon their backs;
He lands us on a grassy stage
Safe from the storms and prelates' rage."

Marvell represented in Parliament his native city of Hull. His
father, who was a clergyman there, lost his life at sea while on a voyage
to marry a young couple that accompanied him. The older Marvell
seems to have had a premonition that he would never return, for as the
boat was leaving he threw his cane ashore crying out, "Ho, for Heaven!"
Neither he nor the young couple ever came back.

Be glad to day, for if, dear heart,
You can be glad just for today,
Tomorrow never comes, you know
And so you will be glad alway.

—From "Good Stories" April 1931

John Mason
d. 1694

"I've found the pearl of greatest price;
My heart doth sing for joy!"*

These are the opening lines of an old hymn still in use, written by a famous divine who is called by Baxter "the glory of the Church of England". His friend Shepherd said of him that he was "a light in the pulpit and a pattern out of it." He was the son of a dissenting minister and the grandfather of the John Mason who wrote a "Treatise on Self Knowledge." He was educated at Cambridge and became the rector of Water-Stratford. He wrote a "Book of Praise" which contained many hymns, some of which came into general use. The close of his life was sensational. About a year before his death he had a glorious vision of the crowned Christ, with a look of unutterable majesty. Mason spoke of this in a famous sermon entitled "The Midnight Cry" in which he predicted the speedy coming of the Lord. A report spread that this stupendous event would take place at Water-Stratford. Crowds gathered in the town from all the surrounding villages until every corner was occupied. Furniture and provisions were brought in and in great excitement the people leaped and danced and sang. This episode was followed by the old man's death, still testifying that he had seen the Lord, that it was time for the nation to tremble and for Christians to trim their lamps. His last words were, "I am full of the loving kindness of the Lord."

---

* The above quoted hymn became a part of my spiritual furnishing during the years that I spent in South Africa. I heard it sung for the first time at the joyous fellowship meetings of the South Africa General Mission in Johannesburg about 1895. The melody used was of a jubilant character, and the singing of that hymn contributed to the atmosphere of glorious joy that characterized those meetings. The experience was unforgetable. I did not know who wrote that blissful hymn until recently. Here is another stanza of it:
> "My Christ, He is the Tree of Life, that in God's Garden grows,
> Whose fruit doth feed, whose leaves do heal;
>   My Christ is Sharon's rose."

There are quaint figures in some of Mason's hymns which remind one of Quarles or of George Herbert. Here are two of his lines:
> "If God does not His Israel save,
> Then let Egyptians mock."

And also these:
> "My soul doth leap, but oh for wings,
> The wings of Noah's dove!
> Then would I flee far hence away,
> Leaving this world of sin;
> Then should my Lord put forth His hand,
> And kindly take me in."

And also these:
> "Man's life's a book of history,
> The leaves thereof are days,
> The letters, mercies closely joined,
> The title is Thy praise."

JOHN MILTON

1608-1674

"Let us with a joyful mind
Praise the Lord, for he is kind."

These are the opening lines of a commonly used hymn
written by the renowned author of Paradise Lost, at the
age of fifteen. Milton's influence on hymn writing has been
slight, as his talents lay in the direction of sacred epics
rather than hymns. He wrote some other hymns but they
do not seem to have been in common use. Milton was born
and died in London. He was educated at Cambridge and
it is said the mulberry tree he planted there as a student
still lives. His first wife left him almost immediately after
their marriage and he contemplated obtaining a divorce* and
marrying again but after two years his wife returned and
had daughters who acted as Milton's secretaries after he
became blind. His blindness caused by over-study was considered by his adversaries as a judgment upon him for his
republican opinions. Milton said of his blindness, "In that
obscurity in which I am enveloped, the light of the Divine
presence more clearly shines." Under Cromwell he held
the position of Secretary of Latin, but from this he was
dismissed at the Restoration when he was poor and blind.
Charles II fined him and ordered his books on Liberty to be
publicly burned. Later Charles would have restored Milton's
position to him, but Milton declined it, as it would have
involved his silence on the subject of Liberty. In his youth†
Milton had dreams of immortal fame which have materialized

---

*About the time Milton contemplated divorce he published some
advanced views on marriage, which might not cause even a ripple of
dissent now, but at the time were regarded as disgraceful and brought
down on him an avalanche of criticism. Without criticising his views I am
not willing either to criticise his wife for leaving him just after marriage.
According to Wilfred Lay in his book "A Plea for Monogamy", the usual
explanation in such cases is ignorance on the part of the bridegroom,
which wrecks at the start the felicity of many a marriage. It is said
that Mrs. Milton's final returning to her husband was because her father
insisted upon it.

† When young, Milton wrote to a friend, "I think (So help me,
heaven) of immortality. I nurse my wings and meditate a flight, but
my Pegasus rises as yet on very tender pinions. Let us be humbly wise."

in his authorship of "Paradise Lost" which it took him
seven years to write. He lived a methodical* life and died
before he was sixty-six. He is buried in St. Giles Church.

ALEXANDER POPE

1688-1744

"What conscience dictates to be done,
    Or warns me not to do,
This help me more than hell to shun,
    That more than heaven pursue."

These lines from a hymn called "The Universal Prayer"†
were written by the poet who is called the first English satirist. Alexander Pope was the son of a linen merchant of
London and was educated as a Roman Catholic, a priest
teaching him the rudiments of Greek and Latin in early
boyhood. Later he went to the Winchester school but at
the age of twelve went to live with his father in Windsor
forest and thereafter educated himself. He had a small
deformed body and an irascible temper. He never married
and was never well. In manhood he lived with his widowed

---

* "His personal habits were simple but majestic. He sat dressed
neatly in black in a small chamber hung with rusty green. He was pale
but not cadaverous. His hands and feet were gouty. He retired at nine
at night and lay until four in summer and five in the winter. Then, if
not disposed to rise, had some one sit at his bedside and read to him.
After rising he had a chapter of the Hebrew Bible read to him. After
breakfast he studied till twelve. After dinner he took exercises, then
played on the organ or bass viol and either had his wife sing to him
or sang himself. Then he studied till six, conversed with visitors till
eight, then took a light supper, smoked a pipe, drank a glass of beer,
and retired." This account would seem to show that the other members
of the family were only small satellites which revolved around the one
great luminary of Milton himself. One wonders if the wife and
daughters liked to be routed out of bed at four or five in the morning
to read to him! Geniuses are not easy to live with, it is said. Yet
was it not a great privilege to minister to such a man as blind Milton?
His daughters did not think so, and have (whether justly or otherwise) gone down in history as undutiful young hussies. Their mother
died in 1653 and three years later Milton married again. This wife
died in 1658 in child-bed and Milton has enshrined her memory and his
grief in a tender sonnet. Later he married his third wife, Elizabeth,
a sensible and practical woman, who wisely sent the rebelling daughters
away for useful training, and they subsequently married. The one who
went to Australia had children, and there may be descendants of Milton
in that part of the world. Elizabeth devoted herself to her wonderful
husband and he had a happy domestic life with her.

† "The Universal Prayer" was written as a conclusion to Pope's
"Essay on Man." Addison speaks of Pope as "a great genius, not
ashamed to employ his art in praise of his Maker."

mother in a little place on the Thames which he beautified
with great care.* He wrote few hymns† which have been
sung. One of these begins, "Vital spark of heavenly flame."
Another of his hymns begins "Teach me to feel another's
woe." He had great success as a writer, and Dr. Johnson re-
counts his fame in the book "Lives of the Poets." He died
at the age of fifty-six and is buried in a vault in Twickenham
church. His friend Bishop Atterbury‡ described him as a
"mens curva in corpore curvo."

Francis Quarles

1592-1644

"I love, (and have some cause to love) the earth;
She is my Maker's creature, therefore good;
* * * * * * * *
But what's a creature, Lord, compared with Thee?"
These opening lines of a hymn entitled "Delight in God
Only" were written by Quarles, that fine old English gentle-

---

* I like to think that this afflicted man with his suffering body had
the relief of a pretty little farmlet of his own, which he made a beauty
spot; and, not having erotic consolation, I am glad he had the resource
of a mother's unchanging love. Pope may not have been a lovable
character, but somehow I feel drawn to his story in sympathy, more
than to the "unco' guid."

† While not excelling as a hymn writer, Pope has contributed to
sacred verse by many sententious epigrams of a high moral strain.
I give here these specimens:
    "For modes of faith let senseless zealots fight;
    He can't be wrong whose life is in the right."

    "All nature is but art, unknown to thee;
    All chance, direction, which thou canst not see;
    All discord, harmony, not understood;
    All partial evil, universal good."

    "Hope springs eternal in the human breast;
    Man never is, but always to be blest."

‡ Pope returned good for evil to Atterbury by praising "his soul
unconquered in the Tower." Atterbury was imprisoned on account of
being mixed up in treasonable plots, but was finally sent into perpetual exile. He went to France where he worked with the Jacobins,
and finally died there.

man whose quaint poems are still a delight.* He lost his
father at the age of seven, was educated at Cambridge and
Oxford and studied law at Lincoln's Inn, which I cannot
learn that he ever practised, but used his legal knowledge
to compose differences that arose among his friends and
neighbors. He was a royalist and was for a time cup bearer
to Queen Elizabeth of Bohemia.† He espoused the cause of
Charles I and his literary material was confiscated by the
Puritans. It is said that his death at the age of fifty-two
was attributed to his chagrin at the harsh treatment‡ he
received at that time. He left a widow and a numerous
family. In his closing hours he gave good advice to his
friends, telling them to have a care of the expense of their
time and every day to call themselves to account. He expressed great sorrow for his own sins, and when his friends
chided him for this he replied, "They be not my friends who
deny me leave to be penitent." He had a peaceful and happy
death after a well-spent life. The charm of his conversation was said " to distill pleasure, knowledge, and virtue
to all who shared his friendship."

Sir Walter Raleigh
1552-1618

"But from this grave, this earth, this dust,
My God shall raise me up, I trust."

This is the closing couplet of an eight-lined poem written
by Sir Walter Raleigh in the Tower of London on the night

---

* Phillips (nephew of Milton) called Quarles "the darling of the
plebeian judgments", referring probably to the popularity of Quarles'
"Divine Emblems" in the cottage homes of England. I give here a
few lines from a little hymn entitled "Secure":
    "Close now thine eyes and rest secure;
    Thy soul is safe enough; thy body sure;
    He that loves thee, He that keeps
    And guards thee, never slumbers, never sleeps.
    The smiling conscience in the sleeping breast
    Has only peace, has only rest."
Some of Quarles' dearest poems are not on religious themes. One
of these, entiled "Love Triumphant" seems to refer to the love story of
himself and his wife. Here are two lines from it:
    "Our firm-united souls did more than twine.
    So I my Best-Beloved's am! So he is mine!"

† This English princess, sister of Charles I, was herself a poetess,
and will be sketched in a future chapter. Quarles later was secretary
to Archbishop Usher, and chronologer of the City of London.

‡ At one period Quarles was driven out of Ireland for his political
opinions. It seems to me that the confiscation of his manuscripts by
the Puritans was a particularly uncalled for hardship. It is no wonder
that Quarles felt deeply the loss of the precious children of his own
brain. Who would not?

before he was beheaded by the order of King James I on an eminently unjust charge. He had in his youth fought for the Huguenots in France. Later he organized the colony of Virginia which he named in honor of Elizabeth, the Virgin Queen. He was a trusted servant of Elizabeth, whose favor he is said to have gained by spreading down his costly mantle for her to walk upon. He was a man of noble presence and moral elevation of character. For his friend Edmund Spenser in 1589 he presented the "Faerie Queen" to Queen Elizabeth. After the accession of James I calamities befell him, for James was his enemy. He was imprisoned in the Tower for thirteen years, during which time he devoted himself to literature.* He was released for a brief time, but that also was full of sorrow. His expedition to Guiana was a miserable failure, and about that time his eldest and favorite son was killed in battle. He returned to England a broken-hearted man—was again imprisoned in the Tower, and his execution quickly followed. He bore imprisonment and death with calm dignity.

THOMAS RANDOLPH

1605-1634

'First worship God: he that forgets to pray
Bids not himself good morrow or good day.
* * * * * * * *
So live with men as though God's curious eye
Did everywhere into thine actions spy."

These lines were written by a young man who died at the

---

* While imprisoned in the Tower he wrote a beautiful poem entitled "My Pilgrimage." Here are some lines from it:

"Give me my scallop-shell of quiet;
My staff of faith to walk upon;
My scrip of joy, immortal diet;
My bottle of salvation;
My gown of glory, hope's true gage;
And thus I'll take my pilgrimage.
* * * * * * * *
Of death and judgment, heaven and hell,
Who oft doth think, must needs die well."

age of twenty-nine. I have not found any other hymns* of his than this one.

GEORGE SANDYS

1577-1644

"You that are of princely birth
Prayse the Lord of heaven and earth."

These opening lines of a metrical version of the 29th "Psalme" were written by one of the translators of the Bishop's Bible. George Sandys was the son of the Archbishop of York. After he was educated at Oxford he devoted himself for some years to travelling in Europe and Asia and published in 1615 a curious account of his experiences. One of his hymns was written at the Holy Sepulchre at Jerusalem. In 1621 he was an emigrant to Virginia where he built the first water mill, the first iron works, and the first ship of that colony, and for a time he was the colony's treasurer. On his return to England he became a member of the privy council of Charles I. He wrote many hymns and paraphrases of the psalms and other portions of scripture† but none seem to be in common use.

---

* I have found a delicious little poem in Bryant's Library of Poetry and Song entitled "Fairies' Song". It is Leigh Hunt's translation from the Latin written by Thomas Randolph. Here is one stanza of it:
"Stolen sweets are always sweeter;
Stolen kisses much completer;
Stolen looks are nice in chapels;
Stolen, stolen be your apples."
What an extraordinary little romance we might envisage about this young man who evidently had experiences in "stolen looks in chapels" followed by "stolen kisses" and "stolen apples." Ah, Thomas, you gave yourself away when you wrote that! What should fairies know about "stolen looks in chapels"?

† The most beautiful poem I have found from his pen is his "Lamentation of David over Saul and Jonathan" from which I cull these lines:
"Thy love was great, oh nevermore
To man, man bore.
No woman when most passionate
Loved at that rate!
How are the mighty fallen in fight!"

WILLIAM SHAKESPEARE

1564-1616

"There's a divinity that shapes our ends
Rough-hew them how we will."

(*Hamlet*)

These lines were written by the pen of the chief literary
glory of England. Shakespeare is not listed as a hymnist
by Dr. Julian, but was certainly a sacred poet whose writings
are marked by the spirit of the Bible.*

THOMAS SHEPHERD

1665-1739

"Must Jesus bear the cross alone"

This hymn as we sing it is a composite production, but
the foundation of it was written by the above named vicar
in the Established Church of England, who became later
a non-comformist preacher near Braintree, Essex, where he
began to preach in a barn in 1690. Seven years later a
chapel was built for his congregation. In connection with
John Mason he published a book of hymns called "Penitential Cries." The first draft of the above hymn was in
that book but the hymn was enlarged by Charles Beecher
and published in the United States in the Plymouth Collection. Prof. George N. Allen of Oberlin added still another
stanza which appears in the Oberlin Manual of Praise
published in 1880.

---

* He was the third son of a yeoman of Stratford-on-Avon, educated
at a grammar school, at the age of fourteen apprenticed to a butcher, at
the age of nineteen married to Anne Hathaway, and six months later a
son was born to the pair. At the age of twenty-two he became a humble
attendant in a theatre. I have read that at first he was employed to hold
horses at the door, but his magnificent powers were soon recognized and
he rose to fame. Some people think that he and his wife were not con-
genial, as he did not bring Anne to London, and he himself seems to
have gone back to Stratford-on-Avon but little. I read somewhere that
Shakespeare had to leave his native town because he had been poaching,
but this may be a slander. Shakespeare did go back near the end of his
life and died there. He does not seem to have left Anne anything by
his will but "the second-best bed."

JAMES SHIRLEY

1596-1666

"The glories of our birth and state
Are shadows, not substantial things."

These lines which begin a majestic poem* on Death which
are said to have "chilled the heart of Oliver Cromwell" were
written by James Shirley, a dramatic author, who was first
a clergyman of the Church of England, but later became a
Roman Catholic. His dramatic works were published in
six volumes. He founded a classical academy in London
where he died from the exposure consequent to the great
London fire of 1666.

SIR PHILIP SIDNEY

1554-1586

"Sing, and let your song be new,
Unto Him that never endeth."

These opening lines of a metrical version of the 96th
Psalm were written by the courtier that was called by Queen
Elizabeth "the jewel of her dominions." Sidney made a
metrical version of forty-three of the Psalms,† which was

---

* Here are some lines from that poem:
"There is no armor against fate.
Death lays his icy hand on kings;
Sceptre and crown must tumble down
And in the dust be equal made
With the poor crooked scythe and spade.
* * * * * * * * *
Only the actions of the just
Smell sweet and blossom in the dust."

† Sir Philip Sidney wrote also verse in other lines. I append here
an early sonnet by him on Sleep:
"Come, sleep, O sleep, the certain knot of peace,
The baiting-place of wit, the balm of woe,
The poor man's wealth, the prisoner's release,
The indifferent judge between the high and low!
With shield of proof, shield me from out the press
Of those fierce darts Despair at me doth throw:
O make me in these civil wars to cease!
I will good tribute pay if thou do so.
Take thou of me smooth pillows, sweetest bed;
A chamber deaf to noise, and blind to light:
A rosy garland, and a weary head;
And if these things, as being thine by right,
Move not thy heavy grace, thou shalt in me,
Livelier than elsewhere Stella's image see."

carried on by his sister Mary Sidney, Countess of Pembroke
after her brother's death, which occurred after the battle
of Zutphen, where he had behaved with conspicuous gallantry. A horse had been shot under him, and as Sidney
was being borne wounded from the battlefield, he complained
of thirst. A bottle of water was procured for him. As he
was about to drink it, he saw a wounded soldier looking
wistfully at the water, and Sidney handed it to his fellow
sufferer, saying, "Thy extremity is greater than mine." His
body was brought to England and buried in St. Paul's
Cathedral. His countrymen were in a passion of grief over
his death. As "sublimely mild, a spirit without spot,*" his
memory goes down through the ages."

EDMUND SPENSER

1553-1599

"And all for love, and nothing for reward,
   O, why should heavenly God to men have such regard?"

These lines taken from his poem on "Angelic Ministry"
were written by "the divine Spenser", a disciple of Chaucer,
whom he calls his "dere maister." Spenser was born and
also died in London and was educated at Cambridge in the
capacity of a "Sizar", (i. e. he was poor and doubtless
waited on tables.) After leaving college he lived in the north
of England and busied himself with poetry, dedicating his
first volume to Sir Philip Sidney, who became his patron.
After Sidney's death Sir Walter Raleigh introduced him
to Queen Elizabeth, but his experiences with that peculiar
lady were not happy ones. For a while he held a political
position in Ireland. At the age of forty-one he married,
but his home was sacked and burned by rebels, his youngest

---

* In the poem by Matthew Royden (found on p. 7 of Whittier's
collection "Songs of Three Centuries") called "Lament for Astrophel"
which was in reality about Sir Philip Sidney, are found these descriptive
lines:
        "To hear him speak and see him smile,
          You were in Paradise the while."
The whole poem is very beautiful.

child burned to death, and he and his wife with difficulty escaped. He was probably very poor at the end of his life. Ben Jonson wrote that Spenser had died at an inn for lack of bread. He is buried near Chaucer in Westminster Abbey. He was a noble-minded gentleman in advance of his age. He has been called "the most poetical of English poets." He wrote "Hymns of Love and Beautie" and it is of both human and divine love that he speaks. There is daintiness, brilliancy, and charm in his poems.

THOMAS STERNHOLD

d. 1549

"On cherub and on cherubim
Full royally he rode,
And on the wings of mighty winds
Came flying all abroad."*

This realistic description of God's agency in a storm is taken from a metrical version of Psalm 18 which my sister's notes characterize as "Sternhold's great hymn." Sternhold, who was "Groom of the Robes" to both Henry VIII and Edward VI is principally known as being a joint author with Hopkins of the first Psalter that was attached to the Book of Common Prayer in England. He did not live to see his work put into use, which did not happen until 1562, thirteen years after Sternhold's death. He started out to make a complete metrical version of the Psalms, but only finished twenty of them. Dr. Julian says that these "should

---

* I used to hear this hymn of Sternhold's sung to a rousing tune in a little country Congregational church in Massachusetts when I was a child, and the imagery of the above stanza appealed to my imagination. I hope I may be excused if I say that I, like Sternhold, made a metrical version of the Psalms, only in my case I finished the whole 150, and had them printed in a pamphlet to my own melodies. I am especially fond of this 18th Psalm, and give here my own stanza which answers to the one of Sternhold's which I have given. Mine is as follows:

"The Lord bowed the heavens and came down,
In pavilion of the darkness who shall find?
He rode upon a cherub and did fly,—
He did fly on the wings of the wind."

I endeavored in the music I composed for this to incorporate the rush and force of the storm the Psalm portrays.

be considered as ballads for the people rather than as poetry."
I have not found many details about the life of Sternhold.
He studied at Oxford but left without getting a degree.

NAHUM TATE

1652-1715

"While shepherds watched their flocks by night
All seated on the ground."

This well-known hymn was written by an Irish Poet
Laureate, son of Rev. Faithful Tate, an Irish clergyman who
wrote verses. Nahum is chiefly remembered as being the
joint author with Nicholas Brady* of a metrical version of
Psalms which was attached to the English Book of Common
Prayer and came into general use. Tate is said to have been
a man of intemperate and improvident life. He died in
London at the age of sixty-three, a refugee from his
creditors.

JEREMY TAYLOR

1613-1667

"Today Almyghtiness grew weak;
Today the Word itself was mute and could not speak."

These lines from "A Hymn for Christmas Day"† were

---

* Nicholas Brady (1659-1726) was for a time chaplain to King
William III. His native town was Bandon, Ireland, and three times
he saved it from burning during the Irish war when he was an active
supporter of King William. He was educated at Oxford and at Dublin
University which gave him the title of D. D. He held various appointments in plurality, but in spite of the income thus derived, his ex-
travagances obliged him also to keep a school. (Wonderful man, to have
so many irons in the fire at once!) It is impossible to tell of the Psalms
of Tate and Brady which were written by the one or the other, but
Tate is generally supposed to have been the poetical workman. "As
pants the hart for cooling streams" and "Through all the changing
scenes of life" come from Tate and Brady's Psalter. Lyte rewrote that
last named hymn, which is sometimes therefore ascribed to him.

† Taylor wrote another "Hymn for Christmas Day" from which I
cull these quaint lines:
"He hath other waiters now;
    A poor cow,
An ox and mule stand and behold
    And wonder
That a stable should enfold
    Him that can thunder."

written by the great English bishop who has been called
"our Shakespeare in theology." He was the son of a
Cambridge barber and entered college as a "sizar," which
shows that he was poor. His career at Oxford was brilliant,
developing his imperial intellect and enthralling eloquence
of which Coleridge said that if he had called Taylor the
most eloquent man that ever lived, Cicero would have forgiven him, and Demosthenes would have nodded assent.
The encyclopaedia speaks of his "inexhaustible imagery,
shining like the glossy purples of a dove's neck." He is
best known as the author of "Holy Living and Holy
Dying."* Dr. Julian says of him, however, that he holds
a very small place in the Antiphon† of England, his attempts
at verse being hampered and shallowed eloquence rather
than poetry. He was a staunch royalist and spoke against
the Puritans. During the Commonwealth he was "sequestered" and filled in the time by teaching school in Wales. I
read also that during the Protectorate he was fined and imprisoned. (I judge not for long.) At this time he lost his
position as Chaplain to the King. He was a splendid scholar
and mighty preacher. After the Restoration he was appointed
Vice-Chancellor of the University of Dublin. He died at
the age of fifty-four and was interred in the Cathedral of
Dromore.

---

* This story is told of the effect of Taylor's "Holy Living and Holy
Dying" on John Keats, who, when meeting death and not a Christian,
requested that book to be read to him by his friend Severn who ministered to him by playing the piano, etc. Through Taylor's book Keats
tried to calm the tumult in his soul, and on Feb. 23, 1821, he said,
"Severn—I—lift me up—I am dying! I shall die easy,—don't be frightened, be firm and thank God it has come." This shows how Taylor's
book helped this beloved young poet to dying peace. I cannot find anything in Keats' poems to be classed as a hymn, but these lines show
his belief in immortality:

"And can I bid these joys farewell?
Yes, I must pass them for a nobler life."

† The unsophisticated reader is invited to enrich his vocabulary
(as I had to) by looking up "Antiphon" in the dictionary.

HENRY VAUGHAN, M. D.

1621-1693

"Give Him thy first thoughts, so shalt thou keep
Him company all day and in Him sleep."

These lines from a remarkable poem entitled "Early
Rising and Prayer"* were written by a Welsh doctor and
poet called "the Silurist."† Henry Vaughan and his twin
brother Thomas were born of a titled family and studied
at Oxford. But their studies were interrupted by the national
troubles. They were hot royalists; Thomas bore arms and
Henry was awhile imprisoned. He later became the village
doctor of Newton, Wales, a place of great natural beauty,
and Dr. Vaughan's poetry is full of expressions showing
his love of nature. His verse resembles that of George
Herbert of whom he said that he was "a convert of that
blessed man." He died at the age of seventy-two and was
almost forgotten for 200 years.‡ His life was then written
by Henry F. Lyte, and his beautiful, thoughtful poems are
receiving attention from hymn compilers and others. He
was an original spirit and writer, and like Wordsworth he
believed that this is not our first state of existence, and that
our souls are haunted by dim memories of a former life.
He published some of his poems in 1650 and Dr. Julian
says that 119 of these have been in use as hymns. They are
not familiar, however, to me. The best of them were
written in a time of affliction.

---

* This poem is too fine and too practical not to be familiar to all.
I cannot refrain from quoting a few lines of it:
"there are set awful hours
'Twixt Heaven and us; the manna was not got
After sun-rising; for day sullies flowers.
    * * * * * * * * *
When the world's up and every swarm abroad,
Keep well thy temper, mix not with each day;
Dispatch necessities; life hath a load
Which must be carried on, and safely may;
Yet keep those cares without thee; let the heart
Be God's alone, and choose the better part."

† Vaughan styled himself "the Silurist" because the ancient inhabitants of South Wales were called Silures. They are described by
Tacitus and are supposedly of Iberian origin.

‡ Let us take courage, dear fellow-failures! After we have been
dead 200 years, possibly someone may discover that we wrote something
worth mentioning and write our lives also, who knows? Nil desper-
andum!

Sir Henry Wotton

1568-1639

"How happy is he born or taught
That serveth not another's will."

These are the opening lines of a poem which has been used as a hymn by the Unitarians. It is entitled "The Happy Life"* and deserves to be engraved on the memories of us all for the truth it expresses. The author was born in Kent and educated at Oxford. He was sent as an ambassador to Venice, and at Augsburg when on his way he wrote in an album, "An ambassador is an honest man sent abroad to lie for the good of his country." He lived for a time at Genoa and was a friend of Beza, the coadjutor of Calvin. Wotton also travelled extensively. He was enmeshed in the political turmoil of England. For awhile he was secretary to Essex† and when that earl was arrested for treason, Wotton had to fly for his life to France. On another occasion he was sent to warn King James I of a plot against his life. Wotton wrote books which are forgotten, but his poems still live. He was the discoverer of the genius of Milton.

---

* This poem ends with these lines:
    "Lord of himself, though not of lands,
    And having nothing, yet hath all."

¶ Wotton's close connection with Essex makes me more interested in him, as the story of that beautiful young man with his pitiful end appeals strongly to me. See Strachey's book on "Elizabeth and Essex."

God is love, that love surrounds me.
   In that love I safely dwell;
'Tis above, beneath, within me.
   God is love, and all is well.
God is love, sweet love!
God is love, pure love!
   That love is mine, and all is well.

—*Credit Lost*

GEORGE WYTHER

(also written Wither)

1588-1667

"Now sing we will Thy praise,
For that Thou dost as well prolong
Our loving as our days."

These lines are culled from a choice little hymn on marriage* written by a Puritan poet who composed over 300 hymns. His best hymns were written in prison where he was put three times (once in the Tower) for what were deemed seditious writings. Twice his life was endangered and it is said that a good-humored remark of Sir John Denham's saved him: to wit, that "His Majesty really must not hang George Wither, because as long as he lives no one will account me the worst poet in England." George Wither was set free. In youth he went for three years to Oxford, but some one persuaded his father that George did not need more education and he was withdrawn " for the plough" that is, for rustic work on the paternal estate. This proved very uncongenial to George who later studied law. From that time he was always printing something either in prose or in verse. His poetry contains many excellencies,† but these are often overlaid with verses that are either indifferent or bad. That he was an honest man and true Christian no one will deny. He sometimes lost his temper in polemics. He was a devoted son of the church of England to the close of his life, yet honestly served non-comformity too.

---

* His marriage (of which this is an anniversary hymn) seems to have been especially felicitous. His wife was Elizabeth, eldest daughter of H. Emerson (a great wit who could write verse too). He was of the same English Emersons from whom Ralph Waldo Emerson was descended. Wither died in London and was buried near the door of Savoy Church on the Strand near which he lived.

† One of Wither's beautiful poems is called the "Rocking Hymn." He had issue and so was interested in babies' lullabies. This lullaby has twelve stanzas, the last lines of them all similar to these I give:
"My pretty lamb, forbear to weep;
Be still, my dear; sweet baby, sleep."
Wither says of it that nurses generally sing children to sleep with unprofitable songs, and that his hymn was prepared to acquaint them and the children with the loving care of their Heavenly Father.

Dr. Edward Young

1684-1765

"A Deity believed is joy begun;
A Deity adored is joy advanced;
A Deity beloved is joy matured."

These lines were written by the author of the "Night Thoughts" that used to be much read once upon a time. Edward Young was the son of an English rector and in time became a rector himself, but devoted himself mostly to literature. His "Night Thoughts" are not lyrical and he can scarcely be classed as a hymnist but rather as a sacred poet. Some of his lines are shrewd and have become almost proverbial.* His marriage to Elizabeth Lee, daughter of an earl, was a very happy one, it seems. His greatest weakness was an inordinate desire for honor, but he was nevertheless a good man and true Christian.

---

* Here are some of his oft-quoted lines:
"At thirty, man suspects himself a fool,
Knows it at forty, and reforms his plan,
At fifty chides his infamous delay;
* * * * * * * * *
Resolves and re-resolves, then dies the same."

"God grant to me that I may see
The beauty of a crooked tree,
The blossom of a humble weed,
The glory of a homely deed.
The pathos of a homeless pup,
The way to lift a brother up.
O grant to me the highest art—
Give me the understanding heart."

—Anon.

CHAPTER VI

THE BRITISH HYMNISTS OF THE EIGHTEENTH CENTURY

"The great revivals have borne witness in song. What would John Wesley have been without his brother Charles? Or Moody without Sankey?

"Somebody has wisely said that one who sings at his work will accomplish a great deal more, and do it better than one who doesn't."

JOSEPH ADDISON

1672-1719

"The Lord my pasture shall prepare
And feed me with a shepherd's care."

These opening lines of one of his well-known* hymns were written by the distinguished author of the "Sir Roger de Coverley Papers" published in the "Spectator".† Joseph Addison, son of Rev. Launcelot Addison, chaplain of the king, was educated at Oxford‡ and originally intended for

---

* The three hymns of Addison's which are familiar to me were in every case used to conclude one of his essays in the Spectator. Besides the one already quoted the others are: "The spacious firmament on high" (erroneously attributed to Andrew Marvell); and "When all Thy mercies, O my God, my rising soul surveys" (also erroneously attributed to Marvell). There is another hymn of his called "The Travellers' Hymn" which Julian says was written in commemoration of deliverance from a shipwreck in the Mediterranean Sea. It begins "How are Thy servants blest, O Lord!"
In December, 1700, Addison took a ship at Marseilles and skirted along the coast, delighted with the myrtles and olive trees which retained their verdure in the winter solstice. Soon a great storm arose in which the captain believed his ship would be lost. Addison fortified his soul against death with devotions. One stanza of this hymn greatly appealed to Robert Burns when a young boy of ten or eleven years. It reads:
"For though in dreadful whirls we hung
High on the broken wave,
I knew Thou wast not slow to hear,
Nor impotent to save."

† The Spectator was "the great, elegant, and popular miscellany of English literature, and Addison's fame is inseparably associated with it." Sir Roger de Coverley is a creation of Addison's gay humor and vivid and gentle imagination, who will live as long as the English literature of that period endures.

‡ Concerning Addison's elementary education I have read that he "as a school boy passed up and down the dreamy garden of the Cathedral hold at Lichfield." This may be of interest to some tourist in England who is tracing out the paths of her illustrious sons and daughters.

the Church, but through his acquaintance with Dryden, he was turned aside into literature and politics, in which he held some official positions including one year as Secretary of State, for which he was temperamentally unfitted and was glad to resign. His health was precarious and amid the plaudits for his literary accomplishments he was led into a "splendid but dismal" *marriage with the dowager countess of Warwick. He died at the age of forty-seven, leaving behind him an unperishable literary record as a writer of sweetness, propriety, and natural dignity of style. He was a man of modesty and true piety, and he helped to reform the manners of his time and to create a class of readers among the middle masses which has since grown prodigious. No one can help loving Addison who reads him.

JAMES ALLEN

1734-1804

"Sweet the moments, rich in blessing,
    Which before the cross I spend."

This useful hymn was written by an earnest but eccentric itinerant preacher who was employed by the Countess of Huntingdon, but who eventually became a Sandemanian† and built a chapel on his own estate at Gayle Yorkshire where he preached until his death. He was at one time set upon by a mob. This hymn was reconstructed into its present

* Lady Mary Wortley Montagu in a letter to the Pope referring both to Addison's marriage and to his appointment as Secretary of State, expressed her fear that a day might come "when he would be heartily glad to resign both." And Dr. Johnson sarcastically remarks concerning the Countess of Warwick that the lady was persuaded to marry him on terms much like those on which a Turkish princess is espoused, to whom the Sultan is reported to announce, "Daughter, I give thee this man for thy slave." It would seem that after marriage Addison put himself in that position, but then, we all of us mostly find ourselves either "the black slave or the white slave" of somebody or other, or else holding someone else in thrall. Addison was timid and awkward in large companies and it was simply impossible for him to attempt debating in parliament, so he got no addition to his happiness from his mistaken step into high life. It was out of keeping with his character and literary pursuits. Retreat alone gave him peace at last. He died at Kensington after a few months' illness.

† The Sandemanians were a sect that believed that under the gospel we are not made subject to the law requiring good works.

familiar form by his friend Walter Shirley, a cousin of
Lady Huntingdon's. Allen was the editor and chief con-
tributor to the Kendall hymn book. He wrote 70 hymns.
One of merit is entitled "Worthy the Lamb."

Rev. John Bakewell

1721-1819

"Hail, Thou once despised Jesus"

This old hymn was written by an English Methodist
evangelist—an associate of the Wesleys and Toplady. He
was born at Brailsford, Derbyshire, and died at the advanced
age of ninety-eight at Lewisham near Greenwich. He was
buried in the Wesleyan burying ground in London. For
some years he conducted an Academy at Greenwich. He
wrote a few hymns of which the one mentioned above is
best known.

Bernard Barton

1784-1849

"Walk in the light; so shalt thou know
That fellowship of love."

This familiar hymn was written by the son of a Quaker,
born in London and apprenticed at 14 to a shopkeeper in
Essex. In adult life he was a banking clerk for forty years in
Woodbridge, England. He was a married man whose wife
died after a year of married life, leaving him with an infant
daughter. He wrote verses for his own amusement and
published four volumes of them. These brought him to the
notice of Walter Scott, Southey, Lamb, Byron, and Coleridge,
and finally, eight years before his death, through the patronage of Sir Robert Peel, he got a pension of 100 pounds a
year. He founded a reading club. His death at the age

of sixty-five was sudden. His daughter after his death published a book of selections from his writings. Some of his hymns and ballads are very fine. One hymn is on "The Sea" and another "On the Sabbath", in which occurs this line:

"Days fixed by God for intercourse with dust."

His hymns are chiefly used by Unitarians.

JAMES BEATTIE

1735-1803

"O pity, great Father of light, then I cried,
From doubt and from darkness Thou only canst free."

These lines culled from a poem called "The Hermit" were written by Scotland's great moral philosopher. Beattie wrote a famous essay on Truth intended as an antidote to the skeptical writing of Hume. He was made Professor of Moral Philosophy at Aberdeen when only twenty-five years old. He is said to have died broken hearted, under the pressure of domestic trials. He was a useful and talented man and the beautiful poems he wrote show his deep love for nature* and his tenderness for animals.† He also wrote a pithy and sarcastic little poem of only eight lines on law.‡

---

* Dr. Chalmers greatly admired the following lines by Beattie:
"Oh how canst thou renounce the boundless store
Of charms which Nature to her votary yields,
The warbling woodland, the resounding shore,
The pomp of groves, the garniture of fields,
*   *   *   *   *   *   *   *   *
And all the dread magnificence of heaven,
Oh how canst thou renounce, and hope to be forgiven?"

† In a poem called "The Minstrel" occur the following lines which might rebuke the women who adorn themselves with the fur or feathers of suffering creatures:
"His heart from cruel sport estranged would bleed
To work the woe of any living thing
By trap or net, by arrow or by sling!
These he detested; these he scorned to wield;
He wished to be the guardian, not the king,
Tyrant for less, or traitor of the field!"

‡ His lines on law are applicable to the big scoundrels who go scot-free:
"Cobwebs for little flies are spread
And laws for little folks are made;
But if an insect of renown,
Hornet or beetle, wasp or drone,
Be caught in quest of sport or plunder,
The flimsy fetter flies in sunder."

BENJAMIN BEDDOME

1717-1795

"Did Christ o'er sinners weep,
And shall our cheeks be dry?"

This old-fashioned hymn often sung in churches two generations ago was written by a faithful Baptist minister of England who was pastor in a small village called Bourton-on-the-water for about fifty-five consecutive years. He wrote about 1,000 hymns.* It was his practice to compose a hymn each week to be sung at the following Sunday morning service in his own church. Montgomery commended his hymns as embodying each of them some one central idea of doctrine or experimental religion with the terseness and simplicity of a Greek epigram. One of his well-known hymns begins:

"My times of sorrow and of joy,"

It was composed to be sung on the morning of Jan. 14, 1778, and by a curious coincidence, Beddome's son, away from home in Edinburgh, died unexpectedly that very day. Beddome desired not to have a long last illness. This wish was gratified. He had been absent only one Sunday from his pulpit when he died at the age of seventy-eight and an hour before his death he was found composing a hymn beginning "God of my life and of my choice."

JOHN BERRIDGE

1716-1793

"Weaned from my lordly self;
Weaned from the miser's pelf;
Weaned from the scorner's ways;
Weaned from the lust of praise;"

These searching lines were written by a bachelor preacher of the Church of England, educated at Cambridge, associated

---

* One well-known hymn of Beddome's begins:
"God in the gospel of His Son
Makes His eternal counsels known."
His hymns were written for his own congregation, not with any view toward publication. He was a contemporary of Isaac Watts.

with Wesley, Whitefield, and Lady Huntingdon. For twenty-five years he rode about 100 miles every week, preaching ten or twelve sermons. When at home his table was ever ready for his hearers, of whom he had thousands flocking to him. His stables were open to their horses. Houses and barns were rented by him for the occupation of the lay preachers that he supported. He was a man of earnest bluntness* and considered eccentric.†

THOMAS BLACKLOCK, D. D.

1721-1791

"Come, O my soul, in sacred lays,"

This is the opening line of an old hymn written by a preacher of the church of Scotland who lost his sight before he was six months old, but his adult facility in composition was so great that he dictated his hymns and sermons as fast as they could be written down. He also wrote a valuable article on Blindness for the Encyclopaedia Brittanica. He was the son of humble parents, but developed into remarkable personality, and notwithstanding his terrible handicap

---

* In a letter of condolence written to Lady Huntingdon on the death of a beloved daughter, he said, "She has gone to pay a most blessed visit, and you will see her again, never to part more. Had she crossed the sea, you could have borne it; but now she has gone to heaven, it is almost intolerable! Wonderful strange love is this! Lament, if you please; but glory, glory, glory unto God says
                                                              John Berridge.
† His eccentricity is shown in his epitaph written by himself as follows: "Here lies the remains of John Berridge, late Vicar of Everton, and an itinerant servant of Jesus Christ, who loved his master and his work, and after running on his errands for many years, was caught up to wait on him above. Reader, art thou born again? (No salvation without a new birth.) I was born in February, 1716; remained ignorant of my fallen state till 1730; lived proudly in faith and works for salvation till 1754; was admitted to Everton vicarage 1755; fled to Jesus for refuge 1755; fell asleep in Jesus Jan. 22, 1793." He was a sanctified genius, brimming with wit, as is shown by this extract from his writings about the unregenerate heart of man: "What a filthy place is here! What a fat idol stands skulking in the corner! A darling sin, I warrant! How it simpers and seems as pleasant as a right eye! And can you find a will to part with it, or strength to pluck it out?"
Berridge was a friend of Rowland Hill; here is an extract from a racy letter he wrote him: "I have suffered from nothing but lapidation and pillory treats, (Most preachers love a snug church and whole skin) and if secularly irregular a storm will follow you, but will do no real harm." "Old Berridge," as he was called, had sympathy with all classes and was very popular.

he became an accomplished scholar and a cultivated, benign, and philosophical thinker. His friendship with David Hume made him feel that he must resign his pulpit. He did one service for the world which deserves to be remembered in connection with his name. He wrote a famous letter which is believed to have deterred Robert Burns from emigrating to the West Indies, and thus presumably saved from oblivion the writings of the greatest lyrist the world has ever seen. I may say I am personally glad I have made this discovery about Blacklock.

WILLIAM BLAKE

1757-1827

"Think not thou canst sigh a sigh,
    And thy Master is not by;
Think not thou canst weep a tear,
    And thy Maker is not near."

These lines were written by the eccentric London artist called by Swinburne the single Englishman of supreme poetic genius of his age. He is recognized today as a most extraordinary personality, but during his life he was believed to be partially insane. He thought he held high converse with the departed spirits of Moses, Homer, Virgil, Dante, and Milton. He illustrated his own poems* with pictures showing a strange fancy which are regarded now as remarkable. He died in poverty and obscurity without public recognition, believing himself to be a martyr to poetic art, but at this late day is crowned with laurels of praise as one of the mighty dead.

---

*I am personally charmed with the sympathy his writings evince for the birds and animals. Here are three such lines:
    "And can he who smiles on all
    Hear the wren with sorrows small,
    Hear the small bird's grief and care?"
    I have myself composed a melody for Blake's exquisite lyric beginning:
    "Little Lamb, who made thee?"
and also for
    "Tiger, tiger, burning bright
    In the forests of the night."
    In his mingling with the spirits of another world, he seems to me to resemble what I have read of Swedenborg.

MICHAEL BRUCE

1746-1767

"To us a child of hope is born;
To us a Son is given."*

This standard hymn was written by a brilliant English
Scotch poet who died† at the age of twenty-one of consumption brought on by his struggle with poverty to obtain an
education in order to prepare for the ministry. He was the
son of a poor weaver and in childhood was employed as a
herd-boy. Later he became a village school master, trying
to earn money to help himself along as a student in
Edinburgh where he became acquainted with James Logan,
a fellow student to whom he entrusted his poems to be
published after his death. Logan eleven years later published
some of Bruce's poems as his own, and there has been much
controversy as to the authorship of certain hymns. That a
young student of so much promise and with a stately style
should be lost to the world through poverty seems to me a
bitter reflection on the regime of capitalism which destroys so
many gifted ones.

RICHARD BURDSALL

1735-1824

"The voice of free grace cries"

This fine old hymn was written by an English Wesleyan
minister. Julian mentions that his memoirs were published
at York. This hymn has gone into many collections and
is familiar.

---

* Julian ascribes this hymn to J. Morison a Scotch minister 1749-
1798.

† Bruce's last composition was a touching poem called "Dying in
the Lord." It begins "The hour of my departure's come."

ROBERT BURNS

1759-1796

"O Thou great Power who reignst above,
I know Thou wilt me hear."

These are the opening lines of one of the few hymns
written by "the Shakespeare of Scotland", the most celebrated
lyrist* of modern times. His "Cotter's Saturday Night"
gives an exact picture of his father. Robert had a limited
education but a sincere reverence for the Bible† which comes
out in various poems. At the age of twenty-seven he came
near going to the West Indies and published his first volume
of poems to get money for the enterprise. It is believed
that a letter written by the blind preacher Blacklock deterred
him from this step. His wife was Jean Armour, his marriage
being publicly ratified when he got some money for his

---

* Burns' hymns are the least important part of his writings. His
lyrics are mostly of nature, of human love, and of the homely comedy
and tragedy of human life. One favorite of mine begins "Ae fond kiss,
and then we sever." I have composed a melody for this and also for
the following little poem by Frederick Knowles called
Burns' Songs
"These are the best of him,
Pathos and jest of him;
Earth holds the rest of him,
There let him lie!
Passions were strong in him;
Pardon the wrong in him;
Hark to the song of him,
Mounting on high!

Each little lyrical
Grave or satirical
Musical miracle
Never can die.
All to our life impart
Echo of mirth or smart,
Heart answers unto heart
In smile or sigh."
This seems to me a summary, both concise and comprehensive, of
Burns in character and writings. It is a work of art in itself for
beauty and skill. I call Burns the "Darling of Humanity." I could
shed tears that he had to die in sorrow and bitterness.

† His deep religious nature, interwoven with his love of the beautiful
comes out in the extract from a letter he wrote a lady friend:—"I have
some favorite flowers in the Spring, among them the mountain daisy,
the harebell, the foxglove, the wild briar rose, the budding birch and
the hoary hawthorn that I view and hang over with particular delight.
I never hear one loud solitary whistle of the curlew, on a summer noon,
or the wild mixing cadence of a troop of gray plovers in an autumnal
morning, without feeling an elevation of soul like the enthusiasm of
devotion or poetry. Tell me, my dear friend, to what can this be
owing? Do these workings argue something within us above the trodden
clod? I am myself partial to such proofs of those awful and important
realities,—a God that made all things, man's immaterial and immortal
nature and a world of weal or woe beyond the grave."

book. During the French Revolution he was regarded as a Jacobin* and this embittered him and induced in him habits of dissipation. He died in poverty, gloom, and broken health, at the early age of thirty-seven.

JOHN BURTON

1773-1822

"Holy Bible, Book Divine!
Precious treasure, thou art mine!"

This hymn was written by an earnest English Sunday School leader, a friend of Robert Hall, the eminent Baptist minister. Burton compiled a hymn book in which were 43 hymns he had himself written.

THOMAS CAMPBELL

1777-1844

"When Jordan hushed his waters still,"
This is the opening line of one of the few hymns written by this Scottish poet of established† reputation as a lyrist of spirit and genius. He was made a poet (rather than a lawyer) by going, after his graduation from college, to the Isle of Mull as a tutor for a year. The grand and desolate scenery around him struck fire within him and we get the sublimity it called out in some of his imperishable poems

* The epithet Jacobin seems to have been used at that period in about the same way that the term Bolshevik is now used and seems to have meant essentially the same thing. As a term of reproach Burns regarded it as unjust and it threw him into melancholy.

† Campbell's own estimate of posthumous fame is striking! Is it correct? He said, "When I think of the existence which I shall commence when the stone is laid over my head, how can literary fame appear to me, or to anyone, but as nothing? I believe that after I am gone justice will be due me in this way,—that I was a pure writer. It is an inexpressible comfort at my time of life to be able to look back and feel that I have not written one line against religion or virtue."

which once read can never be entirely forgotten.* He was
later an eye witness of the battle of Hohenlinden,† hence
his poem on it. He died at Boulogne at the age of sixty-
seven and was buried in Westminster Abbey.

JOSEPH DACRE‡ CARLYLE

1759-1804

"Lord, when we bow before Thy throne,
And our confessions pour,
Teach us to feel the sins we own,
And hate what we deplore."

This well-known hymn was written by a celebrated Scotch
orientalist, born at Carlisle, Scotland, Professor of Arabic
at Cambridge. He accompanied Lord Elgin to Constantinople to explore the literary treasures of the Public Library
in that city, and later extended his journey into Asia Minor
and the islands of the archipelago. He was at one period
of his life Vicar at Newcastle on the Tyne.

---

* Part of Campbell's poem called "Lochiel's Warning" imprinted
itself indelibly on my memory when I was a small child. My older
sisters were attending the district school in our New England hamlet
(called Scotland from some of the early Scotch settlers) and they used
to repeat in my hearing at home this Scotch classic which was in their
school reading book. The sonorous lines
    "Lochiel! Lochiel! beware of the day
        When the Lowlands shall meet thee in battle array."
have echoed and re-echoed in my mind ever since.

† "Hohenlinden" was in my own school reading book at a later
date, and that also is imprinted on my memory, but with my hatred
of war and all its works, I do not like it as well as some of Campbell's
other poems I have since discovered. These tender lines from his
"Gertrude of Wyoming" I greatly admire:
    "Clasp me a little longer on the brink
        Of fate! While I can feel thy dear caress—
        * * * * * * * * *
    Yet seems it, even while life's last pulses run,
    A sweetness in the cup of death to be,
    Lord of my bosom's love, to die beholding thee."

‡ His middle name, Dacre (and also his birthplace Carlisle, near
the family seat of the early Dacres) point to his being a descendant
of that historic feudal family, and in that case a very distant relative
of my own, as I am also descended from the Dacres. In fact, the
Leonard family crest is in reality a Dacre crest, as my ancestor,
Samson Leonard of Hurstmonceaux Castle, had the title of the eleventh
Baron Dacre of the South, which had come to him through the marriage
of Lady Joan Dacre of the North with the Fiennes, and thus the Dacre
crest with the wolf's head on it was used by the early Leonards who
emigrated in the seventeenth century to America.

JOHN CENNICK

1718-1755

"Children of the Heavenly King,
As ye journey sweetly sing."

This familiar hymn was written by a successful hymnist
who was descended from a family of Quakers but reared
in the Church of England. He was for a time an associate
preacher with Wesley and Whitefield, but finally separated
from them on doctrinal grounds and joined the Moravians.
He was born in Reading and died in London at the age of
thirty-seven. He has left a number of hymns which are
still used. One begins, "Jesus, my all, to heaven has gone",
and a well-known grace for the table begins, "Be present
at our table, Lord." He was the original author of the
majestic hymn beginning, "Lo, He comes with clouds
descending!" but the hymn was much amended and improved
by Charles Wesley. Another of his hymns begins, "This is
the way I long have sought—"

THOMAS CHATTERTON

1752-1770

"Almighty Framer of the skies!
O let our pure devotion rise
Like incense in Thy sight!"

The opening lines of his "Hymn for Christmas Day" were
written by the erratic and precocious young genius, Thomas
Chatterton. He was born in Bristol, his father dying before
his birth. The encyclopaedia says of him, "He seems never
to have been young; his intellect was born fully matured."*
From his earliest years he was fond of antiquities "clinging
around old ruins like ivy." At fourteen he was apprenticed
to an attorney who had him eat in a kitchen and chastised

---

* Has this a bearing on the theory of reincarnation?

him with a ruler. He began to forge what purported to be
antique poems and tried to pass them off as genuine. This
led to his dismissal from the attorney's office. He then
went to London and wrote for the papers. Editors inserted his articles but would not pay for them, and
Chatterton's means of life were failing. He tried to get an
appointment on a ship going to Africa, but failed. This
was a last drop in his cup of despair, and he was found
dead in his room by his landlady when she broke into it.
It is believed that he was a suicide by poison. A Dr. Fry was
just on the point of helping him, but was a little too late.
Chatterton's death at seventeen was a loss to the world.
He was buried at St. Andrews, Holborn. Eight years
later his "Miscellanies" were published. There were two
hymns in this book.

SAMUEL TAYLOR COLERIDGE

1772-1834

"He prayeth best who loveth best
All things both great and small;
For the great God who loveth us,
He made and loveth all."

These familiar lines seem hymn-like to me, though "The
Ancient Mariner" from which they are taken is not of course
a hymn. Coleridge wrote his "Hymn before Sunrise" with
its wonderful ascription of praise to God, but the lines I
have quoted come nearer to the heart of man. Coleridge
was one of the "Lake Poets" and the brother-in-law of
Southey. He had one of the finest minds England has produced, but has been compared to an unfinished cathedral,
grand in proportions but defective because incomplete. He
was a vicar's son, born in Devonshire, entered Cambridge
at nineteen, but, being crossed in love, enlisted in the army
under an assumed name. Later he planned to emigrate to
the Susquehanna and restore the Golden Age, but found

to his surprise that money was needed for the enterprise.
He left his family for Southey to care for, went to London,
took opium, and died in childlike humility, conscious of
having wasted his powers. He was a poet, philosopher, and
of exceptional conversational gifts. His son Hartley
Coleridge was also a poet, but less gifted than his father.

WILLIAM COWPER

1731-1800

"Oh for a closer walk with God,
    A calm and heavenly frame!"

These are the opening lines of one of the familiar hymns
of this pathetic hymnist, born in a Hertfordshire parsonage,
who was at various times afflicted with attacks of insanity
that nearly drove him into suicide. He was a shy, sensitive,
child who lost his sweet-faced mother before he was seven
years old. He was then placed in a boarding school where
he was the fag of another boy who bullied him. His sufferings in this school are alluded to in another familiar
hymn* of Cowper's which begins "Hark, my soul, it is the
Lord." He was afflicted with an inferiority complex which
caused him to say to a fellow clerk at the age of eighteen,
"I am nobody and shall always be nobody. You will be
chancellor." This prediction as to his friend came true.
Another of his hymns was written to commemorate an occasion of sorrowful interest. Cowper had an insane delusion
that it was the Divine will for him to go to a certain point
in the river Ouse and drown himself, but the driver of his

---

* The line in this hymn which refers to his boyhood's persecutions
is as follows:
            "I delivered thee when bound."
    There is an amusing story told about this hymn. A mother was in
the habit of singing it to her little six year old daughter at bed time.
One night she sang a different hymn and the child was dissatisfied
and said, "I want the other one." "What other one?" questioned the
mother. The child said, "I want the one about the she-bear." Then
the mother recollected that one stanza of "Hark, my soul, it is the
Lord" contains these lines:
            "Can a mother's tender care
            Cease toward the child she bare?"

vehicle missed his way and Cowper was diverted from his purpose. After this he wrote the hymn beginning:

"God moves in a mysterious way
His wonders to perform."

Another familiar hymn of Cowper's begins, "There is a fountain filled with blood," and another still begins, "Sometimes a light surprises."

Another is

"What various hindrances we meet
When coming to the mercy seat!"*

Cowper recovered his reason before he died and wrote many poems which were published. Cowper would have married a lady named Mary Unwin but for his attack of insanity in 1775. She continued to be his companion to the end—a tender holy attachment. She died four years before he did.

REV. GEORGE CRABBE

1754-1832

"Pilgrim, burdened with thy sin,
Come thy way to Zion's gate."

This hymn was written by a clergyman of the Church of England who is called "the poet of the poor." He knew in personal experience of a struggle with poverty. He was the son of a Suffolk warehouse keeper who with difficulty educated his son for the medical profession. George was apprenticed to a surgeon but disliked the work and went to London with three pounds in his pocket to make a trial of literature. He was at first unfortunate and threatened with arrest for debt. One night he walked Westminster Bridge till daylight in agitation after delivering a letter asking as-

---

* This hymn has also an amusing story. In it come the lines:
"And Satan trembles when he sees
The weakest saint upon his knees."
A mother was teaching this to her small son when he interrupted her with the paralyzing question, "Why does the weakest saint sit on Satan's knees?" This story is recommended to enliven a flagging conversation at a dinner table.

sistance from Burke. The great orator kindly examined Crabbe's poetical compositions* and appointed an interview which resulted in Crabbe's being taken under Burke's own roof where he met such celebrities as Fox and Sir Joshua Reynolds, who presented him with a hundred pound note. By Burke's advice Crabbe took holy orders, became a domestic chaplain to a lord, and was enabled to marry a woman with whom he enjoyed the purest domestic felicity. He was the friend and guest of the distinguished men of his time and obtained uninterrupted public honor. He died at the age of seventy-eight and his son collected and published his writings.

PHILIP DODDRIDGE, D. D.

1702-1751

"Mark the soft-falling snow, and the diffusive rain,
To heaven from which it fell, it turns not back again."

These beautiful lines were written by the gentle dissenting minister and beloved† teacher of a seminary, who has contributed to the world so many of our familiar hymns. These include the following:—

> "Grace, 'tis a charming sound"
> "See Israel's gentle Shepherd stand"
> "Awake, my soul, stretch every nerve,"*

---

* Crabbe wielded a sarcastic pen about unsavory individuals who "carouse and curse and brawl and die" and also those who go to sleep in church. Here are the lines about them:
  "He such sad coil with words of vengeance kept
  That our best sleepers startled as they slept."
  † His simple, unaffected goodness won for him the good will of all. His kindliness is shown in the following little habit of his life. His hymns were not at first printed and he had many requests for a copy of one of them or another. He would write out the desired hymn and present it to the asker with his smile of peculiar sweetness.
  * A funny little story is told of how he got himself up in the morning. He would say over five verses of the hymn "Awake, my soul, and with the sun," and then at the sixth verse would get out of bed. Do we not all have these little personal plays? I must tell here that my playmate of those years, now in her seventies, acknowledged to me recently with a smile that she still uses an infantile device of my own to help her get dressed, as follows: When she and I were children, I invented the following story, that when we dressed ourselves we were dressing a family of four children. The body was the oldest child, the feet were twins, and the head was the baby. This lady still says to herself when dressing, "There, I've got the twins dressed." I have some puerile plays of my own which I will not record here, but will say that in regard to such practises I was reassured by reading in the pages of "Psychology" the advice of the editor who says, "Make a game of it," (that is, of our small personal tasks). So Doddridge was on advanced scientific lines in his manner of rising.

"Thine earthly sabbaths, Lord, we love."†
"O God of Bethel, by whose hand"
"O happy day that fixed my choice"‡
"Do I not love Thee, O my Lord?"
"How gentle God's commands!"

Doddridge was the twentieth§ child of a tradesman in London and was laid out for dead at his birth, but an attendant noticed a slight movement in his little body, and means were taken to restore him. His mother taught him rhymes on the Dutch picture tiles in his home. He became a minister in a humble parish of Northampton where he lived in seclusion, as he said, "like a tortoise shut up in its shell." He continued in this ministry until, in the last stages of consumption, he sailed for Lisbon, where he died at the age of only forty-nine. Few men have done more for the cause of religion than he, through the enduring hymns he has given to the church universal of all succeeding ages, as far as we can tell. His hymns were written for his own congregation and sung by being "lined out." He wrote a book called "The Rise and Progress of Religion in the Soul."*

† This hymn was given by Doddridge in 1736 at the close of a sermon on the text, "There remaineth now a rest for the people of God." The hymn is associated in my mind with the country church I attended in childhood, where I heard it sung by a choir that stood in a gallery at the back of the church, led by a fiddle and a big bass viol. The congregation joined in, turning around in a body and facing the choir during the singing of the hymns.

‡ This hymn by Doddridge has for me an imperishable memory. In the year 1879 my husband, who was then a theological student in Oberlin, had just made his decision to give his life to the work of foreign missions. We were united in that purpose and were very happy in it. One morning he helped me make our bed, standing on one side and I on the other. As we spread on the blankets and quilts we sang together,

"Oh happy day that fixed my choice
On Thee, my Savior and my God,"
I cannot remember any other occasion in my life more filled with pure spiritual joy than that one.

§ At the time of his birth there was only one of those previous nineteen children living, a sister. It would seem by the size of families at that period that wives greatly needed the present day knowledge of birth control. However, if Mrs. Doddridge had possessed that knowledge, she might have deprived the world of the great gift of her twentieth child, Philip. How had she ever lived through so many confinements and bereavements?

* That book of Doddridge's much used in former days, "The Rise and Progress", was written at the suggestion of his friend Dr. Watts. It is good to know that these two great hymnists of the church were not only contemporaries, but also that they were friends.

BOURNE HALL DRAPER

1775-1843

"Ye Christian heralds, go proclaim"

This well-known missionary hymn which was printed in America in 1805 and has appeared in various American collections was written by an English Baptist preacher who was born at Cumnor near Oxford and educated at Bristol Academy under Dr. J. Rylands. He was pastor of a Baptist church at Southampton where he died at the age of sixty-eight.

REV. JONATHAN EVANS

1749-1809

"Hark! the voice of love and mercy
Sounds aloud from Calvary."

The author of this hymn was born in Coventry, England, and lived an irreligious life until he was nearly thirty years of age. He was a worker in a ribbon factory. He became converted and began to speak in public of God's mercy to him, at such times as his secular work permitted. At last he gathered a church around himself, and entered the stated ministry in connection with the Congregationalists. He wrote another hymn which begins, "Come, thou soul-transforming Spirit."

This grace was used very sweetly by children in a day nursery in Des Moines. A picture remains in memory of chubby folded hands, and bowed heads.

"God is gracious, God is good,
And we thank Thee for our food;
By Thy bounty all are fed
Give us Lord our daily bread."

—Anon

John Fawcett, D. D.

1739-1817

"Blest be the tie that binds
Our hearts in Christian love;"

The author of this well-nigh indispensable hymn was converted at the age of sixteen under Whitefield's preaching and became a Baptist pastor of a small church in York. After laboring there seven years he had a flattering call to succeed the celebrated Dr. Gill at a large London church. His wagons were packed with his household goods to go and he preached his farewell sermon to his weeping congregation, but was so moved by their prayers and tears that he unloaded his wagons, saying, "I will not leave you. We will still labor lovingly for the Lord together." In commemoration of this event he wrote the above imperishable hymn. This is a splendid exception to the Marxian doctrine of economic determinism.

Fawcett wrote many other hymns, the most notable of which is

"Lord, dismiss us with Thy blessing"

Also he is the translator of the touching Latin hymn-prayer written by Mary, Queen of Scots the night before her execution.

In his later years he opened a school, and six years before his death he received the degree of D. D. from America, (I think from Brown University.) He died at the age of seventy-eight, a man of a noble record.

James Grahame

1765-1811

"Hail, Sabbath! Thee I hail, the poor man's day!"

This is the opening line of a hymn on the Sabbath which became very popular in Scotland. It was written by the

above-named writer, born at Glasgow, who was educated
by his father's arrangement as a lawyer, but whose heart
was in the ministry, and two years before his death at the
age of forty-six he was ordained as a preacher. This story
is told of the above quoted hymn. It was published in the
Quarterly Review without the knowledge of Grahame's wife,
and no name was attached to it. He brought it and when
he read it aloud, his wife said, "Oh James, if only you
could write like that!" When he told her his secret she
was overwhelmed with surprise and pleasure.

The poet Campbell was Grahame's friend and tells the
following story of a visit they had together at the home of
George Crabbe. They sat up all night in Crabbe's delightful
parlor and agreed to walk to Arthur's Seat at dawn to see
the sun rise. On this walk they talked of serious things,
the beauty of the morning, the recent death of Crabbe's
sister, the proof of God's goodness and benevolence in
creation. When Campbell had retired to his room on
their return to the house, he overheard Grahame singing
in his own room the praises of God with a power and inspiration beyond himself or anything earthly.

THOMAS GRAY

1716-1771

"No further seek his merits to disclose,
  Or draw his frailties from their dread abode,—
  (There they alike in trembling hope repose)
  The bosom of his Father and his God."

These are the closing lines of the immortal Elegy* written
by Thomas Gray who is not listed by Julian as a hymnist
at all, but to my mind he should certainly be classed as a
sacred poet. His childhood's home in London was broken
on account of his father's violent temper which compelled

---

* I have loved the Elegy since childhood when I voluntarily committed it to memory. I know of another child similarly impressed.

his mother to leave her husband. She contrived, however, to give her son educational advantages. Thomas never married, but spent his life either in travel or in the atmosphere of noble libraries. He was offered the Laureateship but declined the honor. He died of gout at the age of fifty-five and is buried beside his mother at Stoke, near Eton, "under the yew tree's shade." The "ivy mantled tower" of the Elegy, at Upton church is falling into decay, though it is a picturesque object still, but it was at Stoke that he wrote, lived, and died. It is said that he polished his elegy for years before giving it out for publication. There are two manuscripts of it in existence. These were sold at auction in 1854 and brought respectively 100 and 130 pounds.

JOSEPH GRIGG

1728(?)*-1767

"Jesus, and shall it ever be
A mortal man ashamed of Thee?"

The writer of this hymn of great power was born in humble circumstances and brought up to mechanical pursuits, but became a Presbyterian minister in London. Later he married a lady of property and retired from the ministry. He died at Walthamstow, Essex. The above quoted hymn is said to have been written when Grigg was only ten years old. If so, it is the most remarkable child composition I know anything about. It will always be known and sung. Grigg wrote another familiar hymn. It begins, "Behold a stranger at the door." He wrote other things in both prose and verse.

---

* This date, although it is the one recorded as that of the birth of Grigg, is probably a mistake. Dr. Julian thinks he must have been born six or eight years earlier.

WILLIAM HAMMOND

1719-1783

"Awake and sing the song of Moses and the Lamb."

This old, familiar hymn was written by an associate of Cennick and other Calvinistic Methodists. He was born at Battle, England, and educated at Cambridge. In 1743 he joined the Moravian Brethren and is buried in the Moravian burying ground at Chelsea. He was a scholar and writer. He translated Latin hymns and wrote an autobiography in Greek which has never been translated. (Why did he not write it in English? How peculiar! No wonder no one took the trouble to translate and publish it.) He published a hymn book and his original hymns are marked by merit and earnestness. He wrote another of our old, familiar hymns. It begins:

"Lord, we come before Thee now.
At Thy feet we humbly bow."

JOSEPH HART

1712-1768

"Come, ye sinners, poor and needy,
Weak and wounded, sick and sore."*

This precious hymn was written by one who had been a wild youth and not converted until he was forty-five years old. He was a teacher of some education and had written a document on the "Unreasonableness of Religion", after which his conscience gave him no peace. He heard a sermon in the Fetter Lane Moravian Chapel on the text Rev.

---

* There is an appealing chorus to this hymn (probably not written by Hart himself) which is found as follows in the Service Hymnal published in Chicago:
"I will arise and go to Jesus! He will embrace me with his arms."
As long as contrite hearts pray for pardon and peace this sincere hymn by Joseph Hart will be sung and loved.

3:10, "Because thou hast kept the word of my patience, I will also keep thee in the hour of temptation" etc. This, and a remarkable view he had of the sufferings of Christ, of which he said, "No one can sense this except by the Holy Ghost", produced in him an amazing change. He became an independent preacher in the old meeting house at Jewin St., London, and wrote many earnest hymns.* He died at the age of fifty-six and is buried in Bunhill Fields Cemetery.

THOMAS HAWEIS

1732-1820

"From the cross uplifted high,
Where the Savior deigns to die,"

This familiar hymn was written by a devoted rector in Northamptonshire for fifty-six years who was also the chaplain of the Countess of Huntingdon and one of the founders of the London Missionary Society. He was deeply interested in Capt. Cook's account of Tahiti and was the means of preparing two missionaries for those islands. He wrote over 250 hymns and collected them for use in churches.† He was educated at Cambridge, at first for a physician and later took holy orders. A Commentary on the Bible and a translation of the New Testament were written by him. He died at Bath where Lady Huntingdon had her chapels.

---

* Another well-known hymn by Hart begins thus:
 "Come, Holy Spirit, come! Let thy bright beams arise."

† Haweis believed strongly in congregational singing, and in the preface to his collection of hymns he complains that in the churches "the voice of joy and gladness is too commonly silent, unless in that shameful mode of psalmody now almost confined to a few persons huddled together in one corner of the church, who sing to the praise and glory of themselves, for the entertainment, or often for the weariness of the rest of the congregation, in absurdity too glaring to be overlooked."

GEORGE HEATH

fl. 1770 d. 1822

"My soul, be on thy guard! Ten thousand foes arise."*

This old hymn was written by a Presbyterian pastor of Devon, England. He wrote other hymns and essays, but seems to be remembered chiefly by this one above mentioned.

DR. SAMUEL JOHNSON

1709-1784

"O Thou whose power o'er moving worlds presides,"

This is the opening line of the translation by the "Founder of English lexicography" of a hymn by Boetheus.† Johnson was the son of a Lichfield book-binder. He had difficulties‡ with obtaining an education. His father§ died insolvent and poverty prevented Samuel from obtaining a degree. At the age of twenty-five he married a widow who had 800 pounds, after which he set going a school where he had a pupil, David Garrick, who later became famous. Johnson afterward went to London and tried writing, but was so miserably remunerated that the wolf was at the door. A turn in his affairs came when he was past fifty and began to report parliamentary debates, and the splendor and pomp of the speeches as they appeared in print must have greatly

---

* This hymn was sung very often in the little Congregational church of my childhood in Massachusetts where my father was a deacon. It has always served as a stimulus to earnest living.

† Boetheus was a Roman philosopher of the fifth century A D. He was executed with horrible cruelty on a false charge. The hymn, though not lyrical in quality, is remarkable for its profundity. These are its closing lines:
"From Thee, great God, we spring; to Thee we tend,
    Path, motive, guide, original and end."

‡ Of his early schoolmaster Johnson said, "He beat me very well," adding, "Without that I should have done nothing."

§ There is a story told of how Johnson punished himself for disobedience to his deceased father by standing out in the rain. (Was it all night? I am not sure and do not wish to stretch the tale.)

astonished the duller statesmen who made them. From that time Johnson's fortunes were on the crest of the wave. In 1750 he edited "The Rambler;" in 1755 he brought out his great dictionary. In 1758 he edited "The Idler." In 1759 he wrote "Rasselas" in the evenings of one week to pay the expenses of his mother's funeral. Later he had so emerged from obscurity that a pension of 300 pounds a year was bestowed on him. He became acquainted with James Boswell who eventually wrote "The Life of Dr. Johnson." He is buried in Westminster Abbey close by the grave of David Garrick. This is the story of a man who "arrived."

Rev. Edmund Jones

1722-1760

"Come, humble sinner, in whose breast"

The writing of this hymn is about the only permanent legacy this useful Welsh Baptist minister of Exeter has left the world, except that from an old record it appears that under his ministry singing was first introduced into the Baptist denomination—a needed innovation indeed! No doubt there were old fossils in the church that opposed this as every other innovation. Some people are built that way! Jones began his preaching at the age of nineteen and died at the age of forty-three.

Keen (or George Keith)

"How firm a foundation, ye saints of the Lord,"

This splendid hymn* is of doubtful authorship. It is usually ascribed to George Keith, a publisher of London, a

---

* When I was in Oberlin College in 1873-7, at chapel prayers each evening sat the long row of our beloved professors on the platform. At one end sat our teacher in mathematics in close range of my vision. This hymn was often sung at this exercise (more often, as I recollect, than any other) and I have a vivid memory of the enthusiasm this teacher put into "I'll never, no never, no never forsake."

son-in-law of the distinguished preacher, Dr. Gill, but Dr. Julian, after much investigation, ascribes it to an unknown author by the name of Keen. The hymn was first published in 1787 in a compilation of hymns called "Riffon's Selection"—the inital "K" was the only identification. In Fletcher's Collection, published in 1822 Riffon's "K" was extended to "Keen" and it is this which determines Julian's opinion as to the authorship. A later collection puts the name Kirkham to this hymn, but by what authority is not known.

THOMAS KELLY
1769-1855

"Hark, ten thousand harps and voices
Sound the notes of praise above!"*

This hymn was written by a clergyman of Dublin, the son of a judge and a friend of Edmund Burke.† Kelly was finely educated, at first for the Irish Bar, but left the law for the gospel. His friends did not like his unconventional way of preaching and treated him with coldness. Of this he said that it would be easier for him to go to the stake than to be obliged to go against those he so dearly loved, but he remained true to his convictions. He was a great writer of hymns, 785 in all. Some of his familiar ones are those beginning:

"Look, ye saints, the sight is glorious!"
"The head that once was crowned with thorns"
"Sing of Jesus, sing forever!"

His hymns are very high in quality.

He finally left the Established Church, and as he had ample means, he built a number of chapels. He was also well known for his liberality to the poor,‡ especially in the

---

* This hymn was the favorite of my late husband, Rev. H. D. Goodenough, who was for thirty-one years a missionary to the Zulus. It was sung at his funeral. When he felt particularly happy he used to sing it, and beat time on the table near him.

† Edmund Burke (1730-1797) was the great humanitarian who prepared the way for the abolition of slavery under Wilberforce. Burke, like Kelly, was born in Dublin and both were educated in the University there.

‡ This story is told of a deserving couple in hard luck in Dublin: The husband said, "Hould up, Bridget, bedad! There's alway Misther Kelly to pull us out of the bog when we've sunk for the last time."

Irish famine. He was much esteemed for his true piety, his amiability, and his support of every noble and worthy cause. His learning was varied, including skill in oriental languages, and composition of music. Death did not come to him until he was eighty-six, a good old age.*

RICHARD KEMPENFELT

1718-1782

"Hark! 'tis the trump of God
Sounds through the realms abroad,
Time is no more."

These are the opening lines of a prophetic poem written by a rear-admiral of Swedish descent in the British Navy, who went down with his ship, the "Royal George," which capsized near Spithead. Kempenfelt was a man of strong religious feeling and an associate of Whitefield and the Wesleys. He wrote several hymns not generally in use. The year before his death he had distinguished himself by the capture of a French convoy on the way to the West Indies. All were lost on board the man-of-war, the "Royal George," about 600 people.

WILLIAM KNOX

1789-1825

"Oh why should the spirit of mortal be proud?"

This poem, written by a young Scotchman born at Firth and educated only at a Parish and Grammar School was a

---

* When Kelly was "sixty years young" Lord Plunkett, an old school fellow met him in the street and said, "You will live to a great age, Mr. Kelly." "I am confident that I shall," was the reply, "as I never expect to die." Kelly's last words were to this effect, "The Lord is my all in all." A beautiful life, a beautiful death, beautiful hymns left behind,—who would not envy such a record?

favorite with Abraham Lincoln* who found the poem in a newspaper with no name attached. Knox tried farming but, not succeeding to his own satisfaction, went to Edinburgh in 1820 and obtained employment in writing for public journals. Walter Scott says of him that "his talent showed itself in a fine strain of pensive beauty." He died at the age of thirty-six.

Bishop Martin Madan

1726-1790

"Come Thou Almighty King!"

These often sung words, set to the stately Italian Hymn of Giardini, are attributed to the above-named English preacher, but on insufficient grounds according to Dr. Julian, who says that there is no evidence that Madan ever composed a hymn, but since he had to do with the compilation of a hymn book various hymns were ascribed to him. Madan was a brother-in-law to the poet Cowper, his wife Judith (née Cowper) did write some original hymns. Madan had some reputation as a musical composer and he wrote a document in which he advocated the practise of polygamy.† He was educated for the Bar but after hearing a sermon by John Wesley on "Prepare to meet thy God" the whole course of his life was changed. He had some difficulty in obtaining Holy Orders, but finally arrived at a bishopric. He had good success in piecing out and altering other people's hymns. Some attribute this hymn to Chas. Wesley. It is found in the British Museum in Whitefield's collection dated 1757.

---

* Lincoln was deeply impressed with the last stanza of this poem as though in anticipation of his own sudden end. It runs as follows:
   "'Tis the twink of an eye, 'tis the draught of a breath
   From the blossom of health to the paleness of death!
   From the gilded saloon to the bier and the shroud!
   Oh why should the spirit of mortal be proud?"
   Twenty-two years after his death Knox's poems were collected and published. Three of his hymns found their way into use for congregational singing. One begins, "The Lord is my Shepherd, He makes me repose".

† Our old Zulu polygamists would have been delighted with his teachings.

Richard Mant, D. D.

1776-1848

"For all Thy saints, O Lord, who strove in Christ to live,"

This hymn was written by a Church of England clergyman who was born at Southampton, England, and became Bishop of Dromore, Ireland. In boyhood he attended the famous Winchester School founded by Wm. Wykeham in the 14th century, and later went to Oxford. He helped to gain his bishopric by his "Bampton Lectures" in which he is said to have been "fencing with the Methodists about notions they never held." He is somewhat largely represented in hymnology, having translated many Latin hymns, made metrical versions of the Psalms, and written original hymns, which are not commonly used. One of these entitled "Prayer on the Death of Friends" is solemn and striking. It is included in the Library of Religious Poetry. The first hymn quoted is No. 1150 in "The New Laudes Domini."

John Marriott

1780-1825

"Thou whose almighty word chaos and darkness heard"

This stately missionary hymn was written by a Church of England clergyman who was born in Germany but educated at Oxford where he took honors. He wrote other hymns not so well known. For two years he was private tutor in the family of a Duke who presented him to the Rectory of a church in Warwickshire, which he retained till his death, but his wife's health necessitated his residence in Devon. He was also curate in various parishes and died at the age of forty-six.

WILLIAM MASON

1719-1791

"Welcome, welcome, dear Redeemer"

This fine old hymn was written by Toplady's successor as editor of the "Gospel Magazine." He was born at Rotherhithe. His useful hymn was not published until he had been in his grave three years. In one sense this was a pity; in another, there is encouragement for some of the rest of us that our efforts may eventually gain recognition and usefulness.

SAMUEL MEDLEY

1738-1799

"Awake, my soul to joyful lays,
    And sing thy great Redeemer's praise."

This familiar hymn was written by a midshipman of the British navy who afterward became a teacher and a popular preacher. He was the son of an English schoolmaster and received a pious upbringing, but did not like the business to which he was apprenticed and joined the navy. He was so severely wounded in an engagement that the surgeon said that only an amputation could save his life. He spent a night in prayer and in the morning the surgeon threw up his hands in astonishment, saying that only a miracle could have wrought the improvement in his condition. After recovering Medley went back to his careless life, but the serious admonitions of his Christian grandfather and a sermon he heard, again restored him to religion and he wrote hymns which he used to print on the broadsides of a ship. The above quoted hymn is an expression of his changed feelings. He wrote two other hymns which are familiar. One begins "Jesus, engrave it on my heart that Thou the one thing needful art." The other begins, "Oh could I speak the matchless worth,"* Medley died at the age of sixty-one after a useful pastorate over a large church in Liverpool. His daughter Sarah published his hymns with a memoir of him.

JAMES MERRICK

1720-1769

"To Thy pastures fair and large"

This favorite hymn of my earlier years was written by a Church of England clergyman whose headaches prevented his active parish work. He was educated at Oxford and died at Reading at the age of 49. He wrote both in prose and verse and published several books. A poem of his called "The Chameleon" won him a place in English literature. Julian lists nine of his hymns.

JAMES MONTGOMERY

1771-1854

"The Lord is my Shepherd, no want shall I know,"

This familiar hymn was written by the honored poet above named. Montgomery was the son of a Moravian† minister in Irvine, Scotland. At the age of sixteen he tried to earn his living in a retail shop, but found the work unsuited to his taste and he made an unsuccessful journey to London

---

* When a child I read a pleasing magazine story called "A singing-school Romance" in which the heroine had a musical rival and lover named Israel. On one public occasion she sang this hymn, changing the line, "And vie with Gabriel while he sings" to "And vie with Israel while he sings." It was a step in the delicious love story. Why can't we get such stories now?

† At the age of six he was sent to a Moravian school where study and recreation were combined and the children taught to regard Jesus, as their brother and friend. He plunged into the world later, but had no peace, although his associates were pure. He wrote to a friend of his despairing thoughts and gained relief through prayer. On his forty-third birthday he wrote to the community at Fulwich where he had been at school and asked for readmission to their connection, which was granted.

to try to find a publisher for his youthful poems. At the age of twenty-one he went to Sheffield as the assistant of a printer and publisher. His chief had to leave England to avoid political persecution and Montgomery carried on his paper, with the result that he got into prison twice; once for printing a poem on "The Fall of the Bastille" and the second time for printing an account of a riot in Sheffield. When he was released he published a book called "Prison Amusements." He rose in public esteem, became a lecturer on poetry, and the earnest advocate of foreign missions. (His father had been a missionary and died on the island of Tobago.) At last he obtained a royal pension of 200 pounds a year. He died in his sleep at the age of eighty-three and was honored with a public funeral. There is a statue to his memory in Sheffield and a stained glass window in the parish church. He wrote 400 hymns.* One familiar one begins, "A poor wayfaring man of grief." Another begins, "Oh where shall rest be found?"; and another, "There is a calm for those who weep." Another of his hymns which had a great attraction for me in early life begins "Let me go, the day is breaking." Another begins "Call Jehovah Thy Salvation."

Other hymns of Montgomery's are these: "Go to the grave in all thy glorious prime."† "At evening time it shall be light." "Forever with the Lord." "Stand up and bless the Lord." "In the hour of trial, Jesus plead for me." "Go to dark Gethsemane."

---

* He was once asked by an attorney which of his writings would live. "None, sir," was the reply, "unless it be a few of my hymns." I think he judged rightly as to the immortality of a good hymn which gets into familiar use.

† This hymn of Montgomery's was in my childhood used at a memorial service for Abraham Lincoln. I was especially impressed with these two lines from it:
"The Christian cannot die before his time
The Lord's appointment is the servant's hour."

THOMAS MOORE

1779-1852

"Come, ye disconsolate, where'er ye languish,"

This surpassingly beautiful hymn was written by the fore-most poet of Ireland. Thomas Moore was the son of a poor trader in Dublin and was educated at Trinity College for the Bar. At the age of nineteen he went to London with his translation of the Odes of Anacreon in his pocket and suc-ceeded after two years in getting them published. Two years later he put out a volume of sweet but licentious verse under the nom de plume of Thomas Little. A certain Lord Morra got him an appointment in Bermuda but Moore did not like the work, turned it over to a deputy, and then traveled in the United States, which cured him of his demo-cratic ideas. Moore went back to England and, because a man named Jeffrey criticised his writings in the Edinburgh Review, the two fought a duel. Neither was killed, and eventually they became friends. Moore's deputy in Bermuda misbehaved and Moore was made responsible for a large sum of money. Lord Landsdowne paid the fine and Moore returned the sum to him later. Moore's home was in a little Wiltshire cottage with old-fashioned windows and trellised doorway hung about with creepers. He wrote Lalla Rookh and the English world applauded. He wrote fugitive poems in which "the tropes both glittered and stung." He travelled on the continent and Byron entrusted to him an autobi-ography not to be published until after Byron's decease. At the solicitation of Byron's family the manuscript was destroyed. Was it a pity? Three years before his death Moore had softening of the brain.

Julian lists twelve hymns of Moore's. Only three of them are familiar to me except the one quoted above. These are the opening lines of the other three:

"As down in the sunless retreats of the ocean"
"Sound the loud timbrel o'er Egypt's dark sea"
"Thou art, O God, the life and light."

The last of these Julian says has attained the greatest popularity. It is a beautiful poem, but my choice would be, "Come ye disconsolate."

REV. JOHN NEWTON

1725-1807

"Glorious things of thee are spoken, Zion, city of our God."

This magnificent hymn was written by the ex-slaver and wanderer* who after his conversion was the associate of Cowper in compiling the book called "Olney Hymns." Newton, born in London, lost his pious mother by death when he was only seven years old. He went to school where he learned the rudiments of Latin† till he was eleven and then went to sea and was shipwrecked on a low, sandy island near Sierra Leone. Here he worked on a lemon plantation for a degenerate man with a black mistress‡ who was cruel to him. He was half starved and ate unwholesome roots to appease his hunger. After fifteen months he got away, but the ship lacked provisions and they were in danger both of starving and sinking before he reached England. On this ship he found a copy of Thomas a Kempis and through it was converted, but spent six more years on the sea, becoming eventually the commander of a slave ship. A great hold upon him at this period for goodness was his faithful love for his future wife, Mary Catlett. Later he dropped his nefarious sea life, studied with Whitefield and Wesley,§ made friends with Hannah More and Wilberforce, settled

---

* In those early, wild days he was on one occasion flogged as a deserter from the British navy.

† He must have learned also the rudiments of geometry, for Julian relates of him that when stranded in Africa he diverted himself by studying geometric problems, drawing the diagrams on the sea sands.

‡ This man and woman on one occasion when he was setting out small lemon trees for them taunted him, saying sarcastically, "You'll be a shipowner some day and eat the fruit of these trees." This insincere prophecy actually was fulfilled in Newton's future history.

§ His studies included Greek, Latin, and Hebrew. He had a wonderful intellect from the start and became a power in both mental and spiritual lines. He was the spiritual father of Scott, the Commentator.

down to an honored and long pastorate,* and wrote many
useful hymns, some of which are,—
"Amazing grace how sweet the sound"
"Come my soul thy suit prepare"
"How sweet the name of Jesus sounds"
"In evil long I took delight"
"Jesus who knows full well the heart of every saint"
"While with ceaseless course the sun"
"One there is above all others"
"Afflictions though they seem severe"
"Safely through another week God has brought us on
        our way"
and this most beautiful of all
        "Quiet Lord, my forward heart,
        Make me teachable and mild."
(This has been one of my favorites since youth and it
almost gave me a shock to discover the strange history of
its author.)

THOMAS OLIVERS

1725-1799

"The God of Abraham praise"†

This stately hymn is the product of a successful itinerant
preacher of Wesley's connection, and that on which his fame
principally rests. He was born in Wales and lost both
parents by death when about four years old. He was thereafter passed around from one relative to another, was apprenticed to a shoe maker and was called by a neighbor "the

---

* Newton preached till he was over eighty. When his eyes were
too dim to keep the place in his manuscript sermon he took his servant
into the pulpit to keep the place with a pointer. One Sunday these
words occurred in the sermon, "Jesus Christ is precious." Newton
purposely repeated the words for emphasis, but the servant, thinking
he had lost his place, whispered, "Go on, go on. You've said that
before." Newton turned upon him saying aloud, "John, I've said that
twice and I'm going to say it again." Then, raising his voice, he said
to the congregation, "Jesus Christ is precious."

† Montgomery says of this hymn, "There is not a hymn in our
language of more elevated thought or more glorious imagery." It is
said to have been written in Westminster, London, at a preacher's house,
and that a Jew found some synagogue music for it. This hymn was
a great source of consolation to Henry Martyn embarking for his
perilous missionary enterprise.

worst boy known in the vicinity for thirty years." Being obliged to leave his native place when he was eighteen on account of his bad conduct, he journeyed to Bristol where the whole course of his life was changed by hearing Whitefield preach on the text, "Is not this a brand plucked from the burning?" Afterward he said of this circumstance, "When the sermon began I was the most profligate young man living. Before it ended I was a new creature."* Olivers joined Wesley at once and travelled about 100,000 miles in itinerant preaching, often meeting with violence and opposition. He was a personal friend of Toplady, but disagreed with him on some doctrinal points. He was buried in Wesley's tomb in London.

EDWARD PERRONET
1726-1792
"All hail the power of Jesus' name!"

The author of this priceless hymn belonged to a family of French emigrés. His father, a whitehaired saint, who died at the age of ninety-one, was associated with the Wesleys. Edward was also at first, and was a bosom friend

---

* He described his experience after his conversion, "I saw God in everything in Heaven and on earth." He was ready to endure any persecution for Christ.

I will never, never leave thee,
I will never thee forsake,
I will guide and guard and keep thee,
For my name and mercies sake.
    I'll be with thee,
    Only all my counsels take.

When the sun of bliss is glowing,
And around thee all is bright,
Pleasures like a river flowing,
All things tending to delight.
    Fear no evil
    I will guide thy steps aright.

When thine earthly path is clouded
Lean on Me in humble prayer,
Through the gloom in which thou'rt shrouded
I will make a light appear.
    And the banner of my love
    I will uprear.

—Credit Lost

of Charles Wesley* but he offended both John Wesley and Lady Huntingdon by writing a satire on abuses in the Church of England which Dr. Julian characterizes as "pungent, salted with wit, and well wrought in picked and packed words", but it roused John Wesley's hottest anger. Wesley also objected to Perronet's insistence that he had a right to administer the sacrament himself and not leave it to the parish priest. Julian says the reader of the Lives of the Wesleys will be "taken captive" by the passages that refer to Perronet's bursting in "full of fire and enthusiasm, yet ebullient and volatile." At last Perronet left the Wesleyan connection and set up a little Congregational church where he could do as he pleased. He evidently had personal means to be able to do this. Also he left a bequest to Wm. Shrubsole for setting the above hymn to the tune of "Miles Lane."† The last stanza of that hymn as it appears in our hymn books was written by some unknown person. Not only are we attracted to Perronet as the author of this universally loved hymn, but because of his independent character and his willingness to suffer persecution‡ for Christ.

BENJAMIN RHODES

1743-1815

"My heart and voice I raise, to sing Messiah's praise,"§

The writer of this hymn in common use was the son of a

---

* John Wesley in a letter to Perronet complains of "Charles and you" as not conforming themselves to the regulations that he (John) had imposed upon them, and says, "I have not one preacher with me, and not six in England whose wills are broken to serve me."

† Personally I like the tune "Miles Lane" better than "Coronation" for Perronet's great hymn. I have heard a great congregation in Johannesburg rolling it to the skies to the tune of Miles Lane with indescribable effect. I have wished congregations in America would use this tune more than they do. The fine tune Coronation was written by Oliver Holden who was born in Shirley, Mass. in 1763.

‡ Wesley has this entry in his diary of an episode in Perronet's ministry when he was only twenty-three years old, where he was "thrown down and rolled in mud and mire. Stones were hurled and windows broken" by the infuriated mob. We see from this the intrepid spirit that was Perronet's and we shall appreciate his splendid hymn all the more. He wrote other hymns (not familiar) and Julian speaks highly of his ability as a hymnist.

§ One stanza of this hymn begins with the words "Jerusalem Divine" and this is used as beginning a separate hymn. After his death people would get together in a small group and sing his "Jerusalem Divine".

Yorkshire schoolmaster and received a good elementary education. He was converted at the age of eleven by hearing Whitefield preach. He had a notable Christian experience. At the age of nineteen his joy in God was so great that it sometimes prevented his sleep. At the age of twenty-two he became one of Wesley's itinerant preachers. People flocked both to hear him preach and sing, as his voice was said to be "like an angel's." In personal appearance, he is said to have had a bald head, a long face, and sparkling eyes. He wrote a number of hymns, particularly for children.

ROBERT ROBINSON

1735-1790

Come, Thou fount of every blessing,"*

The author of this blessed old hymn was born in Norfolk County, England. He lost his father in boyhood, leaving his godly mother in such poverty that Robert was apprenticed to a London barber in his fifteenth year, "an uncongenial position for a bookish and thoughtful lad." During a lark with other boys he heard a prediction as to his future from a fortune-telling woman that set him thinking, and he went to hear Whitefield preach a sermon on the wrath to come that "haunted him blessedly" for three years and resulted in his conversion at the age of nineteen. Eventually he became the pastor of a Baptist church in Cambridge where the famous Robert Hall was afterward pastor. Here he wrote a number of scholarly theological or historical books showing the vehement and enthusiastic glow of passion that belongs to the orator. He retired from the ministry in 1790 and died not very long after, permaturely worn out. His theological views had undergone changes in the direction of Unitarian-

---

* There is a story told that he once heard a lady sing this hymn in a stage coach, and that he burst into tears, saying to her, "I am the unhappy author of that hymn, and I would give a thousand worlds, if I had them, to possess now the feelings that I had when I wrote it." I wish to add here that this hymn has been to me a great source of spiritual uplift. I like it best to the Welsh tune "Hyfrydol," No. 195 in "Songs for Service" published by Rodehever Co., Chicago.

ism (he had come into contact with Dr. Priestly). One biographer says he became a Socinian. Dr. Julian says he was somewhat unstable and impulsive, but speaks in the highest terms of the merits of his hymns.

John Ryland, D. D.

1753-1825

"O Lord, I would delight in Thee,
And on Thy care depend."

The author of the above well-known hymn* was an honored Baptist preacher of Northampton, England. He was so precocious that he read the Psalms in Hebrew at the age of five, and the New Testament in Greek before he was nine, and preached at the age of seventeen. He became the President of a Baptist College at Bristol and received the degree of D. D. from Brown University, Rhode Island. He was one of the founders of the Baptist Missionary Society.

Rev. Thomas Scott

1705-1775

"Hasten, sinner, to be wise;
Stay not for tomorrow's sun."

This well-known hymn was written by the above named independent minister of Ipswich, England. (This is not the commentator of the same name, but is the brother of Elizabeth Scott who also wrote hymns which are in the Yale College library, and who died in Connecticut.) Thomas Scott was the author of many hymns† which were published

---

* Dr. Ryland says of this hymn, "I recollect deeper feelings of mind in composing this hymn than perhaps I ever felt in composing any other." He composed a good many hymns, but as Dr. Julian says of them, "they lack poetry and passion." He is the author of books and discourses.

† One of Scott's hymns closes with this fine stanza:
"Be just and kind; that great command
Doth on eternal pillars stand;
Thus did the ancient prophets teach,
And all that truly know Thee preach."

in a book called "Lyric Poems," the object of which is thus
described by the author, "to furnish a kind of little poetical
system of piety and morals." In this he begins with natural
religion and ends with the millenial reign of Christ on earth.
He may be classed as an "Evangelarian", that is, doctrinally,
while believing that Jesus is the God-appointed Savior of
mankind, he denied the "eternal sonship" of Christ before
the foundation of the world.

Sir Walter Scott, Bart.

1771-1832

"When Israel, of the Lord beloved, out of the land
of bondage came,"

This hymn, taken from the novel Ivanhoe, was written by
this distinguished poet and novelist who otherwise made no
contribution to hymnody.   Walter Scott came of an old
border family and was a sickly child, born in Edinburgh. He
was also lame from childhood, which was for the most part
spent on his grandfather's farm where the foundation of his
literary career was laid.   He was a bold, indomitable little
fellow, with an odd turn for story telling. He left college
after three years, where he did not shine as a student, and
later worked in his father's office as a clerk and then was
called to the bar. At the age of twenty-one he married
Charlotte Carpenter*, a lady of French birth, and thereafter
devoted himself chiefly to literature, in which he became the
idol of his day. He resided at Abbotsford, where summer
after summer, crowds of the noble and distinguished enjoyed
his princely hospitalities.† At the age of fifty-nine he was
smitten with paralysis and taken to Italy, only returning to
his British home (for which he pined) to die, with his chil-

---

* In my genealogical studies I was interested to learn that the first
meeting with his future wife was in the Dacre castle, one of my own
ancestral homes. Charlotte little knew then that in twenty-three years
her husband would receive a baronetcy and she would become Lady
Scott.

† In 1826 Scott suddenly found one morning that he was a bankrupt
with a dying wife. His last years were spent in a desperate struggle
to "owe no one a penny." This effort really killed him.

dren around him and the murmur of the Tweed in his ears.
He was buried beside his wife whom he dearly loved, in the
old Abbey of Dryburgh.

ROBERT SEAGRAVE

1693-1750(?)

"Rise, my soul, and stretch thy wings"*

This standard hymn was written by a reformer in the
Church of England, born in Leicestershire. He became discouraged in his efforts to arouse his parishioners to a true
spiritual life and so eventually he worked outside the
Establishment, preaching at Lorrimar's Hall, Cripplegate,
London, until 1750. He also occupied Whitefield's tabernacle from time to time.

HON. WALTER SHIRLEY

1725-1786

"Peace, troubled soul, whose plaintive moan"

This comforting and tender hymn was written by a cousin
of the Countess of Huntingdon under circumstances of great
affliction.† He was a friend of the Wesleys and Whitefield,
and often preached in their chapels. He was a rector in the
Church of England, and some of his sermons‡ were pub-

---

* This hymn, sometimes erroneously attributed to others, was
printed in Whitefield's hymn book in 1753. It was a favorite in my
New England childhood, and I personally regard it as a strong and
elevating hymn. He wrote some other hymns not so well known. His
hymns were originally prepared for the use of his own congregation.
There seems to be some obscurity about his death.

† The circumstances referred to are as follows: Shirley's elder
brother, Lord Ferrers, murdered a servant who had testified against
him about a matter that had to do with his wife. Ferrers was condemned to the gallows for this murder, and Shirley, Lady Huntingdon,
and the Methodists generally fasted and prayed for his repentance
without avail. Ferrers spent his last night playing piquet with his
prison warden and went unrepentant to his doom. Shirley went back
to his parish a broken-spirited man, and wrote this imperishable hymn
which, with its beautiful melody, may well solace us when we find
ourselves up against the mystery of unanswered prayer.

‡ His hymns were also published, but two well-known hymns have
been ascribed to him which were really written by others. One is
"Lord, dismiss us with Thy blessing." The other is "Sweet the moments rich in blessing", which Shirley recast into its present form,
but did not originally write.

lished. He died at the age of sixty-one and his last days
were peaceful except that his illness was protracted. When
too weak to preach in public he used to sit in his home and
preach to as many people as would come to hear him.

WILLIAM SHRUBSOLE, JR.

1759-1829

"Arm of the Lord, awake, awake!
Put on thy strength, the nations shake."

This magnificent hymn* was written by a shipwright of
Kent, later a clerk in London. He was connected with the
Congregationalists and became one of the directors of the
Bible Society and also of the Tract Society. He wrote over
twenty hymns† which were published singly in various reli-
gious magazines.

CHRISTOPHER SMART

1722-1770

"The world, the clustering spheres, He made,
The glorious light, the soothing shade."

These lines are taken from a poem on the Deity, written
under tragic circumstances by the above named ill-fated
English poet. He had brilliant promise, as he took a poetry
prize for five successive years at Cambridge, then tried to
make a living writing poetry. Through his privations and
dissipations he became insane. In an asylum he was de-

* This hymn is not as well known or as often sung as it deserves
to be. I took a great fancy to it some years ago and have composed a
melody for it, which has been privately printed in a small musical
pamphlet called "Melodies of the People."

† One of Shrubsole's hymns is called "Daily Duties." It is a beautiful morning hymn and is included by the compilers in "The Library of
Religious Poetry," where, however, they attribute the hymn "Arm of
the Lord" to Wm. Shrubsole Sr. instead of Shrubsole Jr., as does
Julian. These two Shrubsoles also should not be confused seemingly
with the William Shrubsole, a London organist, who composed the
stirring tune of Miles Lane for Perronet's hymn "All hail the power."
These three William Shrubsoles seem to be badly mixed, or at least
confusing.

prived of pen, ink, and paper, but wrote the above quoted poem by scratching it with a key on the door of his cell. Smart died eventually in a debtors' prison at the age of forty-eight.

HORACE SMITH

1779-1849

"Contains all creeds within its mighty span
The Love of God displayed in Love of Man."

These lines, (culled from a hymn found in Fox's collection "Hymns and Anthems") were written by a wealthy English stockbroker, a popular and accomplished man noted for his benevolences. He and his brother James wrote a book of clever imitations of noted authors which was used at the opening of Drury Lane Theatre. The book was called "Rejected Addresses." At first there was difficulty in getting it published, but later it ran through sixteen editions and the Smith Brothers got over 1000 pounds for it. (What a pity some poor authors could not be similarly rewarded for their efforts!) In Bryant's Library of Poetry and Song is found a lovely poem called "Hymn to the Flowers*" written by Horace Smith.

---

* This poem closes with these beautiful lines:
"Were I in churchless solitudes remaining
    Far from all voice of teachers and divines,
.My soul would find in flowers of God's ordaining,
    Priests, sermons, shrines."
I hope I may be pardoned for inserting here a stanza of my own on the ministry of flowers. Here it is:
"Thank God for flowers! Oh darlings of the vale,
    Oh kisses of the angels on the sod,
    With fair illumined text ye tell the tale
    That speaks the beauty and the love of God."
May I also be excused by indulgent readers for inserting in connection with Horace Smith's "Hymn of the Flowers" my own poem on "Consider the Lilies" written in my senior year at Oberlin College and printed with my maiden initials as follows:

THE LILIES
By C. L. L. (published in the Oberlin Review May 9th, 1877)

"Consider the lilies how they grow.
They lift their dainty bells of snow
    From broad, dark leaves of green.
No toil is theirs; a shade of care
Their sweet child faces never wear
    Nor sin in them is seen.

Continued on next page

ROBERT SOUTHEY

1774-1843

"Four things which are not in Thy treasury,
I lay before Thee, Lord, with this petition,
My nothingness, my wants,
My sins, and my contrition."

These lines were written by the above named Poet Laureate, who is not counted by Dr. Julian as a hymnist (although his second wife is). Southey was the son of a linen draper who was embarrassed financially. Robert's grandmother sent him to Westminster College from which he was expelled

---

Consider the lilies how they grow.
No palace doth such beauty know
    As theirs of arching trees.
And earthly kings in their parade
And pomp of pride are not arrayed
    In glory such as these.

Consider the lilies how they grow.
From all the summer winds that blow
    They steal the rich perfumes,
They catch the dew and sweet sunlight
In all the fairy cups of white
    Of waxen lily blooms.

Consider the lilies how they grow.
By taking from earth, air, and snow
    The good that each can give,
By drinking in from everything
The life and beauty each doth bring
    The gentle lilies live.

Consider the lilies how they grow.
No tiny root so mean and low
    But feeds on earth's rich moulds.
The broad leaves drink the air and light,
The seed perfects in blossoms white,
    Each part its mission holds.

Consider the lilies how they grow.
Upon the rest all parts bestow
    Their own peculiar good.
They grow by giving back and forth,
The roots send up the strength of earth,
    The leaves send down their food.

Consider the lilies how they grow
By taking and by giving. So
    They rear their airy bells
That honeyed sweets for brown bees hold,
Whence, dusted o'er with pollen gold,
    They fly to fill their cells.

Consider the lilies how they grow
By taking and by giving. Know
    Oh soul, the lesson sweet,
That only in this way, as well
In human life as lily bell,
    Can beauty be complete.

for a trifling insubordination. He must have been something of a rebel in spirit, for he was in sympathy with the French Revolution. He tried to study law but, like our Bryant, found it a distasteful occupation and relinquished it. Then he tried a political secretaryship which was also distasteful and relinquished. Thereafter he depended for his support on literature alone. He and Coleridge married sisters. He wrought with the regularity of a machine, but was happy in his family and friendships. His prose was highly esteemed for its easy and lucid style, and some of his poems are very fine. He worked his brain too incessantly and this probably was the cause of the paralysis and mental stupor which clouded his last years, during which he was tenderly cared for by his devoted second wife.

SAMUEL STENNETT

1727-1795

"Majestic sweetness sits enthroned
Upon the Savior's brow,"

This well known hymn was written by the grandson of the belligerent Rev. Joseph Stennet who was also a Baptist hymn writer of England who declined preferment although his family was large and his salary small. Samuel was born at Exeter and became a prominent Baptist preacher in London, where one of his parishioners and personal friends was the philanthropist John Howard. Stennett was also a contemporary of Isaac Watts and a friend of George III. Stennett wrote the enlivening hymn which I used to hear in my childhood which begins, "On Jordan's stormy banks I stand."

Rev. Joseph Swain

1761-1796

"O Thou in whose presence my soul takes delight"

This beautiful hymn was written by a young Baptist preacher who died at the early age of thirty-five. In his boyhood he was apprenticed to an engraver in London. He became a decided Christian with a poetical and emotional temperament which had expression in the writing of hymns. After a short but popular and useful ministry in London of only five years this career was cut short by death. The above quoted hymn is a rich legacy to the world.

James Thomson

1700-1748

"I cannot go where Universal Love smiles not
    around.

* * * * * * * *

From seeming evil still educing good."

These lines from a religious poem that the author called "a hymn" were written by the above named Scotch poet, who is not classed by Julian as a hymnist at all. James Thomson was the son of a minister and educated himself for the ministry at Edinburgh, but his views changed and he struggled to maintain himself at the age of twenty-five by writing poetry. The merits of his poems in "The Seasons" were finally recognized and brought him friends and patrons and a government office which he held until he died of a neglected cold at the age of forty-eight. He is described as a fine fat fellow, a sharp, accurate observer of men and things, not without his errors, but a loving brother, a fast friend, and of a sweet disposition which endeared him to all that knew him. He gave hope in his last hours that he died in the faith.

AUGUSTUS MONTAGUE TOPLADY

1740-1778

"If through unruffled seas
Toward heaven we calmly sail,"*

This beautiful hymn was written by the author of that dearly loved hymn Rock of Ages† on which his immortal fame rests. Toplady's father was killed during the siege of Carthagena soon after his son's birth. Augustus was educated at Trinity College, Dublin, and was converted under the preaching of James Morris, a Wesleyan itinerant preacher. Toplady writes thus of his conversion: "Strange that I, who had so long sat under the means of grace in England, should be brought nigh to God in an obscure part of Ireland amidst a handful of God's people met in a barn and under the ministry of one who could hardly spell his name." Surely it was the Lord's doing. Toplady became a Calvinistic preacher in London and also was a Church of England clergyman in Devon. He was a strenuous opponent doctrinally of John Wesley and the heated correspondence between these two holy men does not reflect credit on either one. It is to be smilingly noted that although Toplady and the Wesleys quarreled in doctrine, yet "Rock of Ages" by Toplady and "Jesus, Lover of my soul" by Charles Wesley are apt to be placed side by side in hymn books and are associated together. So shall our differences fade away in the light of heaven! Toplady died at the early age of thirty-eight with an overtasked and wasted body. The devout flame of his soul burned brightly till the last. During his last illness he seemed to be in the very vestibule of glory.

---

* This hymn, (so precious to me since childhood) is in reality part of a longer hymn which begins, "Your harps, ye trembling saints." His "Rock of Ages" was sung by the helpless passengers on the Steamer "London" which went down in the Bay of Biscay in 1866. It was sung in their native tongue by Armenian Christians during a massacre in Constantinople. Gladstone wrote a beautiful translation of it into Latin when he was sitting in the House of Commons.

† Toplady named this hymn "A Living and Dying Prayer for the Holiest Believer in the World". I sympathize with him in thinking that there is no human being who does not need Divine indulgence and forgiveness to the end.

To a friend's inquiry he answered with sparkling eye, "O, my dear sir, I cannot tell the comforts I feel in my soul. They are past expression. The consolations of God are so abundant that He leaves me nothing to pray for. My prayers are all converted into praise. I enjoy a heaven already in my soul." Within an hour of dying he called his friends together and asked if they could give him up, and when they said they could tears of joy ran down his cheeks. He said, "No mortal can live after the glories God has manifested to my soul." Toplady is described as fervently leading the devotion of his flock in solemn tones till he and his hearers were in tears. He had an ethereal look in his face, a light form, a musical voice and vivacious manner. He was a truly Christian man.

Sir Aubrey de Vere, Bart.*

1788-1845

"That church which shall not fall,
   From night to morn breathes forth upon the air
   Meek intercession for the souls of men."

These are the closing lines of one of the exquisite sonnets† written by the above named country gentleman of Ireland. He lived most of his life at his ancestral home at Adare where his son who bore his name‡ succeeded him.

---

* There was an earlier Aubrey de Vere, 20th earl in a long line of English earls which included Edward de Vere, 17th earl, who sat in the trials of both Essex and Mary, Queen of Scots. Alas for anyone who had to do with those tragic legal murders! Let those who wish to get the full force of it read Lytton Strachey's thrilling book, "Elizabeth and Essex."

† Our Aubrey de Vere of Ireland wrote also a lovely poem called "The Sisters" which contains this wise admonition:
   "O ye, whom broken vows bereave,
   Your vows to heaven restore;
   O ye, for blighted love who grieve,
   Love deeper, and love more."

‡ The third son of Sir Aubrey de Vere named Thomas Aubrey de Vere, b. 1814, is classed as a hymnist by Dr. Julian. He was one of the professors in the Roman Catholic University of Dublin while Dr. Newman was rector there. Some of his hymns are given in Roman Catholic collections.

Rev. Isaac Watts

1674-1748

"When I survey the wondrous cross
On which the Prince of Glory died"

This immortal hymn was written by the above named hymnist who, with the possible exception of Charles Wesley, has probably contributed more largely* to the hymnology of the church than any other. Watts was the son of a Southampton deacon of an Independent Church who had been twice imprisoned for conscience' sake. When, as a young man,† Isaac complained of the lack of taste in the hymns then sung, he was told, "Give us something better,". so he tried. Here are the first lines of some of his wellknown hymns:

"Joy to the world, the Lord is come"
"There is a land of pure delight"
"God is the refuge of His saints"
"When I can read my title clear"
"My God how endless is Thy love"
"Jesus shall reign where'er the sun"
"Eternal power whose high abode"
"Give me the wings of faith to rise"
"Whene'er I take my walks abroad"
"Alas; and did my Savior bleed"
"How doth the little busy bee"

---

* S. W. Christophers criticises both Watts and Wesley for writing so many hymns—because some are not good. I cannot agree to this view. The poet should write whenever the poetical impulse seizes him, not knowing himself whether the result will be a "gem" or only "paste jewelry." Doubtless when Watts wrote "When I survey the wondrous cross" he was himself unaware that he was surpassing all his other efforts. Hymns are only known as to excellence by the final test of time.

† Watts was the eldest of nine children. A physician, seeing his splendid promise, would have obtained for him a university education had Watts been willing to become a member of the Established Church. He declined this opportunity.

In the beauty of the lilies,
In the mocking-bird's refrain,
In the verdure on the hill-tops,
God expresses life again.

In the beauty of your living,
In the kindly things you do,
In the love you scatter broadcast—
Christ as Love comes forth in you.

—From "Good Stories" April 1931

"Hark from the tombs a doleful sound"
"Come we that love the Lord"
"My dear Redeemer and my Lord"
"Sweet is the work my God, my King"
"Thus far the Lord hath led me on"
"Soon as I heard my Father say"
"Not all the blood of beasts"
"This is the day the Lord has made"
"Begin, my tongue, some heavenly theme"
"Early my God without delay"
"Unveil thy bosom, faithful tomb"
"In all my vast concerns with Thee"
"Hush, my dear, lie still and slumber"
"Come, let us join our cheerful songs"
"Now I lay me down to sleep"*
"Am I a soldier of the cross"
"O God our help in ages past"

Watts was for fourteen years a minister of an Independent Church in London. His health failed in 1712 and he accepted an invitation† to visit in the country and in reality stayed there thirty-six years till his death.‡ He was small in stature, feeble in body, and plain looking. He never married,§ was of a cheerful disposition, fond of children, of high reputation, both as man and preacher. He is called "The founder of English Hymnology."

---

* Of this evening prayer used for 200 years by little children so extensively, some one has written these lines:
"If of all that has been written
I could choose what might be mine,
I would choose that child's petition
Rising to the throne divine."

† This invitation was from Sir Thomas Abney under whose hospitable roof Watts remained for the rest of his life of suffering. Watts composed many of his hymns in a sick room.

‡ As he approached death he said he was waiting God's leave to die and, "It is a great mercy that I have no fear or dread of death. I could, if God please, lay my head back and die without alarm this afternoon or night." He is buried near Bunyan in Bunhill Fields Cemetery, but a monument was erected to him in Westminster Abbey.

§ Watts had in his personal life a great sorrow. He dearly loved a beautiful lady named Elizabeth Singer to whom he proposed marriage, which was declined. Miss Singer in alluding to this said she "loved the jewel but could not admire the casket that contained it." This referred to Watts' lack of good looks. She may have gone farther and fared worse. It would satisfy some curiosity if we could hear how her future life developed. Watts is called the "Melancthon of his day." Hezekiah Butterworth says that "When I survey the wondrous cross" is "the royal jewel of all of Watts' creative work." Julian attributes the child's evening hymn "Now I lay me down to sleep" to Melancthon Woolsey Stryker, 1884. This however must be a mistake. I had it taught to me in my infancy in the eighteen-fifties.

Charles Wesley

1708-1788

"Jesus, lover of my soul, let me to Thy bosom fly;"

This hymn* which embodies the very heart of the Christian religion was written by the "greatest hymnist of all ages", as Julian describes him. He is said to have written 6,500 hymns, not of equal merit, but a great number of them used and beloved.† He was the youngest and eighteenth

---

* This "greatest of all hymns" has many anecdotes connected with it, one of which is this: There was a terrible storm in the English channel. A captain and his crew in despair mistakenly abandoned the ship, hoping by taking the boats to reach the shore in safety. Instead they were all dashed to pieces on the rocks and lost. The next morning the ship was found safely riding the waves, not a soul aboard her, but in the captain's cabin was found his hymn book open to this hymn, "Jesus, lover of my soul" his solace as he went to death.

Henry Ward Beecher said of the hymn "Jesus Lover of my soul". "I would rather be the author of that hymn than to hold the wealth of the richest man in New York. It will go on singing till the trump brings forth the angel band and then I think it will mount up on some lip to the very presence of God." The last evening of Charles G. Finney's life he was walking in his garden and could hear the choir singing "Jesus Lover of my soul" in the church where he had been pastor for forty years. He joined in the singing. Before the next morning he had joined the choir in heaven.

The following lines of comfort concerning those friends who have preceded us into another world were written by Charles Wesley:
"Yet darkly safe with God they sail
His arm still onward bears."

† Here are the first lines of a few of his well-known hymns:
"Arise, my soul, arise"
"Love divine, all love excelling"
"Hark, the herald angels sing"
"Sinners turn, why will ye die"
"Christ the Lord is risen today"
"Jesus the name high over all"
"O glorious hope of perfect love"
"Soldiers of Christ arise"
"Oh, for a heart to praise my God"
"A charge to keep I have"
"Depth of mercy, can there be"
"I know that my Redeemer lives"
"Blow ye the trumpet, blow"
"Ye servants of God, your Master proclaim"
"Light of those whose dreary dwelling"

One of Wesley's hymns which begins:
"Lo, on a narrow neck of land,
'Twixt two unbounded seas I stand"

was written on the rocks at Land's End, England, where the writer could see the English Channel on one side and stormy Atlantic on the other. Montgomery says of it that it portrays "the sublime contemplation of a dying man between this life and the one beyond."

Continued on next page

child of Samuel and Susanna Wesley, born at Epworth, England, where his father was parish clergyman. The years before and after his birth an appalling series of calamities* befell the family, but in spite of straightened circumstances Charles had an Oxford education after the early teaching of his wonderful mother and preparatory training at the Westminster School. At the age of twenty-seven he went with his brother John to Georgia under the auspices of the Society for the Propagation of the Gospel, and on the way came under the influence of Moravian travellers from Germany. This resulted in a tremendous quickening of the spiritual life of both brothers. On their return journey they were overtaken by a mighty storm† in which Charles was

Of his children's hymn beginning "Gentle Jesus, meek and mild," written about 1740, this story is told: An old man over eighty who had long neglected the spiritual life, tried as he lay dying to think of something of comfort. Then he was consoled as he remembered himself kneeling at his mother's knee as a little child, and made the hymn he then repeated his own in the time of death,
"Gentle Jesus, meek and mild, look upon a little child;
Pity my simplicity; suffer me to come to Thee."
One of Wesley's glorious hymns has this story connected with it: In 1737 he had recently received a great quickening of his spiritual life under the ministry of Count Zinzendorf and other Moravians, one of whom, Peter Bohler, visited him in London when he was ill and reproved him for his unwillingness to praise God publicly for receiving "rest to his soul", saying "If you had a thousand tongues you should praise God with them all." This led Wesley to write the familiar hymn, "Oh for a thousand tongues to sing my great Redeemer's praise!"

Two of Wesley's hymns are clearly associated in my mind with my missionary life in Johannesburg. One of them I used to hear sung with uplifting enthusiasm by a great congregation. It begins, "Arise, my soul, arise! Shake off thy guilty fears!" The other is associated with some quiet, tender meetings in the South Africa General Mission where it became very dear to me. It begins:
"Thou hidden source of calm repose."
I have not heard it sung in the United States.

S. C. Gauntlett of the English Salvation Army says that the following hymns were written by Charles Wesley.
"All things are possible to him"
"He wills that I should holy be"
"Come Jesus Lord with holy fire"—and
"Captain of Israel's host—and guide"

* In 1705 the father was thrown into gaol for debt caused by the blowing down of the parsonage barn, the burning of his flax (probably by an incendiary), the stabbing of three cows on whose milk the family depended for food by his enemies who resented his political principles (his wife and possibly himself being a Jacobite). In 1709 the rectory was entirely burned down.

† In this storm the mizzen mast was cut away to save the ship; sheep, hogs, and chickens were washed away or drowned. Wesley, although ill himself, calmed others who were in an agony of fear.

enabled to overcome his own fear and be a comfort to his
despairing fellow-travelers. His victory of prayer and faith
at this crisis was triumphant. A similar triumph of faith
was manifest later when an earthquake shock nearly para-
lyzed with fear his assembled congregation in London, but
Wesley preached calmly on the text, "Therefore will not we
fear though the earth be removed!" At the age of forty-one
he was happily married to Sarah Gwynne. He was an indefatigable worker under his brother John in laying the
foundations of Methodism and endured many persecutions*
in this work. He continued his hymn writing till he was an
old man. Many of his hymns were composed in the saddle†
and only committed to paper when his journey was ended.
His brother John greatly admired Charles' hymns. He died
in London and was buried in the Marylebone Churchyard at
his own wish.

---

* There is an old house in Cornwall with a door having a ponderous
iron knocker. On the door are dents made by a mob which tried to
break in on Mr. Wesley who had taken refuge there. He was rescued
by some sailors who led him out, daring anyone to touch him. Wesley
wrote a curious hymn among these rough Cornish people which they
much enjoyed. It begins,

> "'Listed in the cause of sin, why should a good be evil?
> Music, alas, has too long been pressed to obey the Devil."

† As an old man in London Wesley kept a stock of small cards in
his pocket and, as he jogged along on his little pony, might be seen
now and then jotting down a stanza of the hymn he was mentally
composing. Once his horse stumbled and fell on him, spraining his
hand, which he said "spoiled my hymn writing for that day." Watts,
with great nobility of spirit, said of Wesley's hymn on "Wrestling
Jacob", "It is worth all the verses I have ever written." When Charles
Wesley's feet were "slipping o'er the brink of Jordan" he wrote a
hymn which begins "In age and feebleness extreme, who shall a sinful
worm reclaim?" John Wesley wanted Charles buried in the City Road
Chapel where he had prepared a grave for himself, but Charles said,
"I have lived and I die in the Church of England."

Not so long ago a book hunter at Oxford library unearthed a metrical version of the 119th Psalm by Charles Wesley, which had been
buried in complete oblivion. It is an enchanting and well-sustained
poem which the world had well-nigh lost. Here are two lines of it:

> "Thee I have remembered, Lord, musing in the silent night,
> Loved Thy name and kept Thy word, pure and permanent delight."

Handel composed some of his best music for Wesley's hymns.

John Wesley

1703-1791

"How happy is the Pilgrim's lot!
How free from anxious thought!"

This is known as the "Pilgrim's Hymn"* and was written by the renowned Founder of Methodism, although when John Wesley went to Oxford in 1729 he found already there a little band called "Oxford Methodists" who elected him to be their leader. Here he became associated with George Whitefield. The name Methodists referred to their belief in regularity in the performance of duty. They made a great point of the utilization of time, but there was seemingly no special fervor in their meetings for religious conversation. Probably that feature of Methodism grew out of the spiritual awakening which the Wesley brothers received from contact with the Moravians† later, especially Peter Bohler. After this transforming experience John Wesley toiled incessantly for the spread of a vital, glowing, personal religion, making more converts perhaps than any other man of any age. He died at last in the harness at the patriarchal age

---

* John Wesley wrote the Pilgrim's hymn after a calamitous journey of three or four hundred miles on horse back to Newcastle in 1746. He had encountered a terrible storm, swollen brooks, and unpassable roads which necessitated detours through the fields, and in addition he had been pelted by a mob. Of such trials he wrote these lines:

"Whate'er molests and troubles us
When past, as nothing we esteem,
And pain, like pleasure, is a dream."

The Pilgrim Hymn was a favorite with a well-known character in West England known as "Foolish Dick", who in childhood had not intellect to learn to do anything that required skill. However, after being soundly converted, a remarkable change came upon him, especially in the matter of memory. If a chapter in the Bible or a hymn was read to him, he knew it. He became a useful itinerant preacher, and at the many fire sides that were open to him he would sit and sing the Pilgrim's Hymn, waving his arms in accompaniment. These lines he especially loved:

"No foot of land do I possess,
No cottage in the wilderness."

† John Wesley's first acquaintance with the Moravians (with whom he later broke doctrinally) was on the Georgia trip, during which he wished to marry the daughter of the chief magistrate of Savannah, but gave this up on the advice of the Moravians, wherefore the rejected lady promptly married another man. (Who could blame her?) Her action, however, seems to have displeased John, who refused her admission into the communion, whereupon her husband brought legal action against John, who concluded that Savannah was not a proper place for his activities, and "shaking off the dust of his feet" he left America in a hurry.

of eighty-eight.* John and Charles Wesley worked together and supplemented each other, John being the organizer of the movement, and Charles the hymn writer. Both were powerful preachers and both belonged to that remarkable Wesley family of preachers and poets. Their father, older brother† Samuel, and sister Mehitabel were all sacred poets. John nearly lost his life in the fire which burned the Wesley home when he was six years old. This made a great impression on him. John's marriage and that of his brother Samuel and sister Mehitabel were all unhappy.‡ It seems there was a famous ghost story connected with the Wesley rectory, but I do not know the details.§

HENRY KIRKE WHITE

1785-1806

"Oft in sorrow, oft in woe, onward Christian, onward go!"

This beautiful hymn was found scribbled on the back of one of the college mathematical papers of this brilliant young student after his death from over study in his twenty-second

---

* John Wesley preached in the open air to the age of seventy to congregations numbering 7,000 with a clear, strong voice. He was a picturesque old man, small in stature, with white hair, piercing eye, neat dress. His last words were, "The best of all is, God is with us." After death his body lay in state in the City Road Chapel, London, dressed in his sacerdotal robes and with a Bible in his hands. He was a great preacher. Walter Scott listened to one of his sermons in Kelso Church and went home to meditate on personal religion. Cobden left the world with one of Wesley's lines on his lips. This is one of Wesley's practical mottoes: "Always in haste, but never in a hurry."

† Samuel Wesley, Jr., like the rest, had his religious education from his mother and was her main stay. He also was like a father to his younger brothers and sisters. He was a High Church English Clergyman and disapproved strongly of the innovations of John and Charles, but this did not cause a breach in their fraternal relations.

‡ At the age of forty-nine John Wesley married a widow with four children but later a separation took place. Since I gather that he was an autocrat with his preachers, I can easily surmise that he may have been somewhat domineering with his wife, and they were clearly at an age and a point of development when yielding to the other was not easy.

§ The family of the Wesleys at Epworth were for a considerable time disturbed by loud, mysterious knockings that they regarded as the preter-natural visitations of a "Jacobite Goblin" who did not like to hear Samuel Wesley Sr. pray for the king. They would not vacate their house, however, on this account, and the "goblin", probably discouraged in his attentions, discontinued them.

year. White was the son of a Nottingham butcher and a
superior mother who successfully carried on a boarding school
for girls. Henry was at first apprenticed to a stocking
weaver and later into an attorney's office, but gave all his
spare time to literary pursuits and published a book of poems
at eighteen. Through the influence of a young friend named
Arnold* Henry was converted from atheism to a Christian
experience, and desiring to become a minister, went to
Cambridge† to study, being released from his articles through
the generosity of his employers. At College he so distinguished himself that the highest honors seemed within his
grasp. His untimely death moved both England and America
to sympathy and lamentation. A monumental tablet was
erected in All Saints Church, Cambridge, by a citizen of
Boston, U. S. A. Byron wrote a poetical tribute‡ to his
memory. His picture is preserved for us, showing an intense, sensitive, earnest young face with waving lovelocks
of hair around it and his finely written autograph below.
He has contributed ten hymns to our hymnody, some of
exceeding beauty. One of these, perhaps the best, begins,
"The Lord our God is full of might,"§ another begins, "The
Lord our God is Lord of all."¶

* Arnold was converted through witnessing the triumphant death
of a believer. He did not like to tell White of his change of heart,
fearing ridicule. White noticed his friend's new reserve and inquired
the cause, whereupon Arnold explained his apparent coldness. At this
lack of confidence White exclaimed, "Good God, Arnold, you surely
regard me in a worse light than I deserve." After White's own conversion the friends resumed their close intimacy. White's hymn which
begins "When marshalled on the nightly plain" is supposed to refer
to this crisis in his life.

† During those last two years at college White was accustomed to
sing hymns when he was in a boat on the river Trent. On one occasion he improvised a hymn as he sang.

‡ Byron's lines on White, are these:
"Unhappy White, when life was in its spring
And the young muse just waved her joyous wing,
The Spoiler swept that soaring lyre away
Which else had sounded an immortal lay."

§ This hymn contains these lofty lines:
"Howl, winds of night, your force combine;
Without his high behest,
Ye shall not in the mountain pine
Disturb the sparrow's nest."
I do not see how any Christian can sing those words without ex-
altation.

¶ This hymn contains the line:
"I hear Him in the waterfall."
As a child at singing school I associated this line with the "water-
falls" which were then the fashion in young ladies' hair dressing.

WILLIAM WILLIAMS

1717-1791

"Guide me, O Thou Great Jehovah,
Pilgrim through this barren land."

This grand hymn was written by "The Sweet Singer of Wales," also called the "Watts of Wales." Williams was born in the same year as John Cennick and both were destined to become travelling preachers and to write useful hymns for the Christian Church. Williams wrote his hymns originally in Welsh. Their translations into English were first used in Mr. Whitefield's orphan home in America in a collection called "Gloria in Excelsis" which was republished in England in 1774. Williams wrote (before the day of modern foreign missions) a noble missionary hymn of which the first line is "O'er gloomy hills of darkness."

Williams at the age of twenty-three was ordained a deacon in the Established Church but never took a priest's orders. He was much esteemed in later years as a preacher. His Welsh hymn went through five editions.

WALLACE YOUNG

d. 1751

"When my strength shall decline, and my anguish increase,
And my sins without number in terror I see,
When I turn to Thy mercy for pardon and peace,
Thou Hope of the sinner, shine brightly on me."

This obscure hymnist has expressed in the above lines the need which will come to each of us in turn. The name of the hymn from which this is taken is "Happy Death."

CHAPTER VII

BRITISH HYMNISTS LATER THAN THE EIGHTEENTH CENTURY

"O God, who hast put melody in our hearts, we thank Thee for the songs that help us in our way. Keep us ever in this grace we beseech Thee. And when life grows dark about us give us songs in the night."—Amen.

WILLIAM ALEXANDER, D. D.

1824-1911

"The great poem of this strange existence."

This is a line from the sacred poem called "Up Above" by the Irish Bishop above named who was born at Londonderry and educated at Oxford. He has written and published polished, dignified verses, but very few that can be classed as hymns. His wife, Cecil Frances Alexander, who will be noted in the following chapter is the real hymnist of the family.

HENRY ALFORD, D. D.

1810-1871

"Come, ye thankful people, come!"

This is the opening line of a harvest hymn written by the Dean of Canterbury who was born in London, the son of a rector of the same name. He graduated from Cambridge with honors and is especially distinguished as the editor of the Greek Testament, a noble work into which he put twenty years of labor. His hymn writing was probably a side issue with him, although he published several books of sacred poetry* which are evangelical, but Dr. Julian considers them rather cold. One of his hymns "Forward be our watchword" was composed shortly before Alford's death while he was walking up and down in Canterbury Cathedral. Another of his hymns begins "Ten thousand times ten thousand."

William Allingham

1828-1889

"In trouble for my sin I cried to God,
To the great God who dwelleth in the deeps."

These lines are taken from a profound sacred poem entitled "Levavi Oculos." I think it might be used as a hymn, though Julian does not class the above named poet as a hymnist. The poem of Allingham's called "Sunday Bells" might be used perhaps as a hymn. William Allingham was born at Ballyshannon, Ireland, and at the age of twenty-two published his first book of poems.†

---

* There is one stanza which Alford wrote which is a great favorite with me:

> "My bark is wafted to the strand
> By breath divine;
> And on the helm there rests a hand
> Other than mine."

I consider this beautiful and comforting.

There is also a hymn of Alford's I like which is found in Fox's collection, "Hymns and Anthems." I give below the first and last stanzas of the hymn:

> "Be true to every inmost thought;
> Be as thy thought, thy speech;
> What thou hast not by suffering bought,
> Presume thou not to teach.
> * * * * * * * * *
> Face thou the wind! Though safer seem
> In shelter to abide;
> We were not made to sit and dream;
> The true must first be tried."

† Fox's Hymns and Anthems has two selections from Allingham's pen, scarcely lyrical, but very interesting. One of these contains these lines which remind me of that stately verse in Ps. 119: 165, "Great peace have they which love Thy law and nothing shall offend them."

> "In heavenly sunlight lives no shade of fear;
> The soul there busy or at rest hath peace
> And music floweth from the various world."

Another remarkable poem of Allingham's is called "The Touchstone," which I take it is an allegory showing the fate of a man who, divinely enlightened, applies the Touchstone of Truth to all existing affairs—that he will necessarily be hated by those who uphold the established order, but that Truth lives in spite of all efforts to destroy it. Allingham will probably be best remembered by his delicious poem "The Fairies".

> "Up the airy mountain,
> Down the rushy glen,
> We daren't go a-hunting
> For fear of little men."

Matthew Arnold

1822-1888

"Charge once more then and be dumb!
Let the victors when they come,
When the forts of folly fall,
Find thy body by the wall."

These lines which have the same moral stimulus (to me, at least) as has a rousing hymn, were written by the oldest son of the celebrated Dr. Arnold of Rugby. Matthew held the position of Professor of Poetry at Oxford. He wrote much in both poetry and prose in a subdued but forcible style. He lectured in America in 1885 and his meed of small praise for Emerson caused great commotion and drew out indignant replies. Dr. Julian does not class Arnold as a hymnist.

Philip James Bailey

1816-1902

"Call all who love Thee, Lord, to Thee."

This is the first line of a hymn by the author of a celebrated book called "Festus" which went through ten editions in England and thirty in America. Philip James Bailey was a lawyer, son of the editor of a weekly paper called "The Nottingham Mercury." "Festus" was begun when Philip was in his nineteenth year and completed in three years. His writings are largely not on the earthly plane. "He speaks of universes as other poets speak of buttercups. He is on terms of perfect familiarity with Eternity." The titles of two of his works are, "The Angel World" and "The Mystic and Spiritual Legend." Julian's Dictionary speaks of his compositions* as eminently beautiful.

---

* Here are four of Bailey's fine lines:
"We live in deeds, not years; in thoughts, not breaths;
In feelings, not in figures on a dial;
We should count time by heart throbs. He most lives
Who thinks most, feels the noblest, acts the best."

Sir Henry Williams Baker Bart.

1821-1877

"Oh what, if we are Christ's,
Is earthly shame or loss?"*

This surpassingly beautiful hymn was written by one of
the compilers of "Hymns Ancient and Modern" of which
2,000,000 copies were sold on its publication. Baker was
born in London, educated in Cambridge, and became a Vicar.
He wrote 33 hymns, most of which are characterized by a
tender and plaintive sadness "which reminds one of the
saintly Lyte." Baker was something of a musical composer
and his melodies were harmonized by Dr. Monk. He composed the beautiful melody called "Stephanos" for the hymn
"Art thou weary, art thou languid." One of Baker's exquisite hymns begins, "The King of Love my shepherd is."†

George Linnaeus Banks

1821-1881

"I live for those who love me,
For those I know are true."

This fine hymn which is 209 in "Pilgrim Songs" was
written by an English editor and verse writer born in
Birmingham. The hymn is the joint production of himself
and his wife Isabella, née Varley. He died in London.

---

* This hymn was greatly endeared to me during a period of youthful sorrow.

† Eavon Ellerton, Baker's personal friend, records that the last
audible words on Baker's lips were this stanza from his own hymn:
"Perverse and foolish oft I strayed,
But yet in love He sought me,
And on his shoulder gently laid,
And home rejoicing brought me."

Rev. Sabine Baring-Gould

1834-1924

"Now the day is over; night is drawing nigh;"*

This exquisite evening hymn written in 1865 and included in "Hymns Ancient and Modern" was written by the above named English curate who was born at Exeter and educated at Cambridge. He has written two other well-known hymns. One of these begins: "Through the night of doubt and sorrow, onward goes the pilgrim band." The other begins: "Onward Christian Soldiers."† This was written for his own Sunday school children at Horbury Bridge to march to when they had to walk a whole mile from the church to a place of festivities. The music for this was composed by Sullivan and he feared the tune "was too brassy for church singing."

William Hiley Bathurst

1796-1877

"O for a faith that will not shrink
Though pressed by every foe!"

This precious hymn‡ was written by the above named English clergyman, educated at Oxford, but who resigned his rectory because he could not reconcile his doctrinal views with the Book of Common Prayer. He retired to private life on his paternal estate in Gloucestershire where he devoted himself to writing both in prose and verse. He is the author of 141 metrical versions of Psalms and 206 hymns. His hymns are characterized by simplicity of language and directness of aim.

---

* It is said that "it would be difficult to find any hymnal published in the last twenty-five years in which this hymn does not appear."

† The story is told of a certain Low Church vicar who used this hymn for marching but would not have a cross carried at the head of the procession as was done by High Churchmen. His warden argued in vain for the cross and at last, in protest, arranged for the procession to sing:
     "With the cross of Jesus hid behind the door."

‡ Dr. Julian seems to speak rather disparagingly of Bathurst's hymn writing ability, but I shall have to disagree with him as far as this hymn is concerned. I have a tender memory connected with it. One of my Oberlin schoolmates (named Annette Burr) who called herself my "twin-sister" was especially fond of this hymn. She has been in the better country many years and this hymn still seems a link between us.

RICHARD DODDRIDGE BLACKMORE

1825-

"In the hour of death after this life's whim"

This is the first line of a striking and solemn hymn*
written by the author of "Lorna Doone". Blackmore was
educated at Oxford for the bar, but on account of ill-health
took up the business of market gardening† near London—
combining this with literary pursuits—becoming a foremost
Victorian novelist.

EDWARD HENRY BICKERSTETH

1825-1906

"Peace, perfect peace, in this dark world of sin,"‡

This well-known and beautiful hymn was written by the
author of the celebrated book, "Yesterday, Today, and Forever."§ He was the son of Edward Bickersteth, also a
hymnist, and one of the founders of the Evangelical Alliance,
and a promoter of missions, having been appointed to visit
mission stations in West Africa. The son was educated at
Cambridge and became the Bishop of Exeter. He has ex-
celled as a hymnist. Other hymns of his in common use are
those beginning, "O God the Rock of Ages" and "Thine,
thine forever," also "Till He come, O let the words," and
"Pray, always pray, the Holy Spirit pleads."

---

* This hymn so impressed me that I set it to music. It is printed
under the title "Dominus Illuminatio Mea" in a musical pamphlet of mine
called Melodies of Life and Love."

† Blackmore's wise combinations of mental and physical activity in
order to recuperate in health is worth remembering.

‡ This hymn was written in a few moments and with little effort
after Bickersteth had heard a sermon by Canon Gibbon on the text
"Thou wilt keep him in perfect peace whose mind is stayed on Thee."
Richard le Gallienc says of it, "It would be difficult to name any other
hymn with an equally tranquillizing effect, so filled with a sense of
man's security."

§ This book is on the same great themes that inspired Dante and
Milton. The author had the design of it in his heart for twenty years.
The actual writing took two years only. He wished to awaken deeper
thought on things unseen.

Rev. John Ernest Bode

1816-1874

"O Jesus, I have promised to serve Thee to the end."

This well-known hymn was written in 1869 for the confirmation of his son by the son of a postmaster who was educated at Oxford and became a Rector in the Established Church of England. Bode was also a tutor in his college and delivered the Bampton Lectures. He wrote other hymns, but as far as I am aware only the above has come into common use. He died at Castle Camp at the age of fifty-eight.

Horatius Bonar, D. D.

1808-1889

"I heard the voice of Jesus say,
'Come unto me and rest';"

This is perhaps the best loved hymn among many which this great hymn writer has given to the church. Dr. Bonar came of a family that had representatives among the clergy of Scotland for more than two centuries. His father held a government position in Edinburgh and was a man of deep piety. Horatius was educated in the University of Edinburgh and became a minister in the Free Church of Scotland. His first hymn is perhaps more widely sung than any other that he wrote. It begins: "A few more years shall roll." It is much more sung in England and her colonies than in America. Here are the first lines of some of his other hymns:

"This is not my place of resting"
"Holy Father, hear my cry"
"Yes, for me, for me he careth"
"Make haste, O man, to live"
"Rest for the toiling hand"
"O Light of Light, shine in"
"Fill Thou my life, O Lord, my God"

"No, not despairingly come I to Thee"
"Yet there is room! The Lamb's bright hall of song"
"Go labor on, spend and be spent"
"I lay my sins on Jesus"
"Beyond the smiling and the weeping"
"I was a wandering sheep"*
"Calm me, my God, and keep me calm"
"The cross it standeth fast;"
"In the land of strangers"
"Thy way, not mine, O Lord"
"I hear the words of love"
"Up and away like the dews of the morning"
"Far down the ages now"
"When the weary seeking rest"

It is impossible to speak too highly of Dr. Bonar, either as a hymnist or as a man. His hymns came to him by inspiration. He studied under the celebrated Dr. Chalmers.

BALLINGTON BOOTH

1859-

"The cross that He gave may be heavy"

This hymn is by one of the sons of William Booth, founder of the Salvation Army. Ballington was born at Brighouse, England. He married Maud Charlesworth. For a time he had charge of the Salvation Army's work in the United States, but withdrew in 1896 on account of differing with his father as to the administration and started work of his own called "The Volunteers of America." In this enterprise he has been ably assisted by his talented wife. Their headquarters is at 34 28th St., New York. The above mentioned hymn is 494 in "Christ in Song."

---

* A school girl in Mass. who had laughed at religion—repeated this in a meeting: all eyes were tearful.

BRAMWELL BOOTH

fl. 19th and 20th centuries

"O when shall my soul find her rest?"

This fine hymn was written by the eldest son of the celebrated Booth family who was his father's successor as General of the Salvation Army in England for many years. He was finally deposed when old and ill because it was feared that he would appoint his daughter as his successor, an appointment which seemed to others inappropriate. It was a hard situation; no doubt all were conscientious in it.

HERBERT BOOTH

19th and 20th centuries

"Blessed Lord, in Thee is refuge,
Safety for my trembling soul."

This useful hymn was written by one of the sons of Gen. Wm. Booth of the Salvation Army, who, like all the other children of the family, became an officer in the great organization* started by his parents. This hymn was beloved by Mrs. Booth, the mother of the Salvation Army. She asked when she neared death to have her son Herbert's beautiful hymn sung to her. It is a general favorite in the army's work, but I have not seen or heard it in other religious organizations, as I think it should be. He also wrote "From every stain made clean." "Lord through the blood of the Lamb that was slain" and "Savior hear me while before Thy feet," and "Let me hear Thy voice now speaking."

---

*I think very highly of the world-wide usefulness of the Salvation Army. I first came in contact with it in South Africa and sometimes used to assist in their meetings. I remember particularly one rainy evening in Pieter Maritzburg when I stood with the plucky young officer at a street corner waiting for the audience that did not turn up to the appointed open-air meeting. The young man, undaunted, said to me, "We are looked down on here, but I believe as God sees us we are the biggest thing in this town." I believe he was right, as no other church so ministered to the poor.

Sir John Bowring

1792-1872

"In the cross of Christ I glory"

This triumphant hymn was written by a distinguished man of letters, no less a man of affairs, having been twice a member of Parliament and British Governor of Hong Kong,* as well as filling other government offices. His literary work was of a very high character both in prose and poetry and was done evidently by snatches† in his astonishingly busy life. He was associated with Jeremy Bentham, travelled in many countries including Siam, where he was sent on diplomatic business, and afterward wrote a book on Siam. He wrote many hymns, two more of which are of priceless value to the church. One of these begins, "Watchman, tell us of the night," and the other, "God is love, his mercy brightens." How hard it would be to spare any of his three best hymns! Nothing else written fully takes their place! Bowring had a son‡ who (as well as the father) was a translator of hymns of other languages. Bowring was knighted in 1854 and in 1859 received a government pension and retired from political life. He lived thirteen years more and died at the age of eighty, much honored. Julian attributes to Bowring the hymn "I cannot always trace the way."

---

* While Governor of Hong Kong Bowring ordered an attack on Chinese forts without previously consulting his home government. This was resented in England and led to a change of ministry. In general Bowring was a liberal-minded man. He was a descendant of the old Puritans and spoke for the dissenters. He also advocated free trade.

† The world would have lost much if Bowring and others like him had not snatched time from their ostensible business to follow the instincts of their hearts in literary and artistic lines. Life must have its "bread and roses" both, and when there are lofty desires that come surging up in us that will not down, they should be given scope.

‡ Edgar Alfred Bowring, a younger son of Sir John, was born in 1826 and like his father was a member of Parliament and was a favorite with the Prince Consort. He translated various poems of Schiller, Heine, and Goethe into English.

Matthew Bridges

1800-1893

"Crown Him with many crowns,
The Lamb upon the throne."

The writer of this beautiful hymn which was first printed in his collection "Hymns of the Heart" was born in Essex, England, and was reared in the Established Church, but in early life joined the Romish Communion. He wrote other excellent hymns. Bridges toward the close of his life went to Canada and died there. His hymns were introduced to American collections by Henry Ward Beecher.

Stopford Augustus Brooke

1832-

"When the Lord of Love was here"

This is the finest hymn of an Irish curate born at Donegal and educated at Trinity College, Dublin. He occupied important clerical positions, was chaplain to the British embassy at Berlin, and was Chaplain in Ordinary to the Queen in 1872. He seceded from the Church of England in 1881 and published a hymn book for his congregation. Julian lists 13 of his hymns and says that they are marked by great freshness of thought and tenderness of expression.

Autumn's pale leaves, withered and dying,
Faded their beauty, they last but a day.
Mists of the morning, on the breeze flying,
All things are telling, we're passing away.
Beautiful earth, dearly we love it,—
Though in its bosom we shortly must lie
Teeming with forms, angels might covet
Though in the using they perish and die.
Heaven's our home! Heaven's our home!
Grasping at phantoms not long shall we roam,
Soon we'll be going to heaven our home.
—*Credit lost*

HUGH BOURNE

1772-1852

"Hark, the gospel news is sounding"

This hymn which is much used by the Salvation Army was written by the founder of the Primitive Methodist Society and editor of their first hymn books. Hugh Bourne was born at Stoke on Trent of humble parentage. His father was a member of the Church of England and his mother was a Wesleyan. Hugh was of a strongly devotional turn of mind, and, after obtaining a fairly good education in view of his circumstances, he carried on prayer meetings and a great camp meeting. The Wesleyan Conference did not approve of his methods and excommunicated him, the break occurring in 1810. This led him to organize the Primitive Methodist Society and to compile a hymn book for its use. Julian lists 25 of his hymns. One of his hymns which became familiar to me in South Africa begins, "My soul is now united to Christ, the Living Vine." Julian says the simplicity of Bourne's hymns is their redeeming feature. Wm. Saunders was his partner in the compilation of their joint hymn book.

JAMES DRUMMOND BURNS

1832-1864

"Hushed was the evening hymn"

This is the opening line of a hymn by a Free Church minister of Scotland who was obliged to take a charge at Funchal, Madeira, as ill health prevented him from living in England. He died at the age of thirty-two. He wrote a number of beautiful and pathetic hymns. Two of these are "Still with Thee, O my God," and "As helpless as a child who clings." Julian's Dictionary ranks these hymns very high in literary merit, as having "vivid coloring, delicacy of execution, pensive sweetness, and tenderness."

Frederick Burrington

fl. 19th century

"Dare to be swift, we can but bid
The passing moment ours".

These arresting lines are in one of the two hymns by the
above named obscure author which are included in Fox's
"Hymns and Anthems." I have no data about the author
who was evidently a man of deep, sincere spirit.

Henry Burton

1846-

"Have you had a kindness shown? Pass it on."

This hymn is based on an incident in the life of a famous
London preacher named Mark Guy Pearse who was a
brother-in-law of the writer of the hymn. Pearse when a
boy was shown great kindness by the steward of a ship
because of a former kindness shown to the steward's mother
by the boy's father. The above lines were adopted as a motto
by the International Sunshine Society of New York. The
parents of Henry Burton emigrated from England to
America and Henry was educated at Beloit College. He
became a Wesleyan minister in West Kirby, England, and
wrote a number of hymns which are listed by Julian. One
of these begins, "Come, for the feast is spread." This is
in Sankey's "Songs and Solos." His hymn beginning "O
King of Kings and Lord of Hosts" was written as an ode
for the Jubilee of Queen Victoria and sung at the festival
in Royal Albert Hall in London in 1887.

John Burton

1773-1822

"Holy Bible, book divine"

This old hymn was written by an earnest Baptist Sunday School teacher born in Nottingham, England who was one of the compilers of the Nottingham hymn book which reached its twentieth edition in 1861. There were in this book 43 hymns bearing Burton's signature. I have not been able to discover whether the hymn beginning "Time is winging us away" is by him or by John Burton Jr. Both were hymn writers. He died in Leicester at the age of forty-nine.

John Burton, Jr.

1803-1877

"O Thou that hearest prayer, attend our humble cry."

This well-known hymn was written by a tradesman (cooper) of Stratford, England. He was a deacon in the Congregational Church and wrote for religious periodicals for a long period of years under the nom de plume of "Essex." He wrote many hymns particularly for children, beginning to write hymns at the age of nineteen.

George Gordon, Lord Byron

1788-1824

"The Assyrians came down like a wolf on the fold"

This is the opening line of one of Byron's Hebrew melodies used as a hymn in a few hymnals. Byron of course is not much connected with hymnody. He was born in London in an environment of domestic storm. His father, a captain of the guard, squandered his wife's fortune in debauch and the gambling table and she, taking her dearly beloved little son with her, went to Aberdeen where the two lived on an income of 130 pounds a year till the boy at ten years of age succeeded his grand uncle in a baronetcy. His mother then took him to the ancient family seat at Nottingham (the vicinity where Robin Hood once flourished.) Byron had a series of early love affairs, the first with Mary Duff in Scotland when he was seven, then with his cousin Margaret who died early, then at fourteen with Mary Chaworth whose father had been killed by the grand uncle of Byron whom he had succeeded. These children might have married and so ended the family feud, but they drifted apart. Byron was educated at Harrow and Cambridge. He began to publish poetry which took England by storm, but was meanwhile indulging in revelries from which he tried to escape by marrying Miss Milbanke, the daughter of a baronet. It was an ill assorted marriage and after the birth of her daughter Ada, Lady Byron went to her father and refused to return to her husband. Byron's popular promise turned to fierce criticism and he left England and traveled in Venice, Italy, and finally Greece, to help her in the struggle for independence. From there he published poems of great power, but his health failed and, after an exposure from a storm followed by illness, he died, murmuring of his wife, his sister, and his child. His body, taken to England, was refused burial in Westminster Abbey. He was handsome,— light eyes with sparkles of fire in them, dark eye brows, and a very fascinating manner.

Robert Campbell

1814-1868

"At the Lamb's high feast we sing
Praise to our victorious King."

This translation of a Latin hymn supposed to date from the 6th century is by a Scotch advocate who went from the

Episcopal to the Romish Church at the age of twenty-eight. He found relaxation from his professional duties by writing translations of Latin hymns which he published in a volume called "St. Andrew's Hymns." He died in Edinburgh at the age of fifty-four. He devoted much time to the young and the poor. His hymn translations are "smooth, lyrical, and well-sustained."

Thomas Carlyle

1795-1881

"Lo, here has been dawning another blue day;
Think, wilt thou let it slip useless away?"

This familiar little poem I call a hymn, but Julian says Carlyle is known to hymnology only by his translation of "Ein feste Burg." He was born in Dumfrieshire, Scotland, entered Edinburgh University in his fifteenth year, expecting to become a clergyman, but instead embraced literature as a profession and married Miss Welsh, an accomplished and brilliant scholar, a descendant of John Knox. The pair resided on the wife's property, "the loveliest nook in Britain", near the Irish Sea, among granite hills and black morasses. Here Carlyle elucidated the great questions of philosophy, sociology, and politics, to which he devoted his life, with also his writing on the portraiture of German and other writers. His fondness for the society of Harriet, Lady Ashburton, for a while caused the estrangement of Carlyle and his wife who died suddenly in 1866. This event filled him not only with grief but remorse, as he discovered from her papers that his own selfishness and ill temper had saddened her life. He was offered burial for himself in Westminster Abbey, but preferred to lie with his Scotch ancestors and his wife, and was buried with her. In spite of defects Carlyle was not only a great writer but a man of noble aims. Genius in the end must be forgiven its accompanying short comings.

EDWARD CASWALL

1814-1878

"When morning gilds the skies"

This beautiful translation from a German hymn by an unknown author was written by a clergyman of the Church of England. Caswall was born in Hampshire and educated at Oxford. His wife died in 1849 and the year after he became a Romanist and joined Newman. His life was marked by his loving interest in the sick, the poor, and in little children. He is chiefly known as an able translator of hymns—many of them from the Latin. He wrote a few original hymns* in English which have come into somewhat general use.

REV. JOHN CAWOOD, M. A.

1775-1852

"Hark, what mean those heavenly voices,"

This Christmas hymn found in old hymnals was written in 1819 by an English curate who also wrote 17 hymns which were never published by himself. He was born at Mattock, Derbyshire, of parents in humble circumstances and received in childhood but limited education. At the age of eighteen

---

    * One of these hymns written for a watch night service, is to me surpassingly solemn and beautiful. I became very fond of it during my South African life. I give here two stanzas and the refrain from memory. I have never heard it sung in America and do not think it is generally known, as it deserves to be. The exquisite music to it was composed by Dr. J. B. Dykes.

"Days and moments quickly flying
Blend the living with the dead!
Soon shall you and I be lying
Each within our narrow bed.
  Refrain:
Life passeth soon; death draweth near!
Keep us, dear Lord, till Thou appear;
In Thee to live, in Thee to die,
With Thee to reign in eternity!

Soon our souls to God who gave them
Will have sped their rapid flight—
Able now by grace to save them,
Oh that while we can, we might!

Jesus, infinite Redeemer,
Maker of this mortal frame
Teach, O teach us to remember
Who we are, and whence we came."

he entered the service of a minister and after three years
of study under careful direction he was enabled to enter
Oxford and took his degree in 1801 after which he became
successful in various parts of England.

VERNON J. CHARLESWORTH

1839-

"A shelter in the time of storm"
This is the refrain of a hymn written by the co-pastor of
Newman Hall in London and later the head master of
Spurgeon's Orphanage. Charlesworth was born in Essex
and wrote the "Life of Rowland Hill", also a considerable
number of spiritual hymns 16 of which are listed by Julian.

GILBERT KEITH CHESTERTON

b. London 1874

"The Christchild stood on Mary's knee,
His hair was like a crown,
And all the flowers looked up at him
And all the stars looked down."

These concluding lines of an exquisite Christmas carol
were written by the distinguished writer above named who
has a genius for paradoxes and "swashbuckling."* Chesterton
was born of a family of estate-agents, left St. Paul's School
at the age of seventeen with the view of studying art, but
instead devoted himself to literature. At the age of twenty-
six he published a volume of clever verse called "The Wild
Knight." During the South African War he became widely
known as the writer in the public press of brilliant anti-
imperialist articles and also for his illuminating sketches on
Browning and Dickens. His writings are today a great
power in the world, impetuous, pungent, humorous, never
conventional, and often dogmatic. Chesterton's philosophy
which underlies his writing is violently opposed to that of
the modern age; more power to him! I am very glad indeed to include him among my dear hymnists.

---

* This epithet gleaned from a review, is doubtless inept.

HENRY FOTHERGILL CHORLEY

1808-1872

"God, the all terrible King, who ordainest"

This hymn was written in 1842 for a Russian air by an English author who was born in Lancashire and was subsequently for thirty-five years on the staff of the London Athenaeum. Chorley published novels and songs. The above hymn was imitated in 1870 by J. Ellerton and the two hymns have been intermixed in the use of them. One version of this hymn begins as follows:

"God the all-merciful, earth hath forsaken
Thy ways of blessedness, slighted Thy word."

This version, (possibly partly anonymous) was printed in 1917 by the Pilgrim Press of Boston in a pamphlet called "Selected Hymns of Patriotism."

ARTHUR HUGH CLOUGH

1819-1861

"What is it came ye here to note?
A young man preaching in a boat?"

The poem from which these lines were taken was written by an English poet of whom Emerson said he would "make Tennyson look to his laurels." Clough's father was a Liverpool cotton trader who emigrated to Charleston, S. C., when Arthur was six years old. The boy went back to England, however, for his education at Rugby under Dr. Arnold and later became a tutor at Oxford. At the age of thirty-three he visited America and made the acquaintance of Emerson and Longfellow. Later he took a government position in England, but his health failed in his efforts to assist Florence Nightingale, who was his wife's cousin. He died suddenly at the age of forty-two of a fever in Italy where he had gone with Mr. and Mrs. Tennyson. He wrote both prose and verse, but his poems* are his principal legacy to the world.

ROBERT COLLYER

1823-

"With thankful hearts, O God, we come"

This hymn was written by the pastor for the dedication of Unity Church, Chicago, which was burnt in the great fire of 1870. Robert Collyer was born at Keightley, England, and in early life was a blacksmith. He emigrated to America at the age of twenty-seven. At that time he was a Methodist local preacher but in 1859 he joined the Unitarians and in 1879 became the pastor of "The Church of the Messiah" in New York City. He was a celebrated preacher and widely known as a lecturer.

WILLIAM BENGO COLLYER

1782-1854

"Cease, ye mourners, cease to languish"

This hymn, found in many old hymnals, was written by an eminent evangelical preacher born at Blackheath, England, who began his ministry at the age of twenty with a church of ten members. He was an eloquent preacher who labored with great success and honor—preaching his last sermon about three weeks before he died at the age of seventy-two. He was an amiable man with polished manners, popular alike with rich and poor. A hymn book designed for his own congregation was compiled by him. This contained many of his own hymns.

---

* His poem entitled "As ships becalmed" contains a great truth about the involuntary estrangement which grows up between dear friends at times. I was so taken with it a few years ago that I made a melody for it. This line I especially like, "O neither blame for neither willed." This must be the verdict on most estrangements.

Josiah Conder

1789-1856

"How shall I follow Him I serve!"*

This popular hymn was written by a London author and editor of the Eclectic Review, also a lay preacher and promoter of benevolent enterprises. It is said by Julian that more of Conder's hymns are now in use than of any other Congregational hymn writer except Watts and Doddridge. Julian gives a list of the first lines of 48 of Conder's hymns.† These are among the best known:

"Day by day the manna fell,"
"O shew me not my Savior dying"
"Bread of heaven, on Thee I feed."

This last is extensively used in England as a communion hymn. Conder's wife, Joan Elizabeth Conder, née Thomas, also wrote hymns. Conder wrote much also in prose. He published 30 volumes descriptive of the various countries of the globe. Julian ascribes "The Lord, my Shepherd is" to Conder, but American hymnals ascribe it to Watts.

Barry Cornwall

1798-1874

"Send down Thy sweet-souled angel, God,
    Amid the darkness wild."

These lines from a prayer for a sick child were written by Byran Waller Procter, whose pen name (under which I list him here) was Barry Cornwall. He is considered one of the best of modern English song writers of the school of Keats and Hunt. Bryant's "Library of Poetry and Song" gives 15 of his lovely lyrics,—tender, dainty, musical. He

---

* This hymn is set to a surpassingly beautiful tune by Beethoven called Germany. A dear friend of mine recently deceased, was especially fond of this rich music so that it has a sacred memory for me.

† One of Conder's hymns entitled "The Lord is King" has in it this memorable stanza:
"Alike pervaded by His eye
All parts of His dominion lie,
This world of ours, the world unseen,
And thin the boundary between."
(Yes, thinner than we know.)

was educated at Harrow and later studied law, was for
many years a commissioner of lunacy, but his great work
for the world was song writing. He is not listed by Dr.
Julian as a hymn writer;—that honor, however, is given to
his talented daughter, Adelaide Anne Procter, who will be
noted in the following chapter.

Thomas Cotterill

1779-1823

This hymnist whose name is found in many of the older
hymn collections, was a Church of England clergyman who
was the son of a Staffordshire wood-stapler. He attended a
local boarding school in his boyhood and finally went to Cambridge. He wrote many hymns but few of them became
commonly used. His greatest work was compiling a hymn
book in which some of the great hymns of the church first
appeared,—among these were "Rock of Ages", and "Lo, He
comes with clouds descending". The hymns, however, in
this collection did not bear the names of the authors. This
omission has caused confusion as to the real authorship of
some of them. Cotterill also wrote a book of family prayers
which attained to six editions. He died at Sheffield.

Bishop George Edward Lynch Cotton

1813-1866

"We thank Thee, Lord, for this fair earth"
This hymn, popular in England, was written by a Bishop
of Calcutta who was born in Chester, England. His father,
Capt. Thomas Cotton, was killed in action about a fortnight
after his son's birth. George was educated at Cambridge and
his first appointment was as an assistant master at Rugby.
At the age of forty-five he was consecrated as the Bishop
of Calcutta, the successor to Dr. Daniel Wilson. He was
drowned eight years later while disembarking from a steamer
at Koshtea.

ALLAN CUNNINGHAM

1785-1842

"Come here and kneel wi'me!
The morn is fu'o'the presence o'God,
And I canna pray without thee."

These lines are from a beautiful Scotch poem written by
the son of a stone mason of Dumfriesshire, Scotland. At
the age of eleven Allan was taken from school to learn the
trade of stone masonry. As an apprentice he worked faith-
fully but gave his evenings to writing songs and collecting
traditions. He published some of these which gained him
the acquaintance of Hogg and Sir Walter Scott. Eventually
he went to London and secured a position as foreman in the
studio of the sculptor Chantry, which he held till his death,
but during his career he wielded an indefatigable pen, writing
both prose and poetry, contributing to London papers, and
immortalizing himself by the biography of Lord Burleigh,
the Secretary of State of Queen Elizabeth. He was a
prodigious favorite with Sir Walter Scott, who calls him
"Honest Allan." He was a diligent, earnest man who wrote
the old Covenanters' love songs and a pretty hymn on the
Sabbath.

JOHN NELSON DARBY, M. A.

1800-1882

"O eyes that are weary"

This hymn which is marked usually as anonymous has been
sometimes attributed to the above named Irish hymnist who
was born at Westminster, graduated at Trinity College,
Dublin, in 1819, was called to the bar there but later took
Holy Orders and shortly after allied himself to the Plymouth
Brethren, visiting many parts of the world in that ministry.
He wrote many books on the Bible. The above hymn is used
extensively in America but Julian speaks doubtfully as to
Darby's authorship of it.

Thomas Davis

1804-1845

"Seek them, Christian, night and morn,
Seek them noon and even,
Seek them till thy soul be born
Without stain in heaven."

These lines from a poem on "Holy Habits" were written by a Rector of Worcester, England. He was educated at Oxford for the law, which he gave up after practising for two years. Julian gives the first lines of 28 of his hymns and says they are of considerable merit. He wrote a beautiful poem on "God is Love" and I suppose he is the same Thomas Davis who wrote the delicious love song about "Love in a cottage for Mary and me." The title of this last is "The Banks of the Lee." Davis died at the age of forty-one.

James George Deck

b. Eng. 1802

"Jesus, Thy name I love, all other names above"

This useful hymn was written in New Zealand where the above named author went in 1852 as a minister of the Plymouth Brethren. Deck was educated for the British army and became an officer in the Indian service, but left the cruel business of war for the service of the Prince of Peace. He first took charge of a Somerset congregation at the age of forty-one. Julian gives a list of the first lines of 32 of his hymns and says they are characterized by simplicity and great earnestness. Most of them are unfamiliar to me, but the one quoted above is well known in American collections and also that which begins "O Lamb of God, still keep me near to Thy wounded side." Deck published a collection called "Hymns for the Poor of the Flock." In this is a hymn on the Second advent best known in its rewritten form "Savior hasten Thine appearing."

DAVID DENHAM

1791-1848

"Mid scenes of confusion and creature complaints"

This hymn was written by an English Baptist minister, son of a Baptist minister in the east of London. David began to preach in London at the age of nineteen. At the age of twenty-five he took a charge in Plymouth and other places. Ill health compelled him at last to give up preaching and he sojourned at Cheltenham and Oxford. He died at the age of fifty-seven and was buried in the Bunhill Fields burying ground, London. He published a book of hymns when he was forty-six. This contained one hymn written by his wife.

WILLIAM CHATTERTON DIX

1838-1898

"Come unto me, ye weary, and I will give you rest."

This is the beginning of a hymn written by the above-named author when he was so ill he could scarcely put it on paper, his hand trembled so. Afterward he looked upon the writing of that hymn as the turning point in his recovery. He wrote many hymns; Julian gives the first lines of eighteen of them and says they have not received the attention they deserve. Dix was the son of a surgeon of Bristol and bred to mercantile pursuits and seems to have had only a grammar school education. He was later connected with a marine insurance office in Glasgow. He says of his own hymns that the best known of them were written when he was suffering from some bodily ailment. (I wonder if those were the occasions when the exigencies of business permitted him the requisite leisure for writing.) Dix died at the age of sixty. "The Library of Religious Poetry" embraces several fine poems from his pen.

John Drinkwater

fl. 20th century

"Lord, not for light in darkness do we pray
* * * * * * * *
Grant us the will to fashion as we feel;
Grant us the strength to labor as we know."

These lines are from a fine hymn written by a well-known poet of England.

John East

fl. 1838

"There is a fold whence none can stray,
And pastures ever green."

This familiar hymn was written by the curate of St. Michael's church at Bath, England. He collected sacred poetry and wrote devotional meditations. Julian lists four of his hymns. This hymn is found in one of Bradbury's little Sunday School books.

James Edmeston

1791-1867

"Saviour, breathe an evening blessing"

This immortal hymn was written by a London architect and surveyor who is said to have written 2000 hymns but will probably be longest remembered by the hymn above quoted.* He wrote this after reading in Salter's "Travels in Abyssinia" that at evening in that country the primitive Christians had a plaintive evening hymn, "Jesus, forgive us," which stole from camp to camp. Edmeston was reared

---

* To have contributed this one priceless hymn to our language seems to me enough achievement for one mortal.

as an Independent* but joined the Established Church at an early age. His hymns were many of them written for children.† It was his practice to write hymns to be used on Sunday at family devotions in his own home. He published hymns in various volumes and in a magazine.

JOHN ELLERTON

1826-1893

"Saviour, again to Thy dear name we raise"

This most tender hymn so unique in its use at the closing of religious service and inseparable from spiritual blessing to the believer was written by a vicar in the Church of England. Ellerton was born in London and educated at Cambridge. His many hymns (of which Julian lists 25) are characterized by "elegance of diction and terseness of expression." He has "great sympathy with nature in her sadder moods, loves the fading light and peace of eve, and lingers in the shadows." He lifts the ordinary facts of daily life into stateliness and sublimity by placing them in their relation to heavenly and spiritual realities and values. In 1881 he edited a book of notes on hymns. He wrote a fine variation of Chorley's hymn "God the all terrible."

---

* The maternal grandfather of Edmeston was Rev. Samuel Brewer, for fifty years pastor of an Independent Church in Stepney.

† One of his hymns for children was a great favorite with me when a child in a Massachusetts Sunday School. It begins "Little Travellers Zionward." Dr. Julian lists 19 of Edmeston's hymns. He wrote about 2000 in all.

EBENEZER ELLIOTT

1781-1849

"When wilt Thou save the people?"

This "People's Anthem"* was written by an iron manufacturer of Sheffield, born in Yorkshire. His opinions were
formed largely under the influence of his father. He had
great sympathy with the poor, and denounced the social and
political institutions of the country. He was successful in
the iron business and retired at the age of sixty to an estate
in a rural district where he devoted the last eight years of
his life to writing both prose and verse.

---

* I confess to a passionate fellowship with the views of this "Corn-
law rhymer" whom Julian does not omit altogether but turns him off
with a few cold sentences. I append below the full text of the "People's
Anthem", as I am very fond of it. "The Pilgrim Hymnal" includes it,
but I understand omitted it in a later edition—probably feared it
savored of Bolshevism.

> "When wilt Thou save the people,
> O God of mercy, when?
> Not kings and lords, but nations;
> Not thrones and crowns, but men!
> Flowers of Thy heart, O God, are they,
> Let them not pass as weeds away,
> Their heritage a sunless day.
> God save the people!
>
> Shall crime bring crime forever,
> Strength aiding still the strong?
> Is it Thy will, O Father,
> That men shall toil for wrong?
> "No," say Thy mountains, "No" Thy skies,
> Man's clouded sun shall brightly rise
> And songs be heard instead of sighs.
> God save the people!
>
> When wilt Thou save the people?
> O God of mercy, when?
> The people, Lord, the people,
> Not thrones and crowns, but men.
> God save the people! Thine they are;
> Thy children, as Thine angels fair;
> Save them from bondage and despair;
> **God save the people!**"

Alexander John Ellis

1814-

"When evil thoughts have power, and passion rules
  the hour,
We'll turn our hearts to Thee and shake our
  spirits free."

These lines emphasizing the primary importance of the control of the thought-life, were written by the President of the English philosophical Society. Julian does not list him as a hymnist, but Fox's "Hymns and Anthems" include 13 extracts from his poetical writings. These were more didactic than lyrical, but abound in lofty sentiment and clear expression. Here are a few lines from them:

"Hate is your hell, and love your paradise"
"Holding all God's sons as brothers,
  Self alone, as one of others,"
"Falsehood vanishes when faced."

Major G. D. Ewens

fl. 19th century

"If you want pardon; if you want peace,"

This hymn is attributed to the above writer by S. C. Gantlett of the English Salvation Army.

Frederick William Faber

1814-1863

"Hark, hark, my soul! Angelic songs are swelling."

This exquisite hymn was written by the great hymnist above named. Faber was born in Yorkshire, England, educated at Oxford where he was for a time a tutor, then took Holy Orders in the Church of England and at the age of thirty-two became a Roman Catholic. He died at the age of

forty-nine. The year before his death he published a volume
of his hymns, many of them of great beauty. A few of
Faber's hymns áre in common use. Some of them are as
follows:

"Dear Savior, ever at my side."
"O Paradise, O Paradise, who doth not crave for rest?"
"Faith of our Fathers, living still,"
"I worship thee, sweet will of God."*

Faber's hymns are said by Julian to have "an element
of unreality in them which is against their permanent popularity." Faber is also said to have been a man of
great inward spiritual conflicts. In confirmation of this is a
line of his which reads, "The burden of unquiet life lies
heavy on my head." The picture of him given in F. A.
Jones' book on "Famous Hymns" looks anything but "unquiet." The plump face with the trace of a shrewd smile does
not give the impression of a sensitive, ethereal nature
which his hymns convey. He was probably mercurial in
temperament.

CHARLES LAWRENCE FORD

fl. 1865

"God sends us bitter, all our sins
Embittering, yet so kindly sends,
The path that bitterness begins,
In sweetness ends."

These lines were written by the son of an English artist
of Bath. He was educated at the University of London and
was a contributor to the "Lyra Angelicana."

---

* This hymn is on the whole my favorite among Faber's hymns.
I associate it with the solemn fellowship meetings I attended of the
South African General Mission, Johannesburg. I especially like the
stanza:
"Ill that He blesses is our good,
And unblest good is ill;
And all is right that seems most wrong,
If it be His sweet will."
Faber has also a fine hymn called "The Right must win," the
closing stanza of which has these often quoted lines:
"For right is right, since God is God;
And right the day must win;
To doubt would be disloyalty,
To falter would be sin!"

WILLIAM JOHNSON FOX

1786-1864

"Flung to the heedless winds,
Or on the waters cast,
The martyrs' ashes watched,
Shall gathered be at last."

This translation of a German hymn of Luther's is said*
to have been made by the above named celebrated English
writer and statesman, who was also for part of his life a
Unitarian preacher in London and later the leader of rationalism, also member of the House of Commons, also a member of the Anti-Corn-law League, an advocate of free
trade—helped to found the Westminster Review, and is
considered by Guizot the most finished orator of his time.
The effect of his speeches on the great metropolitan audiences
was electric. When he was a minister of the Court Chapel
in London, Sarah Flower Adams, author of "Nearer, my
God to Thee" was a member of his congregation. He edited
a hymn book in 1841 called "Hymns and Anthems" which
included 13 of his own hymns. These are interesting but
not familiar. I have esteemed it a privilege to have this
Fox's hymn book by me while writing this work. Fox
was the son of a small farmer in Suffolk and as a boy worked
as a weaver. He also worked six years in a bank and then
studied for the ministry under Dr. Pye Smith. He developed into a splendid orator with a great heart for humanity.

---

* The Library of Religious Poetry attributes this hymn to Fox
saying that "it has little of Luther in it," but Dr. Julian does not say
anything about Fox in connection with it. He says it first appeared
in Philadelphia in 1843 in a translation of D'Aubigne's History of the
Reformation and is there said to have been translated by John
Alexander Messenger. It is a splendid production, whoever wrote it.
It is only a paraphrase of Luther's hymn, and the writer of the English
should have the credit of it.

C. W. FRY

fl. 19th century

"Come, Thou burning Spirit, come"

This fervent hymn is claimed by the Salvation Army to be the production of the one of their London workers named above. The hymn is No. 483 in the hymn book compiled by William Booth. However, it appears in "Hymns of the Gospel New and Old" with the initials A. E. S. attached to it. I am not able to unravel the discrepancy. "I have found a friend in Jesus" is sometimes attributed to Fry.

WILLIAM GASKELL

1805-1884

"Press on, press on, ye sons of light,"

This is the opening line of a hymn by the Unitarian minister of Manchester above given. He was a man of cultured mind and literary ability. Julian lists 29 of Gaskell's hymns.* He had a wife perhaps more celebrated than himself. Her maiden name was Elizabeth Cleghorn Stevenson. She was the author of "Mary Barton" and other popular tales and also wrote a biography of Charlotte Brontë.

GEORGE GILL

1820-1880

"Beautiful Zion, built above"

This familiar hymn of childhood's days was written by an Englishman who was born in Devonshire and for some time was missionary in the South Sea Islands where the hymn was written on the island of Mangaia. He later took up pastoral work in England.

---

* Fox's hymn book includes some of Gaskell's hymns. One of these closes with this striking stanza.

"Like them all danger let us brave;
What we deem right pursue;
And e'en the gentle chains of love
Shake off to seek the True."

THOMAS HORNBLOWER GILL

1819-

"Ye people of the Lord, draw near,"

This is one of many hymns by the above-named writer which are listed by Julian, who thinks very highly of them and says they have not received the attention they deserve. The author was a London layman who wrote out of his own personal experience, with quaintness of expression and sweetness of melody. J. Freeman Clarke calls him "a more intellectual Charles Wesley." His life was "singularly devoid of outward incident" but his inward experiences were remarkable.

SIR ROBERT GRANT

1785-1878

"O worship the King all glorious above,"

This stately and well-known hymn was written by a Scotch hymnist, son of a Member of Parliament and director of the East India Company. He was educated at Cambridge, became himself a Member of Parliament, and later the Governor of Bombay where he died after four years in India. His hymns are of great merit, marked by graceful versification and deep feeling. A few of them have come into common use, notably the one beginning, "Saviour, when in dust to Thee." Another not so common but so comforting that we all need it, begins "When gathering clouds around I view." Another still of great worth begins, "O Saviour! whose mercy severe in its kindness."

David Gray

1838-1861

"O Thou of purer eyes than to behold uncleanness,
Sift my soul!"
These lines were written by an untaught Scottish peasant
who died at the age of twenty-three. There is infinite pathos
in the early death of one whose poems evinced such talent.
What might he have given the world had he lived long years?
His poems were published with an introduction by Lord
Houghton.

Christopher Newman Hall

1816-

"I know who makes the daisies."
This is the first line of a hymn written by a prominent
English preacher of great power. He was chairman of
the Congregational Union and when in college at Oberlin
I heard him preach. I shall never forget his graphic description of Christ's healing of the leper—even touching that
loathsome flesh with his tender hand. Hall wrote a tract on
"Come to Jesus" which was translated into 30 languages and
reached a circulation of two millions.

Arthur H. Hallam

1811-1833

"That master light, the secret truth of things,
Which is the body of the infinite God."
These lines were written by the young friend of Tennyson
who will be remembered principally as the one whose early
death at the age of twenty-two inspired Tennyson to write
his immortal poem "In Memoriam." Tennyson and Hallam
were schoolmates and Hallam was engaged to Tennyson's
sister. He went abroad with his father, and in a few weeks
died in Vienna.

George Washington Hangford

fl. 1847

"Speak gently, it is better far
To rule by love than fear.
Speak gently, let no harsh word mar
The good we may do here.'

This hymn was published in Sharpe's London Magazine
in 1848. I have no data about the author. It should be
mentioned that "Heart Throbs No. 1" gives this hymn but
attributes the authorship to David Bates. Julian in his appendix p. 1590 says that this hymn is usually attributed to
Hangford. There seems to be a little uncertainty about the
authorship.

Reginald Heber

1783-1826

"By cool Siloam's shady rill"

This exquisite hymn was written during the college days
at Oxford* by the beloved hymnist who became the noble
Bishop of Calcutta† where he died at the early age of forty-

---

* This hymn was called "Palestine" and was read as a prize poem
at a college commencement at which his aged parents were present.
It was received with such an outburst of applause as is seldom given
to a student. After the exercises were over, young Heber was missing
for a long time. His mother, seeking him, softly opened the door of
his room and found him on his knees breathing his soul out to God
in prayer and gratitude. He was a shrinking, retiring youth, but much
beloved by his mates.

† Heber sailed for India in a troop ship and there are tales of his
kindness to his humble fellow-travellers. He conducted the burial
service of a baby at sea and later went to her cabin to pray and weep
in sympathy for the bereaved mother. Some one asked him if his
first work in the morning was to pray. He replied, "No, to praise.
When the day begins with praise all good things follow." It seems
that Heber went to India alone without his family. There is an echo
of his loneliness in a sweet poem he wrote evidently on the way, which
begins with these words,

"If thou wert by my side, my love
How fast would evening fail,
* * * * * * * * *
If thou, my love, wert by my side,
My babies at my knee—"
This poem gives us a look into the human heart of the man who
gave up so much "to men benighted."

three, being found dead one Sunday night in his cold bath after having that day confirmed 42 persons. This followed a recent attack of fever. "No memory of Indian annals is holier than that of the three years of ceaseless travel, splendid administration, and saintly enthusiasm" of this beloved man who endeared himself to so many eminent friends by "his candor, gentleness, and salient playfulness." He left a precious legacy to the world in the following well-known hymns:

"Bread of the world, in mercy broken"
"Holy, holy, holy, Lord God Almighty"
"The son of God goes forth to war"
"Brightest and best of the sons of the morning"
"Thou art gone to the grave"*
"From Greenland's icy mountains"†
"When through the torn sail the wild tempest is streaming"
"God that madest earth and heaven"

Julian considers the hymn "Holy, holy, holy" as Heber's best, and calls it "a majestic anthem." It seems to me that Greenland's icy mountains which was written in the study and by the request of his father-in-law, Dr. Shipley, has filled as large a place of usefulness as any of his hymns.

Edwin Paxton Hood

1820-1885

"I hear a sweet voice ringing clear
All is well!"

This hymn which became very dear to me a few years ago was written by a self-educated Independent minister of London, a voluminous writer, especially of simple and fresh hymns for children in Sunday Schools. He died in Paris.

---

* This hymn was written on the occasion of the death of his first babe—which was a great grief to him.

† Dr. Shipley one Saturday said to his son-in-law that he was to have a missionary service the following day and desired an appropriate hymn for the occasion. Heber withdrew for about half an hour and came back with the glowing hymn used with such effect ever since in many lands.

Thomas Hood

1798-1845

"O God, that bread should be so dear,
  And flesh and blood so cheap!"

These lines are taken from that immortal poem "The
Song of the Shirt"* written by the poet of laughter and
tears, who is not classed as a hymnist by Julian, but as the
poet of the poor, dear to the heart of God, I cannot omit him.
Hood was born in London and after leaving school was
placed in a counting house. Later he became the sub-editor
of a magazine, and eventually started a magazine of his own,
but he was hampered both by ill health and by pecuniary
difficulties. During his last illness Sir Robert Peel gave him
a pension of 100 pounds a year which after his death was
transferred to his wife. If this pension had come earlier
Hood might not have died at the age of forty-seven, as he
did.

Henry Joy McCracken Hope

1809-1872

"Now I have found a friend"

This hymn was written by an Irish book binder from near
Belfast for many years employed in Dublin, who died
in Dunadry, Ireland. The hymn was privately printed and
seems to have been suggested by one of Mrs. Bonar's.

---

* The pathos of this hymn led me to set it to music some years ago.
His "Bridge of Sighs" is equally pathetic. It was in my school reader
when I was a child, and these lines engraved themselves ineffaceably
on my mind:
  "Owning her weakness, her evil behavior,
    And leaving in meekness her sins to her Saviour."

Bishop William Walsham How

1823-1897

"For all the saints who from their labors rest"

This fine hymn was written by the Bishop of Wakefield, England. He was born at Shrewsbury, the son of a solicitor, and educated at Oxford. He wrote much both in prose and verse, and Julian lists 32 of his hymns. One of these begins: "Summer suns are glowing". Another begins "On wings of living light" and another is:

"O Jesus, Thou art standing
Outside the fast-closed door."

This well-known hymn is associated with Holman Hunt's picture of "Christ at the Door". Bishop How wrote the special hymn for Queen Victoria's diamond jubilee. He has written simple, unadorned and poetical hymns, which have laid firm hold of the church.

Leigh Hunt

1784-1859

"Write me as one that loves his fellow men."

The writer of this line from the classic little poem "Abou Ben Adhem" is not classed as a hymnist, but is listed as a sacred poet,—so I venture to include him here. Hunt was born in London and became, early in life, a literary critic. He was a liberal in politics and had the temerity to write an article reflecting on the obesity of the Prince Regent, for which he had to pay a 500 pound fine and undergo two years' imprisonment.*

* During this confinement he used to hide his prison bars with flowers and had visits from distinguished friends, Byron, Shelley, and Keats. Hunt also wrote poetry in prison. He was a writer of good spirits and cheer. His philosophy is expressed in the sentence, "The sky may be gloomy but there is a bit of blue in it." On the day he was released from prison Keats wrote:
"Kind heart was shut in prison, yet has he
In his immortal spirit been as free
As the sky-searching lark, and as elate."

WILLIAM MELLEN HUTCHINGS

1827-1876

"When mothers of Salem their children brought to
Jesus"
This hymn which is much sung in England was written
for an anniversary of St. Paul's Sunday School by a London
printer and published. He also wrote a hymn beginning,
"We have heard a wondrous story."

REV. JOHN JOHNS

1801-1847

"Hark the loud cannon's roar,
The frantic warriors' call!
Why should the earth be drenched with gore
Are we not brothers all?"

This strong hymn against the iniquity of war* was written
by a Presbyterian minister who labored among the poor of
Liverpool and lost his life at the age of forty-six through an
epidemic of fever, a sacrifice to these self-denying labors.†

---

* Because this hymn is so timely at the present crisis of the world,
and because it seems to be so little known, I give here the remaining
three stanzas of it:
"Want, from the wretch depart,
Chains, from the captive fall!
Sweet mercy, melt the oppressor's heart—
Sufferers are brothers all.

Churches and sects, strike down
Each mean partition wall.
Let Love each harsher feeling drown;
For men are brothers all.

Let Love and Truth alone
Hold human hearts in thrall,
That Heaven its work at length may own
And men be brothers all."
The intrinsic merit of the foregoing hymn bears out the comment
of Julian on this hymn, that Johns was "a man of fine poetic temper-
ament and retiring disposition, but his work among the people called
out his great practical and organizing ability."

† This hymnist has a special interest for me from the way he died,
a sacrifice to his labors for the poor, since I had a son who died similarly in South Africa during the world-wide epidemic of influenza in
1918. Dr. Charles Douglas Goodenough was district surgeon of a large
area in Natal where primitve peoples, natives and coolies, were dying
by the hundreds. Short handed for help, my son struggled with an
overwhelming disaster, and with only about three hours of sleep nightly.
He was so exhausted that when the disease attacked him, he had no re-
sistance left.. When the joyful armistice bells were ringing Nov. 11,
1918, his young soul passed into eternity.

He published three volumes of poems and a few of his hymns
came into common use. Seven of them are listed by Julian.
One of these begins:

"Come, Kingdom of our God."

CAPTAIN JOHNSON

fl. 19th century

"Marching on in the light of God
* * * * * * * * *
A robe of white, a crown of gold."

This hymn, much used by the Salvation army in their
street marches is by one of their captains of whom I have
no data. I take it that he is English. The hymn is catchy
and very familiar. It is included in Thoro Harris's Hymns
of Hope."

JOHN KEBLE

1792-1866

"Sun of my soul, Thou Savior dear,"

This beautiful evening hymn was written by an English
curate, best known as the author of "The Christian Year",
which went through 43 editions* in a little over a quarter of
a century, during which time 108,000 copies had been sold.
He prepared this book when in charge of three little curacies
which altogether did not bring in much more than 100 pounds
a year. He was the son of a Vicar who lived in his own
house in Fairford and educated his two sons entirely until
they entered Oxford where John was elected a "Fellow of
Oriel", a great honor for a boy of nineteen. Later John
was a tutor and examiner at Oxford and resigned this

---

* I have read that before Keble's death there had been 93 editions
of "The Christian Year" published. One writer has prophesied that
this book will live as long as "The Book of Common Prayer" with
which it is thoroughly in accord.

lucrative position on the death of his mother to reside with his father and two sisters* at Fairford. He might have gone with Bishop Coleridge as Archdeacon to the Barbadoes and received 4000 pounds a year, but declined since his father was old and feeble and needed him. Keble was happy on his tiny salary, living in a serene spiritual world of his own as he composed his beautiful hymns. Keble gave the first start to what was called "The Tractarian Movement", noted for the ascetic saintliness of its promoters. It leaned toward the tenets of Romanism, but Keble never joined the Church of Rome.† He married at the age of forty-two‡ and died at seventy-four. Julian ranks his hymns very high and lists 56 of them.§ Keble was in contact with the "Lake Poets."

CHARLES KINGSLEY

1819-1875

"My fairest child, I have no song to give you,
* * * * * * * *
Be good, sweet maid, and let who will be clever."

This pretty poem, often included in hymnals for girls' high schools, was written by the distinguished Canon of Westminster, best known as a novelist, philanthropist and establisher of cooperative associations for working people. He was born in the New Forest at Holm Vicarage, and graduated with honor at Cambridge. Poetry was only a side line with him, but he was a true poet nevertheless. Most of his

---

* Keble had an amusing way of speaking of his beloved sisters. He called Margaret his "wife" and Mary his "sweetheart."

† It was a great grief to him when J. H. Newman seceded to the Church of Rome. He seems to have regarded this as the greatest sorrow of his life, although the deaths of his nearest relations were severe blows. There was a fierce controversy connected with the Tractarian Movement which troubled and unsettled Keble.

‡ His marriage was a happy one and his dearly loved wife survived him only six weeks.

§ One of Keble's beautiful hymns begins thus:
"If cn our daily course our mind
Be set to hallow all we find,
New treasures still of countless price
God will provide for sacrifice."
This hymn is part of one which begins "New every morning is the love."

poetry has little to do with hymnology.* He held strong
opinions on the social anarchy of modern times and this is
reflected in his novels of which "Westward Ho" is considered
the best. Kingsley was chaplain to Queen Victoria.

RUDYARD KIPLING

1865-

"God of our fathers known of old
* * * * * * * * *
Lord God of Hosts, be with us yet,
Lest we forget, lest we forget."

The immortal Recessional was written by the son of an
English gentleman who had a school of art at Lahore, India.
Rudyard was brought to England for his education and
trained at the United Service College at Westward Ho,
Devonshire. At the age of sixteen he returned to India and
was sub-editor of a Gazette. He is the author of many
short and brilliant stories showing a remarkable knowledge
of East Indian life and customs. He also has written many
poems. For years he has resided in London.

---

* "Three fishers went sailing out into the West" is my own favorite
among his entire writings. Who is not familiar with its plaintive refrain:
"For men must work and women must weep,
And there's little to earn and many to keep,
Though the harbor bar be moaning."
This song appeals to me as an immortal production. He wrote it after
a weary day in later life, remembering little religious meetings he had
witnessed in boyhood held on the wharf as the herring fishers were
about to put to sea—their wives, children and sweethearts were there.

Live for something, be not idle,
Look around thee for employ.
                                            —*Credit lost*

KRISHNU PAL

1764-1822

"O thou my soul forget no more
The friend who all thy sorrow bore.
Let every idol be forgot;
But O my soul, forget Him not."

The above lines are a translation of a hymn† written by the first Hindu convert to Christianity. He was a carpenter who fell and broke his arm which was set by one of the missionaries who had toiled in India for six years with no apparent results. This assistance in surgery opened the hearts of this family to receive the gospel message and a wild storm of persecution followed because they had renounced their cast. Krishnu-Pal became a useful and influential Christian and wrote tracts and hymns. His baptism by William Carey was a great event in India. The Governor attended and wept with vast crowds that were present. Krishnu Pal died of cholera at the age of 58.

WILLIAM EDENSOR LITTLEWOOD

1831-1886

"There is no love like the love of Jesus"

This hymn was written by an English vicar who was born in London and graduated at Cambridge in 1854. He published a book called, "A Garland from the Parables" from which the above hymn was taken. His vicarage was at St. James's Bath, England.

---

† Krishnu Pal's hymn was written in the Bengali language and translated into English by Dr. Marshman.

" Into the casket of this day,
Put all things good, and all things gay
That thou canst find along the way."
—*From "Good Stories" for May* 1931

WILLIAM FREEMAN LLOYD

1791-1853

"My times are in Thy hand,
My God, I wish them there."

This familiar hymn was written by one of the secretaries
of the Sunday School Union in England. He was a great
Sunday School teacher and edited a Sunday School magazine. He was born and also died in Gloucestershire.

W. D. LONGSTAFF

fl. 19th century

"Take time to be holy"

This familiar hymn was written by the treasurer of
Bethesda Chapel in Sunderland, England, after a sermon
heard at New Brighton on the text, "Be ye holy for I am
holy." The music to this was written by George Stebbins.

THOMAS TOKE LYNCH

1818-1871

"Gracious Spirit, dwell with me;
I myself would gracious be."

This familiar hymn was written by an Independent
minister of London whose great influence extended far beyond his own congregation. Theological students and
thoughtful people from other churches were attracted by the
freshness and spirituality of his preaching. He wrote many
hymns of which Julian lists 24. They are marked by the
sadness which came from a powerful soul struggling with a
weak and emaciated body. Lynch published a book of hymns
which were attacked by Dr. John Campbell as the "essence
of absurdity". Newman Hall and others defended them
and a bitter hymnological controversy ensued. Time and a

broader criticism have vindicated Lynch's hymns.* Lynch
was the son of an Essex surgeon. Thomas was a delicate
boy, but bright and manly. He wrote poems before he was
thirteen and wished to get them published.† He grew up a
gentle, lovable man, but fearless in controversy with wrong.
He is said to have been of a like spirit with George Mac-
Donald. Before he was old his health gave way and he died
at the age of fifty-three.

HENRY FRANCIS LYTE

1793-1847

"Abide with me, fast falls the eventide,"

This tender hymn was written by the saintly clergyman of
the Church of England above named, on the Sunday evening
after he had preached his farewell sermon and administered
communion to his flock before going away to die in France
at Nice. He gave the hymn to a relative that night and it
was set to music which Lyte had himself composed.‡ He
was born in Kelso, England, and had a much beloved and

---

* I give here a few lines from his hymns which appeal to me:
   "God never is before his time
   And never is behind,
   Hast thou assumed a load
   Which few will share with thee,
   And art thou carrying it for God,
   And shall he fail to see?"
         * * * * * * * * *
   "Remember me, my God, nor let
   My end be my dispraise."

† For his youthful collection of poems Lynch wrote a dedication to
himself which is so delicious and original that I must insert it. Here
it is:
"Dearest Myself,
      As you have had some concern in writing these verses and are
my oldest and most intimate friend, it is but proper that I should
dedicate them to you. I wish you to take them as a token of affection,
rather than of respect. Our relationship of close intimacy makes me
still retain some regard for you, although you have much injured me
and thwarted my designs.—I remain, my dearest myself, your affectionate, though injured companion, I." This was written before he reached
his fourteenth year, and he had in after years many a laugh over it.

‡ Lyte made a metrical version of the Psalms and set them to music
he had composed. He used to teach his flock to sing these, leading the
singing himself.

gentle mother. He had to struggle hard for his education in Trinity College, Dublin, and in the dreary Irish curacy which followed he overtaxed his strength in self-denying labors for widows and children, and in caring for a sick brother clergyman, and himself became a consumptive. He finally settled in a parish in Cornwall among seafaring people, but was a constant sufferer from ill health. His last words were "Peace—joy." He wrote a number of well known hymns. Among these are "Jesus, I my cross have taken" and "There is a safe and secret place." Both of these hymns have been especially precious to me at different times in my life—but each of these times was one of peculiar stress. Lyte's hymns are characterized by tenderness and sadness. Lyte was a married man and Mrs. Lyte also wrote a few hymns.

Nurse Cavell, martyred in Belgium, 1915—shortly before she was shot, joined the British chaplain in singing "Abide with me—Heaven's morning breaks."

John Lyth, D. D.

1821-1886

"There is a better world, they say."

This well-known hymn was written by a Wesleyan minister born at York, England, who became the first Wesleyan minister of Germany, returning to England in 1865 after which he labored at Sheffield, Hull, and other large towns. He published a small volume of poems and a history of Methodism in York. This hymn was written in Stroud, Gloustershire for the anniversary of an infant school. I have a touching memory about it, having heard it sung in Africa by bereaved parents with breaking hearts at the funeral of their only babe. The father was a Church of England clergyman named Booth. I remember their faces as they sang.

Sir Edward Bulwer Lytton

1805-1873

"Thou must believe and thou must venture;
In fearless faith thy safety dwells.
By miracles alone men enter
The glorious land of miracles."*

These bracing lines which close Lytton's fine translation
of a poem by Schiller called "The Longing" are worth repeating again and again as we face the crises of our lives.
Lord Lytton was the youngest son of Gen. Bulwer. He was
born at Norfolk and educated at Cambridge, England. His
principal writings were novels† but he wrote poems‡ also.
At the age of twenty-six he became a member of Parliament
and attached himself to the reform party. At one time he
was Colonial Secretary.

---

* I know a humble, faithful missionary who has entered the "glorious land of miracles." Without physical beauty, good clothes,
brilliancy, or financial backing, she goes back and forth between the
continents telling of the need for evangelization in Africa, and when
she gets ready for another hop across the ocean somebody or other
always provides her with passage money.

† Bulwer's critics were astonished at the cynicism and epigrams
which were woven in his novels and plays.

‡ In a fine poem by Bulwer on The Sabbath occur the stanzas:

"They tell thee in their dreaming school
Of power from old dominion hurled,
When rich and poor, with juster rule,
Shall share the altered world.

Alas, since time itself began,
That fable hath but fooled the hour,
Each age that ripens power in man
But subjects man to power.

Yet every day in seven at least
One bright republic shall be known,
Man's world awhile hath surely ceased
When God proclaims His own.

Six days may rank divide the poor,
O Dives, from thy banquet hall;
The seventh the Father opes the door
And holds his feast for all "

The above lines show Bulwer's cynicism, and despair of any Golden
Age for the world. I am foolish enough to believe there is one coming,
and I have Isaiah back of me for it.

ROBERT, LORD LYTTON

1831-

"Assert thyself and by and by
The world will come and lean on thee."

These lines taken from a poem called "The Artist" were written by the only son of Edward Bulwer Lytton. Neither father nor son is listed as a hymnist by Dr. Julian, and it is with somewhat of an apology that I include them here. However, there is a tonic* in some of their lines which have a similar effect to that produced by a noble hymn.

ROBERT MURRAY McCHEYNE

1813-1843

"When this passing world is done"

This hymn was written by a young Scottish minister of saintly character who died at the age of thirty. Robert McCheyne was born and educated at Edinburgh. He entered high school at the age of eight and took high rank in his classes. He was licensed to preach when he was twenty-two and had a parish of 6000 at Larbert, and later was a pastor at Dundee where he died. He also was a travelling evangelist, preaching in the open air, and was instrumental in the conversion of many people in the revival of 1839. He wrote a few hymns,† some of them in Palestine, where he went on a "Mission of Enquiry" to the Jews.

---

* I give here another stanza of the forceful poem quoted above:
"Be quiet, Take things as they come;
Each hour will draw out some surprise.
With blessing let the days go home;
Thou shalt have thanks from evening skies."
* * * * * * * * *
"Create, create.
Dissection leaves the dead, dead still.
Burn catalogues,—write thine own books."
(It will be seen that I am following this rather startling advice.) I judge that the son was a "chip of the old block."

† One of his hymns was entitled "Jehovah Tsidkenu", meaning "The Lord our Righteousness" which was the watchword of the Reformers. The first line of this hymn is "I once was a stranger to grace and to God." McCheyne was in Dr. Chalmers' class in Edinburgh University. Some of his hymns are of great merit.

GEORGE MACDONALD

1824-1905

"Behind men's hearts and souls doth lie
The infinite of God."

These lines* were written by the distinguished Scotch
Congregational minister above named, who is best known as
a novelist and was also an editor and lecturer. His most
famous novels were "David Elginbrod" and "Robert
Falconer". He wrote a number of valuable hymns, not very
much in use, however. Julian says they are touched with
mysticism which makes them difficult of apprehension. Some
of them are a series on the different beatitudes.

JOHN ROSS MACDUFF, D. D.

1820-

"Everlasting arms of Love—"

This is the opening line of a fine hymn written by an
eminent minister of a church in Glasgow. Both the University of Glasgow and the University of New York conferred on him the degree of D. D. He wrote 31 hymns. One
of them begins "Jesus wept—those tears are over."

---

* These lines are from a "Hymn for the Mother" which has some
striking lines in it. I quote below some of them:
            "Thou knowest what an awful thing
                It is to be a life."
Here is the closing stanza:
            "So, Lord, I sit in Thy wide space,
            My child upon my knee;
            She looketh up into my face,
                And I look up to Thee."

WILLIAM PATON MACKAY, M. D.

1839-1885

"We praise Thee O God
*   *   *   *   *   *   *   *   *
Revive us again."

This familiar hymn was written in 1863 by a Scotch Presbyterian minister born at Montrose. He was educated at the University of Edinburgh for the medical profession which he followed for a time. His parish later was at Hull. He wrote hymns 17 of which were printed in W. Reid's "Praise Book" in 1872. His death at the age of forty-six was the result of an accident.

NORMAN MACLEOD, D. D.

1812-1872

"Courage, brother, do not stumble,
*   *   *   *   *   *   *   *   *
Some will hate and some will love thee,
Some will flatter, some will slight,
Cease from men and look above thee,
Trust in God and do the right."

This fine hymn was written by a Scotch minister born at Campbellton and educated in the universities of Edinburgh and Glasgow. He became one of the Queen's chaplains in 1841. In 1860 he became editor of a periodical called "God's Words" which he continued to edit until his death which occurred in Glasgow at the age of sixty. His writings are numerous and popular. His best known hymn is the one mentioned above which first appeared in 1857 in the Edinburgh Christian Magazine of which he was for a time the editor.

John Marriott

1780-1825

"Thou whose almighty word
Chaos and darkness heard and took their flight."

This stately and imperishable hymn was written by a native of Germany who was educated in England and spent his after life there. Therefore I list him with the British hymnists. He graduated at Oxford with honors and later was a tutor in the family of a Duke who presented him to a curacy which he retained till his death. He was a married man and lived till only the age of forty-six. He published a volume of sermons and wrote several hymns which were not published by himself and they were never issued in book form. The hymn mentioned above is the only one I find which has come into common use.

James Martineau

1805-1900

"A voice upon the midnight air"

This hymn was written in 1840 by a learned Professor of Mental and Moral Philosophy in England, a younger brother of the celebrated Harriet Martineau. He was born in Norwich and had several ministerial positions, a man of great sympathy and insight into the deepest questions of human life. Some Unitarian hymnals were edited by him. Julian lists three of his hymns. His sister's hymns also appeared in his hymn books. He was a Unitarian of the catholic and spiritual type.

GERALD MASSEY

1828-1907

"Ho! trouble-tried and torture-torn,
The kingliest kings are crowned with thorn."

These lines are from a poem entitled "The Kingliest King" written by the above named Christian Socialist. Massey was born of poor, illiterate parents in Hertfordshire and received only a scanty education. He got a few books like Pilgrim's Progress and Robinson Crusoe. In his youth he worked in a silk mill and later in straw plaiting. He began to contribute lyrics to magazines after he fell in love at the age of seventeen. His verses were about the suffering poor and the inequalities of life. The French Revolution stimulated him to try to do something to ameliorate the conditions of his own class, and he started a Reform paper called "The Spirit of Freedom". Charles Kingsley and other philanthropists helped him and called the attention of others to his poetic talent. Later he lectured in England and the United States. In 1868 the English government gave him a pension. He was a "patriot to the core" and is worthy of honor.

RICHARD MASSIE

1800-

"Still on Thy loving heart let me repose,"

This is the opening line of the translation of a hymn by Spitta made by the above-named successful translator of many German hymns. Massie was English and has translated many beautiful hymns of Spitta, Gerhardt and Luther with artistic skill. The first line of one of his translations from Spitta is "I know no life divided."

Rev. George Matheson

1842-1906

"O Love that wilt not let me go,"

This beautiful and tender hymn was written in a few minutes one summer evening in 1822 in an Ayrshire manse and was the fruit of great mental pain.* The author felt he was taking the hymn from dictation rather than being its composer. He graduated brilliantly from the University of Edinburgh and was a preacher and lecturer, although he became blind while a young man.

Albert Midlane

1825-1909

"There's a home for little children
Above the bright blue sky."

This is one of the children's hymns written by a business man of Newport on the Isle of Wight. The hymn was written in 1859 and sung itself around the world in the next ten years. Midlane began to compose hymns as soon as he could read. Before he was nine years old he had composed hymns which so impressed his relatives with their depth and fervor as to give rise to the cheerful belief that he was destined to an early grave. Albert's Sunday School teacher to whom he showed his verses encouraged him to go on writing and gave him invaluable advice about it. He wrote more than 200 hymns and found his recreation in this way. Many of his hymns were published in little Sunday School hymn books. They are useful, pleasing, and spiritual, without reaching the highest poetical excellence.

---

* There is a story current that Matheson was engaged to a young lady of whom he was very fond. When told by a doctor that he was going blind, Matheson offered his fiancée her freedom from the engagement, and she took it—not wishing to have a blind husband. In sore distress at this blow Matheson wrote for sufferers of all time his immortal hymn of Love that will not ever give us up or throw us over.

HENRY HART MILMAN

1791-1868

"Ride on, ride on in majesty!
In lowly pomp ride on to die.
Oh Christ, Thy triumphs now begin!"*

This stately hymn for Palm Sunday was written by the distinguished Dean of St. Paul's and Professor of Poetry at Oxford, a great writer both of prose and verse who was called after his death "the last of the great conversers." Dean Milman was the youngest son of a Baronet who was court physician to King George III. Henry was educated at Oxford where he shone with brilliance as the writer of the "most perfect of Oxford prize poems." He wrote successful plays and delivered the Bampton lectures. His liberal spirit of tolerance† in theology offended the strict ecclesiastics. He wrote historical books which are compared in their splendor of style to the writings of Gibbon. He wrote 13 fine hymns, two of which are, "When our heads are bowed with woe,"‡ and "Brother, thou art gone before us." All Milman's hymns are beautiful and have a classical elegance about them.

ROBERT MONCKTON (LORD HOUGHTON)

1809-1885

"So should we live that every hour
May die as dies the natural flower,
A self-reviving thing of power."

These lines are from a hymn in Fox's "Hymns and Anthems" written by a worthy statesman and poet of England. In politics Lord Houghton was a supporter of Peel.

---

* The triumph of Christ over his foes through his death is reminiscent of the memorable reply of Vanzetti to the judge who sentenced him and Sacco to the electric chair, "The hour of our agony will be the hour of our triumph." So time shall decide in that day when a monument shall be erected in Boston Common to those martyrs for Truth, and men shall stand before it with bared heads and thrilled hearts.

† Milman is said to be the first to take the stand that the Bible should be studied like any other book, and the events of sacred history treated at once critically and reverently.

‡ Julian says of this hymn that it has no peer in the presentation of Christ's human sympathy.

He brought before Parliament the first bill for juvenile re-
formatories and advocated the reform of penal institutions.
He presided over the Social Science Congress in Norwich.
These measures that he advocated as well as his remarkable
poems* show that he was a truly great and noble soul.

John Samuel Bewley Monsell

1811-1875†

"Fight the good fight with all thy might!"‡

This soul-stirring hymn was written in 1863 by an Irish
clergyman, Archdeacon of Londonderry. He was educated
at Trinity College, Dublin, and is considered one of the best
of modern hymnists. Julian lists 72 of his hymns—says they
are bright and musical, but only a few of them are of enduring quality.

Dr. Morgan

fl. 19th century

"All my doubts I give to Jesus"

This useful hymn is attributed as above in Hymns of the
Gospel New and Old (No. 205). Whether the author of
this hymn is Samuel Christopher Morgan, D. D., 1836-1898,
a vicar of the established Church of England, I am unable
to say. Dr. S. C. Morgan was a hymn writer, educated at
Oxford and held appointments in Birmingham and Glouces-
ter. I surmise that he is the author of the hymn in question
but am not positive.

---

* He published two volumes of verse. These are not usually lyrical
enough to be classed as hymns and Julian does not list him as a hymnist
but he should be classed at least as a sacred poet. Here are some of his
lines:
      "Thou, whom each humble Christian worships now,
        Once an idea, now Comforter and Friend,
        Hope of the human heart, descend, descend."
  † Monsell's death was tragic. It was the result of an accident in
connection with the re-building of his church. I have seen two versions
of the story and do not know which is correct. One account is that
Monsell fell from the roof of the church. The other version says that
he was standing in the aisle looking up at the work proceeding above
him, and that some of the material fell down and hurt him.
  ‡ I shall never forget the first time I heard this hymn or the effect
it had upon me. I was on a ship crossing the Atlantic. A company of
splendid young missionaries from England were on their way to
Canada. What power they put into singing that song! Another of
Monsell's hymns begins "Birds have their quiet rest", and another,
"Yes, I do feel, my God, that I am Thine." Another still begins, "Rest
of the weary, joy of the sad."

WILLIAM MORRIS
1834-

"What is this, the sound and rumor?
* * * * * * * * *
'Tis the people marching on."

These lines from a rousing civic song entitled "The March of the People" were written by one of the foremost English poets of the nineteenth century. He is not classed by Julian as a hymnist, but his songs of truth, freedom, and justice have the tonic moral effect of hymns. Morris was educated as a painter, but became a designer of artistic furniture. He wrote both in prose and verse and on various subjects. He was a supporter of Christian Socialism.

EDWARD MOTE
1797-1874

"My hope is built on nothing less
Than Jesus' blood and righteousness.
* * * * * * * * *
On Christ the solid rock I stand,
All other ground is sinking sand."

The author of this useful and well-known hymn was born in London and was converted under the preaching of J. Hyatt in Tottenham Road. Mote became a Baptist preacher. This hymn came to him one day in inspiration as he was walking up Holburn. After he had committed it to writing he saw a brother preacher who asked him to visit his sick wife. Mote complied, sang the hymn in her sick room, where it proved a comfort. Bishop Hall eventually inserted it in a collection of hymns.

FREDERIC W. H. MYERS
1843-1901

"Whose has felt the Spirit of the Highest"*

---

* This line is culled from a fine hymn entitled "Bedrock". It was written by an English poet born at Keswick and who died at Rome. He was a leader in the Society for Psychical Research and Wm. James commends his papers on this subject.

John Mason Neale

1818-1866

"O God, in danger and distress,"

This is the opening line of one of the 66 original hymns
written by the remarkable man whose greatest contribution
to hymnology is nevertheless his translations of the ancient
and medieval hymns of the church, for which all Christians
owe him a deep debt of gratitude. Of this work of translation he wrote, "It is a magnificent thing to pass along the
far-reaching vista of hymns from the sublime, self-con-
tainedness of St. Ambrose to the more fervid inspiration of
St. Gregory—the subjective loveliness of St. Bernard, till all
culminate in the full blaze of glory which surrounds Adam
of St. Victor, the greatest of them all."

Neale was born in London and lost his father by death
when he was five. His early training was under the direction
of his noble and dearly loved mother. He was educated at
Oxford and became a Church of England clergyman, but
was consumptive and not fitted for pastoral duties. He
married and went to Madeira for his health. He founded
a sisterhood at East Grinstead and a home for fallen women.
This met with opposition which culminated in a mob in
which Neale was roughly handled. He died at the age of
forty-eight. One of his hymns begins "Holy Father Thou
hast taught me." Another begins, "Safe home, safe home
in port." This last is a translation from St. Joseph.

Cardinal John Henry Newman

1801-1890

"Lead, Kindly Light."

This precious hymn for all who believe in an over-ruling
Providence* whether they call themselves Christians or not,

---

* I have heard it said that at the Congress of Religions at the
World's Fair in Chicago all stripes of religionists from all over the
world could unite in singing "Lead, Kindly Light." I am personally
very fond of this hymn. I like the tune used in England and her col-
lonies rather than the one most used in America, which is, I think,
very hard to sing.

was written by the intellectual leader* of the Oxford Tractarian Movement in England. Newman was thirty-two years
of age and on the Mediterranean Sea off the coast of
Sardinia during a fierce storm, so homesick that he sat on
his bedside and wept when the hymn was written which is
his chief legacy to the world, although he wrote brilliant
and inimitable prose.† At the age of forty-four he became
a Romanist and was created a Cardinal—the highest office
which it is in the power of the Pope to bestow.

HORATIO LANGRISHE NICHOLSON

fl. 1856

"In the hour of doubt and sorrow"
This is a hymn written by a clergyman of the Church of
England who was educated at Trinity College, Dublin, and
became a lecturer. Julian lists 14 of his hymns.‡

ROBERT NICOLL

1814-1837

"Lord of all life and light,
God save the poor !"§
These are the concluding lines of "The People's Anthem"
written by "Scotland's second Burns" who died¶ at the age

---

* Pusey was the spiritual leader and Keble the poetical leader of
the Tractarian Movement. It was a bitter blow to Keble (and suppose-
ably to Pusey too.) when Newman became a Romanist. There was a
sharp controversy in connection with the step. Cardinal Newman form-
ally recanted all he had said against Rome.

† There is a fine poem Newman wrote which begins:
    "Prune thou thy words, the thoughts control
    That o'er thee swell and throng."

‡ Saunders' "Evenings with the Sacred Poets" tells this story of
one of Nicholson's hymn which begins, "Alone, yet not alone am I":
A mother was in the habit of singing this hymn to her two tiny
daughters who were later separated from her through war. Years after
she was able to identify them as her own children, because when she
sang this hymn to them they remembered that their mother had sung
it to them in their early years. It furnished the clue.

§ More and more the churches must sing these songs of the people
for civic ideals. Julian does not class Nicoll as a hymnist, but I think
he is.

¶ Just before Nicoll's untimely death he, realizing what was ahead
for him, wrote a poem which contained these lines which I think express
an inward wish of many of us:
    "I would be laid among the wildest flowers;
    I would be laid where happy hearts can come."

of tweny-three because he had overtaxed his strength in public labors. His poems are both beautiful and of lofty sentiment. What mother would not be proud to have had him for a son!

Hon. Baptist Wriothesley Noel
1799-1872
"There's not a bird with lonely nest,
    In pathless woods or mountain crest,
    Nor meanest thing that does not share
    O God, in Thy paternal care."

This is the opening stanza of a beautiful hymn on the "Universal Love of God" written by a clergyman born in Leith, Scotland, and brother of the Earl of Gainsborough. He was educated at Cambridge and was for a time Chaplain to Queen Victoria. Eventually he left the Church of England and became a Baptist minister in London. He, in his change of views, was baptized by immersion. He wrote both in prose and in verse.

Hon. Gerard Thomas Noel
1782-1851
"If human kindness meets return"

This is the first line of a familiar hymn written by an elder brother of Hon. Baptist Noel. Gerard Noel, like his brother, was a Church of England clergyman, but eventually became a Canon of Winchester Cathedral. He wrote both in prose and in verse. Julian lists three of his hymns.

Canon Frederick Oakeley
1802-1880
"O come, all ye faithful, joyful and triumphant,"

This is the first line of the most popular translation* of the old Latin hymn "Adeste Fideles" of which the original author or date† is uncertain. This translation is by a clergy-

---

* Julian lists 29 different translations of this stately old hymn.
† This hymn has been ascribed to St. Bonaventura, but it is not found in any of his works. Julian thinks it is of German or French authorship and that it was written in the 17th or 18th century. Another writer calls it a 16th century hymn.

man of the Church of England, born at Shrewsbury, who eventually joined the Roman Communion.

COVENTRY PATMORE

1823-

"The truths of love are like the sea"

This is the opening line of a notable poem entitled "A Wedding Sermon"‡ written by a man of letters born in Woodford, England. Patmore was for a time assistant librarian of the British Museum. He published four books of poems of which Love, both human and divine is the predominant theme.

---

‡ The lines of this poem are arresting, one might almost say startling in their import. I give a few of them:
"In loves of husband and of wife,
Child, father, mother, simple keys
To all the Christian mysteries!
Proclaiming Love even in divine
Realms to be male and feminine.
Christ's marriage with the Church is more,
My children, than a metaphor."
———— "The best delights
Of even this homely passion are
So rare that they who feel them etc."
A similar thought is in the following lines from a poem on "Woman."
"Nuptial contrasts are the poles
On which the heavenly spheres revolve."
Is not this author right in thinking that sex has its basis in eternal verities? Patmore's saying that Christ's marriage with the Church is "more than metaphor" is corroborated by an experience told me by a beloved woman some years ago in one of those rare confidences which are seldom given. She had been seeking in prayer a special endowment for imparting divine health to others when suddenly she was aware that she was in the ecstasy of a transcendent sex experience with some mysterious power—possibly with some faint similarity to what the Virgin Mary must have had on the occasion foretold in Luke 1:35. That my friend's experience was not only a mental one was shown by the fact that it was accompanied by all the vibrations and physical thrills (only in a highly intensified form) that she had known in her particularly felicitous marriage union of former years. This experience, although transporting in blissfulness, was yet almost terrifying, as she knew not what that Power was that held her. It was not a solitary experience, but was repeated with varying intensity during some weeks, but finally disappeared. She felt that her usefulness in the direction that she sought was materially increased thereafter. This experience has been duplicated, I understand, in the lives of some saints of old. It furnishes much food for conjecture as to the possibilities of the future life of the Redeemed. I have related this incident with great hesitancy realizing that it is a subject almost too sacred to be even touched upon. Paul tells us that there are mysteries in heaven of which it is not lawful to speak.

FOLLIOTT SANDFORD PIERPOINT

1835-

"For the beauty of the earth"

This hymn which is used extensively for Flower Services
and for children, was written by an English poet who was
born at Bath and graduated in 1871 at Cambridge. He
published several volumes of verse which included some
hymns.

ROBERT POLLOK

1799-1827

"Where'er a tear was dried,
A wounded heart bound up,—
There was a high and holy place."

These lines were written by a young Scottish poet who
also wrote Pollok's "Course of Time" and died of consumption brought on by over study at the early age of twenty-
eight. He was a graduate of the University of Glasgow
and licensed to preach. His celebrated book went through
20 editions and was highly praised, but the laudations of his
fellow men fell on dying ears. He started with his sister
for Italy in an effort to prolong his life, but only got as far
as Southampton. He is buried at Milbrook where an obelisk
marks his grave. In appearance he was tall, well propor-
tioned, of dark complexion and deep-set eyes where a
smothered light burned hot and flashed out with a meteor
brilliancy when he spoke with enthusiasm. He has left a
memorable description of the exaltation of mind that was
in him as he wrote his poem, parts of which were written

on the tops of his native mountains. He says, "I proceeded from day to day as if I had been in a world in which there was neither sin nor sickness nor poverty." Pollok is a sacred poet rather than a hymnist.

REV. GEORGE RUNDLE PRYNNE

1818-1893

"Jesus meek and gentle, Son of God most high,"

This hymn, well-known in England, was written by the Vicar of St. Peter's church at Plymouth, England. Prynne wrote this hymn in about half an hour one summer evening while his wife was playing for him his favorite music on the piano. It very quickly came into general use, much to the surprise and joy of the author. Prynne wrote several other hymns and published some sermons.

THOMAS RAFFLES

1788-1863

"No night shall be in heaven"

This lovely hymn was written by a prominent English Congregational minister born in London, the son of a solicitor. He was influenced by his pastor to study for the ministry and was ordained in 1808. He was for forty-nine years the honored pastor of the Great George St. Congregational Church in Liverpool. He had much to do with the founding of the Lancashire Independent College. His death occurred in Liverpool. He was married and his son helped to perpetuate his father's many writings. Julian lists 16 of Dr. Raffles' hymns.

George Rawson

1807-1889

"In the dark and cloudy day"

This hymn was written by an English solicitor born in Leeds. He was a Congregationalist and wrote many hymns distinguished by delicacy and refinement which he published in 1876. The compilation of several hymnals was assisted by him. He lived in Leeds and died at the age of eighty-two.

Dr. Andrew Reed

1787-1862

"Holy Ghost, with light divine,
Cheer this saddened heart of mine."

These lines are taken from a familiar hymn by the above named London preacher and philanthropist. He worked at his father's trade of watch-making in his youth and gave his leisure hours to study. He became a preacher of remarkable power and was pastor of an Independent Church in East London for fifty years. He is greatly honored as the founder of five national benevolent institutions. He established the first penny savings bank and schools for the children of sailors. He came in 1834 to America in company with Dr. Matheson as a delegate from the Congregational Union of England and while in this country received the degree of D. D. from Yale College. He wrote many religious books and hymns. His wife Elizabeth (Julian gives it Elizabeed) also wrote hymns.

Trip lightly over trouble;
Trip lightly over wrong.
We only make grief double
By dwelling on it long.

—Credit Lost

SAMUEL ROGERS

1763-1855

"Oh, if the selfish knew how much they lost,"

This is the first line of a hymn included in Fox's "Hymns and Anthems" written by the above named English poet. He was the son of a London banker and wished in early life to devote himself to literature. With a friend, he went to call on Dr. Johnson to talk with the great man about his ambitions, but his courage failed him when his hand was on the knocker. However, Rogers published a book of poems* at the age of twenty-three. He had wealth and lived with his nurse and his cook in St. James Place, where his breakfasts that he served to his friends were more popular than his poems. "Critics might find fault with one, but not the other." He was a stroller in parks and picture galleries and a constant attendant at the opera. He died at the age of ninety-two.

FRANCIS ALBERT ROLLO RUSSELL

1849-

"Christian, rise and act thy creed"

This hymn which appeared in a collection called "Break of Day" published in London in 1893 was written by a Fellow of the Royal Meteorological Society. He was the son of an English earl and was educated at Oxford. Julian lists three of his hymns and classes him as a recent Unitarian hymn writer.

---

* One poem was called "The Wish" and was evidently a favorite with my beloved and romantic "Grandma Nancy", for at the age of fourteen she wrote a little poem modelled on that of Rogers and with the same title. (See Memoirs of the Leonard, Thompson, and Haskell Families" p. 115.) Grandma's poem is to my mind almost or quite as pleasing as Roger's own, and is in no sense a plagiarism, as it expresses a young girl's ambitions rather than a man's.

Joseph Scriven

1820-1886

"What a friend we have in Jesus!"

This hymn, the comforter of multitudes of burdened souls, was written by a native of Dublin who graduated at Trinity College and went to Canada at the age of twenty-five, and died there at Port Hope on Lake Ontario at the age of sixty-six. The hymn was published by H. L. Hastings in 1865. The authorship (according to Mr. Sankey) was discovered in the following way. A neighbor was sitting up with Mr. Scriven in his illness and came upon this hymn in manuscript. Reading it with delight, he questioned Mr. Scriven about it who said he had composed it to comfort his mother in a time of special sorrow, and that he had not intended anyone else to see it. When someone asked Mr. Scriven if he wrote that hymn, he replied, "The Lord and I did it between us." The lady Mr. Scriven was to have married was drowned on the eve of their wedding. He was a man of refinement but he chose humble duties. Once he was walking down a street in Port Hope dressed like a working man and carrying a saw-horse and saw. One who observed him asked another, "Who is that man? I want somebody to saw wood for me." His friend replied, "He won't saw wood for you." "Why not?" was the next question. "Because you can pay for it. Mr. Scriven only saws wood for widows and the sick."

Percy Bysshe Shelley

1792-1822

"Truth its prophet's robe to wear,
Love its power to give and bear."

These lines are culled from a lyric by the dear poet of love and liberty who is not a hymnist in the technical sense, although this poem is found in Fox's "Hymns and Anthems". Shelley was the eldest son of a baronet—a shy, sensitive boy

who got himself into a scrape at Eton by refusing to "fag".
He also was expelled from Oxford for writing a pamphlet
called "A Defense of Atheism." This so irritated his father
that he would not let his imprudent son come home. Another
imprudent step was a rash marriage at the age of nineteen,
after which his father gave him an allowance but never
afterward would have any other dealings with him. In two
years Shelley parted with his wife, who with their two children, went to her father's care and three years later drowned
herself. She had not been an intellectual companion for
Shelley, who had found no fault with her, except that he had
met another woman he had liked better, Mary Godwin, who
travelled with him in ideal felicity, and whom he eventually
married. Shelley tried to regain his children but was
successfully resisted legally by their maternal grandfather.
At twenty-five Shelley left England and resided in Venice
and Italy and made friends with Byron and Leigh Hunt.
At thirty-two he lost his life at sea in a squall. He was a
lovable man whose lovely lyrics will always be a delight. He
was also a defender of the poor and oppressed. Some critics
deny that he was lovable, and count him a disagreeable prig,
who treated his wife abominably.

REV. JAMES GRINDLEY SMALL

1817-1888

"I've found a friend, oh such a friend,"

This well known hymn was written by a native of
Edinburgh educated in the University there. He studied
Divinity under Dr. Chalmers and became a minister of the
Free Church of Scotland. He published several volumes
of poems and hymns and died at Renfrew. He is listed by
Julian in his appendix, p. 1590. The above mentioned hymn
is included in Sankey's "Songs and Solos". It must have
been a satisfaction to Mr. Small that his hymn was in popular use ten years before his death.

Charles Haddon Spurgeon

1834-1892

"Sweetly the holy hymn
Breaks on the morning air."

This prayer meeting hymn was written by the world-famous London Baptist preacher born in Essex, the son of a Congregational minister. He was educated at Colchester and began to preach at the age of seventeen. People thronged to hear him and the great Metropolitan Tabernacle was built to accommodate his vast congregations. He wrote many hymns but only the one mentioned above is of particular interest. I heard him preach once in 1881. On that occasion he began his opening prayer in this way, "O Lord, we lift up our hearts, and Thou knowest what a dead lift that is sometimes."

Joseph Stammers

1801-1885

"Breast the wave, Christian,
When it is strongest."

This hymn, popular in my childhood, was written by an English lawyer who was born, practised his profession, and died at the age of eighty-four in London. His great hymn was published 1830 in a small serial called the Cottage Magazine. He will be remembered in the future from this one hymn—is he not almost an object of envy to have written it? It is found in "The Vestry Chimes" No. 22 but is there set to an unfamiliar tune.

John Sterling

1806-1844

"When up to nightly skies we gaze"
This is the opening line of a hymn written by a Scottish
curate* who was born at the Castle of Kames in the isle of
Bute. He was educated at Cambridge and became a contributor to the London Press. Ill health compelled him to
travel. He wrote several hymns and Carlyle, who wrote
his life, speaks of him as "a little verdant island of poetic
intellect, of melodious human verity." He died at the age
of thirty-eight in the Isle of Wight.

Samuel John Stone

1839-1900

"The Church's one foundation
Is Jesus Christ her Lord."
This standard† hymn was written by a Church of England
curate who wrote many hymns‡ of which Julian lists 49, and
praises him highly as a hymnist. Stone was born in Staffordshire, England, and educated at Oxford. He is buried§ in
the ground of the church where he preached many years,
St. Paul's at Haggerston.

---

* Sterling was for a time curate at the historical Castle of Hurstmonceaux, where his friend Julius Charles Hare was rector. This interests me personally as that castle was built and occupied for centuries
by my ancestors, the historic families of the Monceaux, the Dacres, the
Fienes, and the Leonards. (See "Memoirs of the Leonard, Thompson,
and Haskell families.") This castle, which has been called "A Song in
Stone" has been only a magnificent but melancholy ruin, but has been
partially restored.

† This hymn was written in defense of the faith against the teachings of Bishop Colenso. The lines in the hymn,
"By schisms rent asunder,
By heresies distressed"
refer to the heretical teachings of Colenso which were causing a great
commotion at that period. The Archbishop of Canterbury once remarked
that when he was called to preside at the dedication of a church he
could safely count on two factors of the occasion—viz, cold chicken and
the singing of "The Church's One Foundation". It has been repeatedly
used at great church assemblies. The key note of Stone's songs is Hope.

‡ Another hymn of Stone's beginning
"Lord of our soul's salvation"
was ordered by Queen Victoria to be sung throughout the realm on the
occasion of the Thanksgiving for the recovery of the Prince of Wales.

§ Two days before Stone's death he wrote a letter to F. A. Jones,
the author of "Famous Hymns", excusing his tremulous handwriting,
saying he was nearing death. Jones calls Stone a great man and says
that the Church is poorer for his death.

Canon Hugh Stowell

1799-1865

"From every stormy wind that blows"

This familiar hymn was written by an eloquent clergyman of the Church of England. He was born in the Isle of Man and educated at Oxford. He published a collection of psalms and hymns suitable for use in the English Church. His place of preaching was at Salford, near Manchester, and he was also the Hon. Canon of Chester Cathedral. Julian lists 47 of his hymns. He took great delight in prayer. The above hymn was sung by the 10 martyrs in Cawnpore, India before death.

Thomas Osmond Summers, D. D.

1812-1882

"The morning bright with rosy light
Has waked me from my sleep."

This beautiful morning prayer which so many children (including myself in childhood) have used with great delight and profit, was written by a Methodist minister who was born in Dorsetshire, England. Later he became a missionary in Texas, Alabama, and South Carolina, and was the editor of the Southern Christian Advocate. He wrote the above hymn for his year-old daughter when on a little steamer descending the Tombigbee River. He wrote it on the back of a letter which he mailed at Mobile to her. She was at Tuscaloosa. It was printed in her father's paper and later he wrote an evening hymn for her little sister. Both children died young. The hymns both became great popular favorites.

HENRY SEPTIMUS SUTTON

1825-

"God's love alike is shown.
In what He gives and what denies"

These are the closing lines of a beautiful hymn found in
Fox's "Hymns and Anthems".* It was written by the son
of a book seller and newspaper proprietor of Nottingham,
England. Henry was articled to a surgeon but abandoned
medicine for literature. He was for thirty years the editor
of the "Alliance News". He published books both of prose
and verse. He wrote hymns which have a touch of beautiful
quaintness like the best of the 17th century poets.

CHARLES SWAIN

1803-1874

"The heart it hath its own estate,"

This is the opening line of a hymn written by the "Manchester poet" who began to write for magazines† during
the fourteen years he was connected with the dyeing establishment of his uncle. He later became an engraver.
Swain had Wordsworth, Southey, and Montgomery as his
distinguished friends. When he was fifty-four he had a
pension of fifty pounds a year given him.

---

* Another hymn of Sutton's in this collection ends with this pleasing stanza:

> "Bear thou thy sorrow! Grief shall bring
> Its own excuse in after years;
> The rainbow! See how fair a thing
> God hath built up from tears."

† Some of Swain's poems are beautiful love songs. One begins,
"A violet in her lovely hair." Another is entitled, "Smile and never
heed me."

John Addington Symonds

1840-1893

"These things shall be; a loftier race"

This is the first line of a hymn published in the Methodist Hymn Book, 1901. The author was born at Bristol and educated at Harrow and Oxford. He wrote extensively both in prose and verse, and published several books of poetry. He died in Rome at the age of fifty-three. The poem of which this hymn is part is entitled "A Vista."

Thomas Rawson Taylor

1807-1835

"I'm but a stranger here; Heaven is my home."

This well-known and well-beloved hymn was written by the son of a Congregational preacher. He was born near Wakefield, England, and educated in a Manchester Academy. Between the ages of fifteen and eighteen he was employed first by a merchant and then by a printer. Influenced by strong religious desires he entered the Airedale Independent College at the age of eighteen. While studying he used to go out to villages to preach. Later, for six months he was in ministerial charge of a chapel in Sheffield. This was terminated on account of a failure in health. He died at the age of twenty-eight leaving the above quoted hymn written in his last days as an imperishable legacy to the world. A memoir of him was published after his death which contained a few other hymns, not well known. Taylor was a rarely gifted young man "who learned in suffering what he taught in song."

ALFRED, LORD TENNYSON

1809-1892

"Sunset and evening star, and one clear call for me."

This crowning poem of his life which was written at the age of eighty by the dearest of English poets, was, by the author's direction, placed at the end of all the later editions of his poems. In October of 1889 he had been listening to the moaning of the bay, and after dinner showed to his son the poem which "came in a moment", as he expressed it. His son told him at the time that it was "the crown of his life work." Tennyson explained the "Pilot" as "That Divine and Unseen who is always guiding us." His "Ring out the old, ring in the new," is also classed as a hymn and there are other sections of In Memoriam that I consider as hymns.* The mournful strains of "Late, late, so late, and dark the night and chill' are sometimes sung as a hymn.

Tennyson was the son of a Lincolnshire clergyman and educated at Cambridge. He was appointed poet laureate in 1850 and raised to the peerage in 1884. He lived in a beautiful home in the Isle of Wight among his children and his books, taking wayside rambles in this quiet rural retreat by the sea.

ARCHBISHOP RICHARD CHENEVIX TRENCH

1807-1886

"Some murmur when their sky is clear"

This is the opening line of one of the few hymns left by this thoughtful and eloquent Anglo-Irish Archbishop of Dublin. Trench was born in Ireland during a temporary

---

* One of these is the poem which begins, "Strong Son of God, immortal Love." The whole of In Memoriam is a string of precious pearls.

visit there of his parents, but his childhood was spent in England. On his mother's side he was descended from the French Huguenot refugee, Philip Chenevix. Richard was educated at Cambridge and worked in early manhood in connection with his cousin Robert Boyd on behalf of some exiled Spaniards. The cousin perished by the vengeance of the Spanish sovereign when the scheme was discovered, but Trench, by God's providence, was safe in Gibraltar. Trench married at the age of twenty-five his cousin Mary Trench and entered on his long and honored career as a clergyman in the Church of England. He lost his first born by death— a deep sorrow which gave inspiration to his "Elegiac Poems." He wrote much in prose and verse.* He died in a good old age and left behind him a stainless memory. He was a loveable man, "sweetness and light embodied."

LAWRENCE TUTTIETT

1825-1897

"Father, let me dedicate
All this year to Thee"

This child's hymn for the new year was written by the son of a surgeon of the Royal Navy in England. He was born in Devonshire and was educated at first for the medical profession but later took Holy Orders and became a Church of England clergyman. He published religious books and wrote many hymns about which Julian says that they are characterized by smoothness of rhythm, directness of aim, simplicity of language, and deep earnestness.

---

*His poem on "The Effects of Prayer" has been a great inspiration to me. It begins,
    "Lord, what a change within us one short hour
    Spent in Thy presence will prevail to make."

Rev. Henry Twells
1823-1900
"At even ere the sun did set
The sick, O Lord, around Thee lay."
This surpassingly beautiful hymn* on Christ as the Healer
of Mankind was written by the distinguished clergyman of
the Church of England who was afterward made the Canon
of Peterborough. He is best known as the author of the
above mentioned hymn which has been inserted in most of
the recent standard collections of hymns in both England and
America.

Rev. W. W. Walford
fl. 1849
"Sweet hour of prayer"
This precious old hymn was written by a blind English
preacher and given to the public in 1849. Julian erroneously
attributes it to Frances Van Alstyne but corrects his mistake
in the appendix p. 1591. This hymn was a household favorite
in my childhood's home and we still sing it very often on
Sunday evenings.

John Aikman Wallace
1802-1870
"There is an eye that never sleeps"
The above hymn which appeared in the Scottish Christian
Herald in 1839 and was also published in 1863 by L. O.
Emerson in "The Harp of Judah," p. 124, was written by a
minister of the Free Church of Scotland. Wallace was born
in Edinburgh and died at Trinity, near Edinburgh. Julian's
Dictionary on p. 1231 in error attributes this hymn to James
Cowden Wallace, but acknowledges in the appendix p. 1713
that this is a mistake and gives the authorship to John
Aikman Wallace.

---

* I became acquainted first with this hymn when in the English
colonies of South Africa and grew fond of it. To my mind it fills a
unique need in the Church which no other hymn ever written has met.
   Canon Twells was born at Birmingham, educated at Cambridge and
died at Bournemouth, age seventy-seven.

ALARIC ALEXANDER WATTS

1797-1864

"When shall we meet again"

This is the opening line of a hymn the first stanza of which was written by an English writer and editor of various papers. He was born in Lineton and died at Kensington. At the age of fifty-six he received a royal pension of 100 pounds a year and an appointment at Somerset House. The other stanzas of the above hymn as commonly used were written by S. F. Smith.

WILLIAM WHITING

1825-1878

"Eternal Father, strong to save,
Whose arm doth bind the restless wave,"

This best of hymns for a sea voyage* was written by the master of the Winchester College Chorister School. Some of his pupils have gained great distinction in music. Mr. Whiting was born in London and educated in Clapham. He was not robust, was rather short in stature, and wore spectacles. He was a cheerful man with a quiet humor. His fame rests chiefly on this one great hymn.

WILLIAM WEYNELL WITTEMORE

fl. 19th Century

"I want to be like Jesus."

This is the first line of a well known children's hymn written in 1812 by a London rector—editor of "Sunshine". He also wrote "We won't give up the Bible", in 1839.

---

* During my ten ocean voyages which I have taken in connection with my missionary life in Africa, I have greatly enjoyed this sublime hymn of the sea.

CHRISTOPHER WORDSWORTH

1807-1825

"O day of rest and gladness"

This well-known hymn was written by a nephew of the poet laureate, William Wordsworth, whom he visited regularly up to the time of the latter's death. He was educated at Cambridge and became both a Canon of Westminster Abbey* and Bishop in the Church of England. For a time he was head master of the Harrow School for boys, and it is said that although many of his pupils admired him, yet nevertheless the numbers fell off while he was there in charge. It is also said of him that in theology he was a "bellicose controversialist." He interpreted the scriptures mystically and was particularly fond of the Apocalypse. His many hymns, (most of which are not in common use) resemble those of the Eastern Church.

WILLIAM WORDSWORTH

1770-1850

"Up to the throne of God is borne"

This is the opening line of "The Laborer's Noonday Hymn" written by the foremost poet of nature and human life of his generation. William Wordsworth, the poet laureate who followed Southey, was the son of a Cumberland attorney. His mother died when he was eight years old. He graduated at Cambridge at the age of twenty-one and thereafter devoted himself to literature, although his friends

* Bishop Wordsworth was appointed to this high office by Sir Robert Peel.

wished him to be a clergyman, a calling for which he had an aversion. He passionately sympathized with the army of the French Revolution and travelled in France with friends of the party of the Gironde who were later sent to the scaffold. This fate might have overtaken Wordsworth himself had not difficulties (pecuniary, probably) taken him earlier to England. He wished to live by poetry but found it did not pay and his financial condition was critical. A friend, however, left him a timely legacy expressly that he might have the requisite leisure to develop his poetic talent. So he settled down with his sister Dorothy and with Coleridge got out a book of Lyrical Ballads which was not a financial success, but Wordsworth did not allow himself to be disheartened by the world's neglect. At the age of thirty-two he married his own cousin, Mary Hutchinson, of whom he wrote the poem, "She was a phantom of delight," and the elusive charm of first love never left the married pair whose home life at Grasmere moved on without a jar. He did most of his poetic composition in the open air, and a servant said to a visitor, "This, sir, is my master's library; his study is out-of-doors." He lived a quiet, contemplative life, in close touch with Coleridge and Southey, the three Lake poets being called "the poetic triad." De Quincey and Leigh Hunt were his admirers and finally he was recognized for what he was, a man of lofty genius. He was a tall man, with narrowness and droop about the shoulders, and scarcely dignified carriage. His face told of deep thought and beautiful day dreams. His eyes seemed like windows opening into the spiritual world and emitting "the light that never was on sea or land." His susceptibility to beauty and his mystical communion with nature have profoundly influenced English literature. His poem on "Intimations of Immortality" teaches a previous existence.

John Reynell Wreford, D. D.

1800-1881

"Lord, while for all mankind we pray"

This patriotic hymn, which is a great favorite in both England and America and has gone into many hymnals, was written by an English Presbyterian preacher born at Barnstable in Devonshire.

Wreford had to stop preaching on account of loss of voice. Later, in conjunction with another minister, he opened a school. He spent the later years of his life in retirement in Bristol, where he died. Many hymns were written by him.

Andrew Young

1807-1891

"There is a happy land, far, far, away."*

This hymn was composed by a man who was a successful teacher in Edinburgh for over fifty years. He was educated at the University of Edinburgh and at the age of twenty-three was appointed Head Master of the Niddry St. School which had 80 pupils. He left the position ten years afterwards with 600 pupils enrolled. He then became the English Master of Madras College and was also superintendent of a Sabbath School. One afternoon while he was spending his holidays at a friend's house he heard a little girl playing on the piano a pretty Hindoo tune and he asked her to play it again, saying it would make a fine hymn tune for children. The melody haunted him and the next morning, rising early, he went into the garden and composed the above hymn for the Indian melody to which it is now known all over the world. This is a curious instance of a tune that begot a hymn—rather than the reverse of a hymn begetting the tune. This was probably an ancient melody which arose spontaneously in some heathen heart.

---

* I made a translation of this hymn into Zulu and it was inserted into our Zulu hymn book. My husband, Rev. H. D. Goodenough, translated 16 English hymns into Zulu and they are in use today.

CHAPTER VIII

BRITISH HYMNISTS—WOMEN

"When I have been all but shut up to the curse of a stony heart, some stanza from one of the simple hymns which used to touch and soften me in my childhood has come up from its home in my memory and melted me into childlike tenderness.

Rev. S. W. Christophers.

MRS. SARAH FLOWER ADAMS

1805-1849

"Nearer, my God, to Thee"

This hymn, sung oftener perhaps all over the world* than any other, was written by an English lady of unique and interesting personality who died at the age of forty-four after a protracted pulmonary illness.

Sarah Flower was the daughter of Benjamin Flower† who was imprisoned for a spirited defense of the French Revolution. He was visited in prison by a Miss Eliza Gould, and the friendship thus formed ripened into love, and after Benjamin was released they were married. Their two daughters, Eliza‡ and Sarah were both especially gifted. Sarah wrote poetry and Eliza set her sister's verses to music. Sarah was tall and beautiful, with fine features, vivacious,

---

* On my own travels, on ships and in South Africa, I discovered that this hymn seemed to be universally known and loved. The author had no idea when she wrote this hymn what a gift she was bestowing on humanity and that her name will be immortal through it. It is going from the sublime to the ridiculous to tell in this connection the following story,—A woman once said she used this hymn to boil eggs by. She sang one stanza for soft-boiled eggs and two stanzas for hard-boiled.

† Benjamin Flower was the editor and proprietor of the "Cambridge Intelligencer." His younger daughter Sarah was born at Harlow in Essex.

‡ Eliza and Sarah died only two years apart. Their joint musical compositions were used at their funerals. Sarah's last breath (almost) was employed in unconscious song.

kindly manner, and sparkling wit, strong sensibility, and deep
religious earnestness. She composed her hymns on the impulse of the moment when the spirit moved her. When she
was twenty-nine she married a prominent civil engineer of
London named William G. Adams. She was a member of
Fox's Unitarian* Church in London and contributed 13
hymns to his "Hymns and Anthems" for use in his congregation. She translated Fenelon's hymn which begins, "Living or dying, Lord, I would be Thine."

MRS. CECIL FRANCES ALEXANDER, NÉE HUMPHREYS

1823-

"Jesus calls us o'er the tumult
Of our life's wild restless sea!"

The author of this precious hymn was an Irish lady, the
daughter of Major John Humphreys. At the age of twenty-
seven she married Rev. William Alexander who afterward
became the Bishop of Derry in Ireland. Before her marriage
she published a hymn book for little children which has gone
all over the world. One well-known hymn of hers begins
thus, "There is a green hill far away." Another begins,
"Once in royal David's city."† She wrote about 400 hymns.
Mrs. Alexander also wrote the wonderful poem on "The
Burial of Moses" of which Tennyson said he would have
been proud to have written it.

---

* Although a Unitarian, Sarah's hymns are suited to Christians of
all denominations. "Nearer, my God, to Thee" became widely known
first in America and the idea was prevalent that the author was an
American, which of course is incorrect. As the Titanic was sinking,
the doomed passengers sang "Nearer, My God, to Thee." Those in the
boats heard the song. With his dying breath William McKinley mur-
mured the words "Nearer my God to Thee."

† This hymn was an especial favorite with a little son of mine in
Africa, named Harold. I have a mental picture of the sparkle in his
eyes and his zest in singing it. There is a picture of Mrs. Alexander in
F. A. Jones' book called "Famous Hymns." She wears a stiff little
white cap and looks very serious indeed.

Harriet Auber

1773-1862

"Our blest Redeemer ere he breathed
His tender last farewell,
A guide and comforter bequeathed,
With us to dwell."*

This exquisite lyric was written by an English maiden lady in Berryhead House, Hoddensdon, where she lived with a saintly old lady named Miss MacKenzie, also a writer. Miss Auber was born in London, but in adult life lived in her own interesting but unpretentious house in Hoddensdon which is still standing and where the window is shown, on one pane of which Harriet wrote the immortal hymn quoted above—"a strange manuscript indeed." The picture of this house is shown in F. A. Jones' book on "Famous Hymns." She died at the age of eighty-nine and was buried in the church-yard directly opposite her house. She published at the age of fifty-six a book of her poems entitled "The Spirit of the Psalms." Some of her other hymns have come into common use especially in America. One of these I have known from childhood. It begins, "Hasten, Lord, the glorious time."

Anna Laetitia Barbauld

1743-1825

"Praise to God, immortal praise,"

This is the first line of a well-known hymn which was written by an English lady, the daughter of a dissenting minister and teacher of an academy, Rev. John Aikin. Anna wrote hymns in her youth which were already in use at the time of her marriage at the age of thirty-one to Rev. Rochemont Barbauld, a descendant of a French Huguenot family.

---

* I became acquainted with this hymn during my lonely and sore troubled years in Africa and it was an unspeakable comfort to me.

Her husband, in addition to his pastoral work, conducted a boarding school in Suffolk. Anna was left a widow in 1802 and continued to reside on the scene of her husband's last labors at Newington Green until her death at the age of eighty-two. Her religious principles in youth were formed under the influence of Dr. Doddridge who was for a time a member of her father's household. Her first volume of poetry published at the age of thirty was eminently successful, four editions being called for the first year. Her subsequent writings* were also successful including her hymns for children. One well-known hymn of hers begins "Come, said Jesus' sacred voice."

MRS. EMMA FRANCES BEVAN, NÉE SHUTTLEWORTH

b. Oxford, England, 1827

"Sinners Jesus will receive."

This translation of a German hymn of Erdmann Neumeister's† was made by an English lady born in Oxford, daughter of Philip N. Shuttleworth, a bishop in the English church. She married in 1856 a London banker. She did much good work in the translation of German hymns. Julian says her work has not received the attention it deserves and that her translations are above the average. She translated Terstegan's hymn "Thou sweet beloved will of God."

---

* Probably the most famous poem she ever wrote was on "Life" which was much admired by both Wordsworth and Rogers. I insert it here:

"Life! We've been long together,
Through pleasant and through cloudy weather;
To part is hard when friends are dear,
Perhaps 'twill cost a sigh, a tear.
Then steal away, give little warning,
Choose thine own time,
Say not 'Goodnight' but in some brighter clime
Bid me 'Good morning'."

There is another hymn by Mrs. Barbauld which deserves to be better known than it is. It begins, "Salt of the earth, ye virtuous few", and is found in Fox's "Hymns and Anthems." The stanza I like best and which I think is intensely pertinent to the prophetic words of the advanced thinkers of today, is as follows:

"You lift on high a warning voice
When public ills prevail;
Yours is the writing on the wall
That turns the tyrant pale."

† Neumeister (1671-1756) was an earnest and eloquent preacher of High Lutheranism. He wrote a good many hymns but the one quoted seems to have been most translated of them all.

Mrs. Jane Katherine Bonar

1821-1884

"Fade, fade, each earthly joy,
Jesus is mine."

This beautiful hymn* was written by the wife of the celebrated Dr. Horatius Bonar. Her maiden name was Lundie and she was the daughter of a Scotch minister.

Evangeline Cory Booth

fl. 19th and 20th centuries

"Dark shadows were falling, my spirit appalling"

This is the opening line of a hymn entitled "The wounds of Christ," written by the present Commander-in-Chief in the United States of the Salvation Army. She was born in London of the famous Booth family and has been an officer in the Salvation Army since she was nineteen years old. She was educated at home by private tutors and has as hobbies riding and swimming. Her headquarters are in New York City.

The above quoted hymn was written in London after visiting a fifteen-year-old mother with a dead baby.

Another of her hymns begins "Bowed beneath the garden shades." This was written when she was leaving her much loved work in Canada. Still another of her hymns begins: "Many fears, sins and tears." This was written after visiting in ragged clothes a long-sentence prisoner in Holloway jail. The prisoner had been a minister and said of himself, "I fell as a star from heaven to hell."

---

* This hymn is dear to me and has a sacred association. In 1889 I went with my husband for a parting visit to his old, feeble mother in Wisconsin shortly before our second journey for a series of years of service in So. Africa. I played this hymn to his mother and sang it to her. She liked it much. She never saw her son on earth again after this visit.

JANE BORTHWICK

(and her sister, Sarah, Mrs. Findlater)

1813-1897

"My Jesus, as Thou wilt,"

The above-named Scotch lady is only the translator of this wonderful hymn, the original of which was written by the German hymnist Smolke,—but we certainly should not have the uplift of it, if Miss Borthwick had not put it into English for us,—so she has done the Church an inestimable service by this and other translations. She wrote original hymns but none of them are familiar to me. She was the translator also of some of the beautiful hymns of her Swiss friend Mrs. Meta Hauser-Sweiser, who had seven children and composed her poems in the midst of heavy household cares. Miss Borthwick also translated Zinzendorf's beautiful hymn, "Jesus, still lead on." Jane had a sister Sarah who married a Findlater and who also translated hymns from the German, one of which is Gerard Tersteegen's well-known hymn beginning, "God calling yet! Shall I not hear?"

THE BRONTÉ SISTERS

"I hoped that with the brave and strong,"

This is the first line of a plaintive hymn written by

ANNE BRONTÉ

1820-1849

She was the youngest of the three talented sisters who, after their mother's death lived alone with their eccentric father, Rev. Patrick Bronté. Anne is the only one of the three who is listed as a hymnist by Julian.

CHARLOTTE BRONTÉ

1816-1855

"The human heart has hidden treasures."

This is the first line of a hymn written by the celebrated author of "Jane Eyre." Charlotte was the oldest of the Bronte sisters and was the only one of them who married. This did not occur until 1854 when both of her sisters were dead. She had only one year of married life with Rev. A. Nichols, her father's curate, a little bit of sunshine at the end of a clouded life.

EMILY BRONTÉ

1818-1848

"No coward soul is mine
To tremble in the world's storm-troubled sphere."

These lines were written by the middle one of the three sisters. She was the first of them to die, and their only brother (a source of anxiety) died the same year. Emily was the author of "Wuthering Heights," a gloomy work of genius. The three wove a glamour of romance and fiction around their prosaic life. They are among the most interesting personalities of history.

ELIZABETH BARRETT BROWNING

1809-1861

"Of all the thoughts of God that are,"

This is the opening line of the beautiful hymn on "He giveth His beloved sleep," written by the poetess who stands at the head of English female writers. She was the eldest daughter of Edward M. Barrett, an English country gentleman. Elizabeth was born in London and was a precocious child who wrote an epic poem before she was eleven, and who established her literary reputation in early womanhood by the publication of several books. At the age of thirty-seven she married the poet, Robert Browning. This step was against the wishes of her father.* The pair went to Italy where a son was born to them who took his mother's name, Barrett, rather than his father's. The Brownings had a life of marital felicity in spite of Elizabeth's ill health which continued for years. She wrote many of her poems† on a sick bed. She was slight in figure and had an expressive face with brilliant eyes, and a spiritual personality. She was fascinating in conversation and erudite without pedantry. She is buried in Florence.

ELIZABETH RUNDLE CHARLES

1826-

"Is thy cruse of comfort wasting?
Rise, and share it with another."

These are the opening lines of a hymn by an English lady who has made some important contributions to hymnology, especially in the way of translations from the Latin and German. She was born in Devonshire, and was the daughter of John Rundle, a member of Parliament. Her husband was

---

* It would seem that Mr. Barrett should have thought his daughter at the age of thirty-seven was old enough to make her own choice as to a married partner.

† I append here a Christmas hymn of hers which I think particularly beautiful (although not easily lyrical). It is probably unfamiliar to most of my readers, as to me until recently.
"We sate among the stalls at Bethlehem,
The dumb kine from their fodder turning them,
Softened their horned faces
To almost human gazes
Toward the Newly Born.
The simple shepherds from the star-lit brooks
Brought visionary looks
As yet in their astonied hearing rung
The strange, sweet angel tongue.
The Magi of the East, in sandals worn,
Knelt reverent, sweeping round,
With long, pale beards, their gifts upon the ground—
The incense, myrrh, and gold,
These baby hands were impotent to hold.
So, let all earthlies and celestials wait
Upon Thy royal state!
Sleep, sleep, my Kingly One!"

Andrew Charles, a London barrister. Mrs. Charles is best known as the author of a celebrated book called "The Schönberg-Cotta Family." She also wrote books on various periods of history.

ELIZABETH CECELIA CLEPHANE

1830-1869

"Beneath the cross of Jesus
I fain would take my stand."

This beautiful hymn was written by a young Scotch lady of Edinburgh, the third daughter of Andrew Clephane, a sheriff. She apparently never married and died at the age of thirty-nine. She also wrote the hymn beginning, "There were ninety and nine that safely lay." This was set to music by Mr. Sankey in the following way: He was travelling on a railway when he saw this hymn in a paper and determined to sing it that night at a meeting, near the close of which he doubled up the paper in front of him on the piano and sang it to the great audience, composing the music as he went along. It proved to be one of his most effective songs. I heard him sing it at the Northfield Conference in 1899. The power of the song and his rendering of it were unforgetable.

FRANCES POWER COBBE

1822-1904

"God draws a cloud over each gleaming morn;
Would you ask why?"

These are the opening lines of a beautiful hymn entitled "Rest in the Lord," written by the above-named Irish lady, in reference to a letter in a sad and despairing tone from a friend. Miss Cobbe was the great granddaughter of Charles Cobbe, Archbishop of Dublin. She was a writer principally of prose on current topics. She was a personal friend of Theodore Parker and was with him in Florence during the last days of his life.

Mrs. Elizabeth Codner

fl. 19th century

"Lord, I hear of showers of blessing"*

This familiar hymn was written in 1860 by a lady who was connected with the Mildmay Protestant Mission of London. It was suggested by hearing of the religious revival in Ireland. She published two small books. One is called "The Missionary Ship" and the other, "The Bible in the Kitchen." This latter seems a homely but useful theme. If we need religion anywhere it is in the kitchen. Elizabeth Codner seems not to have left the facts of her personal life on record. She is only remembered by what she has done.

Anna Louisa Coghill, née Walker

1836-

"Work, for the night is coming"

This popular hymn was written in Canada in 1854 before her marriage to Harry Coghill in 1884. She was the daughter of Robert Walker and was born in Kiddermore. The hymn

---

* I myself wrote a hymn on a similar theme to this, and hope it will not seem presumptuous for me to insert it here.

"Grant me a blessing also, O my Father!
Hast Thou one blessing only to bestow?
Filled with rejoicing are the souls about me;
Their cups of joy are filled to overflow.

Why should my heart be still so lone and weary,
When Thou art ever on the giving hand?
Give me a cloudburst of Thy mercy on me,
Drenching with blessing my parched and thirsty land.

Spurn me not, though I have wandered from Thee,
For I am at Thy door, undone and sad,
Giving Thee back my fruitless life, so broken,
Asking Thee now to build, and make me glad.

Dost Thou choose one and turn away the other?
Is there unrighteousness in God, my King?
Are we not all the objects of compassion?
Pity the suffering souls Thou here didst bring!

It is Thy pleasure to receive the sinner;
Like my God to welcome and forgive!
Cause me to drink the river of Thy pleasure.
The matchless love of Christ shall bid me live!
                              (Written by Caroline Leonard Goodenough in 1910.)

was published in a Canada newspaper and passed from there
without any acknowledgment of authorship into Sankey's
"Songs and Solos". This hymn is often printed with her
maiden name as is really more correct, for she was not
married at the time she wrote it or when she published it.

ELIZA COOK

1817-1889

"Father above, I pray to Thee."

This opening line of a child's evening hymn was written
by an English lady, daughter of a Southwark merchant,
who became the editor of a weekly paper called "Eliza
Cook's Journal," which was intended to elevate the people.
She wrote both in prose and poetry.* She died at Wim-
bleton.

JANE COTTERILL, NÉE BOAK

1790-1825

"O Thou who hast at Thy command
The hearts of all men in Thy hand."

This hymn on "Resignation" was written by the daughter
of a Scotch minister, Rev. John Boak. At the age of twenty-
one she married Rev. Joseph Cotterill and lived fourteen
years after her marriage and bore a son who became the
Bishop of Edinburgh. Her husband edited a collection of
hymns, in the appendix of which two of his wife's hymns
appear without signature. The year after Mrs. Cotterill's
death, Montgomery published a hymn collection containing
these hymns to which Mrs. Cotterill's name is appended.

---

* I have from early life been familiar with her poem entitled "The
Old Arm-Chair."

Mrs. Anne Ross Cousin, née Cundell

1824-1906

"The sands of time are sinking"*

This exquisite hymn was written by a Scotch lady, only daughter of David R. Cundell, M. D., of Leith. She married Rev. William Cousin, a minister of the Free Church at Melrose and outlived him. She published at the age of fifty-two a volume of her hymns and poems—some of them very beautiful. Julian, however, says they are "rather meditations than hymns suited for public worship." One hymn she wrote has long been familiar to me. It begins, "Oh Christ, what burdens bowed Thy head."

Frances Elizabeth Cox

fl. 19th Century

"Who are these like stars appearing"

This is a translation from the German of Schenk by a daughter of George V. Cox, of Oxford. She was a well known and successful translator of German hymns. One from Gelbert begins, "Jesus lives no longer now."

---

* This hymn came to my attention in Africa and seemed to fit my own lonely and heart-breaking-experiences, particularly the stanza which begins,
  "Deep waters crossed life's pathway,—
  The hedge of thorns was sharp."
The refrain to this hymn
  "Glory, glory dwelleth in Immanuel's land,"
is said to have been taken from the last words of Samuel Rutherford 1600-1661, a Scotch divine who was shut up in a dungeon for fidelity to the Reformed Faith. He died triumphant in prison. He would have been executed otherwise. The afternoon before his death in reply to the question, "What think ye now of Christ." he said "I shall go away in sleep at 5 by the clock in the morning. O for a well tuned harp! Glory dwelleth in Immanuel's land." He died as predicted.

DINAH MARIA MULOCK CRAIK

1826-1887

"God rest ye, merry gentlemen; let nothing you dismay,
For Jesus Christ, our Savior, was born on Christmas
day."

This pleasing Christmas carol was written by the distinguished author of "John Halifax, Gentleman." Dinah
Mulock was born at Stoke-upon-Trent and was the daughter
of a clergyman. At the age of twenty-three she published
her first novel. At the age of thirty-nine she married George
Lillie Craik, a nephew of the historian of literature of the
same name. Mr. Craik died one year after their marriage
and his wife outlived him twenty-one years. She wrote
many poems* as well as novels. Her poem "Labor and
Rest" is familiar and beautiful.

JANE FOX CREWDSON

1809-1863

"Oh for the peace which floweth as a river,"

This beautiful hymn was written by a Cornish lady,
daughter of George Fox. At the age of twenty-seven she
married Thomas Crewsdon of Manchester. She had a long
illness, during which she wrote her poems and hymns,
"breathing the rich flavor of sanctified affliction." About
a dozen of her hymns have passed into common use. One
of them begins:

"I've found a joy in sorrow,
A secret balm for pain."

---

* Two of these poems have sacred memories for me, "Philip My
King" enchanted me as a very young girl. An older sister bought with
her school teaching money a copy of "Bryant's Library of Poetry
and Song" and brought it to the old farmhouse where I as a child
devoured it mentally. That poem particularly moved me. Another
poem, "Could ye come back to me, Douglas, Douglas," became so moving that I incorporated the name Douglas in that of my beloved youngest son. Now that son has also passed where no word of regret may
reach him and the pathos is increased of that mournful refrain,
"Douglas, Douglas, tender and true."

ADA CAMBRIDGE CROSS

1844-

"Savior, by Thy sweet compassion,"

This is the first line of one of the most beautiful hymns
written by the above-named Norfolk lady, which were published under her maiden name (Cambridge). At the age
of twenty-five she married Rev. G. F. Cross and the pair
went to Australia where the husband labored as a curate.
Mrs. Cross wrote hymns* characterized by sweetness and
simplicity. Mr. and Mrs. Cross came back eventually to
Great Britain.

SARAH DOUDNEY

fl. 1871

"Sleep on, beloved, sleep and take thy rest"†

The author of this elegiac hymn was born near Portsmouth, England, and began to write poems at an early age,
but is known to the reading public mainly through her stories
which were published in magazines. Her hymns are the
least numerous of her writings. Julian lists eight of these.

---

* One hymn of hers contains these lines:
"Lord, Thou hast a holy purpose in each suffering we bear,
Then oh help us each to bear it by Thine own hard life of shame,
Let us suffer well and meekly, let us glorify Thy name."

† This hymn was written to commemorate the death of a friend of
Miss Doudney's Girlhood. The refrain to each stanza is, "Goodnight, goodnight, goodnight." This was suggested by the custom of the early Christians to say Goodnight as they went to martyrdom. I have a vivid association with this hymn. An Irish lady helped me carry on a woman's
shelter in Johannesburg. An illegitimate baby had been left there,
and my friend (whose own child had been separated from her by cruel
circumstances) took this little boy Guy to her heart. When he died she
mourned him, and we used frequently to sing this hymn at her request,
in memory of the beautiful child.

Mary Lundie Duncan

1814-1840

"Jesus, tender shepherd, hear me,
Bless Thy little lamb tonight."*

This lovely child's hymn was written by the daughter of a Scotch minister, who, at the age of twenty-two, married Rev. William Duncan, to whom she was a true helpmeet in his parochial work. She died three and a half years after the marriage,—the result of chill which brought on pneumonia. She left small children for whom she had written several hymns. These were included in a memoir of her which her mother published after her death.

Charlotte Elliott

1789-1871

"Just as I am without one plea"†

This universally loved hymn was written by an invalid lady of London a descendant of the celebrated Episcopal clergyman, Henry and John Venn. Her acquaintance with Dr. C. Malan of Geneva contributed to the spirituality of her character as it appears in the 150 hymns she wrote, a number of which are widely known and include "My God, my Father, while I stray,"‡ and "O Holy Saviour, Friend unseen," and another beginning "My God, is any hour so sweet,-". Miss Elliott, although feeble in body, had a cultured and intellectual mind, imagination, and deep devotion. "For those in sickness and sorrow she has sung as few have done." Another of her hymns begins, "I want that adorning divine."

---

* This hymn was familiar to me in my childhood. It was sung in my family and we all loved it.

† This was written when the author was forty-five. All the family had gone to help in her brother's church bazaar to raise money for the education of the daughters of poor clergymen. Charlotte lay tossing on a sofa, too ill to help, and repining at her apparent uselessness. Then God put a great peace into her soul, and she took a piece of paper and wrote her immortal hymn, "Just as I am."

‡ This is my favorite of Charlotte Elliot's hymns. Its refrain, "Thy will be done", is in accordance with both good stoicism and good Christianity, to accept without repining whatever God allows to come into our lives. This was said to me by my husband's dear college friend, Dr. Wm. G. Frost of Berea College in a time of trial.

"O Holy Savior, Friend Unseen" is a translation of a German Hymn by Fleming.

EMILY E. S. ELLIOTT

1836-1897

"Thou didst leave Thy throne and Thy heavenly crown."

This hymn was written by the above named lady born at Brighton, England and died at Mildmay, London, at the age of sixty-one. She was the daughter of a Church of England clergyman and published a book of hymns for the use of the sick. Some of the hymns gained wide acceptance. For six years she edited "The Church Juvenile Missionary Instructor."

ANN GILBERT, NÉE TAYLOR

1782-1866

"I thank the goodness and the grace"*

Data about Mrs. Gilbert will be found on page 280 in the paragraph about Jane Taylor.

ELLEN LAKSHMI GOREH

1853-

"In the secret of His presence"

This beautiful hymn was written by the daughter of a Brahmin of the highest class who was a Christian convert. Ellen was born at Benares and her mother died the same year. The child was adopted by an English family and educated in England. Frances Havergal assisted her to publish a book of hymns. At the age of twenty-seven she returned to India to take up work among her own country-women.

---

* This hymn written by a sister of Jane Taylor contained the following stanza in which as a child I took a deep interest.

I was not born without a home or in some broken shed,
A gypsy baby taught to roam and steal my daily bread."
The last line I amended as follows: "And steal my gingerbread."
This version conjured up visions of the fortunate gypsy baby engaged in exciting forays and bringing back toothsome spoils.

Dorothy Greenwell

1821-1882

"I am not skilled to understand"
This fine hymn was published in 1873 by the above
mentioned English lady who was commonly known as Dora
Greenwell.* She lived in Rectories and so I assume was a
Rector's daughter. She seems to have been unmarried. She
died near Bristol at the age of sixty-one.

Eliza H. Hamilton

fl. 19th century

"Take me as I am"
This is the refrain of a familiar hymn which is sometimes
(erroneously, as I think) attributed to Stockton, but in
reality, as I believe, the composition of the above named
Scotch lady who had heard this story about a poor, illiterate
girl who had become concerned about her soul at a revival
meeting. She went to the minister who told her she must
read her Bible and pray. She replied "I canna read, I canna
pray, Lord Jesus, take me as I am." Sankey says the hymn
composed on this incident has led to various conversions.

Katherine Hankey

fl. 19th century

"Tell me the old, old story
Of unseen thinks above."†
The author of the above hymn, well-known the world over
written in January, 1866, was an English lady of London

---

† I have a vivid remembrance of the occasion on which I first heard
this hymn. I was a young girl attending the Bridgewater High School
and was being boarded five days in the week in "the village" to be
near my school. One evening my landlady took me and her daughter
Alice to a church social at the home of her pastor, and near the close
of the evening this tender hymn was sung, and there was an accompanying hush in the merry company which left an indelible impression on
my memory.

* In her poem on "The Dying Child" are the lines:
"Four corners are around my bed,
At every one an angel spread;
One to lead me, one to feed me,
Two to take my soul to heaven."

who wrote it when "weak and weary." She was recovering
from an illness. It attracted the attention of Mr. Sankey
who in 1867 sent it to his friend W. H. Doane of Connecticut with the request that he would set it to music, which was
done, when riding in a stage coach one hot afternoon in the
White Mountains, but throwing the words into eight line
stanzas rather than four lines to a stanza. Miss Hankey herself was not pleased with this. That evening it was sung in
the parlor of the hotel. However, what Mr. Doane did,
popularized the hymn which has been translated into many
languages, which was a matter of thankfulness to the author.
Miss Hankey wrote other hymns but none that are as well-
known as this one by which she will always be remembered;
unless it is that other favorite which begins, "I love to tell
the story."

FRANCES RIDLEY HAVERGAL

1836-1879

"Take my life and let it be
Consecrated, Lord, to Thee."

This hymn which is an epitome of the author's character
was written by the daughter of an English clergyman.
At the age of fourteen when in Mrs. Leed's School in
Worcester, Frances gave her heart and life to Jesus whom
she served ever after with a passionate love. She wrote many
hymns. The first lines of some familiar ones I give below:
"I gave my life for Thee"*
"God will take care of you,"
"I bring my sins to Thee"
"Light after darkness, gain after loss,"
"Like a river glorious is God's perfect peace."
"I know I love Thee better Lord."
"True-hearted, whole-hearted, faithful and loyal"

---

* This hymn was written in a few moments on a circular when the
author was a young girl. She did not think it worth copying and was
about to put it in the fire when a sudden impulse checked her. So she
put it in he pocket and later read it to an old woman in an almshouse
who liked it. It became a very popular hymn.

"Lord speak to me that I may speak"
"Who is on the Lord's side?"
"I am trusting Thee, Lord Jesus"
Julian lists 55 of her hymns—a large number when we
realize that she died at the age of 43 at Swansea in
Wales. Although not a great poet, she fills a useful niche in
hymnody.†

DOROTHEA FELICIA HEMANS, NÉE BROWN

1793-1835

"The breaking waves dashed high"

This well-loved song on "The Landing of the Pilgrims"
was written by an English lady born in Liverpool, but at
the age of seven taken to North Wales by her father who
was forced by business trouble to move his family there and
who died not long after. Dorothea was brought up in
romantic scenery and began in childhood to write poetry in
which she was encouraged by her mother. Her first volume
of poems* was published when she was fourteen, and another when she was eighteen. A year later she married Capt.
Hemans of the army, who, although she bore him five sons,
left his family and went to Italy where he died. It was an
unhappy marriage which may account for the vein of sadness
in Mrs. Hemans' poems. Julian lists 22 of her hymns but
speaks slightingly of them. He seems to think she did not
make the Atonement and the Holy Spirit prominent enough
in them! He says she has three ideas pervading her hymns,

---

† When asked how she composed her hymns, she replied, "I never
set myself to write verse. My King suggests a musical line or two,
then I thank Him delightedly and go on with it. The master keeps
the gold and gives it to me piece by piece, just as He will, and as
much as he will and no more. When people talk about 'a gifted
pen' or 'clever verses' I smile to myself, because they do not know that
it is neither, but something more than being talented or clever." I
have heard this interesting story about Miss Havergal,—once she was
on a railway train going to Switzerland when she became aware that
she was listening to the music of a heavenly choir unseen by her
and unheard by those about her. She said the music was unspeakably
beautiful.

* One of her poems is Casabianca. Another which I loved in child-
hood is called "The Graves of the Household." Another is called
"Homes of England" and another of rare beauty is entitled "The
Treasures of the Deep."

viz: the Fatherhood of God, Heaven as our home, and mutual recognition in a future state. (Very good ideas, I think.) Mrs. Hemans died in Dublin at the age of forty-one.*

MARY HOWITT, NÉE BOTHAM

1804-1888

"God might have made the earth bring forth"

This pretty hymn I learned to love in childhood was written by an English lady, daughter of Samuel Botham, a member of the Society of Friends. At the age of nineteen she was married to William Howitt (1795-1879) who also wrote poetry.† The husband and wife, originally of Quaker stock, became at last spiritualists. Their writings were not mostly hymns.‡ They include songs, novels, translations, and contributions to magazines. Both of them lived to a good old age—Mary outlived William by nine years.

AMELIA M. HULL

1825-1882

"There is life for a look at the Crucified One"

This popular hymn was written by an English lady born at Exmouth, the daughter of William T. Hull. She wrote many hymns and poems which she published in six collections. She never married. The above hymn is found in Sankey's "Gospel Hymns."

---

* These lines from her own pen are on her grave in St. Anne's church:
> "Calm in the bosom of thy God,
> Fair Spirit, rest thee now."

Julian says that a burial hymn of hers which begins, "Lowly and solemn be Thy children's cry" is put in more collections than all of her other hymns put together. It is used chiefly in Great Britain. It is unfamiliar to me.

† William Howitt wrote a lovely lyric called "The Departure of the Swallow."

‡ One of Mary Howitt's poems which I greatly admired in chaildhood is called "The fairies of Caldon-Low."

MISS JANE ELIZABETH LEESON

1807-1882

"Saviour, teach me day by day
Love's sweet lesson to obey."

This beautiful hymn was written by a lady who was a member of the Church of England, but who, near the end of her life, became a Roman Catholic. She wrote many hymns, mostly for children. I have given above her dates as given by Julian, but have found them given elsewhere as 1815-1883.

MRS. JEMIMA THOMPSON LUKE

1813-1902 (?)*

"I think when I read that sweet story of old"

This sweetest of children's hymns was written on the back of an envelope in a stage coach in 1841 near Poundsford Park, England, and designed for use in a village school. The author believed it came to her by divine inspiration.† She had been ill with erysipelas. This was two years before her marriage to Samuel Luke, a Congregational minister of Gloucestershire. Mrs. Luke edited a missionary magazine and wrote books for children. She had written for magazines since she was thirteen years old.

---

* I am not sure about the date of her death, but at that time she was between eighty and ninety years old, was living in the Isle of Wight, and had just published in her retirement a fresh and delightful book of reminiscences.

† This hymn has gone all over the world and can never be outgrown. Jemima's father, Thomas Thompson, was the Superintendent of a Sunday School where his own children attended. One Sunday he asked the children to choose the first hymn and they struck up, "I think when I read" etc. Where did that come from? asked Mr. Thompson. "O, Jemima made it," was the reply. The father then sent the hymn to a magazine. I like it best to the tune of the old song, "Believe me, if all those endearing young charms." I loved that music played on the chimes at Ames, Iowa, State College.

Mrs. Margaret Mackay, née Mackay

1802-1887

"Asleep in Jesus, blessed sleep!"

This hymn, the first three words of which inscribed on a tombstone in a rural burying ground‡ in Devonshire furnished its inspiration, was written by a Scotch lady governess of Hedgefield. This is a precious funeral hymn used much in England and America. She was the daughter of a Captain and was married at the age of 18. She did not change her name by marriage.

Mrs. Mary Masters

fl. 1773

"Tis religion that can give
Sweetest pleasure while we live.
Tis religion can supply
Solid comfort when we die.
After death its joys shall be
Lasting as eternity."

These lines were written by an English author* who never studied English grammar and had no education except to

‡ Mrs. Mackay said that the burying ground referred to was that of Pennycross Chapel, only a few miles from a bustling seaport town, but reached through lovely green lanes and surrounded by peace and quiet. Mrs. Mackay's husband, William Mackay, was an officer in the British army, who died in 1845. Mrs. Mackay was a widow forty-two years and died at the age of eighty-five.

* Thomas Scott took an interest in this humble woman. In the preface to her book it says, "Her genius in poetry was always browbeat and discouraged by her parents, and till her merits got the better of her fortune she was shut out from all commerce with the more knowing and polite part of the world." Anyhow, this poor and persistent Mary has got her name into Julian's Dictionary of Hymnology, which is more than some of us college graduates have done or expect to do. Julian says patronizingly of her book of poems that there are two or three things in it worthy of attention.

learn to read and write. She was always discouraged by her parents in her efforts to write poetry. However, in the end she succeeded in publishing a book of her own (Good for her). I should like to see that book! I have not done so.

MARY, QUEEN OF SCOTS

1542-1587

"O merciful Father, My hope is in Thee!
O gracious Redeemer, deliver Thou me!
  My bondage bemoaning,
  With sorrowful groaning,
  I long to be free!
  Lamenting, relenting,
  And humbly repenting,
O Jesus, my Savior, I languish for Thee."

This is the English translation by John Fawcett of the exquisite metrical Latin prayer written by Mary, Queen of Scots the night before her execution at Fotheringay Castle. The pathetic story of the life and death of this beautiful woman wakens sympathy in every gentle heart that hears it. The thrilling tale of Mary's escape from Lochleven Castle through the guidance of "Little Douglas" is told by Alexandre Dumas and may be obtained by sending for the little blue book which the Haldeman Julius Co. supplies entitled, "Mary Stuart, Queen of Scots." George Douglas was her faithful friend, but the rescue he had so skillfully planned was doomed to failure and he lost his own life in her defense.

Mrs. Elizabeth Mills, née King

1805-1829

"We speak of the realms of the blest,*
But what must it be to be there!"

This hymn was written by an accomplished London lady
at the age of twenty-four, shortly before her death and while
she was ill. She was the daughter of Philip King of Stoke,
England, and married a member of Parliament. This hymn
became very popular and was included in nearly every hymn
collection for children in Great Britain and America for
fifty years. The author was esteemed for her amiability and
her tenderness of feeling. She also wrote "Sweet land of
rest for thee I sigh."

Miss Hannah More

1744-1833

"The angry word suppressed; the taunting thought."

This is one of the lines written by an English boarding
school mistress, the daughter of a village schoolmaster. She
believed she had dramatic talent and got introduced to
Garrick who introduced her to Sir Joshua Reynolds, Dr.
Johnson and Burke. Finally she relinquished her ambition
to be a dramatist and devoted herself to writing books of
advice to married people, which was funny since she was
herself a spinster to the end. One of her books is called
"Caleb in Search of a Wife." She also wrote some hymns
and poems for the young and is included among the sacred
poets by one writer. It is pleasing to note that her books
brought her a fortune (which is surely surprising when
compared with the opposite fate of most writers of both
sexes.) Miss More was able to bequeath at her death ten
thousand pounds to charitable and religious institutions.
Should this please the unsuccessful or make them envious?

---

* Philip Philips—the singing pilgrim said of this hymn as he
awaited death in Delaware, O. that it came to him more often than any
other "Why I am left to linger so long is a problem."

Lady Caroline Nairne

1766-1845

"The Land o' the Leal."

This well known and beautiful song was written by a Scotch baroness known as "the flower of Strathern." She was the third daughter of Lawrence Olyphant. At the age of forty she married Capt. W. Murray Nairne (afterward knighted.) Lady Nairne is said to have written her pure verses from being offended at the usual coarseness of popular ballads. She died at her birthplace at the age of seventy-nine.

Hon. Caroline Elizabeth Norton

1808-1877

"Bingen on the Rhine."

This English lady who wrote beautiful poems that are almost (not quite) hymns, and wrote novels also, was the granddaughter of Richard Sheridan, the dramatist, whose great speech in Parliament calling for the impeachment of Hastings was the grandest display of oratory of his age. Caroline's husband, Hon. George Norton, brought action against Lord Melbourne for his intimacy with Caroline, but Melbourne won the case. Caroline later married a titled gentleman named Maxwell.

Miss Marianne Nunn

1778-1847

"One there is above all others"

This well-known hymn was written by a native of Colchester, England. She had two brothers, John and William, both younger than herself, who wrote hymns and were both clergymen of the Church of England. John Nunn in 1817

published a collection of Psalms and Hymns in which was
first published the hymn mentioned above. Its use is very
extensive, especially for children. Miss Nunn never married.
She is remembered for this one hymn.

Catherine Pennefather, née King

1847-1893

"Not now, my child, a little more rough tossing"

This hymn was written by the daughter of Admiral King
of Angley and wife of William Pennefather, who was son
of an Irish Baron and a great philanthropist, the promoter
of the Mildmay Conferences and the writer of many hymns
greatly praised by Julian who lists fifteen of them. Mr.
Pennefather was one of the two men who invited Moody to
come to England to hold meetings. Both of these men were
dead when Moody and Sankey landed at Liverpool. Mrs.
Pennefather was a beautiful character whose public work
was absorbed in that of her distinguished husband. Her
hymn will live. She outlived her husband twenty years.

Mary Bowly Peters

1813-1856

"Through the love of God our Saviour
All shall be well."

This comforting hymn was written by an English lady
born at Cirencester, England, the daughter of Richard
Bowly. She married a Church of England Rector, Rev.
McWilliam Peters. She died at Clifton at the age of forty-
three. Julian lists 26 of her hymns.

Miss Adelaide Anne Procter

1835-1864

"Judge not! the workings of his brain
And of his heart, thou canst not see.
What looks to thy dim eyes a stain,
In God's pure sight may only be
A scar, brought from some well-won field,
Where thou wouldst only faint and yield."

These pungent lines were written by the beautiful and
gentle golden-haired daughter of a London poet* who died
from the severity of her labors for others at the age of
only twenty-nine. Her poems attracted the attention of
Dickens who encouraged her to continue to write. She
has written many beautiful poems, some of which are
familiarly used as hymns. One of these begins,

"My God, I thank Thee who hast made
The world so bright"†

Another begins, "One by one the sands are flowing." She
became a Roman Catholic. She was skilled in music and
languages.

Mrs. Elizabeth Reed, née Holmes

1794-1867

"O do not let the word depart
And close thine eyes against the light."

The author of the above lines was the wife of Rev. Andrew
Reed, D. D., an eminent London Philanthropist, who
founded five benevolent institutions and whose degree was
conferred on him by Yale College in U. S. A. Mrs. Reed
entered deeply into her husband's charitable work. She is
the author of twenty hymns, a few of which, notably the
one quoted above, have come into common use.

---

* Her father's name was Bryan Waller Procter. He wrote under
the nom-de-plume of Barry Cornwall. Adelaide at first used the pen-
name of Mary Berwick.

† Bishop Bickersteth says this beautiful hymn is especially appropriate for the visitation of the sick.

CHRISTINA GEORGINA ROSSETTI
1830-1891 (or 1894)
"Does the road lead up hill all the way?
Yes, to the very end."

These are the opening lines of a beautiful* sacred poem by
the gifted sister of the famous Dante Gabriel Rossetti. The
family was of Italian origin but lived in London where
Christina was born. She received her education at home.
Her verses are profoundly suggestive and lyrical and deserve
a larger place than they occupy in the hymnody of the
church.† She does not seem to have married. She died at
the age of sixty-one. She wrote both in prose and in verse.‡

MARY SHEKELTON
1827-1883
"It passeth knowledge, that dear love of Thine"

This hymn published in 1863 is the best known of those
written by an invalid lady of Dublin who was the Secretary

---

* This poem is a gem which has been a favorite with me since
childhood.

† I here append a Christmas hymn by Christina Rossetti which
I think unique. I do not know how well it would adapt itself to lyrical
purposes.

THE PALING OF THE STARS
"Before the paling of the stars,
Before the winter morn,
Before the earliest cockcrow,
Jesus Christ was born:
Born in a stable,
Cradled in a manger,
In the world His hands had made
Born a stranger.

Priest and King lay fast asleep
In Jerusalem,
Young and old lay fast asleep,
In crowded Bethlehem:
Saint and angel, ox and ass,
Kept a watch together
Before the Christmas daybreak
In the wintry weather.

Jesus on his mother's breast
In the stable cold,
Spotless Lamb of God was He,
Shepherd of the fold:
Let us kneel with Mary maid,
With Joseph bent and hoary,
With saint and angel, ox and ass,
To hail the King of Glory."

‡ "He broke my will from day to day.
He read my yearnings unexpressed
And said me nay."

of the "Invalid's Prayer Union." Her sister collected her
poems after her death in a volume called "Chosen, Chastened,
Crowned."

ANNE SHEPHERD, NÉE HOULDITCH

1809-1857

"Around the throne of God in heaven"

This well-known children's hymn was written by the
daughter of an English Rector. She was born in the Isle
of Wight and married at the age of thirty-four Mr. S. S.
Shepherd of Kent, England, where she died at the age of
forty-eight. She published a book of sixty-four children's
hymns.

ANNA SHIPTON

1815-1901

"Jesus, Master, hear my cry."

This is the first line of a hymn entitled "Blind Bartimeus"
written by the above named author who was noted for her
spirituality and who wrote a number of hymns* which have
passed into common use. One of these begins "Call them
in, the poor, the wretched." Another begins,

"He was better to me than all my hopes
He was better than all my fears."

Miss Shipton died at "St. Leonard's on the Sea" at the age
of eighty-six.

---

* One of her poems is entitled "The First Missionary" and is about
the woman of Samaria with whom Jesus talked. Here are a few lines
culled from that poem:

"Yea, line by line, my life's dark page
He gently read me o'er,
He spoke in wisdom and in love
As man ne'er spake before.
Against my soul, so stained with sin,
No curse of wrath was hurled;
Then knew I, it was Christ the Lord,
The Savior of the World."

SELINA SHIRLEY, COUNTESS OF HUNTINGDON

1707-1791

"When Thou, my righteous Judge, shalt come,"

The author of this hymn has been called the most remarkable woman of her age. She was the daughter of an earl and at the age of twenty-one married an earl. She was at the age of thirty-nine left a widow with a fortune estimated at 100,000 pounds. She used this for the promotion of the Methodist revival and was the spiritual comrade of Wesley, Whitefield,* Watts, and Doddridge, and had a large number of preachers and chapels under her immediate control.† At the time of her death when she was eighty-four years old there were 60 such chapels and in 1851 the connection had increased so there were 109 of them. She had great executive ability.

JANE C. SIMPSON, NÉE BELL

1811-1886

"Star of Peace to wanderers weary"

This well known hymn was written by the daughter of a Glasgow lawyer named James Bell. She wrote for the Edinburgh Literary journal of which her brother was editor, under the nom-de-plume of "Gertrude." In 1837 she married her cousin J. B. Simpson of Glasgow. One of her two hymns which is extensively used, and which has sometimes been erroneously ascribed to other authorship, begins "Go when the morning shineth." She died at the age of seventy-five.

---

* Whitefield was her chaplain and by his will made her the sole proprietrix of his possessions in Georgia, and she organized a mission there, but I have not learned that she went in person. Whitefield was probably not wealthy. He is said to have paid his way at Oxford as a servitor.

† It is said of Lady Huntingdon that "she was not indisposed to play the part of a female pope and that she had quite a passion for carrying her point." I can easily imagine that the males of the species who worked under her were irked by her disposition and qualities which they probably thought ill befitting a female. But since she had the money, she had also the "whip hand." Julian is not convinced she wrote the above hymn.

CAROLINE ANNE BOWLES SOUTHEY

1786-1854

"Launch thy bark, mariner!
Christian, God speed thee."

These lines are from the Mariner's Hymn written by the
talented second wife of the Poet Laureate Robert Southey.
She was the daughter of Capt. Charles Bowles, a retired
officer, and his reduced circumstances made it necessary for
Caroline to earn her living at an early age. She tried
literature and sent a poem to the poet Southey to get help
in its publication. This led to a friendship between the girl
and the poet which eventually brought about their marriage
when Caroline was fifty-three years of age. The pair lived
in a plain looking little house called Greta Hall near an old
bridge over the river Greta. Caroline devotedly nursed the
poet during the paralysis which overtook him later in life,
and her own health suffered in consequence. She wrote after
marriage in connection with her husband. One of her fine
poems is entitled "The Pauper's Death Bed."

"Lord of all pots and pans and things;
   since I've no time to be
A saint by doing lovely things, or
   watching late with Thee,
Or dreaming in the dawnlight, or storming
   heaven's gates,
Make me a saint by getting meals, and
   washing up the plates.
Although I must have Martha's hands,
   I have a Mary mind;
And when I black the boots and shoes, Thy
   sandals, Lord, I find.
I think of how they trod the earth, what time
   I scrub the floor;
.   Accept this meditation, Lord, I haven't
   time for more.
Warm all the kitchen with Thy love, and
   light it with Thy peace;
Forgive me all my worrying and make all
   grumbling cease.
Thou who didst love to give men food, in
   room or by the sea,
Accept this service that I do—I do it unto Thee."
—Written by an English Scullery Maid, name unknown

ANNE STEELE*

1716-1778

"Father, whate'er of earthly bliss†
Thy sovereign will denies."

This immortal hymn was written from the sick bed of an uncomplaining invalid, born at Broughton, Hampshire Co., England, the daughter of Rev. Henry Steele, a Baptist minister. Her many hymns‡ are especially used in the Baptist connection. Anne had an accident in childhood which resulted in life-long suffering. However, she had a lover and preparations for her marriage were made and guests already assembled when tidings came that her lover was drowned. Her consolation in Christ for her sufferings has brought blessing to the Christian world.

QUEEN ELIZABETH STUART (OF BOHEMIA)§

born 1596

"This is joy, this is true pleasure,
If we best things make our treasure,
And enjoy them at full leisure."

˙These lines are culled from the writings of the beautiful and charming English princess, daughter of James I¶ and

---

* Anne was never married, but in accordance with a curious English custom, she is often referred to in hymn books as "Mrs." Anne Steele, as a token of respect. The masculine superiority complex demands that a woman's glory must be a reflected light from the male; therefore she is more important if she is a Mrs. instead of Miss. This tickles my funny bone.

† Anne's father's diary entry Nov. 29, 1751, refers presumably to this hymn as follows: "This day Nanny having sent her composition to London to be printed, I pray God to make it useful and keep her humble." This is enough to make a horse laugh, that poor sick Nanny must not enjoy having her hymns praised lest she should be proud. Probably the father was proud of his daughter's poetry and by a curious self-deception liked to attribute the danger of vanity to her rather than to himself.

‡ One of her well-known hymns begins,
 "Dear Refuge of my weary soul,
 On Thee, when sorrows rise."
 Beside this hymn in an old hymn book my sister, Mary Hall Leonard, wrote, "These are the soft, plaintive utterances of one sorely tried in this earthly life."

§ It may be of interest to note that Julian classes Queen Elizabeth of England as a hymnist because she made a metrical version of some of the psalms. This gentle pastime seems somewhat at variance with other aspects of her strange mixture of characteristics.

¶ She was a granddaughter of Mary, Queen of Scots, and was brought to England as an infant when her father James ascended the throne. Ben Jonson wrote a prophecy about her in which he said, "She shall be the mother of nations." She was an ancestress of Queen Victoria.

sister of Charles I who was beheaded. Elizabeth went as a happy bride to the castle of her husband Frederick, who became the sovereign of Bohemia, but who had to fly into exile after defeat at the battle of Prague, after which the pair lived at the Hague in a state of dependence. They had thirteen children. One was killed in battle; one was drowned; five others died before their mother. Her husband also died thirty years before Elizabeth, who solaced her sorrows by writing hymns. Her youngest daughter, Sophia, was the mother of George I and an ancestress of the present royal family of England. Elizabeth finally went back to England where she had passed her youth. She is accounted a saintly character.

JANE TAYLOR

1783-1824

"When little Samuel woke"

This pretty child's hymn is the joint production of two sisters, Ann and Jane Taylor, born in London where their father was an engraver, and later he became a Congregational minister. These daughters published a book called "Hymns for infant minds". Ann the older of the sisters married at the age of 31 Rev. Joseph Gilbert, a tutor of mathematics in a Yorkshire College.

MISS DOROTHY ANN THRUPP

1779-1847

"Savior, like a shepherd lead us!"

This familiar hymn was written by a London lady who published (at first anonymously) many hymns for children. The above hymn was written ten years before her death which occurred at the age of sixty-eight. Julian lists ten of her hymns.

Mrs. Vokes

fl. 18th century

"Soon shall the last glad song arise."

This familiar old hymn was written by an English lady of whom practically no data have been preserved. Some of her hymns were published in Portsea, England, by a Congregational minister in 1797 and later in Bobell's hymn book in 1806.

Miss Anna Letitia Waring

1820-

"Father, I know that all my life
Is portioned out for me."

This hymn of devotional spirit and intense personality was written by a Welsh lady born in Neath Glamorganshire who published in 1850 a little book of thirty-eight hymns.*

Miss Helen Maria Williams

1762-1827

"While Thee I seek, Protecting Power,
Be my vain wishes stilled."

This brilliant English lady was born near Berwick. Shortly after the French Revolution she went to live in Paris where she was imprisoned for writing in favor of the moder-

---

* Two of her hymns I have been familiar with for many years besides the one first quoted. They are those beginning, "My heart is resting O my God," and "Go not far from me, O my strength." I used to hear these sung at the South African General Mission in Johannesburg and considered them full of depth and sweetness. I should have been glad to know more of the author than I could find. Here are also some of her lines,—
"We need as much the cross we bear
As air we breathe, or light we see,
It draws us to Thy side in prayer,
It binds us to our Strength in Thee."
One of her best beloved hymns begins, "In heavenly love abiding."

ate Republicans called Girondists of whom it was said, "They never accomplished anything." She was released, however, on the fall of Robespierre. She was a writer about French affairs and died at the age of fifty-five in Amsterdam. The above named beautiful hymn is her great contribution to the hymnology of the church. It is sung to the tune of "Brattle Street", which was composed by Pleyel. This is a fine combination of words and music which should be more frequently sung. It has been a favorite with me since childhood.

MISS CATHERINE WINKWORTH

1829-1878

"Lord, hear the voice of my complaint."

This is the first line of one of the many hymns translated from the German by this foremost translator of German hymns. Catherine Winkworth whose work in this line is simply prodigious, was born in London, spent her early life near Manchester, and finally moved with her family to Clifton, near Bristol. She died suddenly of heart disease at the age of forty-nine in Savoy. She was a woman of remarkable intellectual and social gifts, of true piety and of tender and sympathetic refinement. She was interested in the higher education of women. Her translations are executed with conscientious exactitude and show much native poetical ability. Hymnology owes very much to her. She is the author of "Christian Singers of Germany."

CHAPTER IX*

AMERICAN HYMNISTS: MEN

"The songs which are the sweetest and best,—
And sink deepest into the human heart,
Are those which poets do not *try* to write."

Rev. M. E. Abbey

fl. 19th century

"Life is like a mountain railroad
With an engineer that's brave."

Somewhere in the eighteen-eighties, a gray-haired Baptist preacher in the South placed in the hands of Charles D. Tillman of Lyerly, Ga., the breezy song of which the opening lines are given above. Mr. Tillman set the song to a melody which suggested itself to him at once and has been sung with immense popularity. Mr. Tillman sung it for the first time with a guitar accompaniment in a railroad shop in Tallahassee, Fla. At the close of the song he asked how many of the men present wished to start on that railroad journey of which he had been singing. Nearly every hand went up, just as the whistle sounded for them to go back to work. Mr. Tillman says that the whistle was in the very key in which he had been singing. The "powerful" preacher who wrote the song is doubtless long dead. People have forgotten the singer but not the song.

Alfred Henry Ackley

fl. 20th century

"His love is far better than gold "
This hymn was written by a Presbyterian pastor in Wilkes-

---

* I have found difficulty in writing this chapter because so many American hymnists are obscure persons in private life about whom very little is known. I hope the mere mention of them will prove a clue to others in finding out more about them.

Barre, Pa., who has written several popular hymns. One of which is entitled, "Somebody knows." Another is "Every day I need Thee more." He graduated from the Westminster Theological Seminary of Maryland at the age of twenty-two. He studied harmony under Alfred Walker of the Royal Academy of Music, London. He is not an old man and may live to enrich hymnody for many years. His hymns have met with success. His brother Mr. B. D. Ackley is Director of Music in the Churchill Tabernacle in Buffalo.

REV. E. ADAMS

fl. 1869

"Land ahead! Its fruits are waving
Over fields of fadeless green."

This rousing hymn was first published in 1869 in a little Sunday School hymn book called "Bright Jewels" and ten years later was included in a hymnal named "Coronation Hymns." I cannot find anything about the author except his name. The hymn seems to be founded on the dying words of John Adams, the apostle of Pitcairn's Island, whose name was originally Alexander Smith. When this old mutineer of the ship Bounty lay dying after forty years of presiding over the religious community in that paradise of the Pacific, he said, "Land in sight." Someone asked him, "Are you happy?" He replied, "Rounding the cape into the harbor," and later, with his expiring breath, he said, "Let go the anchor!" Hezekiah Butterworth tells this story but gives no clue as to what connection there was, if any, between the John Adams of Pitcairn's Island and the Rev. E. Adams who wrote this hymn.*

---

* My brother-in-law, Dr. C. I. Fisher, in his early manhood taught school in a fishing village on Cape Cod. He described to me the fervor with which the old fisher folk used to sing the hymn "Land Ahead!" It made a deep impression upon him.

John Quincy Adams

1767-1848

"Turn to the stars of heaven thine eyes
And God shall meet thee there."

The above lines are from one of the several hymns written by the sixth* President of the United States whose father, John Adams, had been president before him. John Quincy Adams was born at Quincy, Mass., and educated at Harvard where he was at one period of his life Professor of belles lettres. He was a Unitarian christian who, in the greatest press of official cares during a long and brilliant political career, never forgot or omitted his duties to God. He was a man of sterling character—the champion of the people and the upholder of the right of free speech. He was sent to Congress at the age of seventy-nine and while in the House of Representatives was stricken with paralysis. His last intelligible words were, "This is the last of earth; I am content."

Rev. John Bush Addison

1840—

"There's a stranger at the door;
Let Him in."

This hymn, which was set to music by E. O. Excell, was written by the above-named Methodist minister, a native of Wilson, New York. Mr. Addison did not get his license as a preacher until he was thirty-four years of age, which gives the impression that he did not have early educational advantages. He wrote a number of hymns four of which

---

* John Quincy Adams was a poet as well as a statesman. He made an entire metrical version of the psalms, which, however, was never printed. His most celebrated poem begins.
"Man wants but little here below
Nor wants that little, long."
The closing stanza of this poem is as follows:
"My last great want, absorbing all,
Is, when beneath the sod,
And summoned to my final call,
The mercy of my God."
Written in Washington, Aug. 31, 1841.

are listed by Julian. One of them which is published in Sankey's "Songs and Solos" begins, "I have read of a beautiful city."

FELIX ADLER, Ph. D.

b. Alzey, Germany, 1851

"Sing of the golden city"

This is the opening line of a hymn which was published in the Pilgrim Hymnal in 1904. The author is the son of an eminent Jewish Rabbi and came to America at the age of six. He graduated at the age of nineteen from Columbia College and four years later became Professor of Hebrew and Oriental Literature at Cornell. In 1876 he organized in New York the "Society for Ethical Culture." This was at first composed only of young Jews of liberal tendencies but soon drew large accessions from radicals of other races. Mr. Adler is an original and forceful writer and thinker and has lofty aims and ideals for the elevation of the human race.

JOSEPH ADDISON ALEXANDER

1809-1860

"There is a time, we know not when"

This solemn doctrinal hymn was written by a Professor of Biblical Literature at Princeton, a great Hebraist, a native of Philadelphia. It is part of a poem called "The Doomed Man" which Julian says has "great merit." Another version of this terrible hymn is No. 479 in "Songs of the Sanctuary." It there begins as follows, "There is a line, by us unseen."

Prof. George N. Allen

1812-1877

"Must Jesus bear the cross alone,"

This hymn is of composite authorship.* Prof. Allen altered the first stanza of it to its present form from Thomas Shepherd's "Penitential Cries" published in England in 1693 and later included in an English collection of hymns in 1810. Prof. Allen also added the concluding stanza beginning, "O precious cross, O golden crown." Charles Beecher, brother of Henry Ward Beecher, is said to have contributed three of the stanzas of this hymn, which was published in the "Plymouth Collection" in 1855.

Washington Allston

1779-1843

"To think for aye! To breathe immortal breath,
And know nor hope, nor fear of ending death!"

These lines taken from a sonnet on "Immortality," were written by the distinguished painter-poet above named, who has been called "the American Titian" because of the magical color combinations of his paintings. Allston was born near Georgetown, S. C. At the age of seven he was sent to Newport, R. I., to prepare for college. He graduated from Harvard in 1800 and had studied medicine there, but his real interest was in drawing and painting in which he had shown talent from an early age. In 1801 he went to England where his masters were West and Reynolds. Later he went to

---

* Prof. Allen's name was familiar to me when I was a college student at Oberlin, Ohio, although at that time he was no longer a professor there. This hymn, with which his name is associated, was one very often chosen to open our classes, it being a college custom at that period to begin every recitation with some devotional exercise of praise or prayer.

Rome where he gained a high reputation as a colorist. He
returned to the United States in 1809 and married a sister of
William Ellery Channing. His second wife was a sister of
Richard H. Dana. In 1818 he established a studio in Boston
and painted scripture subjects,—Jacob, Saul, Elijah, Peter,—
one of which (a dead man raised to life by touching the
bones of Elijah) won a prize of 200 guineas in England.
Allston wrote both in prose and verse. His poem, "America
to Great Britain", was called by Sumner one of the choicest
lyrics in the language. He died at Cambridgeport at the age
of sixty-four. Both Coleridge and Samuel Adams were his
friends.

WILLIAM APES

1798-

"God send he angels, take me care;
　He come heself and hear my prayer
　If inward heart do pray.
God see me now, he know me here;
　He say poor Indian neber fear
　Me wid you night and day."

These lines are introduced as a curiosity, but there is a
flavor of genuine piety in them, and, although written by
an Indian, they have also a similarity to the negro spirituals
which is appealing. They are printed in Hezekiah Butterworth's "Story of the Hymns" and were inserted in some of
the Old New England hymn books and used in Methodist
prayer meetings and conferences. The author was the son of
a white man, but his mother was the beautiful daughter of
the Indian King Philip. Apes caused his autobiography and
religious experience to be published. He was born in
Massachusetts.

John Atkinson, D. D.

1835-

"We shall meet beyond the river,"

This very popular hymn, written in 1867 when the author was in sorrow for his mother's death, was the work of a native of Deerfield, New Jersey. Mr. Atkinson became a minister in the Methodist Episcopal Church. This hymn was set to music by Hubert P. Main and published in a Sunday School hymn book called "Bright Jewels." Later it was placed in Sankey's "Songs and Solos. No. 109." I have not found that he wrote other hymns.

Maltbie Davenport Babcock

1850-1901

"Rest in the Lord, my soul."

This hymn was published in the "Pilgrim Hymnal" three years after the untimely death of the brilliant Presbyterian minister who wrote it. Maltbie D. Babcock was born at Syracuse, New York, and graduated from Syracuse University and Auburn Theological Seminary. He held successful pastorates at Lockport, N. Y., Baltimore, and New York City. His short career was memorable for the extraordinary influence of his personality and preaching. He was talented in many different directions. Julian lists five of his hymns* and to these Babcock also composed tunes. He was considered by many as a musical genius. His death at the age of forty-three occurred at Naples when he, with his wife, was returning from a journey to the Holy Land. His biography was written by Dr. C. E. Robinson in 1904. It is highly laudatory.

* One of his hymns begins:
    "This is my Father's world."
    Babcock was in his youth quite a champion base ball pitcher, and the story is told of his taking a bully by the nape of the neck and the seat of his trousers and pitching him over the fence.

LEONARD BACON

1802-1881

"O God, beneath Thy guiding hand
Our exiled fathers crossed the sea."

This is one of the eleven hymns listed by Julian composed
by the above named "Nestor of Congregationalism." The
leader of the Congregational Church in America for many
years in the nineteenth century was born in Detroit, Michigan, and was the son of a missionary to the Indians. For
fifty-seven years he was pastor of a church in New Haven,
Connecticut, and later professor of Theology in Yale Divinity
School. In connection with Richard Storrs he founded the
New York Independent. He was on a Committee that cen-
sured Plymouth Church in Brooklyn for expelling Theodore
Tilton without a formal trial. Dr. Bacon was a brilliant
man of talent, genial, humorous, resolute, and noted for his
fondness for controversy. He was an opponent of Wm.
Lloyd Garrison and of all abolitionists. He had a talented
son named Leonard Woolsey Bacon, b. 1830, who was an
eminent pastor and writer, and who had a remarkable escape
from death when among the Koords of Nestoria, through
the Agha's wife.

REV. THOMAS BALDWIN

1758-1825

"From whence does this union arise?"

This once popular hymn was written by a Baptist preacher
who was born in Bozrah, Connecticut, and died suddenly
when away from home. He was an amiable man, much
beloved. He was at one time a representative in the legislature of Connecticut. Julian lists three of his hymns,

HARRY BARRACLOUGH

fl. 20th century

"My Lord has garments so wondrous fine"
* * * * * * * *
"Out of the ivory palaces
Into a world of woe."

This much used hymn entitled "Ivory Palaces" was written after hearing an evangelist named Dr. Chapman preach on Psalm 45:8. The hymn was severely criticised in an article on "Erotic Hymnody" in the "Christian Century" in October, 1929. It was there said that perfume and eroticism are closely connected, and objection was made to having Christ represented as one whose "garments smell of myrrh and aloes and cassia." It seemed to me that the author of this article was in reality complaining of the imagery of the Bible, rather than of the hymn in question. Anyhow, the hymn "Ivory Palaces", set as it is to a haunting melody, has appealed to the popular heart, and has apparently come to stay—for a good while.

C. M. BATTERSBY

fl. 19th and 20th centuries

"If I have wounded any soul today,
If I have caused one foot to go astray,
If I have walked in my own wilful way,
Dear Lord, forgive."

The above is the first stanza of a lovely hymn entitled "An Evening Prayer" found in Rodeheaver's Songs of Service" No. 179.

REV. CHARLES BEECHER

1815-1900

"We are on our journey home."

This well-known hymn was written by one of the thirteen
children of Lyman Beecher—that remarkable family of
Litchfield, Connecticut. Charles Beecher became a Congregational pastor in Georgetown, Mass., but was also a writer
of religious books and the chief editor of his father's autobiography. He also contributed hymns to the "Plymouth
Collection" of his brother, Henry Ward Beecher.

Some of the stanzas in the hymn* of composite authorship
which begins:

"Must Jesus bear the cross alone,"
are ascribed to Charles Beecher.

FRANKLIN E. BELDEN

"Beautiful City! Haven of peace!"

This hymn was written by the compiler of a hymn-book
entitled "Christ in Song",† which seems to have been used
among the Seventh Day Adventists chiefly. Neither the book
nor the author is mentioned by Julian, and I have no further
details about him except that he is listed as the composer of
the melody to which is sung Miss Abbie Hutchinson's hymn,

"Kind words can never die."
This combination has sunk deep into the heart of the world.

"God knows how deep they lie
Hid in the breast."

W. H. BELLAMY

fl. 19th century

"The home where changes never come"
* * * * * * * *
"O wait, meekly wait and murmur not."

This obscure hymnist, who is not listed by Julian, was
probably an American. His familiar hymn was set to music
by Kirkpatrick, and was published in "Christ in Song."

---

*For further details concerning this hymn, see the paragraph about
George N. Allen.
† I consider "Christ in Song" a remarkable collection as Mr. Belden
has preserved many precious old hymns difficult to find elsewhere.

Rev. George Bennard

fl. 20th century

"On a hill far away, stood an old rugged cross."

This hymn which has become very popular and is by some considered the greatest hymn so far produced in this century was written in 1913 by an evangelist who was born in a humble home in Georgetown, O., but was reared in Iowa in the towns Albia and Lucas. When about 16 years of age his father died leaving the responsibility of the care of a mother and four sisters on his young shoulders. His financial struggles prevented his having much schooling. He married in Illinois and with his wife went into Salvation Army work, but later joined the Methodists. He now travels about holding evangelistic meetings and has written many hymns.

Sanford Fillmore Bennett

1836-1898

"There's a land that is fairer than day,"

*　*　*　*　*　*　*　*　*

In the sweet by and by."

This song, familiar to nearly everyone, was written by a druggist in Wisconsin under the following circumstances: Bennett's friend, Joseph P. Webster, came into the drugstore one day looking very depressed.

"What's the matter?" asked Bennett.

"O, no matter", replied Webster. "It will be all right by and by." Bennett answered jokingly, "The sweet by and by." Then it flashed upon him that the phrase contained the germ of a good hymn, and, turning to his desk he wrote the hymn we know as fast as he could scribble, then handed the paper to Webster, whose eyes kindled. Taking his violin, he played the melody impromptu. In thirty minutes the two friends were singing the hymn together when another friend entered, and on hearing the hymn made this comment, "That hymn is immortal."

Bennett was born in Eden, New York, but the family moved to Illinois where the boy was raised on a farm and attended a district school. Later he taught school, edited a magazine, and was a volunteer in the Civil War. After his episode of being a druggist, he graduated from the Rush Medical School and was a successful doctor, as well as a public-spirited citizen, a gentleman, and a scholar.

W. BENNETT

fl. 19th century

"Thine, Lord, forever, purchased by blood divine"

This fine hymn was written by an author of whom I have no data and whom Julian does not list. The hymn was well set to music by Hubert P. Main and was familiarly sung in prayer meetings in America a generation ago.

LOUIS FITZGERALD BENSON, D. D.

1855-1930

"Open the door to the Saviour"

This hymn of invitation was written by a Presbyterian minister born at Philadelphia and educated at the University of Pennsylvania, who practised law for seven years before taking up theological studies. He did pastoral work after his ordination for six years and then resigned to devote himself to literary work in Philadelphia. He has edited a series of hymnals for the Presbyterian church and "his researches and publications are thorough and praiseworthy." His hymns* are thus far not very well known but deserve attention. He was considered a leading authority on hymnology, and was one of the few honorary members of the Hymn Society, and also a prolific writer and occupied a prominent position in the church and in educational circles.

* One of Benson's hymn begins "Not of this fold Thine other sheep obey Thee."

George Washington Bethune

1805-1862

"Tossed upon life's raging billow"

This first and favorite hymn* of the above named eminent divine was written when the author was only twenty years old and was on a voyage to the West Indies for the benefit of his health. Dr. Bethune was born in New York and became the pastor of Dutch Reformed churches in various cities, including Utica, Philadelphia, and Brooklyn.

Peter Philip Bilhorn

1861-

"There comes to my heart one sweet strain,"

This well-known hymn† was written by a gifted evangelist and gospel singer, born at Mendota, Illinois, 1861. Bilhorn's father was killed in the Civil War, and at the age of eight the boy had to leave school to help his mother. The family moved to Chicago when the boy was eighteen, and his fine voice was an attraction in concert halls. In 1881 he was persuaded to attend the revival meetings being held in Moody's church. On the twelfth night he was converted and took part in city mission work, at the same time studying music under Professor George F. Root. Later he began work among the cow boys of the West, devoting his talents to the singing of the gospel.

---

* He is the author of several well-known hymns. One of these begins, "It is not death to die, to leave this weary load." Another begins, "There is no name so sweet on earth." He is also the translator of a lovely German hymn which contains these lines,
"Where I have Thee, there is my fatherland
* * * * * * * * * *
And in all human kind, long lost brothers there I find."
Dr. Bethune died in Italy where he had gone for his health. The day before he died he wrote, as is supposed, an exquisite hymn entitled. "He died for me." Philip Schaff in "The Library of Religious Poetry" ranks this hymn very highly, and says it deserves a place beside "Rock of Ages" and "Jesus, lover of my soul."
I found these lines of Bethune's which I like,
"And song to me is company,—
Good company when I am lonely."

† Mr. Bilhorn has written other hymns. One of these is, "The best friend to have is Jesus." He has a ranch in California, but the Bilhorn Brothers manufacture in Chicago a useful little folding organ used in many missionary lands. The hymn "There comes to my heart one sweet strain" is sometimes ascribed to Roblin.

WILLIAM BILLINGS

1746-1800

"Let tyrants shake their iron rod."

This hymn was written by a poor tanner in Boston, who died leaving a destitute family. He was, however, a friend of the distinguished patriot Samuel Adams, 1732-1803. He published patriotic songs during the Revolutionary War. His airs were of a merry and popular nature. He had no instructions but melodies were ever running through his mind.

J. M. BLACK

fl. 19th century

"When the trumpet of the Lord shall sound,
* * * * * * * *
And the roll is called up yonder,
I'll be there."

This hymn, which has had a great popularity in gospel meetings, was written by the president of a young people's meeting, and was suggested by the failure of a young girl to respond to her name at roll-call. Mr. Black went home and composed both the hymn and tune that evening.

F. A. BLACKMER

fi. 19th century

"Once I thought I walked with Jesus
* * * * * * * *
O the peace my Savior gives."

This hymn which I found in "Hymns of the Gospel New and Old" became familiar to me in the meetings of the South African General Mission in Johannesburg. I have no data about the author and he is not listed by Julian. Another of his hymns is entitled "Numberless as the sands."

Philip P. Bliss

1838-1876

"Light in the darkness, sailor,

*   *   *   *   *   *   *   *

Pull for the shore!"

This is one of a multitude of popular gospel songs composed and sung by this sweet singing evangelist who, with his wife, was burned* to death in the terrible railroad disaster of Ashtabula, Ohio, when a bridge collapsed under his train. P. P. Bliss was born in Clearfield, Co., Pennsylvania, but went to Chicago in 1864 in the employ of George F. Root the musician, under whom he conducted musical institutes and led choirs. In 1874 he joined D. W. Whittle in evangelistic work, to which he contributed (although a poor man) the royalty on his gospel song books which was worth $30,000. Julian lists 48† of his hymns and says he stands next to Fanny Crosby as a writer of this class of hymns.

* Mr. Bliss was returning to his work after a visit to his aged mother. Flames quickly enveloped his wrecked train, from which Mr. Bliss extricated himself, but lost his life in his ineffectual effort to rescue his wife. No trace of the bodies of either was ever found. A monument to their memory was erected by the Sunday Schools of Great Britain and America at Rome, Pennsylvania, a little hamlet some miles from any railway, near which P. P. Bliss was born. His death made a profound impression on the whole country.

† I give here a list of the first lines of some of the best known of the songs of P. P. Bliss.
"Man of sorrows, what a name!"
"Standing by a purpose true,"
"Ho, my comrades, see the signal,"
"Sing them over again to me,"
"I am so glad that our Father in Heaven"
"I will sing of my Redeemer,"
"Brightly beams our Father's mercy,"
"At the feet of Jesus,"
"Come, sing the gospel's joyful sound,"
" 'Tis the promise of God full salvation to give,"
"Only an armour-bearer,"
"Have you on the Lord believed? Still there's more to follow."
"Almost persuaded now to believe"
"Repeat the story o'er and o'er"
"More holiness give me,"
"Whosoever heareth, shout, shout the sound!"
"Down life's dark vale we wander"
"How much owest thou?"
"The whole world was lost in the darkness of sin,"

S. Earl Taylor tells of the thrilling effect of the hymn, "The light of the world is Jesus," upon the natives of India when frightened by the darkness of an eclipse.

FRANK BOTTOME

1823-1894

"O bliss of the purified,"*

This well-known hymn was written by a minister of the
Methodist Episcopal Church in America. He is listed here,
although in reality he was born in Derbyshire, England and
went back there before his death at the age of sixty-one.
Julian lists 49 of his hymns. Bottome helped to compile
several hymnals.

DR. W. RUSSELL BOWIE

"Lovely to the outward eye

Seemed Jerusalem to lie."

This hymn was written in 1909 by a clergyman who was
later the rector of Grace Episcopal Church in New York
City. It is found in "Hymns of the Living Age." Dr.
Bowie also wrote a hymn beginning, "O holy city seen of
John." These moving lines were written by Bowie:
"Hark how from men whose lives are held
More cheap than merchandise,
From women, struggling sore for bread
From little children's cries
There dwells a sobbing human plaint—
That bids thy walls arise."

WILLIAM BACHELOR BRADBURY

1816-1868

"Cast thy burden on the Lord
And He shall sustain thee and comfort thee."

The music of this lovely anthem† was written by a native
of Maine who became the compiler of many Sunday School

---

* One Sunday evening in my childhood I sat with my chum-sister
on a low stone wall and we sang together this hymn which we had
recently learned. A chipmunk sat up on its haunches for a long time,
near us, apparently entranced with our music.
† This anthem is found in "Christ in Song", No. 685. It was often
sung on Sunday morning by the great choir in the First Church of
Oberlin when I was a student there. I was greatly moved by its
sweetness and stateliness which made a lasting impression upon me.

hymn books which had for a time great popularity. One of Bradbury's tunes which should immortalize him is that to which "Sweet hour of prayer" is commonly sung. Bradbury was the conductor of musical conventions and one of these was attended by Ira D. Sankey when a young man. From this incident Sankey got his first impression of the power of sacred song, which doubtless contributed largely to his choice of a musical career in mission meetings.

CALEB DAVIS BRADLEE

1831-1897

"Our fathers' guide, our ways decide
This day!"

This hymn was written by a Unitarian minister, son of a Boston merchant. He was named for his maternal grandfather who was the first speaker of the United States House of Representatives and one of the electors of George Washington. Our hymnist named above was A. B. from Harvard in 1852 and A. M. in 1853. He married Caroline Gay and the pair had three children. He inherited ample means and his home was one of hospitality and good cheer. He contributed to many good causes. Although not adopting a clerical dress, he was at once recognized as a minister. His pastorates in Boston and Dorchester were early experiments of the Institutional Church. He had just preached his farewell sermon at Dorchester in prospect of taking a new pastorate at Brookline when he was taken suddenly ill and died the same day. His classical attainments were many and varied including the ability to write in both French and Italian. Several good hymns were written by him and Samuel Elliot calls him "one of the heralds of a liberal faith." His paternal grandfather, Nathaniel Bradlee was one of the "Indians" who over threw the tea in the "Boston teaparty."

John Gardiner Calkins Brainerd

1796-1828

"To Thee, O God, the shepherd Kings"

This poem, entitled "An agricultural hymn" and published in a Congregational hymnal in 1845, was written by a friend of John G. Whittier. Brainerd was born at New London, Connecticut, and educated at Yale. For some time he practised law at Middletown, Conn. At another time he edited a paper called "The Commoner". He published a book of poems.* He died at the early age of thirty-two and Whittier wrote his memoir.

Jonathan Huntington Bright

1804-1837

"Should sorrow o'er thy brow
Its darkened shadow fling,
There's rest for thee in Heaven."

This beautiful hymn entitled "Caelo Quies" was written by a Massachusetts author, a native of Salem, who died at the early age of thirty-three. He wrote for the press under the pen-name of "Viator". This poem is found in the "Library of Religious Poetry."

---

* One beautiful poem of his is on Niagara. Here are two lines from it:
                    "It would seem
        As though God poured thee from His hollow hand
        And hung His bow upon thine awful front."

CHARLES TIMOTHY BROOKS

1813-1883

"God bless our native land,
Firm may she ever stand
Through storm and night."

This national hymn* was written by a Unitarian minister
during the time when he was studying in the Harvard Divinity School, 1833-5. Brooks was born in Salem, Mass., and
became a talented writer and translator from the German.
He held pastorates at Nahant, Mass.; Augusta, Maine;
Windsor, Vt.; and Newport, R. I., where he died at the
age of seventy after a pastorate of thirty-seven years and ten
subsequent† years spent in literary work. At the last he was
nearly blind. His wife was a Newport lady. They had five
children.

PHILLIPS BROOKS, D. D.

1835-1893

"O little town of Bethlehem"‡

This lovely Christmas hymn was written by the wonderful
Bishop of Massachusetts, who died in Boston, adored and
honored by all who knew him. One of Scotland's foremost
sons, Principal Tulloch, said of his preaching, "I was
electrified. I could have got up and shouted." Dr. S. Weir
Mitchell said of his character that of all men he had ever met

---

* This hymn is said to be a translation from the German. Another
hymn which Brooks translated from the German of Seidl begins,
"'Lord, Thou art great'! I cry, when in the east
The day is blooming like a rose of fire."

† Brooks had a bronchial trouble which necessitated his spending
winters at the South, and he took a ten months voyage to India for his
health, which was not thereby improved. In his enforced leisure he
wrote poetry.

‡ This hymn was written in 1868 for his Sunday School. He had
spent the Christmas of 1866 in Bethlehem of Judea. It is said that he
had in early life a defect in speech which he overcame, and that he
became famous through his prayer at the opening of the Centennial in
Philadelphia. This last, however, is only partially true, as he was
famous in Massachusetts before that. He was instrumental in keeping
the hymn, "How firm a foundation"—in the Episcopal hymn book, and
made a speech in committee emphasizing the value of the association
with such hymns.

he regarded Phillips Brooks as the one man entirely great. It is difficult to analyze his power, but there was no one but felt and responded to the nobility of his nature and the majesty of his spirit.* From his mother he drew most largely his inspiration and the grandeur of his life.

JOHN E. BROWN

fl. 19th century

"Since my soul is saved and sanctified,
    Feasting, I am feasting,
    Feasting with my Lord."

This hymn was written by a worker in the Holiness movement. He had a brother, L. O. Brown, who worked with him. The above hymn has been used effectively in certain mission assemblies.

WILLIAM CULLEN BRYANT

1794-1878

"Oh deem not they are blest alone
Whose lives a peaceful tenor keep."

This comforting hymn (although to sing it is apt to bring the tears) was written by the "Wordsworth of America." Bryant was born at Cummington, Mass., educated at Williams College, and in early life practised law,† which he did not like and soon abandoned for literary pursuits. At

---

* In my early teens I twice heard Brooks speak. His solemn old year sermon on the text, "The harvest is passed, the summer is ended, and we are not saved," which I heard the night of my fifteenth birthday, struck deep into my soul. I was much impressed both by his commanding personality and his physical beauty.

In later years I have been interested to learn that Brooks was a descendant of John Howland of the Mayflower (as I am also) and that he is connected with my family by various other lines, including those of Otis, Jacob, and Gorham.

† Bryant studied law in West Bridgewater, the ancestral town both of his family and of my own, between which there are genealogical links, both through the Bryants and Aldens, my family being descended from Joseph Alden, third child of John and Priscilla, who settled in Bridgewater as a first proprietor in his father's right.

one period he was editor of the New York Evening Post. He continued his active labors to the age of eighty-three and finally died from the effects of a fall and exposure after the delivery of an oration in Central Park, New York. He left the world without a stain on his name, a beloved poet,* an honored citizen, a pure patriot. At the age of sixty-four, when he had snowwhite hair and a flowing beard, he received the rite of baptism in Naples in 1858. He was a descendant of John and Priscilla Alden of Mayflower fame, through their seventh child, Zachariah.

HERBERT BUFFUM

1879-

"Lord, I have started to walk in the light
* * * * * * * * *
I'm going through."

This gospel hymn† was written by an American hymnist born in La Fayette, Ill., and converted in a Methodist church under the preaching of a Capt. Lee. At the age of seventeen Buffum began to preach on the Pacific coast and was known as the "Boy Preacher." In this enterprise he had phenomenal success. He began at eighteen to publish his gospel songs as sheet music. Mr. Buffum has a wife and three children. He constantly travels as an evangelist and has preached much in small towns in Kansas.

---

* Some of Bryant's poems are immortal. The greatest of these is probably "Thanatopsis" written at the age of nineteen. His "Forest Hymn" is surpassingly beautiful, and so is that poetic gem, "Lines to a waterfowl", the closing stanza of which was often on the lips of my eldest sister as she neared her end,
"He who from zone to zone
Guides through the boundless sky thy certain flight,
In the long way that I must tread alone,
Will lead my steps aright."
When an octogenarian, Bryant wrote the lovely poem beginning,
"As shadows cast by cloud and sun
Flit o'er the summer grass."

† This hymn has been much used in the Holiness movement. Publishers vied with each other in efforts to own the song.

Stephen Greenleaf Bulfinch, D. D.

1809-1870

"Holy Son of God Most High,

*   *   *   *   *   *   *   *

Even Thy word of might appears
Less resistless than Thy tears."

These fine lines are from a hymn on the miracles of Christ written by a Unitarian minister who was a native of Boston, Mass., but went at the age of nine to live in Washington, D. C., his father being the architect of the capitol building there. Stephen Bulfinch was a graduate of Harvard and held pastorates in various Unitarian churches, including those in several New England towns and in Charlestown, S. C. He wrote a number of hymns* which are characterized by solid and tranquil piety and by intellectual merit. Julian says of them that "they deserve a wider circulation than has been accorded to them." Mr. Bulfinch died at East Cambridge, Mass., at the age of sixty-one.

Bishop George Burgess

1809-1866

"The harvest dawn is near,"

This hymn, said to be widely used, was written by a native of Providence, R. I., who became eventually an Episcopal Bishop in Maine. He studied two years in Germany and died at sea near Haiti at the age of fifty-seven. It is said of him that he literally "walked with God." He wrote a metrical version of the Psalms and various hymns.†

---

* One of his hymns begins, "Hail to the Sabbath Day." As a writer of hymns he had few superiors in his generation.

† The following extract from one of his hymns seems almost prophetic of his death at sea.

"While o'er the deep Thy servants sail,

*   *   *   *   *   *   *   *

If life's wide ocean smile or roar,
Still guide them to the heavenly shore
And grant their dust in Christ may sleep,
Abroad, at home, or in the deep."

William Henry Burleigh

1812-1871

"Lead us, O Father, in the paths of peace."

This beautiful hymn was written by a Unitarian reformer, a descendant of William Bradford of the Mayflower. He was born at Woodstock, Conn., apprenticed to a printer, and became in manhood the publisher in Pittsburg, Pa., of "The Christian Witness" and "The Temperance Banner." Later in Hartford, Conn., he edited "The Christian Freeman." From 1849 to 1855 he was agent for the New York Temperance Society, and from 1855 to 1870 was Harbor Master in New York City. He wrote poems and hymns which appeared in various periodicals and collected his verse in a volume in 1841. After his death his widow enlarged and republished the book. Julian lists 14 of his hymns and says of them that they are used more widely in other denominations than in Burleigh's own, and also that they are more used in England* than in America.

John Burroughs

1837-1921

"Serene I fold my hands and wait
Nor care for wind nor tide nor sea;
I rave no more 'gainst time or fate,
For lo! my own shall come to me."

This fine poem entitled "Waiting", which to my mind has the essence of a hymn of faith†, was written by the eminent American naturalist above named. He was born and reared

---

* The most popular of his hymns in England begins thus, "Still will we trust, though earth seems dark and dreary." Burleigh's hymns are full of sweet thought and felicitous expression.

† I append here some other stanzas of this hymn which was so endeared to my late husband that he had it pinned on the wall near his desk.

"I stay my haste, I make delays,
For what avails this eager pace?
I stand amid the eternal ways
And what is mine shall know my face.

Continued on next page

on a farm at Roxbury, N. Y., and was of English and Irish ancestry. He says of himself that he belonged to the open air, and loved nature with a love passing all the books of the world. However, he left home at the age of seventeen, got a little schooling, and taught country schools for eight or nine years. Then he obtained employment as a vault keeper in Washington, D. C. and later was sent with two others by the United States Government to London in charge of $3,000,000 in United States bonds to be exchanged through the Jay Cooke syndicate. After his return to this country he was appointed a United States bank examiner. In 1874 he left the commercial world behind him and purchased a small fruit farm on the Hudson River, giving his summers to farm work and his winters to literary work. He wrote of common things, but his writings made his readers wish to get out of doors and roam about and realize how glorious a world we live in,—even when the trees are bare and the ground covered with snow. He died at the good old age of eighty-six, much beloved.

RICHARD BURTON

1861-

"Christmas tide; it is so warm and sweet—
A whole world's heart at a baby's feet."

These are the closing lines of a pretty Christmas hymn written by a native of Hartford, Conn., son of a minister. Richard Burton was educated at Johns Hopkins University and also taught old English there. At the age of twenty-seven he married, then travelled in Europe for a year, 1889-90.

Asleep, awake, by night or day,
The friends I seek are seeking me;
No wind can drive my bark astray,
Nor change the tide of destiny.

The stars come nightly to the sky;
The tidal wave unto the sea;
Nor time, nor space, nor deep, nor high
Can keep my own away from me."

Some people have debated whether John Burroughs should be counted as a Christian, but this hymn indicates faith in Providence.

Later he became professor of English at the University of Minnesota for nineteen years, resigning that position in 1925 to devote himself to literature. His home subsequently was at Englewood, N. J. He is the author of many beautiful poems, which cannot, however, be classed as hymns. One poem with a semi-hymnlike quality is called "Black Sheep." It is given in "Heart Throbs, No. 1."

C. F. Butler

fl. 19th century

"Since Christ my soul from sin set free
This world hath been a heaven to me.
* * * * * * * *
Where Jesus is, 'tis heaven there."

This hymn, not listed by Julian, was copyrighted by James M. Black and published in a collection called "Christ in Song." (No. 224). This author is probably an American.

Hezekiah Butterworth

1839-1905

"O Church of Christ, our blest abode,"

This hymn was written by an American writer who was on the editorial staff of the Youth's Companion for twenty-five years. He was born at Warwick, R. I. He wrote a book called "The Story of the Hymns" published by the American Tract Society. He was a pleasing writer. A children's hymn of his, entitled "Christ's Lambs", begins, "Little ones of God are we."

Prof. William Herbert Carruth

1859-

"A fire mist and a planet,
A crystal and a cell,
*   *   *   *   *
Some call it evolution,
And others call it God."

These lines are from a celebrated poem of religious tone written by a native of Ossawatomie, Kansas. Carruth was educated at the University of Kansas and at Harvard, where he became a professor of German. Later he took the position of Professor of English at Stanford University, California.

Dr. R. Kelso Carter

fl. 19th century

"Standing on the promises of Christ, my King,"

This familiar hymn was written by a professor in the Military College at Chester, Pa. He was also licensed to preach by the Methodist Episcopal Church and was active in leading camp meetings. Later he became a medical man by profession. He wrote novels as well as hymns. One of his hymns begins, "Cross of Christ, lead onward." He generally composed the music to his own hymns.

Dr. E. T. Cassel

fl. 19th century

"I am a stranger here
*   *   *   *   *
On business for my King."

This hymn, by an author of whom I have no data, is No. 27 in "Jubilant Praise" where it is called "Dr. Chapman's Campaign Hymn." It was copyrighted by E. O. Excell. Cassel also wrote "Loyalty to Christ."

John White Chadwick

1840-1904

"It singeth low in every heart,"

This is the opening line of a hymn* of exquisite beauty and tenderness, written by a Unitarian minister, a native of Marblehead, Mass. John W. Chadwick was perhaps the most distinguished graduate which the Bridgewater Normal School† ever had. He later graduated from the Harvard Divinity School‡ and became pastor of a church at Brooklyn, N. Y., and also a writer for periodicals. He published a book of poems and The life of William Ellery Channing and The life of Theodore Parker. His beautiful hymns§ are included in many Congregational and Unitarian collections. He died in Brooklyn at the age of sixty-four.

Edwin Hubbell Chapin

1814-1880

"Our Father, God! not face to face,"

This hymn was written by a distinguished Universalist preacher, the pastor of the Church of the Divine Paternity in New York City. He was born in Union Village Washington, N. Y., and educated in Bennington, Vt. In his earlier years he was eminent as a lecturer. With J. Q. Adams he edited a prominent Universalist collection of hymns entitled "Hymns of Christian Devotion."

---

* This hymn was written in 1876 for the 25th anniversary dedication of his church in Brooklyn.

† It is a matter of personal interest that Mr. Chadwick graduated from this excellent school in my own native town where five sisters and my only brother graduated.

‡ Mr. Chadwick wrote for his graduating class at Harvard in 1864 a hymn which is characterized by Julian as "one of superior merit". The first line of this is as follows: "Eternal Ruler of the Ceaseless round."

§ One of Chadwick's fine hymns is "A Harvest Song", beginning, "O Thou whose perfect goodness crowns."

CHILSON

fl. 19th century

"How much of joy and comfort,
How much of real cheer,
The dear Lord in His kindness
Gives to His children here."

This is the first stanza of a hymn which was familiar to me in childhood. It is No. 58 in "Vestry Chimes" where it is marked "Poetry by Chilson." I have no other clue to the author.

JAMES FREEMAN CLARKE, D. D.

1810-1888

"Dear Friend whose presence in the house"

This is the opening line of a beautiful hymn written by the above-named Unitarian minister. Dr. Clarke was born at Hanover, New Hampshire, and graduated at Harvard. He was at one time pastor of "The Church of the Disciples" in Boston where he edited a hymn book for the use of his church. Later he went to Louisville, Kentucky, where he edited a journal called "The Western Messenger." He was a powerful writer of theological books.* Julian lists seven of his hymns. When dying† at Lakewood at the age of seventy-eight, he asked to have Lyte's hymn "Abide with me" read to him, then "stepped through the open door into the yet higher life beyond,"—"a heart like a fountain of sunbeams."

---

* I have been particularly impressed with his noble book on "The Ten Great Religions." One of the services Clarke rendered to the Christians of America was in introducing to them Sarah F. Adams' immortal hymn, "Nearer My God to Thee."

† "When his soul began to lay aside the clay, it was not a time of decay but of transfiguration,—ever more faith, more hope, more love." Although in childhood he had a violent temper, in manhood he could not retain a drop of bitterness. No one was more ready to say with sweet humility, "Forgive me."

THOMAS CURTIS CLARK

1877-

"Free us, God of all the worlds,
From the narrow bonds of hate;
To the dreams of brotherhood
May our land be consecrate."

This fine hymn entitled "New Battle for Freedom" was written by one of the editors of the "Christian Century" and a writer in both prose and verse. He was born in Vincennes, Indiana, and now makes his home in Maywood, Illinois.

JOHN R. CLEMENTS

1868-

"Somebody did a golden deed,"

This popular hymn was written by a practical man in the grocery business who has written several hymns that are well known.

I list Mr. Clements with the American hymnists, although he was in reality born in Ireland, but was brought in his infancy to the United States and is identified with this country. He was educated in a rural school, and his religious aspirations were formed through his contact with the Christian Endeavor movement. He has a pleasing and genial face. Julian does not list his hymns.

S. O'MALLY CLUFF (OR CLOUGH)

fl. 1874

"I have a Saviour, He's pleading in glory,
For you I am praying,"

This useful gospel hymn was published in Ira D. Sankey's "Songs and Solos." Julian mentions it, but I have no information about the author. Sankey found this hymn in a leaflet in Ireland, and set it to music in 1874.

Oscar Clute

1840-1901

"O love of God most full, O love of God most free"

This hymn is found in the Pilgrim Hymnal published 1904.

Samuel Valentine Cole, D. D.

1851-

"O Thou who sealest up the past,
    The days slip from us, and the years
    Grow silent with their hopes and fears,
    'Tis Thine to keep all things at last."

This New Year's hymn was written in 1887 by a New England minister, a native of Machiasport, Maine. Mr. Cole graduated at Bowdoin College and Andover Theological Seminary. In 1897 he became president of Wheaton Seminary. In 1901 he published a book of poems which contained the above-mentioned hymn. This was included also in "The Pilgrim Hymnal" published in 1904.

Daniel C. Colesworthy

1810-1893

"A little word in kindness spoken,"

This hymn is one of two listed by Julian as being written by the above-named editor, printer, and bookseller, born in Portland, Maine, where he in manhood edited a paper called "The Portland Tribune." Later he removed to Boston. He published several volumes of verse and Sunday School hymns.

Moncure Daniel Conway

1832-1907

"O heart, my heart, when clouds of fate
Shroud thy fair sky and on thee beat,
With childlike trust, attunéd wait;
Win from each storm its music sweet."

This is the closing stanza of a hymn written by an obscure and almost forgotten writer who was first a Methodist and became later a Unitarian minister. The "clouds of fate" certainly overhung his stormy career. He was driven from Virginia, his native state, on account of his political opinions, and dismissed from a Washington church because of his position about slavery. After this he became a lecturer on emancipation in Ohio, New England, and in London where he served a Unitarian church. He was the son of a slave holder, and during the Civil War period he colonized his father's slaves at Yellow Springs,* Ohio. He wrote many books and was at one time editor of a paper in Boston called "The Commonwealth."

George Cooper

b. New York City 1840

"There are lonely hearts to cherish"

This is one of the useful hymns in Ira D. Sankey's "Songs and Solos." I do not find any further facts about the man who wrote it.

---

* It is a matter of regret to me that I did not know about this heroic man during the two months I spent at Yellow Springs, Ohio, in 1927, putting a book through the Antioch Press. How eagerly, had I known, should I have obtained data about him!

Rev. W. D. Cornell

fl. 19th or early 20th century

"Far away in the depths ot my spirit tonight,

* * * * * * * *

Peace, peace, wonderful peace,"

This hymn which is found in "Christ in Song" (No. 210) was written by some obscure minister of whom I have no further data. He is not mentioned by Julian, and was probably an American. His hymn is greatly beloved.

Maxwell N. Cornelius, D. D.

fl. 19th century

"Not now, but in the coming years

* * * * * * * *

Sometime we'll understand."

This hymn, which has been a comfort to many, was written by a Presbyterian minister who was brought up on a Pennsylvania farm and learned to be a brick mason. In erecting a house his leg was broken and had to be amputated. When the doctors were about to operate, Cornelius requested that he might play a tune on his violin, as it might be his last. He played a melody so sweet that the physicians wept. Cornelius survived the operation, but was maimed for life. He then went to college, and became the pastor of a church at Altoona, Pa. Later he went to California for his wife's health and he built the largest Presbyterian church in Pasadena. Those who subscribed the money failed, and Cornelius had to meet their obligations, but cleared the church of debt. His wife died and he preached the funeral sermon and read the above hymn at the close. It was later published in a paper where Major Whittle read it and gave it to McGranahan who set it to music.

CHRISTOPHER CHRISTIAN COX, M. D.

1816-1882

"Silently the shades of evening"

This beautiful twilight hymn was written by a Maryland physician born at Baltimore who practised medicine there in his adult life. In 1861 he became a Brigade Surgeon in the United States Army. His home was then in Washington, D. C. He was a member of the Protestant Episcopal Church. The above-mentioned hymn was popular in my childhood days. Julian lists one more of his hymns which begins, "The burden of my sins, O Lord,".

ARTHUR CLEVELAND COXE

1818-1896

"Saviour, sprinkle many nations."

This superb missionary hymn was written by the Rector of St. John's Church in Hartford, Conn., who became later the Bishop of the Western Diocese of New York. Arthur Coxe was born in Mendham, New Jersey, and was the son of an eminent Presbyterian minister. He wrote a number of well known hymns; one begins, "In the silent midnight watches,". Julian calls this an "impressive moral poem." Coxe also wrote these well known lines,

> "O where are kings and empires now,
> Of old that went and came?"

Bishop Coxe was a man of "over scrupulous modesty."* He was a member of the hymnal committee of his church and he refused to permit his own lyrics to be inserted in the American Episcopal Hymnal. These are used, however, in the English edition and in the collections of all other denominational hymnals in America. Bishop Coxe had a rare and abiding charm about his personality, although one writer says of him that he was "brilliant rather than weighty, and ornamental rather than solid."

---

* Bishop Coxe said, "Alas, I feel pretty sure I have never produced one hymn, justly so called." In this I think posterity will entirely disagree with him. F. A. Jones calls the second stanza of "Saviour, sprinkle many nations" one of the very finest in the English language.

WILLIAM CROSSWELL, D. D.

1804-1844

"Lord, lead the way the Saviour went."

This hymn, written for the Sisters of Mercy of the Howard Benevolent Society of Boston, is considered by Julian as the best American hymn for benevolent occasions. The author was an Episcopal rector in New York and Boston. In the latter city he died suddenly at the age of forty in his church at the close of a service. Instead of rising from his knees at the close of the collect he sank to the floor and expired. This occurred in the Church of the Advent, of which he was the founder.

Dr. Crosswell was born at Hudson, N. Y., and graduated at Yale where he studied law, but eventually took Holy Orders. His memoir was written by his father who was a clergyman in New Haven, Conn. His hymns are characterized by gracefulness and sweetness. One of these begins,

"The lilied fields behold! What king in his array
Of purple pall and cloth of gold shines gorgeously as they?

CHRISTOPHER PEARSE CROUCH

1813-1892

"Thought is deeper than all speech;
Feeling deeper than all thought."

These lines are from the pen of the son of William Crouch, a distinguished Chief Justice of the United States. Christopher Crouch was born in Alexandria, Va., and graduated at the Columbian College in Washington. He studied theology and preached for seven years, but became later a landscape painter and a writer for the best periodicals. His later home was in Cambridge, Mass. Schaff's Library of Religious Poetry contains several beautiful poems by him.

William Orcutt Cushing*

1823-

"O safe to the Rock that is higher than I"

This hymn of which the author said it was the outgrowth of many heart conflicts and soul yearnings, with the history of many battles behind it, was written by a native of Hingham, Mass. Cushing wrote a number of gospel hymns† which were printed in Sankey's "Songs and Solos." There is a hymn beginning, "There'll be no dark valley when Jesus comes," of which Cushing composed the first line and Sankey the rest. Julian ascribed it to the joint authorship of the two. Cushing's Sunday School hymn beginning,

"When he cometh, when he cometh
To make up his jewels,"

was once sung at a novel impromptu international concert in the steerage of a great Atlantic liner. A service was being held for the emigrants and a hymn was wanted that everybody knew. It was found that nearly everyone knew "Jewels."

Richard Henry Dana

1787-1879

"A voice within us speaks the startling word,
'Man, thou shalt never die.' "

These lines are culled from a beautiful sacred poem entitled, "The Husband's and Wife's Grave" written by the poet, novelist, and editor above named. He was the son of Judge Francis Dana, Chief Justice of the Commonwealth. He was

---

* Some hymn books give the name as W. W. Cushing.
† Some of these are:
  "Beautiful Valley of Eden"
  "Ring the bells of Heaven"
  "We are watching, we are waiting"
  "Down in the valley with my Saviour I would go"
  "Under His wings"

A story is told of the last mentioned hymn that a dying man in western Massachusetts asked to have it sung to him, and said that his conversion was due to hearing it sung in former years.

born in Cambridge and rusticated from Harvard because of his implication in what is known as the "Rotten Cabbage Rebellion." He never returned to Harvard where he had been a poor scholar. He devoted himself to literature, started the "North American Review", and became a writer of great merit, both philosophical and imaginative. He was a member of the Congregational Church, and was an opponent of Channing. He had a country home on Cape Ann. He was for fifty years an invalid, but died at an advanced age.

Samuel Davies, D. D.

1724-1761

"Great God of wonders, all Thy ways"

This is the opening line of one* of the hymns in the style of Watts written by the Successor of Jonathan Edwards as President of Princeton Seminary. Davies was born at Newcastle, Delaware. He was sent at the age of twenty-nine to England to solicit funds for the College of New Jersey. In this he was successful. After the defeat of Braddock he preached a sermon on the disaster to which he appended this prophecy about Washington, "That heroic youth, Col. Washington, whom I cannot but hope Providence has preserved for some important service to his country." Davies died at the early age of thirty-seven.

Frank M. Davis

fl. 19th century

"Savior, lead me lest I stray"

This hymn, No. 436 in the Service Hymnal, and also the music to which it is set, are by the above named author.

---

* This hymn has been included in more than a hundred collections.

HENRY MORTON DEXTER, D. D.

1821-1890

"Shepherd of tender youth, guiding in love and truth,"

This beautiful translation of the earliest Christian hymn by Clement of Alexandria was made by a prominent Congregational minister born in Plympton, Mass. Dr. Dexter was for many years the editor of the Congregationalist and wrote many standard books on Congregationalism. He lived in Boston and had a brilliant intellectual life.

CHARLES ALBERT DICKINSON, D. D.

1849-1907

"O golden day so long desired
Born of a darksome night."

This inspiring Christian Endeavor hymn sung by great masses of young people was written as an expression of thankfulness after a terrific storm on the Atlantic as the above named author was returning with Dr. C. E. Clark from England where they had been promoting the Christian Endeavor movement. Dr. Dickinson was born at Westminster, Va., and graduated at Harvard in 1876. He held successive pastorates at Portland, Lowell, and Boston, where he was the first exponent of the Institutional Church, developing a great bee-hive of Christian industry on many lines. Later, on account of failing health, he went to Sacramento, Cal., where he was pastor for two years before his death. He was a lovable man, full of good cheer and friendliness. In early life he established at his birthplace in Virginia a useful home for boys and girls.

George Washington Doane, D. D.

1799-1859

"Softly now the light of day"

This well-known hymn was written by a native of Trenton, N. J., who became an Episcopal Bishop in his own state. He graduated at Union College, Schenectady, N. Y., after which he was successively Professor at Trinity College, Hartford, Conn., Rector in Boston, and then for twenty-seven years Bishop of New Jersey. He was one of the great prelates of his time, a man of exceptional talent and force of character. No rain or cold could keep him from his appointments. His energy was a ceaseless fire within him. He also had the ability to sleep anywhere at will. He went through severe* troubles which left their mark on his later writing.†

William Croswell Doane, D. D.

1832-1913

"Ancient of Days, who sittest throned in glory,"

This hymn, written in 1886 for the bicentenary of the city of Albany, is the composition of an Episcopal Bishop born in Boston. Wm. C. Doane was a son of Bishop George W. Doane. He was a writer of both prose and verse and was a D.D. of Oxford and an L.L.D. of Cambridge.

---

* At one time Bishop Doane was obliged to go into bankruptcy on account of the great charitable institutions he had founded, but he assigned all his own property to his creditors.

† Julian lists 19 of his hymns; one of these is considered one of the great English hymns. It begins, "Thou art the Way to Thee alone." A child poem beginning " 'What is that, mother?' 'The lark, my child.' " was a great favorite in my early childhood.

William Howard Doane

1831-

"No one knows but Jesus."

This hymn was written by a native of Preston, Conn., who was a mechanical as well as a musical genius,—a somewhat unusual combination of talents. Mr. Doane patented more than seventy inventions, but he is chiefly known as the composer of the tunes of many popular Sunday School and gospel hymns,* a thousand melodies. He studied for the musical profession at Woodstock, Conn., under eminent masters, and obtained the degree of Doctor of Music. He became well-known as the trainer of choirs and made his home in Cincinnati, Ohio, where he was superintendent of a large Baptist Sunday School. He edited eight hymn books.

John A. Dorgan

1836-1867

"Thy sneer I can forgive
  Because I know the strength of destiny;
  Until my task is done I cannot die,†
  And then I would not live."

This is the concluding stanza of a poem called "Fate" found in Whittier's "Songs of Three Centuries." The author was a talented Philadelphia lawyer who died of consumption at the age of thirty-one. The poem is scarcely a hymn, but virile Christian spirit is in it.

---

* These melodies include those of—
    "Near the Cross"
    "Safe in the arms of Jesus."
    "Rescue the perishing"
    "Pass me not, oh gentle Saviour."
    "Tell me the old, old story."
  † In similar vein my brother-in-law Dr. C. L. Fisher used to say, "Man is immortal till his work is done; then how quick he snuffs out."

George Duffield, Jr., D. D.

1818-1888

"Stand up, stand up for Jesus,"

This hymn, which has been sung until nearly threadbare, was written by a Presbyterian minister of Detroit, Mich. The inspiration came to the author from the dying message of the young pastor of the Church of the Epiphany in Philadelphia, named Dudley Tyng. He had been the leader of a great union prayer meeting in a mighty revival season. He died as the result of a terrible accident. When nearing death he was asked if he had any message for his ministerial brethren, and he replied, "Tell them to stand up for Jesus." He was too sick later to know his family. He was asked, "Do you know Jesus?" He said, "I know Jesus; I have a steadfast trust in Jesus." Then he was asked, "Are you happy?" He replied, "Perfectly happy." He was buried amidst 10,000 weeping people. In his life he had been much persecuted for pleading the cause of the slave. This hymn, which incorporates the message of this devoted soul, is a precious legacy which Dr. Duffield has bequeathed to the world. Duffield was born at Carlisle, Pa., educated at Yale, and held pastoral charges at various places. Julian lists five of his hymns.

Paul Lawrence Dunbar

1872-1906

"O lil' lamb out in de col',
De Mastah call you to de fol' "

This pretty hymn in negro dialect was written by the first full-blooded negro to distinguish himself in literature. (Dumas in France and Pushkin in Russia were mulattoes, not full-blooded negroes.) Dunbar's parents were slaves. His father escaped from slavery in Kentucky and went to Canada. His mother was freed by the events of the Civil

War. Their son Paul was born in Dayton, Ohio. The father, who was a plasterer, taught himself to read. He died, leaving his wife and son to struggle with poverty. Paul supported himself as an elevator boy and later as an assistant in the Library of Congress, writing his verse as a recreation. In 1898 he married and after that he devoted himself entirely to literature. He published a book of poems to which W. D. Howells wrote an introduction, highly commending Dunbar's genius. At the age of only thirty-four Dunbar died in his home in Dayton, Ohio, of tuberculosis.

Timothy Dwight

1752-1817

"I love Thy kingdom, Lord,"

This standard hymn was written in 1800 by the prominent theologian whose name is considered by Julian the most important one in early American hymnology. Dwight was the grandson of Jonathan Edwards, and was for twenty-two years the president of Yale College, which was his own Alma Mater. His birthplace was Northampton, Mass., and he was a precocious child who learned the alphabet at one lesson, and at eight years of age was ready for the freshman class at Yale in Latin and Greek, but did not enter until later, his mother having wisely opposed his frenzy for the classics by diversions in history and geography. It is not altogether surprising, after these intellectual feats in childhood, that we learn that he was not really a well man ever; that he was seldom free from bodily pain. However, in spite of this chronic condition, Yale's greatness begins with his presidency when he was forty-three years old. Julian lists fifteen of Dwight's hymns and speaks well of them, but there seems to be a difference of opinion as to his real intellectual power. One writer characterizes him as fertile in the production of "respectable ideas" which are sufficiently commonplace but not original. We get on the one hand a picture of a sort of George Babbitt personality, thrust into prominence by heredity and environment. On the other hand we find him highly eulogized as an illustrious writer and educational leader. One of his hymns begins, "While life prolongs its precious light."

SIDNEY DYER

1814-1898

"Time is earnest, passing by,"

This hymn is sometimes attributed to Joseph Dyer, an English hymnist, but its authorship is doubtful. It first appeared anonymously in 1857.

Sidney Dyer was born at White Creek, N. Y. From 1831 to 1840 he served in the United State Army. Later he was a Baptist missionary to the Choctaw Indians. Later still he was a pastor in Indianapolis, and then was secretary of the Baptist Publishing Society. Sixteen of his hymns were included in "The Southwestern Psalmist." The well-known hymn beginning, "Work for the night is coming," is often attributed to this author but Julian says the real author is Anna L. Walker of Canada. Dyer wrote a hymn on the same subject; hence the confusion.

EL NATHAN

19th century

"There shall be showers of blessing,"

This hymn, and also" Why not now" which appears over the above signature, was written by Major D. W. Whittle. El Nathan is an early nom de plume used by him. "Come on the wings of the morning" is also attributed to "El Nathan."

Ralph Waldo Emerson

1803-1882

"God said, 'I am tired of kings;
I suffer them no more;
Into my ear the morning brings
The outrage of the poor'."

This is a stanza* of the "Boston hymn" written by "The Sage of Concord." Emerson was the eighth in succession of a long line of Puritan ministers. He was born in Boston where his father died when Ralph was seven years old. He entered Harvard at fourteen but did not distinguish himself as a student. Later, at the age of twenty-nine, he resigned his position as a Unitarian minister because of scruples against administering the Lord's Supper. He then devoted himself to writing† and lecturing. Much of his inspiration was gained through the transcendent movement. Although not a reformer in the technical sense, he took a progressive view of public questions such as anti-slavery and woman's suffrage. In 1847 he went to England where he was warmly received. At the age of seventy-nine he died in Concord.

Prof. O. E. Excell

1851-1921

"Do you know the world is dying
For a little bit of love?"

This popular hymn was written by a native of Uniontown,

---

* Other stanzas of this hymn are as follows:
"I will divide my goods,
    Call in the wretch and slave,
None shall rule but the humble,
    And none but toil shall have.
* * * * * * * * *
My will fulfilled shall be,
    For in daylight as in dark
My thunderbolt has eyes to see
    His way home to the mark."

† In his latest publication he says, "Unlovely, nay frightful, is the solitude of the soul which is without God in the world. In this chill, houseless, fatherless, aimless case is the man who hears only the sound of his own footsteps in God's resplendent creation." He called himself a Christian theist.

Pa. When he was twenty he married and the pair moved
to the Pacific coast where Excell worked as a brick mason
but studied music in spare hours. He had a way of singing
about his work and had a remarkable voice of natural range
and power. One day Sam Jones, the evangelist, happened
to visit the place where Excell was working and was so attracted by the voice that he engaged him as his chorister,
with the result that they worked together for twenty years.
In 1881 Mr. Excell began to publish hymn books* and at
the time of his death was selling 100,000 hymn books an-
nually. He was also a great leader of multitudes in song.
He would sometimes lead 20,000 or 50,000 people in singing. He died at the age of seventy in the Wesley Memorial
Hospital in Chicago. He was a man of great sympathy and
courtesy. One of his close associates said of him that he
had never been known to lose his temper before an audience.
He had a kind smile and had a true faith in God.

Rev. Harry Webb Farrington

1880-1930

"I know not how that Bethlehem's Babe
From sin should set me free."

This hymn, which is considered one of the ten best produced in America in the first quarter of the twentieth century
(as published in a list given in the Western Christian Advocate in 1928) was written by a minister who was born in
the British West Indies. He lost his mother early and was
thrown on his own resources. He has become a favorite
speaker to school children. It is said of him that he has
addressed three million of them. One of his hymns is en-

---

* Some of his well-known hymns are these:
    "Since I have been redeemed."
    "My Father knows."
Excell also composed the music for the following well-known hymns:
    "Jesus bids us come"
    "Count your blessings"
    "Let the Saviour in"
    "Heavenly sunlight"

titled "The Men in Air." Others are "Dear Lord who sought at dawn of day," "We tarry Lord, do not depart." "Almighty God Thy power has wrought." "Our Father made the lovely earth." "Lord rend the veils of creed and race," and "Strong righteous Man of Galilee."

EUGENE FIELD

1850-1895

"There burns a star o'er Bethlehem town,"

This Christmas hymn was written by the witty journalist called "The Chicago Humorist." Field was born in St. Louis, Mo., and graduated at the Missouri State University. He has published several books of verse which abound in delicate pathos. He is the author of several hymns which have come into common use, and of many poems for children.

THE HYMNS OF LONG AGO.

"There's lots o' music in 'em, the hymns of long ago;
An' when some gray-haired brother sings the ones I used to know,
I sorter want to take a hand—I think o' days gone by,
'On Jordan's stormy banks I stand, and cast a wistful eye.'

There's lot o' music in 'em—those dear, sweet hymns of old.
With visions bright of lands of light and shining streets of gold;
And I hear 'em ringing—singing, where memory dreaming stands,
'From Greenland's icy mountains to India's coral strands.'

They seem to sing forever of holier, sweeter days,
When the lillies of the love of God bloomed white in all the ways;
And I want to hear their music from the old-time meetin's rise,
' 'Till I can read my title clear to mansions in the skies.'

We hardly needed singin' books in them old days; we knew
The words, the tune of every one the dear old hymn book through!
We had no blaring trumpets then, no organs built for show.
We only sang to praise the Lord, 'from whom all blessings flow.'

If I can only hear 'em, I'll pass without a sigh
To Canaan's fair and happy land where my possessions lie."

—*Anon*

JAMES THOMAS FIELDS

1817-1881

"Thou who has called our being here,"

This is the opening line of a child's hymn written by an eminent editor of the "Atlantic Monthly." Fields was born in Portsmouth, N. H., and, after receiving a high school education, became a clerk in a Boston book store, where he seemed to know intuitively what sort of book it was a customer wanted. He began to write early with "that indefinable quality which distinguishes a literary artist from a literary artisan." He became a partner in the publishing house of Ticknor and Fields. Through repeated visits to Europe he had a wide acquaintance with literary men abroad. He published books in both prose and verse and lectured in the United States. He died in Boston at the age of sixty-four.

REV. C. M. FILLMORE

fl. 19th century

"Tell mother I'll be there"

This useful hymn was written by a minister of the Christian Church. He had a brother, James H. Fillmore who was a music publisher and also a farmer brother named Fred. All three were fine men and all three wrote hymns.

JAMES FLINT, D. D.

1779-1855

"Happy the unrepining poor."

This hymn, which appeared in Sewall's "New York Collection" in 1820 was written by a Unitarian minister who was born at Reading, Mass. and graduated at Harvard. His first pastorate was at East Bridgewater*, Mass., and his next pastorate at Salem. Julian lists thirty-nine of his hymns.

---

* This connection with East Bridgewater interests me, as this place was originally part of my native town of Bridgewater.

Daniel S. Ford

1822-1899

"The bread that giveth strength I want to give;
The water pure that bids the thirsty live.
I want to help the fainting day by day;
I'm sure I shall not pass again this way."

This is the first stanza of a poem found after his death
in the desk of the proprietor and editor of "The Youth's
Companion."* Although it is not sure that the poem was
written by Mr. Ford, yet it had been evidently handled
and kept by him a long time. It gives such a true picture
of the character and daily life of this useful man, patient,
wise, tender, tactful, that I venture to place it under his
name, though it is probably anonymous. It is found in
Heart Throbs No. 1.

James Freeman

1759-1835

"Lord of the worlds below,"

This hymn, based on Thompson's "Seasons", was written
by the pastor of King's Chapel in Boston. Freeman was
the first avowed preacher of Unitarianism in the United
States. He was born at Charlestown, Mass., and was a
graduate of Harvard. He helped to change the historic parish
in Boston from Episcopacy to the then new ways of teaching and discipline.

---

* Ford bought "The Youth's Companion" from its founder, N. P.
Willis.   When Mr. Ford died the paper had 500,000 subscribers.
   The poem above quoted is found on p. 106 in "Heart Throbs" No. 1.
I admired it sufficiently to set it to music.

J. E. FRENCH

fl. 19th or 20th century

"We find many people who can't understand
Why we are so happy and free.
*   *   *   *   *   *   *   *   *
Oh, this is like heaven to me."

I have no data beyond his name about the writer of this little religious ditty which is sung with gusto in certain humble assemblies. The critics who despise such doggerel would be happier, perhaps, for the experience which it embodies, which effervesces with fervor and ecstasy.

WILLIAM GOODELL FROST, D. D.

1854-

"Thou dear Disposer of my ways,
　　My fathers' God and mine,
Who leadst through bright or clouded days
　　With tenderness divine,

I bless Thee for my priceless part
　　In being, thought, and power,
And heavenly calls that reached my heart
　　In youth's inspiring hour;

That I have heard Thy prophets speak
　　And seen Thy kingdom grow,
And shared the toil, and on my cheek
　　Have felt the battle's glow.

But from that field of glorious strife,
　　Thou didst recall my way,
Taught me Thou didst not need my life,
　　Showed me how brief earth's day.

Now since from weakness' deathlike swoon
　　Thou givst a second birth,
With chastened joy I'd seize the boon—
　　Feel heaven more near than earth."

This beautiful hymn entitled "Recovery" was written by the man who for twenty-eight years was President of Berea College, Ky., foremost in the work for the mountain region. He was born at Leroy, N. Y., and named for his grandfather, Wm. Goodell, a co-worker with Whittier and Garrison for anti-slavery. Pres. Frost was educated at Oberlin where he became Professor of Greek, and where his three sons by his first marriage were born, their mother being Louise Raney. They are now filling useful positions in the world. By his second marriage to Eleanor Marsh* there were two children, the son being a victim of the World War, leaving a terrible sorrow in that beautiful home. The only daughter married a doctor and lives far away.

NATHANIEL LANGDON FROTHINGHAM, D. D.

1793-1870

"O God, whose presence glows in all,"

This is the opening line of an ordination hymn written by the pastor for thirty-five years of the Unitarian church in Boston, his native city. Dr. Frothingham was an attendant of this same church for twenty years more after his strength and sight failed. He was a graduate of Harvard, and an accomplished scholar and a courteous gentleman. Julian lists three of his hymns.†

---

* Mrs. Frost has been a most efficient helper to her talented husband in his wonderful work for the world at Berea. These two have been personal friends of my deceased husband and myself from our college days in Oberlin, and I have had the privilege of visiting their charming home many times. Dr. Frost's eloquence in public addresses has always been an inspiration to me.

† Here are three of his lines that please me,

"Cast thy bread upon the waters;
Crave from Fortune no indenture;
Boldly on, and venture, venture."

He published two volumes of poems, translations from the German, showing a refined taste and an elegant diction.

Octavius Brooks Frothingham

1822-1895

"Thou Lord of Hosts, whose guiding hand,"

This is the opening line of a hymn written by the leader of the "Free Religious Movement." Octavius B. Frothingham was born in Boston and was the son of Dr. N. L. Frothingham, and like him a Unitarian minister. His preaching was eloquent and impressive, and he ranked high as a scholar. He held pastorates at Salem, Mass., Jersey City, and New York City. He published many prose books on religion of the rationalistic type. Julian mentions two hymns of his. He is called "brave and brilliant."

William Henry Furness, D. D.

1802-1896

"Feeble, helpless, how shall I"

This is the opening line of one of many hymns* written by a classmate of Emerson who was born at Boston and became in 1824 the pastor of Dr. Priestley's church in Philadelphia. His pastorate lasted fifty years. When he had written 1500 sermons he stopped counting. He was a friend of the slave and an ardent supporter of the anti-slavery cause. He never went to Europe. At the age of twenty-three he married Miss Jenks of Salem. They had a son named for his father, who became a successful portrait painter in Philadelphia. Among his sitters were his father, Lucretia Mott, Charles Sumner, and other celebrities. The son died at the age of thirty-nine while the father lived to the age of ninety-four, the sole survivor of the class of 1820 at Harvard.

---

* One of his hymns begins, "Slowly by Thy hand unfurled," and another begins,
> "O for a prophet's fire,
> O for an angel's tongue."
The Quaker's doctrine of the inner light is thus expressed by Furness,
> "That I may henceforth heed whate'er
> Thy voice within me saith."
Julian lists fifteen of his hymns and songs. Some of them have great merit.

CHARLES S. GABRIEL

fl. 19th and 20th centuries

"When all my labors and trials are o'er
* * * * * * * *
O that will be glory for me."

This hymn* known as "the glory song" was, with its music, written by a hymnist characterized by George B. Stebbins as "the most gifted and brilliant writer of gospel hymns for forty years." This is an arresting statement. Julian does not list this author at all, but Gabriel has written several well-known hymns. Among these are "He lifted me" and "I never will cease to love Him," and "Where the gates swing outward never".† Charles Gabriel was born in the late eighteen fifties on an Iowa farm in a little board shanty and went to school in the winters only sitting on log benches without backs. He began to write hymns in early boyhood. At the age of seventeen his mother gave him from her scanty store $25 and he went away to seek his career in California where he became a self-made man. In 1892 he came to Chicago with a wife and baby, a plug hat, a cane, and $16 in cash, and found employment assisting Dr. J. F. Berry to prepare an Epworth League Song Book. Since then he has compiled or assisted to compile 35 books of gospel songs partly in connection with E. O. Excell. One of his hymns begins, "There's a call comes ringing o'er the restless wave."

WILLIAM CHANNING GANNETT

1840-

"He hides within the lily
A strong and tender care."

This is the best known hymn of a Unitarian preacher,

---

* This song was inspired by the frequent ejaculations of "Glory!" by an old man known as "Old Glory Face." It was the campaign song of Torry and Alexander in Australia, New Zealand, and Tasmania. More than a hundred million copies have been printed, many translations made.

† This hymn was suggested by the words of Gabriel's son as he said good-bye, going to the World War.

born in Boston, educated at Harvard, and in 1889 becoming the pastor of a church in Rochester, N. Y. Julian lists ten of Gannett's hymns and says that they are characterized by poetic beauty and loving sympathy, and that they are widely appreciated in America and to some extent in Great Britain.

WILLIAM LLOYD GARRISON

1805-1879

"Unto the winds and waves I now commit
My body, subject to the will of heaven."

These are the opening lines of a splendid sonnet entitled, "On leaving my native land for England." It cannot be classed as a hymn, yet it is included in "A Library of Sacred Poetry." Garrison, the philanthropist and writer for the anti-slavery cause, was born at Newburyport, Mass., and died in New York at the age of seventy-four. He was imprisoned on account of his efforts in behalf of the slaves and while in jail he wrote a remarkable sonnet on "The Free Mind," also found in "The Library of Sacred Poetry." He lived to see slavery abolished by constitutional amendment. He was the editor of the Liberator, and was received with distinction in England. Oswald Garrison Villard is his grandson and seems to be a "chip of the old block."

RICHARD WATSON GILDER, L. L. D.

1844-1909

"In myriad forms, by myriad names"

This hymn, printed in a collection called "In Excelsis" and sung at the presentation of the Egyptian obelisk to the city of New York in 1881, was written by the associate editor with J. G. Holland of Scribner's Monthly from its beginning in 1870, and after Mr. Holland's death, Mr. Gilder became editor-in-chief. He published several books of poems and three of his hymns are in use in hymnals. He was born at Bordentown, N. J. and educated at a seminary in Flushing, L. I.

Rev. Joseph Henry Gilmore

1834-1918

"He leadeth me, oh blessed thought"*

This well-known hymn was written in 1859 by the pastor of a Philadelphia Baptist church. He had been giving that Wednesday evening a lecture on the twenty-third psalm, and later was with his wife in the parlor of one of his deacons. The hymn was written there and given to his wife, who, without his knowledge, sent it to the "Watchman and Reflector." It was set to music by Wm. B. Bradbury. Later, when Mr. Gilmore was applying for the pastorate of a Rochester church, he was surprised to find that his hymn was already in use there. Mr. Gilmore was a native of Boston and a graduate of Brown University. He became Professor of Hebrew at Newton Theological Seminary at the age of twenty-seven, and at the age of thirty-four was made Professor of Logic in Rochester University, New York. He wrote music as well as composed hymns.

H. L. Gilmour

fl. 19th century

"My soul in sad exile was out on life's sea,
* * * * * * * *
I've anchored my soul in the Haven of Rest."

This pretty and useful hymn was written by a dentist who for twenty years conducted an orchestra at Ocean Grove Camp Meeting in New Jersey. The hymn is found in "Christ in Song" No. 211.

---

* It may be of interest to note that this hymn was running in my mind during the first night that I ever spent on a railroad train. I was sixteen years old and was on my first journey from Massachusetts to Oberlin to enter college there. It was a great step into the unknown to me, and my whole life since then has been shaped from that event from which grew my marriage and my career in African mission work. Later in Africa I wrote a poem on this hymn and its fulfillment in my own life. This was published in a small volume of my poems called "Natal Lilies."

WASHINGTON GLADDEN, D. D.

1836-1916

"O Master, let me walk with Thee,"

This much used and valued hymn was written in 1879 by a Congregational minister born in Pottsgrove, Pa., and educated at Williams College. He was for a time editor of the "New York Independent," and of "Sunday Afternoon." In 1882 he became the pastor of the First Congregational Church in Cincinnati. He was a distinguished leader among Congregationalists. I believe, however, that his fame will eventually rest upon the authorship of the above-mentioned hymn of great beauty and power.

Dr. Gladden took a spirited stand against the receiving by the missionary board of his denomination a large donation from John D. Rockefeller, calling it "tainted money" because he thought unscrupulous methods had been used in Rockefeller's business. Dr. Gladden did not win out in this controversy, but he showed in it his indomitable courage and honesty.

ADONIRAM JUDSON GORDON

1836-1895

"O Spirit's anointing, for service appointing"

This hymn was written at the request of a hundred college students at the Northfield Bible School in 1886 who had given themselves to the work of foreign missions. The author was Dr. Gordon, the beloved pastor of the Clarendon St. church in Boston. He was born at New Hampton, N. H., and graduated at Brown University. He was a descendant of John Robinson of Leyden. The hymn* beginning, "My Jesus, I love Thee," is sometimes erroneously attributed to Dr. Gordon who found it in a London hymn book and set it to music.

---

* This popular hymn was sung with great power in a train en route for Chicago at the time of the Columbian Exposition. The singers were a husband and wife. Another of Gordon's hymns begins, "O Holy Ghost, arise,".

F. M. GRAHAM

fl. 19th or early 20th century

"There was a time on earth
When in the book of heaven
* * * * * * * *
The old account was settled long ago."

This popular gospel hymn was written by the above named obscure hymnist about whom I have found no data except that the music of the hymn was also composed by him. It is No. 122 in "The Air-Pilot Hymnal". It is often used in revival meetings.

FREDERICK A. GRAVES

1856-1927

"O my brother, do you know the Saviour,
* * * * * * * *
There's honey in the Rock for you."

This taking gospel hymn was written by a devout layman who lived in Zion City, presumably one of Dr. Dowie's congregation. He has a son in the business of gospel hymn publishing in St. Louis.

Mr. Graves has written many hymns, two of which are familiar to me besides "The honey in the Rock." The title of one of these is "He was nailed to the cross for me" and the other is "He'll never forget to keep me." I had the pleasure of meeting Mr. Graves once in his home. He had a very pleasing personality and both he and his wife had had remarkable healings which are described in a pamphlet entitled "The New Gift." Mr. Graves was born in Williamstown, Mass. His father died when he was six years old. His widowed mother placed him (before her death which occurred soon after) with a Mr. Russell who lived on the Connecticut River near Northfield. At the age of twenty-one Frederick went to Minnesota to join an elder brother. He had developed both a religious character and proficiency in singing, and was engaged by an evangelist as a singer in gospel meetings. He and his wife published a little hymnal.

JAMES M. GRAY, D. D.

1851-

"Not silver nor gold hath obtained my redemption."

This hymn was written by a preacher connected with the Moody Church and Bible Institute of Chicago—one of the trustees of that great and useful institution. Dr. Gray's home was in Chicago and he is the author of many religious books. He is an opponent of Christian Science and seems to connect Spiritualism with the fallen angels.

THOMAS GRAY, JR. M. D.

1803-1849

"We come in childhood's innocence,"

This is one of the children's hymns written by the above-named Unitarian doctor of Boston. He was born in Roxbury, Mass., the son of a Unitarian preacher. He graduated at Harvard at the age of twenty, and after traveling in England and on the continent, settled down to professional life, eventually exchanging the practise of medicine for chemistry. His hymns are commended by Julian as of more than ordinary merit. One hymn which is popular with children begins, "Goodnight, goodnight, our song is said." His death at the age of forty-six seems premature.

HERMANN HAGEDORN

1882-

"Friend of the free, when man's weak barriers fall,
Thou art a wall, great Lord! Thou art a wall!"

These lines taken from the "Hymn of the Free Peoples"
were written by an instructor of English at Harvard, his
alma mater. Professor Hagedorn was born in New York,
and has written both in prose and verse. In 1908 he married
Miss Dorothy Oakley of Englewood, N. J., and the pair
have five children.

JOHN B. HAGUE

1813-

"Hark, sinner, while God from on high doth entreat
    thee."

This hymn of warning was written by a Baptist preacher
who was born at New Rochelle, New York. In 1845 he
took up educational work and became a member of an
Episcopal church. He edited a hymn book to which he contributed seven hymns of his own.

EDWARD PAYSON HAMMOND

1831-1910

"I feel like singing all the time;
My tears are wiped away."

These are the opening lines of a well-known hymn
written by a successful evangelist born in Ellington, Conn.
Mr. Hammond edited a hymnal called "Hymns of Prayer
and Praise" and is the author of a few hymns* of his own.
He was sent by General Howard to hold meetings in Alaska.

---

* The hymn "Go and tell Jesus" is sometimes attributed to Hammond
and sometimes to Selina S. Gibbs. Hammond is called the children's
evangelist, and the first mentioned hymn was suggested to the author
by the testimony of a young girl who was converted in his meetings.
Mr. Spurgeon was very fond of this hymn and it was sung in his
tabernacle in London on one occasion when Hammond conducted a meeting and 8,000 were present and 3,000 turned away for lack of room.
The hymn was also used in Hammond's meetings in Norway, Sweden,
Jerusalem, and Alaska.

SAMUEL YOUNG HARMER

1809-

"In the Christian's home in glory
* * * * * * * * *
There is rest for the weary."

This well-known hymn was written in 1856 for a camp meeting collection. The author was born at Germantown, Pa., and was the son of a member of the Society of Friends. Samuel, Jr. became in 1847 a minister of the Methodist Episcopal church after spending several years as local preacher and Sunday School worker. The hymn is given in "Christ in Song", No. 928.

THORO HARRIS

b. 1874

"Are you trusting Jesus all along the way?
* * * * * * * * *
More abundantly."

This hymn was written by a publisher of gospel song books who has for many years resided in Chicago. He was the son of a doctor in Washington, D. C. who died when the boy was eight years old, and the upbringing of the family fell entirely to the mother from that point. Thoro was full of music from his infancy. He began to compose melodies at the age of five and by the time he was six was writing them down in his own fashion. His family were originally Congregationalists, but when Thoro was twelve years old an evangelist of the Seventh Day Adventists was preaching in Washington and this family were among the converts to that doctrine. For twenty years Thoro kept Saturday as the Sabbath. When he was fifteen he went to college at Battle Creek, Mich. (the college which was later removed to Baring Springs). He studied harmony and afterwards graduated

at a Normal School in Washington and taught for four years
thereafter, during which time he married and three children
were born of this union. His wife died at their home in
Chicago in 1922, and the three children are now grown. The
one daughter is married in Chicago and the sons are also
there. In 1927 Mr. Harris re-married and his good wife
Freda is his companion in all his labors in the shipping of
his multitudes of gospel hymnals to various parts of the
country. His first hymn book was published in Boston in
1902 and soon after this he relinquished the teaching profession to throw himself entirely into the perilous financial
adventures of earning a living for himself and family in the
publishing of gospel hymns where his heart was. He is and
always has been in very moderate circumstances, but is working along the lines of his heart's desire, which is certainly
one of the prime requisites of happiness in this life. A year
or two before the World War broke out Mr. Harris was
drawn by a remarkable experience into the Pentecostal movement where he has remained, and his hymn books are mainly
compiled for this connection. He has composed many hymns
and tunes. He is a kind and genial man, and I greatly prize
his friendship.

Rev. Louis Hartsough

1828-1894

"I hear Thy welcome voice,"*

This deservedly popular hymn was written by a Methodist
preacher who was born at Ithaca, N. Y. At one period of
his life his health became impaired and he was sent by the
Bible Society to work in the Rocky Mountain region. His
wife was the first woman to sit on a jury in a murder case
in Utah. In 1859 Mr. Hartsough edited a hymn book. His

---

* This hymn was written during a revival at Epworth, Ia. It was
published in Sankey's "Songs and Solos" in 1878. Sankey said of it
that it "proved to be one of the most helpful of the revival hymns." I
have a memory picture of my sweet-faced daughter playing this hymn
on a little folding organ at morning worship in her cottage home among
the cornfields of South Dakota.

later years were spent at Mt. Vernon, Ia. He was a man of deep piety. There was never a day in his home without family worship. He was greatly beloved.

JEFFERSON HASKELL

1807-

"My latest sun is sinking fast,
*   *   *   *   *   *   *   *   *
O come, angel band, come and around us steal;
O bear us away on your snowy wings
To my immortal home."

This hymn on old age* was written by a native of Thompson, Conn., and published in "J. W. Dadmun's Melodeon" in 1860—No. 11, also in "The Golden Shower" in 1862. Julian mentions this hymn in his appendix.

HORACE LORENZO HASTINGS

b. 1831-

"Shall we meet beyond the river
Where the surges cease to roll?"

This voluminous writer was born at Blandford, Mass. He wrote hymns and preached in his seventeenth year, and labored as an evangelist. He established a monthly paper called "The Christian." Many of his hymns were published in it. He wrote at least 450 hymns. The above hymn was set to music by Elihu S. Rice, a clerk in a hardware store who later became a preacher.

---

* It seems strange that a hymn on old age should have been a special favorite with Sunday School children, but so it has been reported to me by my husband and his sister who were familiar with the hymn in their childhood and were particularly fond of the chorus. The hymn is interesting to me as having been written by one who was probably a kinsman, judging from his name and the locality where he lived.

Thomas Hastings

1784-1872

"Hail to the brightness of Zion's glad morning,"

This fine millenial hymn was written by a native of Washington, Litchfield Co., Conn. When Hastings was two years old his father moved to Clinton, N. Y., where the boy grew up in rough frontier life with small educational privileges. However, he early developed a talent for music and began to teach at the age of twenty-two, devoting himself especially to the improvement of church music. He went in 1823 to Utica where he conducted a musical journal on religious lines. In 1832 he was called to New York City where he took charge of several church choirs and spent the remaining forty years of his life in great and increasing usefulness and repute. He wrote hymns as a corollary to his music work. Julian does not consider him a great poet but says that for fifty years more of his hymns were in common use than those of any other one writer. Julian lists 56 of them. The following are the first lines of several of the most familiar ones. He wrote the music as well as the words of the first one.

"Child of sin and sorrow."
"He that goeth forth with weeping."
"Gently Lord, Oh gently lead us."
"Today the Saviour calls"
"O tell me, thou life and delight of my soul."

John Hay

1838-1905

"The people will come to their own at last,
God is not mocked forever."

These lines were written by the distinguished diplomat who was instrumental in giving back to China for the education of her youth the indemnity granted to the United States after the Boxer Rising, a gracious act which endeared our country to China. In his early manhood he was the private secretary and biographer of Abraham Lincoln. In later life he was Secretary of State under Roosevelt. Wm. Allen White said of him, "His halo never flickered." He was born at Salem, Ind., and graduated at Brown University.* In his college days he had the ambition to be a poet. His son says of him, "Fate took the choice out of his hands and turned the bard into first a writer, and then a maker of history." However, I believe he will perhaps be remembered by his delightful book of "Pike County Ballads", especially the poem "Jim Bludsoe" which George Eliott is said to have recited with tears at a London dinner party calling it one of the finest poems† of the English language.

HAYWARD

fl. 18th and 19th centuries

"Welcome, delightful morn; Thou day of sacred rest,"

This fine Sabbath hymn was probably written by an American. I have no data about him, not even his initials. I have been familiar with the hymn since childhood. The tune, "Lischer", to which it is set, is an inspiring one. It was printed in 1806 in Dobell's "New Selections" and was repeated in 1887 in "Hymns of the Faith", New York. Julian mentions him on p. 1570 but gives no data. The "Index of Authors" given in "The New Laudes Domini" says of Hayward, "There the trail ends." It seems pathetic that one who has contributed one of the finest of our Sabbath hymns should have so dropped out from the knowledge of his fellow men. "Only remembered by what he has done."

---

* His grandfather David A. Leonard (who was my own great uncle) was a graduate of Brown and class poet, as was also Hay in the same college. Since Hay was my second cousin I take a personal pride in telling this incident of his boyhood (never before published, as I think). John was a dutiful lad who, enveloped in a big apron, used nightly to help his mother with the supper dishes, for which his boy companions derided him as a sissy. One night when they came around his home with scornful remarks, John treated them to a plentiful shower of dish water which they did not appreciate unless later on as they watched his career.

† Another lovely poem of Hay's named "The Stirrup Cup" is found in "Heart Throbs" No. 1. It begins,

"My short and happy day is done;
The long and lonely night comes in;
And at my door the pale horse stands
To carry me to distant lands."

Frederick Henry Hedge, D. D.

1805-1890

"Beneath Thy hammer, Lord, I lie"

This fine hymn was written by the son of a man who was a Professor in Harvard for 38 years. The son was born in Cambridge, Mass., and graduated at Harvard at the age of twenty. He later became a Professor of German and Church History at Harvard. He was a man of independent thought, who distrusted systems and hewed a path beyond the convention of theology. In 1853 in connection with a Doctor Huntington he published a hymnal entitled "Hymns for the Church of Christ" which has been used by the Unitarians.

Rev. Clifton J. Hicks

fl. 1925

"There is a book of grace divine"

This is the opening line of a worthy hymn written by the pastor of the Geneva Presbyterian Church in So. Norfolk, Va. It is sung to the tune Materna.

Thomas Wentworth Higginson

1823-

"The land our fathers left to us"

This hymn was written by a Unitarian minister and author who was born at Cambridge, Mass., and educated at Harvard. After eleven years of service as pastor he retired from the ministry and devoted himself to literature with marked success, being a leading contributor to the "Atlantic Monthly." He also published some prose books. He wrote a few hymns.

Julian lists four of them. During the Civil War he was colonel of the first negro regiment raised in South Carolina. Also he was at one period captain of the 51st regiment of Massachusetts and was wounded. He was a friend of Emily Dickinson and parts of an interesting correspondence with the unique poetess have been preserved.

Rev. Elisha Albright Hoffman

1839-1929

"I must tell Jesus all of my trouble"

This precious although humble gospel hymn* was written by a pastor in Lebanon, Pa., born in Orwigsburg, Pa., the son of a minister of the Evangelical Association. He was reared in the atmosphere of holy joy and song, the family being accustomed to spend some time, perhaps half an hour, singing hymns each morning at worship. The son was destined to contribute many hymns† to the church.

Oliver Holden

1765-1844

"They who seek a throne of grace"

This well-known hymn was written by one of the pioneers of American psalmody. He was born at Shirley, Mass., and was in his youth a carpenter. Subsequently he became a music seller in Charlestown. He edited a hymn book in

---

* This hymn which has been a great comfort to me in a time of stress, was written under these circumstances: Mr. Hoffman was calling on a parishioner in trouble. Wringing her hands she said to her pastor, "What shall I do?" He replied, "You must tell Jesus," Her sad face lighted up and she exclaimed, "Yes, I must tell Jesus." On his return home Mr. Hoffman immediately wrote this hymn.
   † Some of the familiar hymns written by Mr. Hoffman are these:
      "What a wonderful Savior is Jesus, my Lord!"
      "Have you been to Jesus for the cleansing power?"
      "What a fellowship, what a joy divine,"
      "Whosoever receiveth the crucified one."
      "Down at the cross where my Savior died"

which twenty-one of his own hymns were printed with the signature "H". He is best known probably as the author of the grand tune "Coronation", through which the hearts of countless thousands have poured out their adoration to the Lord of All. In this he has done enough for one man to do for the uplifting of the human race. I feel a glory and pride in him as a native of my own state.

JOSIAH GILBERT HOLLAND

1819-1881

"For summer's bloom and autumn's blight"

This hymn was written by the above-named editor and author. J. G. Holland was born at Belchertown, Mass., and was the author of several successful books, especially "Bittersweet" and "Katherina" which were very popular in my childhood days. In "Bitter-sweet" was a hymn entitled "A Song of Faith" which begins

"Evil is only the slave of good;
Sorrow the servant of joy."

Holland was for some time on the editorial staff of "The Springfield Republican" and became in 1870 the founder and editor of "Scribner's Monthly," the idea of which he conceived during a two years' trip to Europe. He was widely known as a lecturer. His residence in winter was in New York City, in summer on one of the Thousand Islands which he purchased and called the name of his home there Bonnicastle. Holland was the son of a poor man whose character is sketched in a poem called "Daniel Gray." The father was unable to assist his ambitious son in acquiring an education, but after many struggles Josiah graduated with honor from the Berkshire Medical College in Pittsfield. He showed a talent for writing at an early age and made that his profession.

John Haynes Holmes

1879-

"O God whose smile is in the sky"

This fine hymn* was written in 1907 by the pastor of a Unitarian church in New York City. Dr. Holmes was a native of Philadelphia and graduated at Harvard. He opposed the entrance of the United States into the World War and thundered his objections from pulpit and press to all reactionary policies, yet for some mysterious reason he passed through that grievous epoch without being jailed for his utterances. In 1917 he became the director of the Civil Liberties Bureau and in 1919 he left the Unitarian denomination and became pastor of Community Church. He is a contributing editor of "The World Tomorrow", edits "Unity", and is one of the fearless and forward-looking prophets of our age. He is a wonderful preacher, an ardent pacifist, and a man to glory in. "He is far too salty to win acclaim from conventional universities and has never had a doctor's degree laid on his quizzical brow."

Oliver Wendell Holmes, M. D.

1809-1894

"Lord of all being, throned afar,"

This majestic and imperishable hymn was written by one of the great literary geniuses of America. Dr. Holmes was born at Cambridge, Mass., and was the son of a minister and educated at Harvard where he became in 1847 the Professor of Anatomy. He is not chiefly considered in the light of either a doctor of medicine or as a hymn writer, though he was both of these. He is generally remembered as a

---

* Another of his hymns written in 1908 begins, "O Father, thou who givest all" another begins. "O God, whose love is over all." This is found in "Hymns of the Living Age", No. 83.

writer of sparkling and witty prose and verse*, and something of a philosopher as well. The hymn above mentioned
may be his greatest contribution to the world. Another
well-known hymn he wrote begins, "O Love Divine, which
stooped to share". There are also two religious poems, one
on "Robinson of Leyden" and the other on "The Chambered
Nautilus" which call out the noblest sentiments and enthu-
siasms of the soul of man.

JOSIAH HOPKINS, D. D.

1786-1862

"O turn ye, O turn ye,
For why will ye die?"

This well-known hymn of exhortation was written by a
minister who started out as a Congregationalist but ended as
a Presbyterian pastor. He was born at Pittsford, Vt., and
died at Geneva, N. Y. He was the editor of a hymn book
called "Conference Hymns" and contributed original hymns
to the "Christian's Lyre" in 1860 from which the above hymn
was taken.

EDWARD HOPPER, D. D.

1818-1888

"Jesus, Savior, pilot me"

This much-beloved hymn† published in 1871 was written
by a New York minister of "The Church of Sea and Land",
a graduate in 1842 of Union Theological Seminary. He will
always be remembered as the author of the above mentioned
hymn.

---

* When Dr. Holmes was about to lecture to the Oxford students in
England, one young scalawag called out to him as he stood on the
platform, "Did you come in the 'One-hoss Shay,' sir?" In the same
year (1809) that Holmes was born, Lincoln, Gladstone, Tennyson, Dar-
win and Elizabeth Barrett Browning were also born.

† Major Whittle sang this hymn to a dying soldier in Tampa, Fla.,
who had heard it sung previously by a beloved sister in Michigan. He
asked, "Will Jesus pilot me into the haven of rest?" and Whittle said,
"Yes, he will." Then said the soldier, "I will trust him with all my
heart." When Whittle called the next day he was told that the soldier
had passed out in the night.

Frederick Lucian Hosmer

1840-

"O beautiful, my country,"

This is the opening line of one of the 56 hymns* written by a minister who is called by Julian "The most powerful hymnist among Unitarians for twenty years. Mr. Hosmer was born in Framingham, Mass., and educated at Harvard. He was at one period pastor in Berkeley, Cal. Julian lists 27 of his hymns.

R. E. Hudson

fl. 19th century

"Are you ready for the Bridegroom
When He comes?"

This hymn which is found in "Hymns of the Gospel New and Old" was used considerably in the South African General Mission in Johannesburg in the eighteen hundred and nineties. Julian does not list the hymn or the author. Hudson also wrote "My life, my love, I give to Thee." This is 406 in the Service Hymnal and the music was composed by C. E. Dunbar. Hudson copyrighted this hymn which is in common use.

George C. Hugg

fl. 19th century

"Walk in the light the Lord has given"

This hymn, which was frequently used in the South African General Mission in Johannesburg, is by an obscure author unlisted by Julian. The hymn is to be found in "Hymns of the Gospel New and Old."

---

* I cull these lines from his hymns:
    "One thought I have, my ample creed,
        So deep it is and broad,
    And equal to my every need,—
        It is the thought of God."
One of his hymns begins thus, "Father, we look to Thee in all our sorrow." Another begins,
        "I cannot think of them as dead
        Who walk with us no more."
Another of Hosmer's hymns begins, "I came not hither by my will." This is a special favorite in my own home.

Asa Hull

fl. 19th century

"I do believe, I now believe."

This familiar chorus was written by a shrewd American business man who published "The Vestry Chimes."

William Hunter, D. D.

1811-1877

"My heavenly home is bright and fair"

This is one of several familiar hymns* written by a native of Ireland whom I have ventured to class with American hymnists because he came to America at the age of six and his life work was in this country where he obtained a college education and became Professor of Hebrew in Allegheny College. At another period of his life he was a Methodist minister at Alliance, Ohio. He wrote 125 hymns and edited three hymn books. Some of his hymns have been translated into various Indian languages.

D. W. C. Huntington

fl. 19th century

"O think of the home over there."

This gospel hymn was written by an obscure hymnist about whom I have no data. He was probably an American. The hymn was set to music by Tulleus C. O. Kane. It is No. 607 in the Service Hymnal.

---

* Two others of his well-known hymns are those beginning "The great physician now is near", and "Joyfully, joyfully, onward I move."

Frederic Dan Huntington

1819-1904

"So heaven is gathering one by one."

This burial hymn was written by a Unitarian minister born at Hadley, Mass., graduated at Amherst College and Harvard University Divinity School, and later University Preacher at Harvard and Bishop of Central New York. He edited with Dr. Hedge a Unitarian hymnal and a collection of Sacred Poetry. Julian lists four of his hymns.

Prof. George Huntington

1878-

"Two empires by the sea,
Two nations great and free,
    One anthem raise!
One race of ancient fame,
One tongue, one faith we claim,
One God, whose glorious name
    We love and praise."

This is a hymn on world peace written by the President of Robert College, Constantinople who is also President of the Board of Managers of the American Chamber of Commerce for the Levant. Dr. Huntington was born at Gorham, Maine, and educated at Williams College and Hartford Theological Seminary.

Charles William Johnson

1865-

"I hear a voice that speaks to me;
I sense a presence I cannot see."

These are the opening lines of a hymn entitled "Companionship" written by a citizen of Springfield, Mass. (128 Orleans St.) This public-spirited gentleman at the time when dis-

armament was the uppermost need of the world, put out
peace envelopes which bore the motto, "Build friendships,
not warships for national defense." He sells these at the
cost of 500 for a dollar—an astonishing low figure, thus
scattering broadcast the thought of peace for a war-weary
world. Mr. Johnson was born at Dumnerston, Vt., and is
in the business of making hand colored flower pictures which
are very beautiful. He began to write hymns at the age of
forty-nine. One of these he calls his "lily poem." It was
suggested by a sermon he heard from his pastor on "The
lily that grew from the mud", a message he passed on to
many young soldiers as they went forth into the filth and
strain of the World War, and some came back undefiled in
consequence. He is now working enthusiastically for "a
lasting peace" which is the title of one of his hymns. Another
is entitled "The Larger Patriotism". He is an unusual man
working on original lines.

SAMUEL JOHNSON, M. A.

1822-1882

"Onward Christian, though the region
Where thou art be drear and lone."

This choice hymn was written by a native of Salem, Mass.
and graduate of Harvard who founded a free church at Lynn
of which he was the pastor for seventeen years. Although
not officially connected with the Unitarian denomination,
yet he associated with that body, and in connection with
Samuel Longfellow edited a hymn book popularly known
as "that of the two Sams." He died at North Andover at
the age of sixty. Julian lists fifteen of his beautiful hymns
which deserve to be more widely used than they are. One
of these begins, "Savior, in Thy mysterious presence kneeling,".

C. P. Jones

fl. 19th century

"When pangs of death seized on my soul
* * * * * * * *
I would not be denied."

This gospel hymn, both words and music, was composed by an obscure American hymnist of whom I have no data. It is not listed by Julian but has been widely used in revival meetings in America. It is found in the "Air-Pilot Hymnal" No 123. C. P. Jones also wrote both words and music of "Deeper, deeper in the blood of Jesus." This is found in "The Air-Pilot Hymnal" No. 8. Another found in the "Service Hymnal" (No. 391) begins, "Jesus Christ is made to me all I need."

L. E. Jones

fl. 19th century

"Would you be free from your burden of sin,
There's power in the blood."

This well-known hymn* was written by an obscure writer about whom I have no data except that I have read that he used the name Edgar Lewis as a nom-de-plume.

R. Jukes

fl. 19th century

"My heart is fixed, eternal God,
Fixed on Thee."

This hymn I associate with Salvation Army Holiness meetings. I have no data about the author. It was set to music by Sweeney and is No. 97 in "Hymns of the Gospel New and Old." I consider it an effective hymn.

---

* This hymn is found in "Christ in Song", page 27. Mr. Jones is the composer of the tune as well as the words.

E. W. KELLOGG

fl. 19th century

"We three kings of Orient are"

This good Christmas hymn is No. 61 in "Happy Voices." It is said to be taken by permission from "The Morning Star", a collection I have never seen. There is no information about the author. I list him among the Americans, as Julian does not give him.

FRANCIS SCOTT KEY

1779-1843

"Praise, my soul, the God that sought thee."

This is one of several hymns written by the celebrated author of "The Star Spangled Banner." He was born in Frederick Co., Md. and educated at St. John's College, Annapolis. He was a lawyer who practised at Washington, D. C., and in the late years of his life was District Attorney of the United States. He was a sincere Episcopalian Christian, and America may well be proud of her distinguished son. A slave holder by inheritance, he did all a minister could do for the chatttels on his plantation, helped them in trouble, defended them in the courts, held religious services for them, and organized a scheme of African colonization. He died in Baltimore at the age of sixty-two. There is a bronze statue over his grave.

JOYCE KILMER

1886-1918

"No longer of Him be it said
He hath no place to lay his head."

This hymn is found in "Hymns of the Living Age" No. 175. The author was a young soldier who was killed in the World War. His widow Alice Kilmer has published books of poems.

J. M. KIRK

fl. 19th century

"I am watching for the coming of the glad millenial day
* * * * * * * *
O, our Lord is coming back to earth again."

This advent hymn is not listed by Julian and I have no data about the author. He was probably an American. It is 109 in "The Air Pilot Hymnal".

WILLIAM J. KIRKPATRICK

fl. 19th century

"I've wandered far away from God."

The author of this gospel hymn was a resident of Philadelphia who was in youth a carpenter's apprentice. In 1861 he went into the Union Army. Then after the war he was in business for ten years, then gave up everything else to write and publish sacred music. With John R. Sweeny he published hymn books. Sweeny died first* and Kirkpatrick married Sweeny's widow. He is not listed by Julian.

SIDNEY LANIER

1842-1881

"Into the woods my master went"

This striking poem, used in some collections as a hymn, was written by a Georgia poet who was one of the earliest Confederate volunteers in the Civil War. He was of Huguenot descent and graduated from Oglethorpe College at the age of eighteen. Soon after he was in command of a blockade runner which was captured and Lanier was a prisoner over five months. After the war he practised law with his father awhile, had charge of a country Academy for a time but had lung trouble and moved from place to place

---

* I have read this story about Kirkpatrick's death,—viz, that he died sitting in his chair at four A. M. and that a poem on heaven that he had just written was found beside him. This is so identical with a story told of E. Hopper that I wonder!

to find better health. For four years he tried the climate in Texas, then went to Maryland, devoting himself to music and literature. He was flutist in symphony concerts, gave lectures on poetry, and wrote a cantata for the centennial exhibition in Philadelphia in 1876. In early life he was a Presbyterian, but gradually lost sympathy with organized Christianity. He died at the age of thirty-nine at Lynn, N. C. His poems* were collected by his widow.

Eden R. Latta

fl. 19th century

"Blessed be the fountain of blood
* * * * * * * *
Whiter than the snow."

This hymn which was included by Sankey in "Songs and Solos" without authorship, is listed under the above name by Julian who says that the authorship is unknown. Latta was probably an American. It is 104 in "The Air Pilot Hymnal."

William Leggett

1802-1840

"O Jesus, bring us to that rest,
Where all the ransomed shall be found
In thine eternal fulness blest,—
While ages roll their cycles round."

This is the closing stanza of a beautiful hymn entitled, "Meeting Above," written by an associate of the poet Bryant who wrote a tribute to his memory. Leggett was born in New York City and became a political writer of eminence. For a while he was a midshipman. He published a book called "Tales of a country schoolmaster" and also started a

---

* His poem on "The Marshes of Glynn" is a favorite with me and I have set part of it to music in a booklet called "Melodies of Life and Love." I like these lines:
"As the marsh hen so secretly builds on the sod,
I will build me a nest on the favor of God."

magazine named "The Plain Dealer" which fearlessly defended the right of free discussion and denounced those who mobbed the abolitionists. Van Buren appointed him agent to Guatemala but he died when preparing for his departure at the age of only thirty-eight.

Edgar Lewis

fl. 19th century

"Just lean upon the arms of Jesus

* * * * * * * * *

Lean on His arms, trusting in His love."

This hymn was published in "Christ in Song", No. 502, but I have no data concerning the author. The hymn was copyrighted in 1903 by D. B. Towner who was for many years the singer at the Moody Institute in Chicago. There are indications that Edgar Lewis is a nom-de-plume for L. E. Jones.

Nicholas Vachel Lindsay

1870-

"Star of my heart, I follow from afar."

This is the opening line of a lovely Christmas hymn written by the above-named American poet of distinction. Lindsay was born in Springfield, Ill., educated at Hiram College, Ohio, and at the Art Institute of Chicago. He became a lecturer for the Anti-saloon League. He took a walking trip from Illinois to New Mexico distributing tracts and speaking on "The Gospel of Beauty". He has published books of poems. He has a charming personality.*

---

* I learned this about him from my son, Dr. Aubrey W. Goodenough of Colorado Springs, who had the joy of entertaining Mr. Lindsay a year or two ago. The young daughter of that home has become exceedingly foud of his poetry, and when I saw her last summer she repeated to me poem after poem of his which she had committed to memory.

Since that visit my beloved son who was Prof. of English in Colorado College has passed to another world, but the passion for poetry he inspired in his daughter is her priceless legacy to her, this applies also to his pupils.

Abiel Abbot Livermore

1811-1892

"A holy air is breathing round"

This is the first line of a communion hymn written by a Unitarian minister who was a native of Wilton, N. H., the son of a farmer. He graduated at Harvard in 1833 and held various pastorates—at Keene, N. H., Cincinnati, Ohio, and Yonkers, N. Y. In 1863 he became the President of the Theological Seminary in Meadville, Pa. and later edited an estimable collection of hymns. In 1890 he retired to his ancestral home in Wilton, N. H., where he died. He was a man of sincere piety, tolerant, cordial, and with a sunny smile and sympathy with the pleasures of young people.

John D. Long

1838-

> "I would, dear Jesus, I could break
> The hedge that creeds and hearsay make,
> And like the first disciples be
> In person led and taught by Thee."

This is the opening stanza of a sweet little hymn written by the 28th governor of Massachusetts, who later went to Congress where he proved himself a polished debater. He was born at Buckfield, Maine, and entered Harvard College at the age of fourteen, where he distinguished himself for brilliance. He was greatly respected in his political career.

Henry Wadsworth Longfellow

1807-1882

"Tell me not in mournful numbers"

This is the opening line of the "Psalm of Life" written by our distinguished American poet when he was a young man,

and published in his "Voices of the Night." Longfellow
was born at Portland, Maine, into a Unitarian family, and
was the son of a judge. At the age of fourteen he entered
Bowdoin College and was a classmate of Nathaniel
Hawthorne. He became Professor of Belles Lettres at
Harvard. His name is a household word wherever English
is spoken. He was highly honored in England. Both Cambridge and Oxford bestowed degrees upon him and his bust
is placed in that temple of honor, Westminster Abbey. There
was one terrible tragedy in his family. The clothing of his
second wife caught fire from a lighted candle and she died
from the effect of the burns. Longfellow was buried in
Mount Auburn cemetery. The plot of ground opposite his
Cambridge residence is made into a park. His statue is
erected in Portland, his native city. He is not essentially a
hymnist, though he wrote a few poems which have been used
as hymns, especially one which begins, "I heard the bells on
Christmas day."

Samuel Longfellow

1819-1892

"O Life, that maketh all things new,"

This is the opening line of one of the many lovely hymns
written by a younger brother of Henry W. Longfellow.
Samuel, like his brother, was born in Portland, Maine. He
was educated at Harvard and became a Unitarian minister,
holding pastorates in various cities. He edited a hymn book
with Samuel Johnson. His hymns* are widely used among
Unitarians. They are full of spiritual depth and sweetness.
It is impossible for a soul that knows God to sing them
without an inward blessing.

---

* I quote these lines from one of his hymns found in the Pilgrim
Hymnal, No. 272.
    "Look backward, how much has been won!
    Look round, how much is yet to win!
    The watches of the night are done;
    The watches of the day begin."

Dr. Edmund S. Lorenz

fl. 20th century

"Amid the trials which I meet"

This appears to have been written many years ago by the above named publisher of Gospel Hymns in Dayton, Ohio, who is called by the editor of "The Christian Century" the "Dean of gospel hymn writers." This particular hymn appears in various early hymnals under the nom-de-plume E. D. Mund.

James Russell Lowell

1819-1891

"Are we pledged to craven silence?
We have nobler duties first."

These spirited lines from a poem called "Stanzas on Freedom" which might be appropriately used as a hymn on some occasions, were written by the distinguished man of letters above mentioned. Lowell was born at Cambridge, Mass. and graduated from Harvard at the age of nineteen—the class poet. He was the successor there of H. W. Longfellow as Professor of Belles Lettres. Later he was U. S. Minister to Spain and England. At one period of his life he was the editor of the Atlantic Monthly. The spirit of the reformer burned within him. He is everybody's dear poet. Although not primarily a hymnist, I do not feel like leaving him out.

POTENTIA

"Thou canst not fail! The future all unknwon
Lies in thy power; its secrets are thy own.
There's not a task that thou canst not fulfill,
Strong in the thought, as thou thyself shalt will."

—*C. B.* 1880.

Robert Lowry, D. D.

1826-1899

"Shall we gather at the river?"

This dear hymn* of our childhood was written by a Baptist minister who was born at Philadelphia and educated at Lewisburg University, where he later became Professor of Rhetoric. He had much to do with the publishing of Sunday School hymn books and is the author of the following familiar hymns:

"Where is my wandering boy tonight?"
"Weeping will not save me,"
"My home is in Heaven; my rest is not here."
"My life flows on in endless song." (Music by the author)
"One more day's work for Jesus."
"Low in the grave he lay"
"Shall we know each other there?"
"What can wash away my sin?"†

George Lunt

1803-1885

"Pilgrims and wanderers, hither we come;
  Where the free dare to be, this is our home."

These lines are the refrain after each stanza of the beautiful Pilgrim hymn written by the above named Massachusetts lawyer, who was educated at Harvard and served several years in the legislature of his native state. He was for a time principal of a high school in Newburyport, and later practised law in that town. At one time he was U. S. Attorney under President Taylor. After this he was the

---

* Dr. Lowry was a delegate in 1880 to the Robert Raikes centennial in London and was given an enthusiastic reception as the author of "Shall we gather at the river?" which was written on a hot summer day in Brooklyn in 1864 during an epidemic of sickness when many friends of the author were passing away. The question of meeting them in a future world was pressing on his soul and, seating himself at the organ, he poured out the words and the music as if inspired.

† This hymn was first introduced at a camp meeting at Ocean Grove, N. J.

editor of "The Boston Courier." He wrote some books in
a brilliant style. One was "Radicalism in Religion." Another
was "Three Eras of New England." He also published three
volumes of verse. He was a finished writer.

J. B. MACKAY

fl. 19th century

"Is there anyone can help us?

*   *   *   *   *   *   *   *

Yes, there's One, only One."

This hymn which is No. 522 in "Christ in Song" was
written, both words and music, by the above named author.
The hymn is sometimes attributed to Peter Bilhorn.

BASIL MANLY, JR.

1825-

"There is a light which shines from heaven."

This is one of about forty hymns written by the above-
named Baptist preacher of South Carolina. He was born in
Edgefield Co. educated at the State University of Alabama,
and held important appointments in Charleston, S. C. and
elsewhere. In connection with his father, Basil Manly, Sr.,
he edited "The Baptist Psalmody" in which nine of his
hymns appeared.

DANIEL MARCH, D. D.

1816-1909

"Hark, the voice of Jesus crying,"

This hymn was written in 1868 on the impulse of the
moment and sung from manuscript at the close of a sermon

on "Here am I; send me." Is. 6:8. The author was a Congregational minister of Philadelphia who was born in Millbury, Mass., and graduated at Yale in 1840. He lived to be very old—over ninety. The hymn was published in a Methodist Episcopal hymn book in 1878 and was also included in Sankey's "Songs and Solos." It is sometimes confused with the hymn beginning "If you cannot on the ocean" by Ellen Gates. Julian says it was the latter hymn and not the one by Dr. March that was sung in the U. S. Senate by Philip Phillips in the hearing of President Lincoln which moved him to tears and which he asked to have repeated later.

Edwin Markham

1852-

"God show us love's great way,
And lead us day by day
    To love's great ends;
Oh may our country be
One shelter of the free,
    One house of friends."

This is the concluding stanza of a hymn entitled "New America" written by our beloved contemporary poet. He was born in Oregon City and went early to California where he supported himself in a life of poverty and struggle, blacksmithing, farming, herding cattle and sheep in boyhood. Finally he went to the San José Normal School and other schools, taking special studies in literature until he became a Superintendent of Schools. In 1900 he wrote "The Man with the Hoe" which gained world-wide attention and has been called "The battle cry for the next thousand years." Markham has published many books of poetry. He now lives in New York State.

SAMUEL WESLEY MARTIN

1839-

"The gospel bells are ringing,"
This gospel hymn* was written by a native of Plainfield,
Ill. Julian mentions this hymn.

W. C. MARTIN

fl. 20th century

"To Jesus every day I find
* * * * * * * *
The half cannot be fancied."
This popular hymn is found in Rodeheaver's collection
"Songs for Service" as is also "The name of Jesus is so
sweet", both attributed to W. C. Martin. See Mrs. C. D.
Martin Chapter 10.

LOWELL MASON

1792-1872

The name of this wonderful musical genius is scattered
through our hymnals as the composer of many of our
standard tunes, such as the tune to "Safely through another
week." His reputation was made in 1823 when, as a bank
clerk in Savannah, Ga., a lady sent her son to ask him to
compose a tune for Heber's hymn "From Greenland's icy
mountains." In one half hour he returned with it. The
tune was written at a stroke, like the hymn itself. Mason was
born at Medfield, Mass., and found a way to develop his
musical talent although employed in bank business in his
earlier years. He is called "the father of American choir
singing." The American Academy of music was founded
by him.

---

* I have a very distinct association with this hymn. I had a little
nurse maid to help me with my first baby who sang it over and over
to the child for many days until melody and words are unforgetable.

Rev. John B. Matthias

fl. 19th century

"I saw a way worn pilgrim
* * * * * * * *
Then palms of victory, crowns of glory."

This effective hymn which is not listed by Julian is found in the "Service Hymnal" No. 333. It is also No. 24 in "Gospel Gems" published by George D. Russell of 125 Tremont St., Boston, Mass. I have no data about the author except that he composed the melody as well as the words of the hymn. I take it that he is an American but am not positive about it.

Rev. J. J. Maxfield*

fl. 19th century

"I do not ask for earthly store
Beyond a day's supply."

This was a favorite hymn in Moody's Scotland campaign. The choirs would gather at the station and sing this hymn at Moody's departure.

Rev. R. H. McDaniel

fl. 20th century

"What a wonderful change in my life has been
wrought,
Since Jesus came into my heart!"

This hymn, which was greatly used in the revivals conducted by Rev. W. A. Sunday, was written by a minister of the Disciple Church. Even in his boyhood he was accustomed to lead the song service in enthusiastic prayer and testimony meetings, and the above mentioned hymn has carried with

---

* This is not in Julian. I do not know whether the author is American or British.

it a wave of joy which has thrilled great throngs.*   Mr. McDaniel is a truly consecrated man whose hymns are the expression of a deep personal experience.

Rev. Wm. McDonald

1820-1901

"I am coming to the cross."

This much used hymn which was published in the American Baptist Praise Book in 1871, was written by an American author.   He also wrote,

> "I am coming to Jesus for rest,
> * * * * * * *
> I believe Jesus saves."

This hymn is found in "The Air Pilot" No. 77, published by Thoro Harris of Chicago.

James McGranahan

fl. 19th century

This colleague of Major Whittle's in the gospel of song did not know the Major until the day they met at Ashtabula, Ohio, soon after the tragic death of P. P. Bliss.   It proved to be a turning point in McGranahan's life.   He had previously been a successful worker in Institutes and Conventions.   After conference with Whittle and after making it a subject of prayer, he decided to give his life to gospel work with voice and pen.   He was associated with Moody and edited fifteen hymn books.

---

* At the end of Mr. Sunday's campaign in Des Moines, Ia., many thousands gathered at the railroad station to bid him good-bye; hundreds of those who had been converted at the revival were present and this hymn was then sung, but they changed the refrain to "When Jesus came into my home."

John Hugh McNaughton
1829-

"There is beauty all around
When there's love at home."

This heaven-breathing song was written by a writer of
Scottish parentage, born at Caledonia, N. Y., in the beautiful
Genessee valley. Mr. Sheppard, the song publisher, tells
this incident about him. One morning Mr. Sheppard
wondered at the throngs of people in his store all asking to
buy a song which had been sung at a concert the previous
evening; among them a tall slim young man was pacing up
and down with folded arms. Presently he stepped up to Mr.
Sheppard with his keen steel-blue eyes glittering and inquired, "Will the proprietor tell me what he pays for the
manuscript of such a song as these people are buying?" "A
good deal," Mr. Sheppard, "for a song that makes people
cry, as that one did last night, but let me tell you, young
man, not one song writer in a hundred makes such a hit."
"Ah, indeed," said the young man as he left the store. A
few days afterward Mr. Sheppard received a manuscript song
and with it this laconic note, "That other song I gave you.
If you want this one, the price is named on the corner." The
price was outrageous, but Mr. Sheppard paid it and never
regretted it.* H. W. Longfellow wrote afterward to Mc-
Naughton, "Your poems have touched me very much. Tears
fall down my cheeks as I read them." 450,000 copies were
published of some of McNaughton's songs. One of them
was entitled "Belle Mahone"; another, "A Faded Coat of
Blue."

C. Austin Miles
fl. 20th century

"I came to the garden alone,
          *   *   *   *   *   *   *   *
For He walks with me and He talks with me."

This popular hymn written by the above-named author,

---

* Mr. McNaughton's inherited Scotch thrift appears in this shrewd
bargain.

is coupled with Harry Barracleugh's hymn, "Ivory Palaces" as savoring of "eroticism" and the critics are very hard on both. However, the public knows what it likes, and the hymn will certainly be used in spite of the critics.

E. F. MILLER

fl. 19th century

"O mourner in Zion, how blessed art thou!"
This useful hymn which is found in "Hymns of the Gospel New and Old" was written (both words and music) by an obscure author of whom I do not know either the nationality or the sex.

JOACHIM MILLER

1841-1913

"A weakness for the weaker side,—
A siding with the helpless weak."
These lines, culled from the beautiful poem entitled "Walker in Nicaragua", were written by a poet whose real name was Cincinnatus Heine Miller. He was born in Indiana, but was taken in boyhood by his parents to Oregon, and became a miner in California. He was a volunteer in General Walker's Nicaragua expedition in 1855 and lived an adventurous life among the Indians on the Pacific coast. He attemped to study law, was appointed County Judge in Oregon, edited a paper in Empire City which was suppressed by the authorities for disunion sentiments, and finally went to England where he was accepted for a time as a "lion." It is by a stretch of the imagination that he is included here as a hymnist, but the lines quoted above seem to me to reflect the attitude* of Christ and to include Miller, if not as a hymnist, at least among the sacred poets.

---

* These lines of Miller's also show the tender spirit of Christ:
"Is it worth while that we jostle a brother?
* * * * * * * * *
God pity us all in a pitiful strife."

WILLIAM AUGUSTUS MUHLENBERG, D. D.

1796-1877

"O cease, my wandering soul,
On restless wings to roam."

This beautiful hymn set to an appealing melody called
Adrian, was written by an Episcopal clergyman and philanthropist of the noblest type, who was born in Philadelphia
and was a grandson of Henry M. Muhlenberg, the patriarch
of Lutheranism in America. William Muhlenberg graduated
at the University of Pennsylvania and served churches in
Pennsylvania and New York. He started an enterprise which
he called St. Johnsland for the benefit of the children of
the poor and for the aged. He had a genuine poetical gift
which was not largely used. Julian lists 12 of his hymns and
says the best known of these is the one beginning, "Savior
who Thy flock art feeding." Another well-known hymn of
his begins, "I would not live always."* He died, poor, and
suffering from lapse of memory, at the age of eighty in St.
Luke's Hospital.

ELIAS NASON

1811-1887

"Jesus only when the morning"

This hymn was written about 1856 in Natick, Mass., by
the above named Congregational minister, who published it
with original music in the Boston "Wellspring." Nason was
born at Wrentham, Mass., and graduated at Brown University. He was a teacher in Georgia and in Massachusetts
before he became a preacher. He was also a lecturer and the

---

* There is a story told (also denied by others) that the occasion of
writing this lovely lyric was the breaking up by her relatives of his
prospects of marriage with a woman he deeply loved. The first version
of the poem was written in a lady's album, then printed in 1826 anonymously in the Episcopal Recorder. Dr. Muhlenberg was soon after on
a hymn book committee, one of whom, a satirical critic, opposed the
insertion of the hymn, not knowing the author. Dr. Muhlenberg therefore voted against the selection of his own hymn, but his friend, Dr.
Onderdonk, secured its insertion and it came into popular use.

author of several biographies. In conjunction with Dr. Edward Kirk he published "Songs for Social and Public Worship."

John G. Neihardt

fl. 20th century

"Let me live out my years in heat of blood!
Let me die drunken with the dreamer's wine!
Let me not see this soul-house built of mud
Go toppling in the dust—a vacant shrine!

Let me go quickly like a candle light
Snuffed out just at the heyday of its glow!
Give me high noon—and let it then be night!
Thus would I go.

And grant me when I face the grisly Thing,
One haughty cry to pierce the gray Perhaps!
O let me be a tune-swept fiddlestring
That feels the Master Melody—and snaps."

This is the best known lyric of the first American poet, I believe, to be regularly elected a state poet. Nebraska thus honored her son a few years ago by act of the legislature. Mr. Neihardt has published a book of epics of the West which has been pronounced by a critic as "profoundly notable in the development of American poetry."

Rev. David Nelson

1793-1844

"My days are gliding swifty by"

This popular hymn, written in 1835 by a Presbyterian minister, has a thrilling story told by Mr. Sankey about its composition. Nelson was born near Jonesborough in East

Tennessee and at the age of seventeen graduated at Washington College, Va., then took his M. D. degree in Philadelphia. He served as a surgeon in the War of 1812. In 1823 he resigned infidelity and medicine and became a preacher in Missouri. Becoming convinced of the sinfulness of slavery, he said he would rather live on baked potatoes and salt than hold slaves. This angered his slave holding neighbors who drove him away and would have harmed him, but he escaped their hands and hid in bushes by the Mississippi River, opposite Quincy, Ill., where he had friends who came across the river and rescued him from extreme peril. His pursuers had passed the very clump of bushes where he was and had stuck their guns into it, but had passed him by unperceived. It was while in this hiding place that Nelson composed mentally the lines of this hymn, which was afterward set to music by Prof. George F. Root, who could not understand why such a simple tune should have become so popular. Mr. Nelson founded two labor colleges, one at Greenfields and the other near Quincy, Ill.

ASAHEL NETTLETON

1783-1843

"Come, Holy Ghost, my soul inspire."

This hymn, which appeared in a compilation known as "Village Hymns" edited by the above named Connecticut evangelist, is sometimes attributed to Dr. Nettleton's authorship, but Julian thinks on insufficient grounds, saying that "Nettleton could appreciate a good hymn, but it is doubtful if he ever did or could have written one." Nettleton was a graduate of Yale and licensed to preach, but never was settled over a congregation. He preached in Massachusetts, Connecticut, New York, and Great Britain. More hymns of the older American writers have passed from Nettleton's "Village Hymns" into English collections than from any other source.

Edwin Nevin, D. D.

1814-1868

"Always with us, always with us,"

This familiar hymn was written by a native of Shippensburg, Pa., who graduated in theology at Princeton in 1836. He was first a Presbyterian minister, then Congregational, and finally, after a rest of six years on account of ill health, he took up a pastorate at Lancaster, Pa., and later at Philadelphia. Julian lists 79 of his hymns.*

William Newell, D. D.

1804-1881

"Changing, fading, falling, flying
From the homes that gave them birth,
Autumn leaves in beauty dying
Seek the mother breast of earth."

This lovely hymn, written for the consecration of the Cambridge Cemetery, is by a Unitarian minister born at Littleton, Mass., and educated at Harvard. He was a pastor at Cambridge for nearly thirty-eight years. He wrote 11 hymns† which have gone into collections.

James Nicholson

fl. 19th century

"Lord Jesus, I long to be perfectly whole"

This hymn was written by an American Methodist minister and is found in Sankey's "Songs and Solos."

---

* One of these which begins "O heaven, sweet heaven," was written after the death of a beloved son. So many hymns have been the fruit of personal sorrow.

† One of these hymns begins, "All hail, God's angel, Truth," and another, "Serve God and be cheerful."

Nathaniel Niles

1835-

"Precious promise God has given

* * * * * * * * *

I will guide thee with mine eye."

This useful hymn was written in 1871 by a lawyer who was on his way to business in a street car going from his home in Morristown, N. J., to his law office in New York. The hymn was written on the margin of a newspaper and was probably the most important thing Mr. Niles ever did in his life. He was born in South Kingston, R. I., and was educated in Providence.

Frank Mason North, D. D.

1850-

"Where cross the crowded ways of life"

This hymn, said to be included in more standard hymnals than any other hymn of the 20th century, was written at the suggestion of Prof. Caleb T. Winchester of Wesleyan University, who had heard Dr. North preach a sermon on the text, "Go ye therefore into the highways." In this sermon Dr. North described the crowds in Union Square, New York City. This suggested the first line of this notable hymn which was published in 1905. Dr. North was born in New York City and became the secretary of the Methodist Union.

Andrews Norton, D. D.

1786-1853

"Where ancient forests widely spread,
Where bends the cateract's ocean-fall,
On the lone mountain's silent head,
There are Thy temples, God of all."

This is the opening stanza of one of the few hymns*

---

* Julian calls his hymns "Meditations in verse." One of these begins,
"My God, I thank Thee. May no thought". Another begins,
"Oh, stay thy tears, for they are blest
Whose days are past, whose toil is done."

written by a distinguished scholar, controversalist, and critic, who was born at Hingham, Mass., and died at Newport, R. I. Dr. Norton was the successor of Dr. Channing in a professorship at Harvard Theological School. He was a Unitarian and opposed the doctrine of the Trinity, but also opposed Theodore Parker's Naturalistic Theology. He wrote a powerful prose work on the genuineness of the gospels.

Nathaniel Norton

fl. 19th century

"Come unto me; it is the Savior's voice."

This hymn was written by a man of culture and extensive reading who had until that night never made a public profession of religion. In an after meeting held by George F. Pentecost, this man rose and acknowledged Christ as his Savior, then went home and wrote this hymn.

Cyrus S. Nusbaum

fl. 19th century

"Would you live for Jesus?
* * * * * * * * *
Let Him have His way with thee."

This hymn which is No. 396 in the Service Hymnal was written by the above named obscure hymnist who is also the composer of the tune to which it is set.

Rev. Johnson Oatman, Jr.

1856-1930

"When storms of life are round me beating
* * * * * * * * *
I want to be alone with God."

This beautiful hymn was written by a Methodist minister who lived in New Jersey. It was first published by Kirkpatrick whose songs were later bought by the Hope Publishing Co. of Chicago. Mr. Oatman it said to have written 5,000 hymns and to have more of his pieces* in the gospel song books than any other writer. In 1916 he believed his best songs were yet to be written.

Rev. Samson Occum

fl. 18th century

"Awaked by Sinai's awful sound"

This hymn was written by a remarkable Indian† preacher who in boyhood was converted under the preaching of George Whitefield. Occum was educated at Lebanon, Conn., and labored among the Indians of Long Island and also among the Oneidas of New York. He went to England to raise money for schools and while there attracted much attention. He raised $10,000, which is said to be the foundation of Dartmouth College.

W. A. Ogden

fl. 19th century

"I've a message from the Lord, Hallelujah!"

This hymn, of which the above named author composed both words and music is found in "Hymns of the Gospel New and Old." It is not listed by Julian.

---

* Here are the titles of some of his well-known hymns:
"No, not one."   "Higher Ground."
"Deeper Yet."   "Count your blessings."
The following lines are the first stanza and chorus of one of his hymns which personally I like very much:
"If thou would'st have the dear Savior from heaven
Walk by thy side from the morn till the even,
There is a rule that each day thou must follow,—
Humble thyself to walk with God.
Refrain. Humble thyself and the Lord will draw near thee,
Humble thyself and his mercy shall cheer thee,
He will not walk with the proud or the scornful,
Humble thyself to walk with God."
This hymn appears in the hymnal "Heavenly Praises" published by Thoro Harris of Chicago.

† I came across a picture of this man in a book called "Pioneer Hymn-writers" opp. p. 55.

TULLIUS CLINTON O'KANE

1830-

"Who are these beside the chilly wave?"
* * * * * * * *
Washed in the blood of the Lamb."

This familiar gospel hymn was written by an American writer, a musician, tall, splendid looking,—straight. The hymn is found in "Christ in Song." No. 890.

KENNETH G. OLSEN

1886-

"Have faith in God; His word is true,"

This hymn of merit was written by a hymnist descended from the old Viking stock of Norway. He was born at Stoughton, Wis., and graduated at the University of Wisconsin, after which he taught English and public speaking for eight years until failing sight stopped him. This trouble with his eyes began in boyhood and induced him to sit at a piano and improvise music. He married a lady who had been educated at the Oberlin Conservatory of Music, and with her aid Mr. Olsen has been able to harmonize his many original hymns,* which have been used of God in gospel meetings. He is now connected with the Christian Workers' Union—headquarters at Framingham, Mass.

---

* One of Mr. Olsen's inspirational hymns is entitled, "Sweeter because 'tis true." He is interested in the composition of both words and melodies and in the ministry of sending them by radio. He also assists in the editing of "Word and Work."

HENRY USTIC ONDERDONK, D. D.

1789-1858

"The Spirit in our hearts"

This hymn in extensive use among Episcopalians was
written by a Bishop of Philadelphia who did large and useful
service to hymnody both as an author and a compiler. In
1844 he was suspended from the House of Bishops on account of intemperance but was restored in 1856. He did
not, however, resume the duties of his office, but died two
years later, presumably (like so many of us) a broken-spirited
man. Dr. Onderdonk was born in New York City, graduated
at Columbia College, and took a degree in medicine in Edinburgh. Julian lists 12 of his hymns.

EDGAR PAGE

fl. 19th century

"I've reached the land of corn and wine,"

This hymn, given in Sankey's "Songs and Solos" is attributed to the above named author, as is also the hymn beginning "Simply trusting every day", but both these hymns are
in Sankey's book "My Life and Sacred Songs", published
in 1906, attributed to E. P. Stites, but without any explanation as to the change in his ascription of authorship. This is
a puzzler, but Mr. Sankey is now beyond our asking him for
an explanation.

D. K. PALMER

fl. 19th century

"Angry words, oh let them never
From the tongue unguarded slip."

This useful hymn of admonition, much needed by us all,
was evidently written by a connection of Dr. Horatio
Richmond Palmer who set the above words to music. But
whether D. K. Palmer is a man or woman I do not know.
The hymn is not listed by Julian. It is found in Christ
in Song No. 581.

Dr. Horatio Richmond Palmer, Mus. Doc.

1834-1907

"Yield not to temptation."

This well known hymn* was written in 1868 by a choir master in a Baptist church. Later he conducted with efficiency and acceptance the singing in the great Chautauqua assemblies of Bishop John H. Vincent. Later still he organized the Church Choral Union and had a choir of 4,000 at a sacred concert given in Madison Square Garden in New York. He was born in Sherbourne, New York, and died at his home at Park Hill on the Hudson in his seventy-third year. He was a beloved, enthusiastic man of magnetic personality. He held from Chicago University the degree of Mus. Doc. He was the son of a musician. At the age of seven he sang alto in a choir and at the age of seventeen was organist and choir-master. His birth place was Sherbourne, N. Y.

Ray Palmer, D. D.

1808-1887

"My faith looks up to Thee,"

This standard hymn† was written by a prominent Congregational minister when he was a young man in the theological seminary. One day he met on the streets of New York the well known music composer Lowell Mason, who said to him, "I am getting up a hymnal. Have you a hymn to contribute?" Palmer replied by taking the above hymn written in pencil out of his pocket and asking, "How will this do?" Mason read it over as they stood in the street, then said, "Mr. Palmer, you may do many things in your

---

* This hymn was on one occasion used to quell an uprising of the women prisoners at Sing Sing, N. Y. A lady sang it in a clear, strong voice, the tumult subsided, and the women went quietly to their cells. Dr. Palmer composed the tune to this and to numerous other hymns for hymn books. He is also the author of a hymn called "Galilee" for which he got the inspiration through a visit to the Holy Land.

† The author said of this hymn that it was born in his heart and demanded expression, that he wrote it with little effort and tender emotion, and ended the last lines with tears. It has been translated into many languages among them Tamil and Tahitian.

life, but I think you will be longest remembered as the author
of 'My faith looks up to Thee'." Later on Mr. Palmer made
some fine translations from Latin hymns. One of these
from Bernard of Clairvaux begins, "Jesus, thou joy of
loving hearts." Another from the Latin hymn probably by
Thomas Aquinas begins, "O bread to pilgrims given." Ray
Palmer was born at Little Compton, R. I., held a pastorate
in Albany, N. Y., and finally resided in Newark, N. J.

Rev. J. Edgar Park, D. D.

1879-

"We would see Jesus; lo, His star is shining."

This hymn, which is considered one of the best that the
present century has produced, was written in 1913 by the
above named author. It is included in the hymnal called
"Hymns of the Living Age," No. 132. Dr. Park was born
in Belfast, Ireland, and perhaps should be listed as a British
hymnist, but as his active life has been largely in the United
States, I venture to place him here. He is a Congregational
minister and has been President of Wheaton College. His
home is in Norton, Mass. He is a married man with six
children. His wife is a Massachusetts lady.

Rev. John Parker

fl. 19th century

"God holds the key of all unknown,
    And I am glad."

This beautiful hymn set to music by George Stebbins and
found in Gospel Hymns No. 5, was written by the above
named American pastor.

THEODORE PARKER

1812-1860

"And they who dearest hope and deepest pray,
  Toil by the Light, Life, Way which Thou hast
    given."

These lines, taken from a hymn on Jesus, were written by the eloquent and fearless reformer* above named. Parker was born in Lexington, Mass., where his grandfather had been captain of the militia in the famous battle of 1775. Parker was brought up on a farm and went to district school. At the age of seventeen he began to teach school and supported himself through Harvard College. Later he was a Unitarian pastor at North Roxbury, but became leader of an independent society which worshipped at Music Hall in Boston. He was an ardent anti-slavery lecturer. He died from tuberculosis in Florence, Italy, at the age of forty-eight.

JOHN HOWARD PAYNE

1791-1852

" 'Mid pleasures and palaces though we may roam,
  Be it ever so humble, there's no place like home."

This is given as a hymn in "Christ in Song", No. 738. Julian does not list it. It is said that Payne wrote this in a foreign land and that he did not have any home at the time. He was born in New York City, the son of a doctor. His mother was a converted Jewess. His father became bankrupt and John supported himself early as a clerk and later became an actor. He finally became United States Consul at Tunis where he died. His remains were brought back to the United States in 1883 and he is buried at Washington, D. C.

---

* Here are some lines from his pen:
   "I shudder not to bear a hated name,
   Wanting all wealth, myself my sole defense;
   But give me, Lord, eyes to behold the truth,
     * * * * * * * *
   Give me the power to labor for mankind;
   Make me the mouth of those who cannot speak."
Parker held a very liberal theology.

ANDREW PRESTON PEABODY, D. D.

1811-1893

"Behold the western evening light."

This hymn was written by the chaplain of Harvard University and editor of the North American Review 1854-63. He was born in Beverly, Mass., and became a Unitarian minister of abounding charity and rhetorical grace, highly esteemed as a thinker and writer and for his beneficial influence over successive classes of students at Harvard, where he resigned his position in 1881.

WILLIAM BOURNE OLIVER PEABODY

1799-1848

"Who is thy neighbor? He whom thou
Hast power to aid and bless."

The writer of this hymn was a native of Exeter, N. H., a graduate of Harvard and the pastor for twenty-seven years of the Unitarian Church at Springfield, Mass. He was a man of rare accomplishments and consummate virtue, whose loveliness of character "impressed many outside his own sect." He wrote a number of hymns, five of which are listed by Julian. He had a twin brother, Oliver William Bourne Peabody, who also was a Unitarian minister and wrote hymns. The brothers resembled each other in looks, voice, manner, and qualities of mind—a remarkable instance of "identical twins."

CORICE C. PEARL*

1856-

"We shall meet them; we shall meet them,
Over on the other side."

This hymn was written by a business man of Norwalk, O.,

---

* The Pearls are descended from a notable English family that settled in West Boxford, Mass. in early days. Two rooms from their home of beauty and refinement are reproduced in the Fine Arts Building in Boston from materials brought from that house, including a great fireplace with its mantel seven feet long, and elegant antique furniture.

who was also curator of the Historical Society of that town
for many years. Mr. Pearl is a genial person with a wonderful faculty of making friends wherever he goes, and as
the hymn shows he considers friendships eternal. His birthplace was Berlin Heights, O. where his father was a school-
teacher and later had a store. Both father and son used
verse-writing* as a recreation.

Rev. George B. Peck
fl. 19th century
"Come, come to Jesus!
He waits to welcome thee."

This hymn, not listed by Julian, was written by an obscure
hymnist, probably an American.

Sylvanus Dryden Phelps, D. D.
1816-
"Saviour, Thy dying love Thou gavest me"

This master hymn was written by the minister of a Baptist
church in New Haven, Conn., who later was the editor of
a Hartford paper called "The Christian Secretary." Mr.
Phelps was born in Sheffield, Conn., and graduated at
Brown University in 1844. He wrote poems which were
published and several hymns appear in various collections.
The one quoted above, written in 1862, is the best known.
Dr. Lowry wrote a letter to Dr. Phelps on his seventieth
birthday in which he said, "It is worth living seventy years
for, even if nothing comes of it, but one such hymn as
'Saviour, Thy dying love.' Happy is the man who produces
one song which the world will keep singing after its author
shall have passed away." Julian lists 13 of his hymns. Two
of these are the ones beginning:
"Once I heard a sound at my heart's dark door",
and
"Sweet is the hour of prayer."

---

* Mr. Pearl's beautiful lyric entitled "My Violin" will probably be
included in an anthology now in preparation by the Quill Club of
Colorado Springs of which Mr. Pearl is a member.

PHILIP PHILLIPS

1834-1895

"I have heard of a Saviour's love"

This hymn was published in Sankey's "Songe and Solos" and was written by the above named "Singing Pilgrim", as he was commonly called. Phillips was born at Chautauqua Co., N. Y., and in youth was engaged in farming but early devoted himself to the work of a singing evangelist. In this capacity he visited most of the English speaking countries. He also edited several hymnals. When nearing death in Delaware, Ohio, he wrote, "You see I am still in the land of the dying. Often in the night seasons I have real visions. The lines that come to me most often are,

"We speak of the realms of the blest,

*   *   *   *   *   *   *

But what must it be to be there!"

ARTHUR TAPPAN PIERSON

1837-

"With harps and with viols there stand a great throng"

This hymn which was published in Sankey's "Songs and Solos" and also in "Laudes Domini", was written by the above named Presbyterian minister who had pastorates in Binghamton, New York, and Detroit. He was widely known for his power and consecration in service. Julian lists four of his hymns. He was born in New York City.

JOHN PIERPONT

1785-1866

"God of our fathers in whose sight"

This hymn is one of the many written by a Boston Unitarian pastor born at Litchfield, Conn., and educated at Yale

College and Harvard Divinity School. His advocacy of anti-slavery, temperance, and other reforms led to his withdrawal from the Boston pastorate, but he took a pastorate at Troy, N. Y., and later at Medford, Mass. During the Civil War he was chaplain of a Massachusetts regiment. Later he was employed until his death in the Treasury Department at Washington. He was tall, handsome, a genuine poet, a man of zeal and energy. He died suddenly at Medford, Mass. Julian lists 19 of his hymns. He also was a writer of other poems and he edited school reading books. One of his well known poems begins, "The Pilgrim fathers, where are they?" Another which begins "I cannot make them dead" is characterized by Julian as "exquisitely touching and beautiful."

Dr. William S. Pitts

fl. 19th century

"There's a church in the valley by the wildwood,"

This lovely hymn about the little brown church of his childhood was written by the above named author who composed the music as well as the words. The piece is found in "The Service Hymnal", No. 740.

Edgar Allen Poe

1811-1849

"Thank heaven the crisis, the danger is past
* * * * * * * * *
And the fever called living is conquered at last."

It is by a stretch of the imagination that the celebrated author of "The Raven" is called a hymnist, although he did write a hymn to the Virgin Mary. He was born in Boston, second son of a romantic couple of stage people who died early. Edgar was adopted by a man named Allen who was displeased with him and disinherited him. This threw him into literature to support himself and the destitute and beauti-

ful cousin Virginia Clemm whom he married and who died
early of consumption. Her mother tenderly cared for the
pathetic pair in a home of extreme poverty. The "loved and
lost Lenore" was a friend of his youth, a certain Mrs. Helen
Stannard, the mother of a boy schoolmate. To her he con-
fided his boyish sorrows and when she died he used to visit
her grave nightly, lingering longer when the nights were
dreary and cold. Poe was dissipated,—drinking and gambling,—but there was a strange fascination about him and
those who knew him most loved him the best. Some critics
consider Poe the most remarkable poetic genius America has
produced.

WILLIAM C. POOLE

fl. 1913

"Just when I need Him most,"

This popular hymn was written by a native of Maryland
from Quaker stock. He was raised on a farm, but in adult
life has been a preacher in Wilmington, Del., and has been
the Superintendent of the Anti-Saloon League of Delaware.
He has written about 500 hymns. This writing he considers
as a recreation from heavy cares and responsibilities which
might otherwise be depressing. He says of himself that he
has been living at high pressure since he was fifteen years
old, but that he has been composing verses since he was
twelve.

LEWIS GLOVER PRAY

1793-

"When God upheaved the pillared earth"

This hymn was written by a native of Quincy, Mass., who
was in youth an apprentice in a shoe store, but became a
member of the State Legislature. He was a life long Sunday School worker and compiled the first Sunday School
hymn book with music for the Unitarians. One of his hymns
begins, "Come when the leaves are greenest."

Rev. James Proctor

Probably 19th century

"Nothing, sinner, great or small,
Nothing, sinner, no."

These familiar lines, not listed by Julian, are attributed to the above named minister.

Anson D. F. Randolph

1820-1896

"I would be joyful as the days go by,
Counting God's mercies to me."

These lines were written by the above named prominent New York publisher. He was born at Woodbridge, N. J. His poems were collected by his brother and published by Charles Scribner. Mr. Randolph was educated in the public schools of New York and was a man of practical tastes. He died at Westhampton, Long Island. One of his hymns is found in a few collections. It begins, "Weary, Lord, of struggling here." This is listed by Julian.

Isaac Ogden Rankin

1852-

"Light of the world's dark story"

This is one of the hymns* written in 1900 by the literary editor of the "Congregationalist" and included in the "Pilgrim Hymnal." Mr. Rankin was born in New York City and graduated at Princeton and at Union Theological Seminary.

---

* Another of his hymns begins,
          "We should go singing, singing,
              Along the pilgrim road."
I have seen the tender gospel hymn,
          "Are you weary, are you heavy hearted?
                Tell it to Jesus,"
attributed both to Isaac and to Jeremiah Rankin. Julian does not list this last mentioned hymn at all and I am not sure by which of the Rankins it was written.

JEREMIAH EAMES RANKIN, D. D.

1828-1904

"God be with you till we meet again."

This popular good-bye* hymn was written by a Congregational minister of Washington, D. C., who was for several years President of Howard University. He was born at Thornton, N. H., and educated at Middlebury College, Vt. Another of his hymns begins, "Are you weary, are you heavy hearted?"

ROSSITER WORTHINGTON RAYMOND, PH. D.

1840-1901

"Far out on the desolate billow"

This pretty song was written by a mining engineer, a contributor to scientific journals, who was born in Cincinnati, Ohio, graduated at Brooklyn Polytechnic, and also studied in Germany. He served in the Civil War with the grade of captain. Dr. Raymond was a Congregationalist and associated with the Plymouth Church in Brooklyn. Julian lists six of his hymns.

---

* I had this story about this hymn told me by a lady who claimed to know the facts. She said it was slipped into the hand of Dr. Rankin's daughter just as she was about to sail with her mother for Europe. The father was anxious lest the excitement to which she was going should be detrimental to her spiritual life. Sankey, however, denies that the hymn was written for any special occasion and Dr. Rankin says that the last stanzas were written later than the first ones.

Francis Brewster Reeves

1836-1922

"There dawns a day on every heart
When earthly pleasures cloy"

This fine hymn is one of many* written by the President of the Girard National Bank of Philadelphia—who also held many positions of public trust. He was born at Bridgeton, N. J. and in later life became a ruling elder in the Presbyterian church and Superintendent of a Sunday School. In 1892 he was commissioned to distribute a cargo of food in Russia, for the relief of famine sufferers, and the Emperor Alexander III recognized his personal services by a costly gift. Mr. Reeves was the author of a book on "The Evolution of our Christian Hymnology."

Eben Eugene Rexford

1848-

"O where are the reapers that garner in"

This is one of the four hymns by the above named writer which are included in Sankey's "Songs and Solos". E. E. Rexford was born in Johnsburg, N. Y., went to district school, then taught two years and went to Lawrence University at Appleton, Wis., where he took a degree. He then devoted himself to literary work. He was floricultural editor of the "Ladies Home Journal" for fourteen years. I have seen the song "Silver Threads among the Gold"

---

* The first line of some of Mr. Reeves' hymns are as follows:
"Wake my soul in joyful measure."
"In the still air a voice calls soft and clear."
"Let not your heart be with trouble oppressed."
"Accept dear Lord our praise!"
"We thank Thee Father that Thy love for all."
"On all who would, God's grace implore."
"God give our President."
"Heavenly Father, God of Nations."
"O why should we, heavy laden be."
The last mentioned hymn was written on a train when returning from the funeral of Robert DuBois who was for 28 years leader of a choir at Bridgeton, N. J. This information was obtained for me by Dr. John Wurts of Germantown, Pa., whose encouragement in this arduous undertaking (as also the interest of his beloved wife) has been of incalculable help to me.

attributed to him (whether correctly I cannot say). His first poem was written and published when he was fourteen. I have seen his picture, showing a pleasant, kindly face. He was an organist for many years in a Congregational Church in Wisconsin. One of his hymns is entitled "The Beacon Light."

Rev. Charles Francis Richardson

1851-1913

"It is the Holy Ghost
Who takes man's body for His temple fair,
And he who guards it with most constant care
Shall please its tenant best."

These lines are culled from a poem* on temperance by the above named author and Professor of English at Dartmouth College, his alma mater. Professor Richardson was born in Holliwell, Maine, and some of his hymns have been published in hymnals.

Daniel C. Roberts, D. D.

1841-1907

"God of our fathers, whose almighty hand
Leads forth in beauty all the starry band"

This hymn was written in 1876 by an Episcopal clergyman born at Bridge Hampton, Long Island, N. Y. Before his ordination Dr. Roberts served as a private in the Civil War. He was a graduate of Gambier College and was eventually Rector at Concord, N. H. The above hymn is used in various hymnals.

---

* These lines inculcate a neglected truth. Is it Herbert Spencer who says "The first duty of man is to be a good animal?"

CHARLES SEYMOUR ROBINSON, D. D.

1829-1899

"Savior, I follow on, guided by Thee"

This standard hymn was written by a Presbyterian minister who was born at Bennington, Vt., and graduated at Union Theological Seminary, New York. He was at the time the minister of the American Chapel at Paris, France. He edited two standard hymnals, "Songs of the Sanctuary" and "Laudes Domini." His death took place in New York.

REV. WADE ROBINSON

fl. 19th century

"Loved with everlasting love"

This beautiful hymn found in one of the Northfield Hymnals was written by an author of whom I have no data.

HOMER RODEHEAVER

1880-

"Somebody cares"

This is the title of a well-known gospel hymn written by one of three Rodeheaver brothers who are carrying on one of the largest gospel publishing companies in our country. Homer Rodeheaver was born in Union Furnace, O., but was taken in infancy to East Tennessee where he spent his boy-hood, working in log and saw mill camp and in coal mines. He attended crude mountain schools, but later worked his way for a part of four years in Ohio Wesleyan University. For five years he was musical director with Dr. W. E. Biederwolf and then for twenty years was in the same capacity with Rev. Wm. A. Sunday. He has written several gospel songs.*

---

* One of his hymns is "O, how He saves," and another is "Carry On." He also wrote some popular songs that had to do with the World War. One was, "We'll be waiting when you come back home," and another, "Good-bye France, Hello Miss Liberty."

Charles B. J. Root

fl. 19th century

"Abiding, O so wondrous sweet"

This hymn which was sung in the South African General Mission in Johannesburg is by an obscure hymnist. The hymn is found in Hymns of the Gospel New and Old.

George F. Root

1820-1895

"She only touched the hem of His garment"

This well known hymn was written by a doctor of music who is best known as the composer of popular songs which include "Just before the battle, mother," and "The battle cry of Freedom." Mr. Root was a native of Sheffield, Berkshire Co., Mass., and died at Bailey Island, Maine. He had a gracious and engaging personality and was beloved by all. He was also a devout Christian. Once when with George Stebbins he pointed to a Bible lying on the table and remarked that he regarded the Word of God as the chart of his life. He composed the melodies to which we sing various well known hymns. The words of four hymns found in "Sankey's books were also written by him. One of these begins, "Why do you wait, dear brother?" Another of his hymns begins, "Come to the Savior make no delay."

F. H. Rowley

fl. 19th century

"I will sing the wondrous story"

This familiar gospel hymn which is found in Sankey's collection No. 5 is by an obscure hymnist who is not listed by Julian. The hymn was set to music by Peter Bilhorn.

J. Edward Ruark

fl. 20th century

"You may have the joybells ringing in your heart"

This gospel hymn is by an author of whom I have no data. It is familiar and found in Rodeheaver's Songs for Service.

J. F. Rushing

fl. 19th century

"Christian, the morn breaks sweetly o'er thee
And all the midnight shadows flee,
* * * * * * * *
Away, away, leave all for glory."

This hymn* is No. 680 in Christ in Song" and is there set to music by the author of the words.

Abram J. Ryan

1834-1886

"Life is a burden, bear it;
Life is a duty, dare it;
Life is a thorn crown, wear it
Though it break your heart in twain."

These lines were written by the poetic priest of the Southland. Like Henry Timrod, Ryan was a poet of the lost cause of the South. He was of Irish descent, and some of his poems are very beautiful. Here are two lines from one of a hymn-like quality,

"And a cross gleams in our pathway; on it hangs the crucified,
And he answers all our yearnings by the whisper, "Follow me."

---

* I like this hymn so much, that I often sing it to a melody of my own, when I am working around the house.

REV. T. RYDER

fl. 19th century

"Buried with Christ and raised with Him too"

This hymn, which is No. 309 in "Hymns of the Gospel New and Old" was written by an author of whom I have no data. Julian lists a Rev. H. J. D. Ryder, an English hymn writer, but I suppose the two are not identical.

REV. J. H. SAMMIS

fl. 19th century

"When we walk with the Lord,
* * * * * * * * *
Trust and obey."

This well-known hymn was written by a native of Brooklyn, N. Y., who in his 22nd year went to Loganport, Ind. He became a Y. M. C. A. secretary. Later he attended Lane and McCormack seminaries and was a Presbyterian pastor in several cities of the middle west. Eventually he went to Los Angeles, Cal. His hymn is widely used, but Julian does not list either the hymn or its author. The suggestion for the hymn was given by Professor Towner from a testimony given in one of Mr. Moody's meetings at Brockton, Mass., by a young man who said, "I'm going to trust and I'm going to obey." Professor Towner jotted down that sentence and sent it to Mr. Sammis who wrote the chorus of the hymn first.

IRA D. SANKEY

1840-1908

"There'll be no dark valley when Jesus comes"

All but the first line of this much used hymn was written by the beloved gospel singer, Mr. Sankey, who generally ascribes the hymn to W. D. Cushing who wrote the first line of it. Julian lists it as of composite authorship. Mr. Sankey is not primarily a hymnist though he wrote nine hymns,* but he composed the music of many hymns written by others and beautifully rendered in song by himself. He was born in Edinburg, Pa. His father was a state legislator and banker. Ira's voice attracted the attention of Mr. Moody at a Y. M. C. A. convention in Indianapolis. At the close of the meeting he sought out Sankey and asked what was his employment. When Sankey told him he was employed in a bank, Moody said, "You will have to give that up. I have been looking for you eight years." So it transpired that Sankey went to England and .Scotland with Moody and sang before Queen Victoria and got a deathless name and crown through the harvest of souls won to Christ through his singing. He tells in his book about his tragic experience in escaping from the Chicago fire.

MINOT JUDSON SAVAGE

1841-1918

"O Star of Truth down-shining,"

This hymn was written by a Unitarian minister of Boston, who was born at Norridgewock, Maine, and graduated at Bangor Theological Seminary. With H. M. Dow he edited a hymnal called "Sacred Songs for Public Worship" to which he contributed 46 of his own hymns, some of which appeared later in other hymnals. Julian lists eight of his hymns. He was a Congregational minister for six years before he became a Unitarian pastor.

---

* The last hymn of which Mr. Sankey wrote both words and music was composed especially for the memorial service held for **Mr. Moody** in Carnegie Hall in New York. It was based on Moody's last **words,** "Earth recedes, heaven opens before me. God is calling me and I must go." The first line of this hymn is as follows:
  "Out of the shadow land, into the sunshine."
Mr. Sankey sang it at the above named meeting.

CHARLES H. SCOTT

"Open my eyes that I may see"

This fine hymn which is 174 in the "Service Hymnal" was written, both words and music, by the above named writer.

EDMUND HAMILTON SEARS

1810-1876

"Calm on the listening ear of night"

This hymn, which was considered by Oliver Wendell Holmes as one of the finest ever written, was composed by a Berkshire clergyman, born at Sandisfield, Mass. Dr. Sears wrote also another well-known hymn which begins, "It came upon the midnight clear." He is also the author of a book entitled "The Fourth Gospel the Heart of Christ." He died at Weston, Mass., where his last pastorate was held. He had previously been a pastor at Wayland and at Lancaster, Mass. He was a graduate of the Harvard theological school and, although connected with the Unitarians, he always held to the absolute divinity of Christ. His views were rather Swedenborgian than Unitarian. His two Christmas hymns rank with the best and are in extensive use on both sides of the Atlantic.

KNOWLES SHAW

fl. 19th century

"Sowing in the morning
* * * * * * * * *
Bringing in the sheaves."

This well known hymn which is No. 443 in the Service Hymnal is by the above named obscure author.

L. Shorey

fl. 19th century

"I have a friend so precious"

This hymn by an obscure author is entitled "My Lord and I" and found in "Jubilant Praise" No. 69.

Gordon D. Shorney

fl. 20th century

Mr. Shorney does not class himself as a hymnist but as the President of the Hope Publishing Co. of Chicago, he is intimately connected with hymnody, and is such a fine friend in this undertaking of mine, I cannot omit him.

Ernest Warburton Shurtleff

1862-1817

"Lead on, O King Eternal,"

This hymn, which was written as a parting hymn for the class of 1887 at Andover Theological Seminary, was written by a native of Boston. He held Congregational pastorates at Palmer and Plymouth in Massachusetts and later in Minneapolis, Minn. The above hymn has appeared in various collections.

A. B. Simpson

fl. 19th century

"The mercy of God is an ocean divine
* * * * * * * *
Launch out into the deep."

This hymn was written by the founder of the Christian Alliance of New York. He was a saintly character and promoted greatly the work of foreign missions. His great camp meetings held yearly at Old Orchard, Maine, were precious occasions to the throngs who gathered there. He published a hymnal in which were several of his own hymns.*

W. T. SLEEPER

"A ruler once came to Jesus by night,"

This solemn hymn was written by a preacher of Worcester, Mass. on a suggestion by George C. Stebbins who, in his book, "Reminiscences and Gospel Hymn Stories" relates an incident connected with this hymn, that on its being sung in a street meeting in St. Joseph, Mo., it was the means of conversion of one of the listeners. Sleeper† also wrote the fine hymn beginning,

"Out of my bondage, sorrow and night,
Jesus, I come to Thee."

SAMUEL FRANCIS SMITH, D. D.

1808-1895

"My country, 'tis of thee,"

Our national anthem§ was written by a Baptist minister of Newton, Mass. He was educated at Harvard and was a scholarly and graceful‡ writer, a pure and gentle character.

* One of these begins, "Once it was the blessing, now it is the Lord." Another begins, "I have learned the wondrous secret." This is to be found in "Christ in Song," No. 562.

† Mr. Sleeper's initials are sometimes given as W. W. I am not sure which way is correct.

‡ He also wrote three other well known hymns, viz—
"The morning light is breaking"
"Today the Saviour calls"
"Softly fades the twilight ray."

§ Since I wrote the above, Congress has made "The Star Spangled Banner" the national anthem, much to the disapproval of pacifists.

On many public occasions he was the guest of honor* as
the author of the national anthem. He had a happy old age
and died suddenly and painlessly on a seat in a railroad car
in the eighty-eighth year of his age.

H. G. Spofford

fl. 1874

"It is well with my soul."

This hymn was written by a Chicago lawyer in commemoration of the death of his four children by drowning due
to the collision of the French steamer Ville de Havre in
1874 with a large sailing ship. Their mother, when she
knew the steamer was sinking, took her children to the deck
and prayed with them. She herself was picked up and
cabled to her husband, "Saved alone." The pair went to
Jerusalem and founded a colony who lived there waiting for
the Lord's return.

Charles Sprague

1791-1875

"Gay, guiltless pair,
    What seek ye from the fields of heaven?"

This lovely sacred poem entitled "The Winged Worship-
pers" was suggested to the author by two swallows that
flew into a church during service. Sprague was a teller in
a Boston bank whose father was one of the party that threw

---

* On one occasion he visited the Board of Trade in Chicago and
although sitting in the gallery, he became the center of notice. Suddenly
the trading on the floor ceased and from the wheat pit came the song,
"My country 'tis of thee." Dr. Smith arose from his seat and bowed.
He was then led to the floor by the Secretary, and, with heads uncovered,
the members sang the rest of the hymn. Dr. Smith had a son who was
a missionary in Burmah. He had the joy of hearing "The morning
light is breaking" sung by the Burmese Christians in their native
tongue. His classmate at Harvard, Oliver Wendell Holmes wrote of him
"there's a fine youngster of excellent pith. Fate tried to conceal him
by naming him Smith."

over the cargo of tea in Boston harbor in 1773, the famous
"Boston tea-party." Charles was educated in the public
schools and received various honors for his poems and ora-
tions. His writings were published in 1855. Most of his
poems are not sufficiently lyrical to be called hymns.

GEORGE C. STEBBINS
1846-
"Christian, walk carefully, danger is near."

This hymn, which seems to have been originally by an
anonymous writer, was arranged and set to music by the
above named fellow worker with Moody and Whittle in
evangelistic meetings. Mr. Stebbins is not primarily a
hymnist, but rather a composer of music to which very many
of our best known gospel hymns are set, as is shown in
"Gospel Hymns No. 5" which he edited in company with
Sankey and James McGranahan. One of Stebbins' most
beautiful tunes is that to which Fanny Crosby's glorious
hymn is set which begins, "Some day the silver chord will
break." Another of Stebbins' beautiful melodies is the one
to which is set the hymn beginning, "In the secret of His
presence." It is said that Mr. Stebbins left his father's farm
to devote himself to the ministry of gospel song. He was a
consecrated man who lived in Brooklyn, N. Y.

E. P. STITES
fl. 19th century
"Simply trusting every day"

This hymn was written by a Chicago man. It was handed
as a newspaper clipping to Mr. Moody in 1876. He passed
it over to Sankey to write the music for it. Sankey assented
provided Mr. Moody would vouch for the doctrine of the
hymn. Mr. Moody said he would, so the music was written.
The story is told of the comfort the hymn was to a sick
woman in great suffering. Both this hymn and another have
been attributed to Edgar Page. (See note on Edgar Page.)

Rev. John Hart Stockton

1813-1877

"Come, every soul by sin oppressed."

This gospel hymn was written by a Methodist preacher who also set the hymn to music. It was used by Sankey who changed the chorus to the one now most familiar. Sankey tells the story of using this hymn in London where eight persons were converted through hearing it.

Whitley (?) Stokes

fl. 19th century

"Hover o'er me, Holy Spirit,
* * * * * * * *
Fill me now."

This hymn, published in 1907 by L. E. Sweeney, was evidently written by an American, but whether it was Dr. Whitley Stokes is not ascertained. Julian does not list this hymn. It is found in "Christ in Song" No. 308. The author is there simply given as "Stokes." (No initials).

Nathan Strong, D. D.

1748-1816

"Almighty Sovereign of the skies"

This hymn for national thanksgiving was written by a Congregational minister, a native of Coventry, Conn., a graduate of Yale and subsequently the pastor of the First Congregational Church of Hartford. He won much repute by an essay on "The Doctrine of Eternal Misery Consistent with the Infinite Benevolence of God." (I have not read it and cannot say whether it is convincing or not.) Julian says of him that his services to American hymnology have been very great. Six of his hymns were published in Nettleton's "Village Hymns."

Melancthon Woolsey Stryker, L. L. D.

1851-1905

"Death cannot make my soul afraid."

This hymn was written by a Presbyterian minister born in Vernon, N. Y. and pastor at various places, Auburn, Ithaca, Holyoke, and Chicago. He was joint editor with H. P. Main of "The Church Praise Book" in 1882. Julian lists 28 of his hymns and says that they are massive and rugged, full of dogmatism and fire, and that in spite of some defects, a few of them will live. He was President of Hamilton College at one period of his life.

Leonard Swain

1821-1869

"My soul, weigh not thy life"

This hymn and also the one beginning "My soul, it is thy God" was written by a Congregational minister who was born at Concord, N. H. and educated at Dartmouth College and Andover. His pastorates were at Nashua, N. H., and at Providence, R. I. The above hymns appeared anonymously in 1858 and for a long time their authorship was unknown.

Timothy Swan

1758-

This eccentric genius, born at Worcester, Mass., was the composer of the tune of China to which is set the hymn of Watts which begins, "Why do we mourn departing friends?" The wild and thrilling notes of this tune make children weep. Swan's only course of study lasted three weeks. He was apprenticed to a hatter in Northfield and while at work he composed psalm tunes of great originality.

William Bingham Tappan

1794-1849

" 'Tis midnight and on Olive's brow"

This beautiful standard hymn* was written by a missionary of the American Sunday School Union who was born at Beverly, Mass. At the age of sixteen Tappan was apprenticed to a clock maker in Boston. At the age of twenty-one he went to Philadelphia and became a licensed preacher for the Congregationalists and went later to Cincinnati in Sunday School Union work. Eventually he returned to Boston and finally died suddenly in West Needham, Mass., of cholera.

Bayard Taylor

1825-1878

"Not so in haste, my heart,"

This hymn† entitled "Wait" is ascribed in the Pilgrim Hymnal to the distinguished author and traveler above named. Taylor was born at Kennett Square, Pa., and got his education in local schools and academies. He never went to college. He began early to contribute to papers and was on the editorial staff of the New York Tribune a large part of his life. At the age of nineteen he took a pedestrian tour through Europe and sent back to the Tribune letters describing his journey, and later went to Syria, Egypt, Calcutta, and China, joining the expedition of Commodore Perry to Japan. At the age of thirty-two he married Mary Agnew

---

* This was set to music by Wm. B. Bradbury. While in Philadelphia Tappan wrote at the age of twenty-four another well-known hymn which begins, "There is an hour of peaceful rest." This hymn was reproduced in England and on the continent.

† This hymn was published in a newspaper first in 1876 and signed B. T. It is not found in any of Taylor's books. Julian expresses some doubt as to whether Taylor wrote it. He did write some other poems of a somewhat hymnlike quality but not really hymns. One of these entitled "The Voyagers" closes with these fine lines,
"We sail no faster for our hopes
No slower for our fears."
He also has a fine poem on "The Old-fashioned Choir" which closes with this line, "Blessed song, blessed Sabbath, forever, amen." I had the pleasure at Oberlin of hearing Taylor lecture.

of his home town. He was a popular lecturer, the author of
many books, a man of social qualities and fine presence. In
1878 he was appointed United States Minister to Germany
and died in Berlin the same year. His body was brought
back to his native town for burial.

George Lansing Taylor, D. D.
1835-

"Dare to do right, dare to be true"
This hymn which first appeared anonymously in W. B.
Bradbury's Golden Censer in 1864, was written by a Methodist minister who was born at Skaneateles, N. Y., and
graduated at Columbia College in 1861 and received his D.D.
from Syracuse in 1876.

Will L. Thompson
1849-1911

"Softly and tenderly Jesus is calling"
This gospel hymn* was written by a choir leader whose
home and birthplace was in East Liverpool, Ohio.

Henry David Thoreau
1817-1862

"I will not doubt the love untold
    Which not my worth nor want hath bought,
    Which wooed me young, and wooed me old,
    And to this evening hath me brought."
These are the concluding lines of a poem on "Inspiration"
by a celebrated genius of Concord, Mass. I feel hesitancy
about including him with the hymnists. (Julian does not and,

---

* Another of Thompson's hymns begins,
            "There's a great day coming
        * * * * * * * *
                Are you ready?"
Another is, "Jesus is all the world to me." He was connected with the
Thompson Music Co. of Chicago.

so far as I know, no hymn of his has ever been included in a hymnal) but the above lines seem to me to have a hymnlike quality. Thoreau graduated at Harvard at the age of twenty. He never married, and supported himself in a bare living by mechanical work, giving all the time possible to the study of nature, close at his doors. He never went far from home, but became an authority on the natural phenomena about him. His writings are forceful and full of the appreciation of beauty. He was a vegetarian and eccentric* in his opinions.

HENRY TIMROD

1829-1867

"Ye winds, keep every storm aloof,
And kiss away the tears they weep.
Ye skies that made their only roof,
Look gently on their houseless sleep."

These lines are culled from "The Orphan Hymn" by a poet of the lost cause, born at Charleston, S. C., who died at the age of thirty-eight of tuberculosis. Timrod was a victim of the Civil War by which both his health and his fortunes were crushed. His beautiful poetry† was being printed as he lay in his last illness and the proof sheets he had been looking over were spattered with his blood as his breath left his body.

---

* There is an amusing story told of him. At one time he was put in jail for refusing to pay a tax which he considered unjust. While incarcerated he had a visit from his friend Ralph Waldo Emerson, who inquired on his arrival, "What are you doing in here, Henry?" Thoreau replied, "What are you doing out there, Ralph?"
Thoreau has lately been compared with Kant as one who made the most of himself by "getting into ruts". i. e. confining his activities to a very limited space. Here is a saying of his, "Sell your clothes and keep your thoughts."

† Timrod's poetry greatly appeals to me. I quote here a few of his choice lines:
"The simplest record of thyself hath worth."
"The time must come wherein thou shalt be taught
The value and the beauty of the past."
"There is no unimpressive spot on earth,
The beauty of the stars is over all."
"A lofty hope, if earnestly pursued,
Is its own crown, and never in this life
Is labor wholly fruitless. In this faith
I shall not count the chances."

Henry Tucker

fl. 19th century

"Call the children early, mother."

This hymn by the above named author is found in one of Bradbury's little collections. It was sung familiarly in my childhood in Sunday School.

H. L. Turner

fl. 19th century

"It may be at morn when the day is awaking"

This hymn is found in "Christ in Song" No. 867. It is not in Julian.

Henry Hallam Tweedy, D. D.

"Eternal God whose power upholds

Both flower and flaming star,"

These are the opening lines of a prize missionary hymn recently copyrighted by the National Hymn Society, headquarters at 105 E. 22nd St., New York City. It was written by a professor in the Yale Divinity School. It is the second prize hymn Dr. Tweedy has written. To me it seems the latest born of the great hymns of the ages.

Rev. Edward Smith Ufford

fl. 19th century

"Throw out the life line across the dark wave,"

This gospel song of which Dr. Cuyler said that it had more electricity in it than any other he had heard, was written by a Baptist minister who was born in Newark, New Jersey. The song was prompted by witnessing a drill of the life saving station at Point Allerton near Boston,—seeing the life line flung out by the crew.* Ufford went home, wrote the song, then sat down at his organ and composed the tune to it in fifteen minutes. His melody was arranged by George C. Stebbins and copyrighted by Bigelow and Main in 1890. Julian does not list it. Mr. Ufford made a world tour, singing his own hymn and using a life saving apparatus to illustrate his lectures. He was a fine Christian character.

THOMAS COGSWELL UPHAM

1799-1872

"I would love Thee, God and Father,"

This hymn,† translated from one of Madame Guyon's, was written by a notable Congregational minister born at Deerfield, N. H., educated at Dartmouth College and Andover Seminary, and for forty-two years Professor of Mental and Moral Philosophy at Bowdoin College. His text book on Mental Philosophy was widely used. He published a volume of poems and a biography of Madame Guyon. Julian lists 8 of his hymns and several of them were included in hymnals. His death took place in New York when he was seventy-five years old.

---

* Sankey's account of the way this hymn was written differs slightly. He says that Ufford was living near the ocean in Massachusetts and was looking at a wreck. He tells several anecdotes about the usefulness of the hymn and life line as an illustration. Here is one of them. The captain's brother fell overboard from a steamer and was drowning. The vessel was reversed and a life line thrown to the man in the water who caught hold of it, tied it around his body, and cried, "Pull away." "Have you hold of the line?" called the captain. Back came the answer, "The line has hold of me."

† This beautiful hymn was a favorite in my childhood's home.

Louis Untermeyer
fl. 19th and 20th centuries

"God, though this life is but a wraith,
Although we know not what we use,
Although we grope with little faith,
Give me the heart to fight and lose."
This is the opening stanza of a hymn called "Prayer" by
the above named liberal author.

J. W. VanDeVenter
1855-

"Looking this way"
This is the title of an appealing song about our departed
friends. It was written by a man born in the country in
Michigan and educated mostly in country schools. He wrote
about 100 hymns.* The one mentioned was a great favorite
with Ira D. Sankey. VanDeVenter's home was latterly in
St. Petersburg, Fla.

Dr. Henry Van Dyke, Jr.
1852-

"O Maker of the mighty deep,"
This hymn, published in 1908, which has been rated as
one of the ten best produced in America during the 20th
century so far, was written by the distinguished author and
clergyman above mentioned. Dr. Van Dyke was born in
Germantown, Pa., and graduated at Princeton with high
honors. He held a Congregational pastorate at Newport,
R. I., 1878-82. Then he was pastor of the Brick Presbyterian
church in New York. Later he was a lecturer in Paris, and
minister to the Netherlands 1900-1902. He has written
many books of both prose and poetry and is highly thought
of. His home is in Princeton, N. J.

---

* Another of his hymns begins, "All to Jesus I surrender." This
hymn is not listed by Julian.

JONES VERY

1813-1880

"Wilt Thou not visit me?
The plant beside me feels Thy gentle dew."

This lovely hymn was written by "a Unitarian clergyman without charge." Jones Very was born at Salem, Mass., graduated at Harvard, and was a tutor there for two years. He spent most of his life at Salem, Mass., devoting himself to literature. Many beautiful sonnets and other poems have come from his pen. One of his hymns is found in "The Pilgrim Hymnal." It begins, "Father, thy wonders do not singly stand." Another begins, "O heavenly gift of love divine." Julian lists 9 of his hymns.

HOWARD ARNOLD WALTER

1883-1918

"I would be true, for there are those that trust me;
I would be pure, for there are those who care;
I would be strong, for there is much to suffer;
I would be brave, for there is much to dare;
I would be friend of all—the foe—the friendless;
I would be giving and forget the gift;
I would be humble, for I know my weakness;
I would look up—and laugh—and love and lift."

This immortal* song was written by a native of New Britain, Ct., who, it is said, "romped through Princeton, clutching class and scholastic honors right and left, graduating cum laude in 1905 and receiving the Master's degree in 1909. In the seminary he garnered every prize in sight, including the fellowship he used for a year in Glasgow and Edinburgh." He was ordained in 1910 and in 1912 went to

---

* This song is especially endeared to me as in the strong, tender lines linger the cadences of a beloved son's rich baritone voice as he sang it to his parents on his parting visit to his dying father in 1927. I have had an interesting letter from Elizabeth Garrett who set the song to its beautiful music.

India as Y. M. C. A. National Secretary. In 1910 he married Marguerite B. Darlington of Brooklyn, N.Y., and three children were born to them. Always Mr. Walter's pen was busy and he had several books in preparation at the time of his death, which took place at Lahore, India, in 1918.

HENRY WARE, JR., D. D.

1794-1843

"Lift your glad voices in triumph on high"

This hymn used widely among Unitarians* was written by a Unitarian minister, co-pastor with Ralph Waldo Emerson of the Second Unitarian Church in Boston at one period of his life. Henry was born in Hingham, Mass., and was the son of a Unitarian minister of the same name. He graduated with high honors at Harvard and was later Professor of Pulpit Eloquence in the Harvard Divinity School. Later still he was editor of "The Christian Examiner". He seems to have done his work under a terrible handicap of physical suffering for many years. He died at Framingham at the age of forty-nine.

WILLIAM FAIRFIELD WARREN, D. D.

1833-1929

"Out on an ocean all boundless we ride"

This hymn, beloved by children,† was written by a Methodist minister of high repute and scholarship, born in Williamsburg, Mass. Wm. F. Warren graduated at the age of twenty at the Wesleyan University of Middletown, Ct.

---

* He wrote many hymns which rank very high among Unitarians. Julian lists 14 of them and says they are of more than usual merit. The last hymn he wrote was against slavery and begins, "Oppression shall not always reign."

† This hymn, which is found in "Christ in Song" No. 740, was sung nearly every Sunday evening in my childhood's home. No hymn was a greater favorite. A touching story is told in "Stories of the Christian Hymns" by Silas S. H. Paine of a little boy in Harpoot, Turkey, who had been bitten by a mad dog, and between the awful paroxysms of hydrophobia he asked to have his favorite hymn, "Out on an ocean", sung to him and joined in the singing.

He was for a time Professor of Systematic Theology in Bremen, Germany, then returned to America in 1866 and was appointed President of Boston University in 1873. He published works on theology and logic. Another of his hymns begins, "I worship Thee, O Holy Ghost."

HENRY S. WASHBURN

1813-

"Let every heart rejoice and sing"

This hymn, which has been used both at home and abroad, was written by a business man born at Providence, R. I., who spent his boyhood at Kingston, Mass., and was educated at Brown University. Subsequently he was a manufacturer in Worcester and Boston, and became President of the Union Mutual Life Insurance Co. He was active in public matters and wrote several songs and hymns. Denominationally he was a Baptist.

REV. DAVID A. WASSON

1823-1887

"O thou God's mariner, heart of mine,
Spread canvas to the airs divine,
Spread sail! and let thy fortune be
Forgotten in thy destiny."

These lines, culled from a beautiful* poem entitled "Seen and Unseen" which contains hymn-like stanzas, were written by a little known American poet. David A. Wasson was born in Maine, was a teacher at nineteen, spent one year at Bowdoin College, and then went to sea as a common sailor for his health. Later he studied for a Congregational minister at Bangor Theological Seminary. His theological views

---

* This poem is found in Whittier's collection "Songs of Three Centuries". Here are two more of its fine lines:
"And all God's argosies come to shore,
Let ocean smile or ocean roar."

changed and he became pastor of an Independent Church at
Bangor, and later, for a few months, supplied the Society
of Theodore Parker in Boston. Failing health caused his
retirement from the ministry and he was employed for four
years in the Boston custom house. Then he went to Germany
and wrote much for reviews.

Rev. G. D. Watson

fl. 19th century

"I hear my dying Savior say
'Follow me'."
This hymn which is in "Hymns of the Gospel New and
Old" is set to the tune of "Maryland, my Maryland." It is
by an author of whom I have no data.

C. F. Weigelm

fl. 19th century

"O I love to walk with Jesus
* * * * * * * *
I will follow where He leadeth."
This hymn which is No. 85 in Jubilee Songs published by
Thoro Harris is by an author of whom I have no data. I
have seen the name spelled also Weigle. It is sung familiarly
in gospel meetings.

Marcus M. Wells

1815-1895

"Holy Spirit, faithful guide,"
This useful hymn, first published in 1864 by T. E. Perkins
of New York in a collection called "The Sacred Lute" is
there attributed both as to words and music to M. M. Wells.
I have no further data about him. The hymn is now in
many collections and is indispensable.

REV. ROBERT WHITAKER

1863-

"My country is the world"

This splendid hymn was written by a free lance social
evangelist who was born at Padiham, Lancashire, England,
but who has been so long in the United States that I venture
to list him among the American hymnists. Mr. Whitaker
began to preach at the age of twenty, was ordained in 1887,
but has not been serving any church since 1923. His
pacifist activities resulted in 1918 in his being jailed in Los
Angeles for 94 days. During this imprisonment he wrote
a fine hymn entitled "Whatever Is." Other persecutions
which he suffered on account of his pacifism included being
mobbed in Los Angeles and being disinherited of an estate
in San José worth $100,000. Mr. Whitaker has served either
officially or unofficially many radical groups and causes, especially the "Civil Liberties Union." At present he is devoting himself to writing for labor and religious periodicals.
He is married but has no children. His home is at Los
Gatos, California. He has written a number of hymns.

JOHN GREENLEAF WHITTIER

1807-1892

"We may not climb the heavenly steeps"

This exquisite hymn which enriches every standard hymnal
was written by our best beloved Quaker poet, honored the
world over. "The barefoot boy" was born in Haverhill,
Mass., and lived on the same spot. He never married but
lived with a maiden sister, carrying on the ancestral farm,
combining this primitive work with his writing and work
for the anti-slavery cause. For one year, 1838, he published

in Philadelphia a paper called "The Pennsylvania Freeman", but this was terminated by a mob which sacked and burned his printing office. He died at Hampton Falls, New Hampshire. Julian lists 31 of his hymns,*

MAJOR DANIEL WEBSTER WHITTLE

1840-1900

"Dying with Jesus, by death reckoned mine,

* * * * * * * * *

Moment by moment I'm kept in His love."

This hymn† was written by a Civil War veteran who was also a well known evangelist in the closing years of the nineteenth century. Major Whittle was born at Chicopee Falls, Mass. In the fifties he went to Chicago where he was employed by the Wells Fargo Express Co. In 1861 he enlisted in the Civil War, was with Sherman in his march to the sea, was in the staff of Gen. O. O. Howard who became his life

---

* One of the most beautiful of these is that which begins:
"Dear Lord and Father of mankind,
Forgive our feverish ways."
I append here a sonnet by Lincoln Hully which gives a just estimate of Whittier's superlative character.
"Though snow-bound all his years by circumstance,
Shut in by narrow duties and by creed,
He knew the simple, natural things that breed
Contempt for masks and all the ills of chance.
Brought up to bear life's burdens, in the trance
Of silence at the Quaker meetings, deed
Meant more than word to meet one's deepest need,
And conquer life and time's most fitful dance.

Behind the poet's fascinating dreams
Of duty, honor, dignity, and grace,
There stands the nobler poem of the man.
From eyes that never blanched there daily streams
A light that glows upon his gentle face
Wrought on our Maker's finest, noblest plan."
As Whittier lay dying he whispered, "Love, love to all the world."
Some one recited to him his poem "At Last" written in his old age,
"When on my day of life the night is falling."

† This hymn was suggested by a remark of Varley, the English evangelist, who said he did not like "I need Thee every hour" very well because he needed Jesus every moment. So Whittle wrote the hymn and his daughter Mary set it to music. It was copyrighted both in England and Washington on the same day. The South African saint, Andrew Murray, adopted it as his favorite hymn and used to have it sung every day when the plates were changed at dinner. Whittle wrote some hymns under the nom-de-plume "El Nathan". "While we pray and while we plead" is one of his. Another of Whittle's hymns has for its chorus, "O, the crowning day is coming by and by." Six of his hymns are in Sankey's "Songs and Solos."

long friend, and was wounded at Vicksburg. With his arm still in a sling he returned to Chicago and attended one of Moody's meetings where he was called on to speak and was given three cheers. Whittle then was for a time the Treasurer of the Elgin Watch Co. but through Moody's influence he gave himself to evangelistic work. His wife and his daughter Mary (who later married Moody's son Will) used to sing in his meetings. During the Spanish War Whittle went into the southern military camps where he broke down with the work and hardships of camp life. He spent his last years in the home of his married daughter Mary at Northfield, Mass. Whittle was a manly, self-sacrificing Christian, sincere and loyal.

C. B. WIDMEYER

fl. 20th century

"Come and dine, the Master calleth"

This somewhat effective gospel hymn was written by an obscure author. This hymn is found in "The Air Pilot Hymnal No. 6. Widmeyer is the composer of both words and melody.

SAMUEL WILLARD

1776-1839

"Cease, my heart, to dread tomorrow"

This hymn of the liberal faith was written by an American writer who for twenty-seven years was blind owing to too much study by a dim light.

Theodore Chickering Williams

b. 1855

"When thy heart with joy o'er flowing"

This useful hymn* was written by the Head Master of
Hackley School, Tarrytown, New York. Mr. Williams was
born at Brookline, Mass., and educated at Harvard for the
Unitarian ministry. He was pastor of All Souls Chu~ch,
New York, for fourteen years, after which he engaged in
educational work. Julian lists six of his hymns taken from
a hymnal edited by Mrs. F. C. Williams called "Amore Dei."

Nathaniel Parker Willis

1807-1867

"Sleep safe, O wave-worn mariners"

This hymn was written at sea when the author was tossed
by waves. He was born at Portland, Maine, the son of the
Nathaniel Willis who started the "Boston Recorder" which
afterward became "The Congregationalist". He was also
the founder of "The Youth's Companion." The son was
educated at Yale and was later appointed attaché to the
American legation at Paris, visiting Greece and Turkey. He
married the daughter of a British officer and while in
England he fought a duel with Captain Marry. When he
was thirty-two years old he returned to New York where
he published a paper and wrote dramas. His wife died and
his second marriage was to a daughter of Hon. Joseph
Grinnell of Massachusetts. He did much graceful† literary

---

* This hymn closes with these two fine stanzas:
"Hast thou borne a secret sorrow
    In thy lonely breast?
Take to thee thy sorrowing brother
    For a guest.
Share with him thy bread of blessing,
    Sorrow's burden share;
When thy heart enfolds a brother
    God is there."

† Some of Willis's poems, while not hymns, belong to the realm of
sacred poetry. One of these is "The Healing of the Leper". Another
tells that most pathetic tale of "Hagar in the Wilderness". Another
called "Two Women" is full of pathos. Willis had a talented sister who
wrote under the nom-de-plume of "Fanny Fern." He had also a brother
who was a musical artist. It was evidently an unusually gifted family.

work during a long, brave struggle with consumptive illness.
He died at Idlewild on the Hudson. He is called a "poet of
society."

H. L. WILSON

fl. 19th century

"For the Lion of Judah shall break every chain"

This is the refrain of a song which is sung familiarly in
the Salvation Army marches. The first line of the hymn is
"'Twas Jesus my Savior who died on the tree." The author
is obscure and Julian does not list him or the hymn.

WILLIAM WINTER

1836-1917

"Come with a smile, when come thou must,
* * * * * * * *
And waft me from a work that's done
To peace that waits on thy command
In God's mysterious better land."

This charming poem entitled "Azrael", parts of which
might be used as a hymn, was written by a native of Massachusetts, a graduate of Harvard Law School, who moved
to New York in 1859 and became a dramatic editor of the
New York Tribune. He published some volumes of verses
of peculiar gracefulness.

WILL ELLSWORTH WITTER

1854-

"While Jesus whispers to you 'Come,
Sinner, come.' "

This invitation hymn was written in 1877 by a school
teacher in Wyoming Valley, New York. He was staying

on a farm and was in spiritual anxiety for two of his pupils. It was on a Saturday afternoon, and while he was bunching hay the words and tune of this hymn seemed to sing themselves into his soul. He had been recently touched by the death of P. P. Bliss and had prayed that he might be useful to write hymns that would touch hearts. Witter went home and wrote down the hymn which had been composed while in the hay field, with the conviction that they were the God given answer to his prayer. Witter was born near La Grange, New York, and became eventually a Baptist preacher.

Samuel Wolcott, D. D.

1813-1886

"Christ for the world we sing"

This standard hymn was the first one written by a Congregational minister who was then fifty-five years old. The occasion of writing it was after seeing the mottoes "Christ for the World" and "The World for Christ" in green letters over the platform at a Y. M. C. A. convention. After that Dr. Wolcott composed about 200 hymns but none of these are familiar. Julian does not list them. Samuel Wolcott was born at So. Windsor, Ct., and educated at Yale and Andover. He was for a time a missionary in Syria. After his return to America he held various pastorates and was at one period the secretary of a Missionary Society in Ohio. He died in Longmeadow, Mass., at the age of seventy-three. He will probably be longest remembered as the author of "Christ for the world we sing."

L. B. WOODBURY

fl. 19th century

"Ho! reapers of life's harvest,
Why stand with rusty blade?"

Both words and music of this hymn were composed by the above named author about whom I have no other data. The hymn is not listed by Julian. It is included in "Christ in Song" No. 622. The hymn was a favorite with President Garfield and was sung at his funeral.

JOHN H. YATES

fl. 19th century

"Encamped along the hills of light."

This hymn, set to music by Sankey and much used in Christian Endeavor meetings, was written by an obscure author.

H. J. ZELLEY

fl. 20th century

"He rolled the sea away"

This is the title of a gospel hymn found in Rodeheaver's "Songs for Service". I have no data about the author.

CHAPTER X

AMERICAN HYMNISTS: WOMEN

"A good hymn is a more valuable contribution to Christian literature than vast tomes of theology, for it will sing to the ages after the tomes are mouldering on the shelves."

MRS. OPHELIA ADAMS

fl. 20th century

"I love to think my Father knows
Why I have missed the path I chose."

These are the opening lines of a comforting hymn written by the above named obscure author. The hymn is No. 39 in Excell's "Jubilant Praise."

LUCY EVELINA AKERMAN, NÉE METCALF

1816-1874

"Nothing but leaves, the spirit grieves
Over a wasted life."

This hymn, which was greatly used in Great Britain by Sankey,* was written by a Unitarian lady who lived in Providence, R. I., where she also died. It was suggested by hearing a sermon by M. D. Conway, and was first published in the "Christian Observer" in 1858. It was set to music by S. A. Vail. Mrs. Akerman was the daughter of Thomas Metcalf of Wrentham, Mass. She married Charles Akerman of Portsmouth, N. H.

---

* Sankey sang this hymn at a meeting in Birmingham, England, where a lady who heard it was convicted that her life had been "nothing but leaves". It became a turning point, and she founded a rescue home for girls where hundreds of them were converted.

MARY A. BACHELOR

fl. 19th century

"Go bury thy sorrow; the world has its share."

This useful hymn was written by the daughter of a minister while she was staying with a beloved brother who was also a minister. One day she told her brother about a matter that troubled her. Afterward her conscience reproached her for adding to his many cares, and she went up to her little attic bedroom and wrote the above hymn. P. P. Bliss found it in a newspaper and set it to music, according to one account, but in "The Notes of Joy" the music is ascribed to Mrs. J. F. Knapp. Julian says the authorship is open to doubt.

MRS. URANIA LOCKE BAILEY

fl. 19th century

"The mistakes of my life have been many"*

I have no details about the lady who wrote this useful hymn, which was written about 1871. Sankey in his "Story of the Hymns" tells of a lawyer (probably Mr. Henry Durant, although he does not name him) who used to ask for this hymn in the Moody revival meetings in Boston. This man had ignored God until his only child, a boy, had died. This affliction led to his conversion and to his founding Wellesley College. Moody and Sankey purchased a perpetual scholarship at Wellesley for some girl at the Northfield school.

---

* This hymn was a favorite with my deceased husband, Rev. H. D. Goodenough, who used often to quote it and who translated it into the Zulu language and had it incorporated into the Zulu hymnal to use among the Zulu Congregational churches in South Africa. I am told that this hymn is much sung and prized by the Zulus, in a letter received from my eldest son, Leonard D. Goodenough, who has settled in Natal. He remarked very truly that the sentiment of this hymn "we may all take to ourselves".

Mary Ann Baker

fl. 1874

"Master, the tempest is raging"

This hymn was written by a young lady of Chicago who had been requested by Dr. H. P. Palmer to write some hymns to accompany the Sunday School lessons he was preparing, one of which was about Christ stilling the tempest. Miss Baker had recently gone through a terrible struggle with rebellion against God concerning the death under distressing circumstances of her beloved and only brother, who had died at a distance from her where he was trying to regain health in a warmer climate. The hymn which recounted the stilling of the tempest of emotion in her own soul, was used during President Garfield's sickness and at some of the many funeral services held for him throughout the United States. Miss Baker was a Baptist and a worker in the temperance cause.

Katherine Lee Bates

1859-1929

"O beautiful for spacious skies"

This hymn which has surely immortalized its happy author, was written in 1893 at Colorado Springs after a day on Pike's Peak. It is considered by many people—including Amos R. Wells—as the finest and most appropriate national hymn which America possesses. Miss Bates graduated at Wellesley College in 1880 and became Professor of Latin and English Literature in her alma mater. She has written some other hymns. One of these (No. 144 in "Hymns of the Living Age") begins "Hosanna to the Son of David."

Mrs. Lydia Baxter

1809-1874

"Take the name of Jesus with you,
Child of sorrow and of woe."

This hymn was written by an invalid lady, a Baptist, who

was born at Petersburg, N. Y. She also wrote a hymn beginning "One by one we cross the river," and about three years before her death she wrote "There is a gate that stands ajar," much sung by Sankey* and connected with the incident of a wayward girl who returned to her home one night and found that the door had been left unlocked every night during her absence, hoping for her return.

ADA BLENKHORN
fl. 19th century

"Let a little sunshine in"
This is the refrain of a familiar gospel hymn set to music by Gabriel and copyrighted and printed in "Jubilant Praise" by Excell. I have no data about the author.

MARY G. BRAINERD
fl. 19th century

"I know not what awaits me"
This beautiful hymn entitled "Confidence and Joy" which was published in the Methodist Sunday School Hymn Book in 1879, was written by the above named lady, about whom no details have been obtained. The hymn was found in the trunk of P. P. Bliss after he was killed. The trunk reached Chicago safely, with the music in it which Bliss had composed for this hymn.

ANNA HEMPSTEAD BRANCH
fl. 19th or 20th centuries

"I lay me down with sighs and tears, after a barren day,
Yet every morning I awake, innocent and gay!"†

---

* Sankey tells the story of the conversion of a young Scottish girl through this hymn at a watch night service. She was hurt in a railroad accident a month later and was found with a copy of Sankey's "Songs and Solos" in her hand opened to this hymn. She was carried to a cottage where she died shortly after the accident.

† The above lines open a lovely poem on "The Blessed Hands of Sleep", so dear to me that I have framed it, and placed it on the wall of my room. It expresses my appreciation of God's marvellous gift to us of sleep, better than any other I know. I have no data about the author.

Carrie E. Breck

1855-

"Look all around you; find someone in need,
* * * * * * * *
Help somebody today."

This much used hymn was written by the busy mother of five daughters. She was reared in Vermont but after her marriage to Frank A. Breck she went to live in Portland, Ore., "the city of roses." This hymn was set to music by Charles H. Gabriel. Mrs. Breck has written another well known hymn which begins, "Face to face with Christ my Savior." Her hymns were composed largely while she was about her housework.

Mary Brown

fl. 19th century

"It may not be on the mountain's height
* * * * * * * *
I'll go where you want me to go, dear Lord."

This hymn was adopted by a class of over 100 missionary nurses at Battle Creek, Mich., as their class hymn. They used to sing it every Sabbath afternoon. These nurses were from all over the world, and when they parted they agreed that in their different fields they would continue to sing this hymn.*

---

* I have a very vivid recollection of the first time I heard this hymn sung. It was at a missionary meeting, and the singer was a lady who was blind. The effect of her singing was profound. This hymn also was sung repeatedly on public occasions in the town of Rochester, Mass. where I live, by a lovely young soloist named Winifred Lewis, whose sudden and early death was a cause of deep sorrow to the whole community.

PHOEBE HINSDALE BROWN

1783-1861

"I love to steal awhile away
From every cumbering care."

The author of this well known hymn was the first woman in America to write a hymn of wide popularity. She was the daughter of George Hinsdale and was born in Canaan, N. Y. She was left an orphan at·two years old, and thereafter lived with a relative where her life was full of drudgery and privations which crushed her spirit. At the age of eighteen however, kind friends assisted her to school privileges at Claverack, N. Y., where she united with the Congregational church. At the age of twenty-two she married a house painter named Timothy H. Brown, and her married life, (which was unhappy) was spent at Ellington, Ct., thirty years of it, and at Monson, Mass. It was at Ellington in 1818 that Mrs. Brown wrote the above hymn. With husband and children she lived in two small rooms where there was no privacy, so she was accustomed to retire for prayer toward night to a brookside where there were trees and alders. One night a wealthy woman whose house she passed, said to her harshly in the presence of company, "Why do you come at evening so near our house? If you want anything, why don't you come and ask for it?" Mrs. Brown, deeply grieved, went to her wretched home, took a child on her lap, and wrote the above hymn. It was printed in Nettleton's "Village Hymns" in 1824. In 1850 Mrs. Brown went to live with her daughter in Henry, Ill. Her son, Samuel Robbins Brown, D. D. was the first American missionary to enter Japan.

Hattie E. Buell

fl. 19th century

"My Father is rich in houses and lands
* * * * * * * * *
I'm the child of a King."

This gospel hymn by an obscure author was sung in 1883 by Peter Bilhorn at Blunt, So. Dak., on a wharf boat on the Missouri River on which he was taking a trip with his little organ. Bilhorn sang the same hymn in Moody's church in Chicago. When he had finished a man in the audience rose and said that he had heard Mr. Bilhorn sing it two years before at Blunt, So. Dak., and it had set him to thinking, which resulted in his conversion, and that he was at the time he spoke studying for the ministry.

Etta* Campbell

fl. 19th century

"What means this eager, anxious throng?
* * * * * * * * *
Jesus of Nazareth passeth by."

This hymn was written in 1863 when a revival was in progress in Newark, N. J., conducted by Rev. E. P. Hammond. One afternoon the address was on the text, "Jesus of Nazareth passeth by." Etta Campbell was present and soon after wrote this hymn, which is said to have been instrumental in the conversion of hundreds of people, particularly in Edinboro when Sankey sang it at the Moody meetings. Miss Campbell was a teacher in Morristown, N. J.

Julia A. Carney, née Fletcher

1823-

"Little drops of water, little grains of sand"

This popular children's song was written in 1845 by a teacher in the primary schools of Boston, Mass. It is some-

---

* Her name is sometimes given as Emma instead of Etta.

times erroneously ascribed to Rev. Cobham Brewer (1810-
1897) of London, England, who in 1848 published a later
version of the poem. Mrs. Carney, however, is the one who
should probably have the credit of authorship.

ALICE CARY

1820-1871

' Life with its dark and dreadful ills
Recedes and fades away."

This hymn was written in New York shortly before her
death after an illness of terrible suffering by the elder of
the two Cary sisters, dear to the hearts of Americans. They
were born on a farm eight miles north of Cincinnati, Ohio.
Alice began to write for the press at the age of eighteen.
Some ten years later she had an affair of the heart which
shattered her health and wounded her spirit, and in 1850
she removed to New York City where she was soon joined
by her sister Phoebe, who was the housekeeper in the charming home they established, a rendezvous for cultivated and
literary people. They were entirely dependent on their
earnings from their writing but Horace Greeley was their
patron and they thus maintained themselves for twenty
years. The sisters were Universalists and these two lines
culled from the writings of Alice embody their belief,

"I feel, I know that God is love,
And knowing this, I know it all."

After the death of Alice, Phoebe aged rapidly and grew
gray. She said "It seems to me a cord stretches from Alice's
heart to mine."

PHOEBE CARY

1824-1871

"One sweetly solemn thought
Comes to me o'er and o'er."

This universally loved* hymn was written in 1852 in a little third story back bedroom one Sunday noon after the author had returned† from the Church of the Puritans." Phoebe wrote both in prose and verse, most of her works being issued in connection with her life long companion, her sister Alice. Neither of them were ever married. Phoebe was the more robust and self-reliant of the two and had more humor. She died at Newport, R. I. three months after her sister, broken down with grief at her sister's death.

MRS. E. D. CHENEY

fl. 19th century

"At first I prayed for light,—could I but see the way,
How gladly, swiftly would I walk to everlasting day!
And next I prayed for strength that I might tread the road
With firm, unfailing feet and win the heaven's serene abode.
And then I asked for faith. Could I but trust my God
I'd live enfolded in His peace, though foes were all abroad.
But now I pray for love, deep love for God and man,
A living love that will not fail, however dark His plan,
And light and strength and faith are opening everywhere,
God waited patiently until I prayed the larger prayer."

This beautiful‡ hymn was set to music by C. E. Kettle and is found in "Christ in Song", No. 830. I insert it in full but know nothing of the author.

---

* This story is told of this hymn: A young man named Harry was gambling with an old man in a Chinese gambling den. Harry was losing money, but began to sing softly to himself, "One sweetly solemn thought." The old man started up, saying, "My mother used to sing that, and this is the last time I shall ever gamble." He gave Harry back his money and left the old life behind. Both men were converted through the incident. Phoebe Cary's poem, "I said if I might go back again", made a great impression on me in my youth.

† Phoebe had been listening to a solemn sermon on the brevity of life preached by George B. Cheever.

‡ This hymn was especially admired by my deceased sister, Mary Hall Leonard.

MARTHA* A. W. COOK, NÉE WALKER

1806-1874

"In some way or other the Lord will provide"

This hymn, written by a Boston lady, wife of Rev. Parsons Cook, who was the editor of a paper called "The Puritan Recorder", was published in 1864. It is included by Ira D. Sankey in his "Songs and Solos".

SUSAN COOLIDGE

fl. 19th century

"Every day is a fresh beginning;
Every day is the world made new;
You who are weary of sorrow and sinning,
Here is a beautiful hope for you."

This hymn of hope found in "Heart Throbs No. 1" was written by Sarah Chauncey Woolsey, whose nom-de-plume was "Susan Coolidge." She was born in Ohio, a descendant of Jonathan Edwards and niece of President Woolsey of Yale. Most of her life was spent in New Haven, Ct., and Newport, R. I. She wrote with marked talent in both prose and verse.

FANNY J. CROSBY

1823-1915

"Some day the silver cord will break,
* * * * * * * *
And I shall see Him face to face."

This hymn† was written by the blind woman, a Methodist,

---

* Her name is given by Julian as E. D. Martha Cook.
† I had the great privilege of hearing Sankey sing this hymn at Northfield,

who has been called "the queen of gospel hymn writers." Fanny Crosby lost her sight at the age of six weeks through the mistake of a doctor who ordered hot poultices put on her eyes for the inflammation from a cold. When she was twelve she entered the Institution for the Blind in New York City, and after her graduation she became a teacher there for twelve years. In 1858 she married another teacher, Alexander Van Alstyne, a musician and also blind. She wrote about 2,000 hymns and some* songs which were not hymns. It is said that 100,000,000 copies of her songs have been printed. Certainly they are scattered through multitudes of books. She had a serious, appealing face. Her marriage was happy. The hymn "Rescue the perishing", which became a battle cry for Christian workers throughout the world, was written after visiting a mission in one of the worst districts of New York. Sankey and others tell many stories of the way her hymns† have resulted in conversions. "Safe in the arms of Jesus" rang in the soul of Bishop Harrington when he was in the hands of a mob in equatorial Africa that was bent on taking his life. This hymn was written to fit a melody composed by W. H. Doane who had asked Fanny Crosby to write some words to fit his tune. Dr. George Duffield said just before his death, "I rather think her talent will stand beside that of Watts and Wesley." Rodeheaver says, "Her name will live as long as people sing the gospel." She lived in her later years in Bridgeport, Ct., where at the age of eighty she was still writing hymns.

---

* "Rosalie, the Prairie Flower" and "There's music in the air" were Fanny Crosby's compositions but she wrote under various noms-de-plume.
    † The following are some of her familiar hymns:
        "Blessed assurance; Jesus is mine"
        "Pass me not, oh gentle Savior"
        " 'Tis the blessed hour of prayer"
        "Come, great Deliverer, come"
        "Never be sad or discouraged" (Christ in Song No. 560)
        "To the work, to the work; we are servants of God"
        "Jesus, keep me near the cross"
        "We shall reach the summer land by and by"
        "Sweet are the moments of blessing"
One nom-de-plume Fanny Crosby used was Grace J. Francis; under this was published, "Hold thou my hand." After her marriage her hymns were published as by Frances Van Alstyne.

Mary Stanley Bunce Dana, née Palmer

1810-1883

"I'm a pilgrim and I'm a stranger"

This well loved hymn was written by a daughter of Rev. Benjamin M. Palmer, at the time of Mary's birth pastor of the Congregational Church at Beaufort, S. C. In 1814 Dr. Palmer became pastor of the Circular Church of Charleston, S. C., and Mary was educated in schools there and in northern seminaries. In 1835 she was married to Charles E. Dana of New York who died at Muscatine, Ia., four years later. Mrs. Dana then returned to Charleston where she established her reputation as a poet* 'and writer for periodicals. In 1848 she married Prof. Robert D. Shindler of Shelby College, Ky. Her husband in 1869 began his rectorship at Nacogdochies, Texas, where Mrs. Shindler died fourteen years later. She had published two collections of poems. She is sometimes known as Mrs. Dana and sometimes as Mrs. Shindler.

Lizzie De Armond

fl. 20th century

"If your heart keeps right,"

This gospel song was written by a widow with eight children whose necessity compelled her to write for papers and magazines. Her articles found a ready market. She has written various Sunday School hymns and dialogues.†

---

* One of her familiar poems begins, "Flee as a bird to your mountain." Another much used begins,
   "Come, sing to me of heaven,
         * * * * * * * * *
      There'll be no more sorrow there."
Some persons consider her best hymn the one beginning, "Prince of Peace, control my will." One pathetic hymn has for its refrain, "Pass under the rod."

† Charles H. Gabriel's pamphlet, "The Singers and Their Songs," shows a picture of Mrs. De Armond. She has a pleasing face. She also wrote the hymn with the refrain,
   "It was for me the Savior died
      On the cross of Calvary"

Margaret Wade Campbell Deland

1857-

"Blow golden trumpets sweet and clear"
This hymn was written by a native of Pittsburg, Pa.,
whose mother died in her infancy. Margaret was brought
up in an uncle's family. She became a teacher of design in
New York City. She married Lorin Deland. Mrs. Deland
is best known as the author of "John Ward, Preacher."

Mary Demorest, née Lee

1838-1887

"I am far frae my hame"
The author of this hymn was born at Croton Falls, N. Y.
She had a Scotch nurse, so became familiar with the Scotch
dialect. This hymn was suggested by a story she heard of a
certain Scotchman named John MacDuff who took his homesick wife back to the Scottish home from America. Sankey
tells the story in his book "My Life and Sacred Songs." He
used to sing the hymn in the Moody meetings. The
Demorests went to Pasadena, Cal., and Mrs. Demorest died
there. She wrote the hymn when she was twenty-three years
old.

Emily Dickinson

1830-1886

"If I can stop one heart from breaking,
    I shall not live in vain.
If I can ease one life the aching,
    Or cool one pain,
Or help one fainting robin
    Into his nest again
    I shall not live in vain."
These lines were written by "the great New England
mystic," "a gentle, terrific soul," counted by some as the

greatest woman poet of modern times. She was born at Amherst, Mass.,the daughter of a lawyer, Edward Dickinson, a pillar of the church who went to Congress for two years. Emily went for a short time to Mt. Holyoke Seminary, but, for some unknown reason, packed her belongings and went home. In her early twenties she went to Philadelphia where she fell completely in love with a married man, made the great renunciation, and rushed desperately home to shut herself up for thirty years, thereafter scarcely setting foot beyond her own door step. Only a very few of her strange poems were published before her death; she evidently did not write for fame but for self expression. In 1924, sixty years after most of them were written, her collected poems appeared. (There had been some little volumes previously.) Her writings have made a tremendous sensation on both sides of the Atlantic. Her preoccupation is with the inner life and God and eternity.

MARY LOWE DICKINSON

1839-

"We should fill our lives with the sweetest things
If we had but a day."

This poem, which has a hymn-like quality, was written by a native of Fitchburg, Mass. Miss Lowe married John B. Dickinson and survived him. She was prominent in religious and literary circles, was professor of Belles Lettres in Denver University and President of the National Council of King's Daughters. At one period she was assistant editor with E. E. Hale of a magazine called "Lend a Hand". Mrs. Dickinson published two books of poems.

Mary Baker Eddy

1827-1910

"Shepherd, show me how to go,
    O'er the hillside steep,
How to gather, how to sow,
    How to feed Thy sheep.
I would listen to Thy voice
    Lest my footsteps stray.
I would follow and rejoice
    All the rugged way."

This beautiful hymn* was written by the celebrated founder of the Christian Science Church. Mary Baker was born at Bow, N. H., near Concord. Her parents were Congregationalists and Mary herself joined this church, but was dismissed in good and regular standing at her own request in 1875. At an early age she married Col. George Glover by whom she had one son. In 1866 she "discovered" Christian Science and began to teach and practice mental healing. After Col. Glover's death she married Dr. Asa S. Eddy who died in 1882. Mrs. Eddy established in Boston the First Church Scientist which has numerous branches.

Mary E. Edgar

fl. 20th century

"God who touchest earth with beauty,
    Make me lovely too,
With Thy spirit recreate me,
    Make my life anew."

This is the first stanza of a pretty hymn which was published by the American missionary magazine. I judge that the author is an American. She is not listed by Julian.

---

* Mrs. Eddy wrote a number of hymns. One of these which I like very much, begins, "O gentle Presence, peace, and joy, and power." In one stanza of this the author evidently drew on her own experience. It runs as follows:

"O make me glad for every scalding tear,
    For hope deferred, ingratitude, disdain;
Wait, and love more, for every hate, and fear
    No ill, since God is good, and loss is gain."

One of her followers said of her autobiography, "It made me cry to read it."

LIZZIE EDWARDS

fl. 19th century

"I must have the Savior with me"
This hymn, which is 541 in "Christ in Song" was set to
music by John R. Sweeney. It is said that Lizzie Edwards
is a myth and that she represents only an early nom-de-plume
of Fanny Crosby's. I am not able to verify this statement.
It is however certain that Fanny Crosby did write under
various noms-de-plume.

CATHERINE HARBISON EALING, NÉE WATERMAN

1812-

"Come unto me when shadows darkly gather"
This beautiful hymn* was first published in 1839 in "The
Christian Keepsake Annual". The author was an Episcopal
lady who, at the age of twenty-eight, married George J.
Ealing of Philadelphia. Her poems were collected and
published in 1850 in a book called "The Broken Bracelet."

M. P. FERGUSON

fl. 1897

"Joys are flowing like a river"
* * * * * * * *
Blessed quietness! Holy quietness!"
This hymn† was written by the founder of the Peniel Mission in Los Angeles. It is No. 366 in "Christ in Song." It
was copyrighted by L. L. Pickett of Wilmore, Ky., in 1897.

---

* Julian says this hymn is widely known, yet it is somewhat difficult to find it in any recent hymnals, but I found it in "The Methodist
Hymnal" and it was in 1865 published in "Hymns of the Ages," 3rd
series, but without the author's name. The hymn also appears in

Hymnal of the Reformed Church	1920
Hymns of Worship and Service	1921
The American Hymnal—Century Co.	1919
In Excelsis—Century Co.	1917

My mother was very fond of it and it was imprinted in my childish
memory from hearing her sing it about her work.
† I heard this hymn sung in South Africa soon after its first publication. A devout lady of Pietermaritzburg, Natal, sang it in her home
with a shining face and much feeling.

ALICE A. FLAGG

fl. 20th century

"Point us the way, O voice of the Divine,
* * * * * * * * *
We need Thy comfort, voice of the Divine,
From holy writ or sacred songbook lore;
We will creep in and sit at Jesus' feet;
Show us, dear Church of Christ, the Open Door."

The above extracts are from a lovely hymn entitled "The Church" which was published in the "American Missionary." The hymn should become a standard one in the hymnals.

ANNIE JOHNSON FLINT

fl. 20th century

"His grace is great enough to meet the great things
* * * * * * * * *
His grace is great enough to meet the small things."

This pretty hymn is printed on a card published at Eden, N. Y., by Helen A. Casterline. Annie Johnson Flint also wrote "Have you come to the Red Sea place in your life?" and also "We are the only Bible the careless world will read."

ELIZA LEE FOLLEN, NÉE CABOT

1787-1860

"God, Thou art good; each perfumed flower"

This is one of many hymns* written by a Boston lady, daughter of Samuel Cabot. At the age of forty-one she married Professor Charles Follen, who in 1840, after twelve years of married life, perished aboard the "Lexington" which was burnt in Long Island Sound. Mrs. Follen outlived her husband twenty years and finally died in Brookline, Mass.

---

* Julian lists several of her hymns. One of these begins, "How sweet to be allowed to pray!"

In 1854 she was in England and while there published her second volume of children's poems which was entitled "The Lark and the Linnet." Mrs. Follen was a Unitarian. Among her voluminous writings are various translations of poems from the German.

SARAH MARGARET FULLER

1810-1850

"Jesus, a child, his course began"

This children's hymn was written by one of the most remarkable* women which America has produced. Margaret Fuller was the daughter of Hon. Timothy Fuller and was born at Cambridgeport, Mass. She wrote Latin verses at the age of eight. She had a fine education and after her father's death she assisted the family by private teaching and became a lecturer and writer for the "New York Tribune" under the patronage of Horace Greeley. In 1840 she edited "The Dial". In 1847 she was married at Rome to the Marchese Ossoli. While in Rome she took charge of a hospital. In July, 1850, she and her husband and their new-born infant were drowned in a ship wreck in sight of New York—a hurricane wave burst over their ship.

MRS. ELLEN H. GATES, NÉE HUNTINGTON

fl. 1860

"If you cannot on the ocean"

The author of this hymn,† a sister of a noted financier, was born in Torrington, Ct. The hymn was written in the winter of 1861-2 in Elizabeth, N. J. one afternoon when

---

* Margaret Fuller went to England in 1846 and made distinguished friends. One of these was Carlyle. From England she went to Paris and became the friend of George Sand. She was "strong-minded," that is, she advocated "woman's rights." In religion she was a Unitarian. One of her short poems is printed in "Hymns and Anthems" published in London by W. J. Fox for use in his chapel.

† This hymn was a favorite with Lincoln who especially liked the last stanza, which closes with these lines:
"Though they may forget the singer,
They will not forget the song."

the author had been watching the falling of snow. The words "came to her" and she had a presentiment that "although the hymn was a simple little thing, it had wings and could fly." Later Miss Huntington married Isaac G. Gates and lived in New York City. She is the author of several well known hymns. One of these was written at the request of Philip Phillips* to embody Bunyan's story of Christian and Hopeful entering heaven. The first line is as follows: "I will sing you a song of that beautiful land." Another is, "Come home, come home, you are weary at heart."

SELINA S. GIBBS

fl. 19th century

"Go and tell Jesus, weary, sinsick soul."

I have no data about the author of this familiar gospel hymn, which is by some ascribed to E. P. Hammond.

MISS SIDNEY† GILL

fl. 1854

"I want to be an angel"

This hymn was written by a very young lady who was teaching in an infant Sunday School of Dr. Joel Parker's church in Philadelphia, of which she was a member. She had been telling the little ones about angels when a lovely little girl exclaimed, "O, I want to be an angel". This child died only a few days later, and under the strong impression made upon the young teacher, this hymn was written and sung in the school. The family did not know how it came to be printed in a Dayton, Ohio, newspaper. It came into use in all English speaking countries and was a great favorite with children.

---

* Phillips, with his little boy in his lap in 1865 set this hymn to music. It was later used at the child's funeral and also at his own, where it was sung by Sankey, who was his friend.

† The name Sidney is odd for a woman, but comes down from a Welsh ancestress.

CAROLINE GILMAN, NÉE HOWARD

1794-

"Is there a lone and dreary hour?"

This hymn, in extensive use among Unitarians, was written by a Boston lady who became the wife of Dr. Samuel Gilman, (1791-1858), who was also a hymn writer and pastor of a Unitarian church in Charleston, S. C.

CAROLINE L. GOODENOUGH

1856-

"Take thy life quietly, oh hard pressed soul!
These storms of pain and fear that o'er thee roll
In one brief year shall quite have passed from sight,
Leaving serene and clear thy pathway bright.

Take thy life quietly, let faith's calm ray
Point through the midnight drear to breaking day.
Hold fast the Hand of Love that thee doth guide,
Thy way leads straight above, whate'er betide.

Take thy life quietly, for God doth reign,
He knows the reason why of all our pain.
Some day we'll see and own in worlds of light
That all life's weary way, God led us right."

This is one of the many hymns* written by the author of this book.

---

* It has been my solace during a long and eventful life to write hymns for self-expression. Many of them I have set to music. For any further details I would refer the enquirer to my book "Memoirs of the Leonard, Thompson, and Haskell Families."

HANNAH FLAGG GOULD

1789-1865

"Day of God, thou blessed day"

This hymn for Sunday was written by a native of Lancaster, Vt. who in youth went with her family to live in Newburyport, Mass. She published a book of poems, five of which are listed as hymns in Julian's dictionary.

LOUISE IMOGENE GUINEY

1861-1920

OUT IN THE FIELDS WITH GOD

"The little cares that fretted me,
    I lost them yesterday
Among the fields above the sea,
    Among the winds at play.
Among the lowing of the herds,
    The rustling of the trees,
Among the singing of the birds,
    The humming of the bees.
The fears of what may come to pass,
    I cast them all away
Among the clover-scented grass,
    Among the new-mown hay,
Among the husking of the corn
    Where drowsy poppies nod,
Where ill thoughts die and good are born,
    Out in the fields with God."

The above lovely poem* carries its own appeal. She also wrote a unique Christmas hymn entitled "Tryste Noel" which I have set to music.

---

* My sister's friend, Jean Kennedy, associates this poem with the passing of her father who died plowing "out in the fields with God,"— a passing which one might almost covet.

Ida A. Guirey

fl. 20th century

"Jesus; Rose of Sharon, bloom within my heart
Beauties of Thy truth, and holiness impart."

This hymn was written by an author of whom I have no data. The music to which it is sung is by Charles Gabriel. It is beautiful over the radio.

Elvina Mable Hall

1818-

"I hear the Savior say,
'Thy strength indeed is small."

This hymn, written in 1865 on the fly leaf of a hymn book in a Methodist Episcopal choir in Baltimore, Md., by a native of Alexandria, Va., was published in Sankey's* "Songs and Solos" and is much used in America and England.

Jane E. Hall

fl. 1881

"The love that Jesus had for me"

This hymn, which was published in Sankey's "Songs and Solos" and is also found in "Hymns of the Gospel New and Old", was written by a native of Brattleboro, Vt. She also wrote the music for her hymns.

"When the grass shall cover me,
Head to foot where I am lying.
* * * * * * * *
You will say how kind she was,
You will say how true she was,
When the grass grows over me."

This is from an anonymous poem on p. 273 of "Songs of Three Centuries".

---

* Sankey tells a touching story of the effect of this song which was sung in an open air meeting in the hearing of a wayward young woman who had been wandering most of that day in the streets with nowhere to go. It induced her to go to the city missionaries who found a place for her. She died soon after in a hospital repeating this hymn.

Louisa Jane Hall, née Park

1802-

"Never, my heart, wilt thou grow old;
My hair is white, my blood runs cold,
And one by one my powers depart—
But youth sits smiling in my heart."*

The author of this brave hymn on old age was born at
Newbury, Mass. Her father became teacher of a young
ladies' school in Boston and the daughter herself went to
Boston to live in 1866 after the death of her husband, Rev.
E. B. Hall of Providence, R. I. to whom she had been
married twenty-six years.

Mary C. D. Hamilton

fl. 20th century

"Lord, guard and guide the men who fly
Through the great spaces of the sky."

This hymn was printed in 1917 by the Pilgrim Press in a
pamphlet entitled "Selected Hymns of Patriotism." It seems
to be a needed hymn for special occasions.

Phoebe A. Hanaford

1829-

"Cast thy bread upon the waters"

This standard hymn was written by a Universalist preacher
born on Nantucket Island, Massachusetts. She was at the
time a settled pastor in Jersey City, New Jersey.

---

* Other stanzas of this hymn are as follows:
"Downhill the path of age? Oh no!
Up, up, with patient steps I go.
I watch the skies fast brightening there;
I breathe a sweeter, purer, air.

Beside my road small tasks spring up,
Though but to hand the cooling cup,
Speak the true word of hearty cheer,
Tell the lone soul that God is near."

Mrs. Annie Sherwood Hawks, née Sherwood

1835-

"I need Thee every hour"

This familiar hymn* was written by a Baptist lady born
at Hoosack, N. Y., who in adult life resided in Brooklyn,
N. Y. She wrote about 400 Sunday School hymns of which
the one quoted is the best known. It has been translated into
many languages. It was a comfort to her in the twilight of
her life when her eyesight was poor. She married in 1857
Charles H. Hawkes, and the pair had three children. This
hymn was written in the midst of household cares. Mrs.
Hawkes died at Bennington, Vt., having lived there with a
daughter after her husband's death.

Marianne Hearn

fl. 19th century

"When my final farewell to the world I have said
* * * * * * * * *
Will anyone there at the beautiful gate
Be waiting and watching for me?"

At one of Moody's meetings in Farwell Hall, Chicago, a
testimony was given by a man who said that his conversion
was due to hearing this song by which his stony heart was
softened.

Mrs. S. M. I. Henry

fl. 19th century

"I know my heavenly Father knows
The storms that would my way oppose."

I have no data as to the author of this well known hymn.

---

* "I need Thee every hour" was sung in a Sunday School Convention in 1872. It was sung in the meetings in Chicago at the time of
the World's Fair.—A remark of the English evangelist Varley at that
time about this hymn led Major Whittle to write "Moment by Moment."

ANNIE HERBERT

fl. 19th century

"When the mists have rolled in splendor,
* * * * * * * *
We shall know each other better
When the mists have rolled away."

This hymn, No. 893 in "Christ in Song", was first sung in the Free Trade Hall of Manchester, England, in 1883 by Sankey. It was one of the most popular of those he sang. It is mentioned by Julian, but no information is given about the author other than her name. I do not know whether she is American or British.

(MISS) ELIZA EDMUNDS HEWITT

1851-

"There's a word of tender beauty
In the sayings of our Lord
* * * * * * * *
While his eye is on the sparrow
I shall not forgotten be."

This exquisite hymn was written by a Sunday School worker in the Calvin Presbyterian Church of Philadelphia, her native city. Her career as a teacher in her earlier years was cut short by a spinal malady which made her a shut-in sufferer for a long time. In her slow convalescence she wrote hymns which attracted the notice of John R. Sweeney, a former chorister of her church. Some of her well known songs are the following:

"There is sunshine in my soul today"
"Will there be any stars in my crown?"
"Stepping in the light"
"More about Jesus would I know."

She and Fanny Crosby were personal friends.

GRACE WEBSTER HINSDALE, NÉE HADDOCK

1833-1902

"O what can little hands do
To please the King of heaven?"

This children's hymn which was published in 1868 in a
book entitled "Daily Meditations for Children" was written
by the daughter of one of the Yale professors. She married
a New York lawyer named Theodore Hinsdale. Under the
pen name "Farin" she contributed to the periodical press.
She is listed by Julian.

CHARLOTTE G. HOSMER

fl. 20th century

"In loving kindness Jesus came
* * * * * * * * *
From sinking sand He lifted me."

This popular hymn in Gospel meetings is No. 94 in Rodeheaver's collection "Songs of Service." It was set to music
by Charles H. Gabriel.

JULIA WARD HOWE

1819-1910

"Mine eyes have seen the glory of the coming of the Lord,"

This hymn which was characterized by Rudyard Kipling
as the "terrible" Battle Hymn of the Republic, was written
in December 1861, after the author had watched a review of
the Army of the Potomac near Washington which was interrupted by an attack of the enemy. Deeply impressed,
Mrs. Howe sprang from her bed during the night and wrote
this immortal song which was sung by thousands of camp
fires during the war. Mrs. Howe showed the song to James
T. Fields who bought it for five dollars and published it on

the first page of the Atlantic Monthly for February 1862.
James Russell Lowell had declined to publish a poem by
Mrs. Howe on the ground that "No woman could write a
poem," but it is doubtful whether he ever wrote anything
which stirred the popular heart* like the Battle Hymn of
the Republic. It was sung by the inmates of Libby Prison
when they heard the news of the victory at Gettysburg. This
story was told by the chaplain C. C. McCabe, who was one
of the prisoners.

Mrs. Howe was born in New York City, the daughter of
Samuel Ward. She married at the age of twenty-four Dr.
Samuel G. Howe, a Boston philanthropist. She wrote much
both in prose and verse, and became one of the best known
women in European countries. She was an ardent supporter
of peace and of woman suffrage and of settling international
disputes by arbitration.

(Miss) Abbie Hutchinson

fl. 19th century

"Kind words can never die"
This imperishable hymn which was set to music (a haunting melody) by F. E. Belden, is printed in "Christ in Song"
No. 739. Julian lists her, and the hymn, but gives no light
on her identity. I judge, however, that she was an American
lady.

Abby Bradley Hyde

1799-1872

"Dear Saviour, if these lambs should stray,"
This touching hymn published in Nettleton's "Village
Hymns" and widely used, was written by the above named
Massachusetts lady, a native of Stockbridge. She married at
the age of nineteen Rev. Lavius Hyde of Salisbury, Mass., a

---

* In 1910 Julia Ward Howe went at the age of ninety-one to the
great hall of Smith College to receive the degree of Doctor of Laws.
2000 white-clad girls like a flock of doves, and the whole audience, rose
and sang "Mine eyes have seen the glory of the coming of the Lord."

Congregational minister. She died in Andover. Julian lists
five of her hymns*.

HELEN HUNT JACKSON, NÉE FISKE

1831-1885

"Not as I will"

This hymn† was written by that beloved singer whose
grave on Cheyenne Mt. near Colorado Springs (her last
home) is visited as a shrine. Helen Hunt Jackson was the daughter of Prof. N. W.
Fiske of Amherst, Mass. She married first Major E. B.
Hunt, a United States engineer. Their home was in Newport, R. I., and here Helen began to write for periodicals
over the signature "H. H." At the age of thirty-two she
was left a widow. After thirteen years of widowhood she
married Wm. S. Jackson, a banker of Denver, Colorado.
Her death at the age of fifty-four occurred in California.

MARY D. JAMES

fl. 19th century

"My body, soul, and spirit,
* * * * * * * *
My all is on the altar,
I'm waiting for the fire."

This hymn which is used effectively in consecration meetings was written by an obscure author. Julian does not list
her or her hymns. She also wrote the hymn, "O Blessed
Fellowship divine" and another beginning "All for Jesus"
which is found in a collection called, "Familiar Songs of the
Gospel."

---

* One of her hymns begins, "Say, sinner, hath a voice within?" Mrs.
Hyde says of it that it was written down from her lips by a young
sister when she was not able to hold up her head from the pillow. All
of her pieces in Nettleton's "Village Hymns" are signed "Hyde". She
wrote about fifty hymns.

† Julian does not list her as a hymnist and most of her sweet verses
are not hymns, but some of them could be classed as sacred poetry. I
give here four lines culled from her poem on "The Pilgrim Fathers."
"And if it be that it is saved,
Our poor republic, stained and bruised,
'Twill be because we lay again
Their corner stones which we refused."

Sophie Jewett

1861-1909

"Lord, we praise Thee for our brother Sun"
This is the first line of a translation of Francis of Assisi's
"Song of the Sun" by the above named Assistant Professor
of English at Wellesley College. Sophie Jewett was born
at Moravia, N. Y., and educated at Buffalo. She wrote some
books, in one of which, named "God's Troubadour", this
translation appears.

Mrs. James G. Johnson

fl. 19th century

"O word of words the sweetest
Come, O come to me."
This hymn was set to music by McGranahan and pub-
lished in Sankey's "Gospel Songs" No. 6.

Emily Chubbuck Judson

1817-1854

"Hear, O my God, one earnest prayer;
Room for my bird in Paradise;
And give her angel plumage there."
These are the concluding lines of a lovely sacred poem
written by the third wife of the celebrated missionary,
Adoniram Judson. Emily Chubbuck was born in Morris-
ville, N. Y., became a teacher in Utica, and wrote for the
press with the nom-de-plume of Fanny Forrester. At the
age of twenty-nine she married her illustrious husband and
went with him to Burmah. Two years later was born to
them in that foreign land, the daughter of whom the above
lines were written. When the child was two years old, her
sick father was carried on a litter to a ship, in the vain hope
that a sea voyage would restore his health. His wife Emily
was herself unable to accompany him. Dr. Judson died

almost within sight of the mountains of Burmah, and his body was committed to the deep. So ended a life of thrilling experiences for the introduction of Christianity to Burmah, which included nearly two years of indignities and barbarities in a death prison. His wife Emily returned to America, and devoted herself to revising her husband's memoirs. Whether the little daughter lived to accompany Emily I do not know. Emily herself died only four years later than her husband, her fame being both assured and eclipsed by his. Emily can scarcely be classed as a hymnist but I include her as a sacred poet of very great interest.

Mrs. Mary A. Kidder, née Pepper

1820-1905

"Lord, I care not for riches,
Neither silver nor gold,
* * * * * * * *
Is my name written there?"

This hymn, found in Sankey's "Songs and Solos"* was written by a native of Boston. She was a member of the Methodist church and resided for forty-six years in New York City. She died in Chelsea, Mass., at the age of eighty-six.

Harriet McEwan Kimball

1834-

"The day is ended,—ere I sink to sleep"

This is the opening line of a lovely hymn† entitled "All's Well", written by a native of Portsmouth, N. H. Miss Kimball was a Roman Catholic. Julian lists six of her hymns.

---

* There is another hymn of Mrs. Kidder's in the same collection, the first line of which is, "We shall sleep, but not forever."
† The closing stanza of this hymn is as follows:
"At peace with all the world, dear Lord, and Thee,
No fears my soul's unwavering faith can shake.
All's well, whichever side the grave for me
The morning light shall break."

Lucy Larcom

1826-1893

"When for me the silent oar
Parts the silent river,"
This beloved hymn, published in 1858, is by a favorite
American poetess. Lucy Larcom was born at Beverly Farms,
Mass., and in girlhood worked in the mills where she was a
frequent contributor to "The Lowell Offering", a periodical
conducted by the mill operatives. Later she went to school
in the Monticello Female Seminary at Alton, Ill., then be-
came a teacher at Wheaton Seminary, Norton, Mass., and
at Bradford Academy. Then she did editorial work in "Our
Young Folks" which merged with "St. Nicholas". She as-
sisted Whittier in editing three books; one of these was
"The Songs of Three Centuries." She also published four
volumes of her own poems and an autobiography entitled "A
New England Girlhood." Some of her other hymns are
those beginning:
"Hand in hand with angels
Through this world we go"
"O God, Thy world is sweet with prayer"*
"For the wealth of pathless forests"
"If the world seems cold to you."
Julian lists 11 of her hymns. She went back in woman-
hood to live at Beverly Farms where she was born.

Mary Artemisia Lathbury

1841-1913

"Day is dying in the west"
This hymn of surpassing beauty† was written by a Chautauqua teacher of whom Rev. E. E. Hale said, "She has a

---

* This hymn is in the "Pilgrim Hymnal".
† Another of her exquisite hymns which is found in most of the
standard hymnals begins
"Break Thou the bread of life,
Dear Lord, to me,"
Another begins, "Children of yesterday, heirs of tomorrow". Another
begins "O Shepherd of the nameless fold". Miss Lathbury died at
East Orange, N. J.

marvelous lyric power which not five people in a century
show, and her chance of having a name two hundred years
hence is better than that of most writers in America." Mary
A. Lathbury was born in Manchester, N. Y., the daughter
of a Methodist minister. At the age of eighteen she spent
one year at an art school in Worcester and then engaged
in teaching various schools in Vermont and New York. When
she was thirty-three years old Dr. Vincent engaged her as
assistant editor of the Methodist Episcopal School publications. She also contributed to various young people's magazines and is the author of 11 hymns which were published
in 1894 in a collection called "The New Era of Song." She
was a friend of Frances Willard, and was a member of the
"New Jerusalem Church."

MARY HALL LEONARD

1847-1921

> "On His altar lay it down,
>   Burden hard to carry,
> He, the world's strong burden-bearer,
> Of thy grief the willing sharer,
>   Though relief may tarry."

This is the first stanza* of a hymn by the above named

---

* Other stanzas of this hymn are as follows:

> "On His altar lay it down;
> If he ask thy treasure,
> For each earthly joy he taketh
> Holy recompense he maketh
> In unstinted measure.

> On His altar lay it down,
> Boon of thy vain longing,
> Not in wrath this strange denial,
> Seest thou not from out this trial
> Richer blessings thronging?

> On His altar lay it down
> In full resignation.
> Loving heart for service lowly,
> Leave it on the altar holy
> As thy glad oblation."

New England teacher and writer who was born on a farm†
in Bridgewater, Mass., and became the author of nine books,
four of poetry,‡ three southern stories, a local history, and
two on grammar and education. She was a woman of keen
intellectual power and of diversified talent in many directions.
Her death occurred in Rochester, Mass., on the ancestral
farm where her mother was born.

SARAH WHITE LIVERMORE

1789-1874

"Awake, oh Church, thy strength put on"

This is one of many hymns written by the above named
teacher born at Milton, N. H. She was one of the first to
establish Sunday Schools. Miss Livermore was a Unitarian.
She died at the age of eighty-five at her birthplace.

EMILY B. LORD

fl. 20th century

"Maker of earth and sea and sky,
 Creation's sovereign Lord and King,
 Who hung the starry worlds on high
 And formed alike the sparrow's wing,
 Bless the dumb creatures of Thy care,
 And listen to their voiceless prayer."

This remarkable prayer for the dumb animals was printed
in "The Friends' Intelligencer" of March 10, 1928.

---

† This author was the sister of the writer of this book and further
details concerning her may be found in "Memoirs of the Leonard,
Thompson, and Haskell Families", by Caroline Leonard Goodenough.
There is also a sketch of her and her portrait to be found in the National
Cyclopedia of American Biography, published by J. T. White and Co.
‡ In her collection of poems entitled "Rest and Unrest" there are
published two other hymns of hers. One begins, "In His temple, God
I saw". The other begins, "I thank Thee, Lord, that Thy best gifts are
free." This hymn was read at her funeral, which occurred two days
before Thanksgiving Day.

MARIA WHITE LOWELL

1821-1853

"After our child's untroubled breath
Up to the Father took its way
* * * * * * * * *
A blissful vision through the night
Would all my happy senses sway,
Of the good Shepherd on the height
Or climbing up the starry way
Holding our little lamb asleep."

These lines* were written by the first wife of James
Russell Lowell—a beautiful and gifted woman who died at
the age of thirty-two. She was born at Watertown, Mass.,
was an ardent supporter of anti-slavery, and contributed to
a magazine called "The Liberty Bell."

MARY WHEATON LYON, NÉE WHEATON

1844-1892

"My heart is tired, so tired tonight"

This hymn of deep feeling was written by a native of
Fabius, N. Y., who graduated from Cazenovia in 1865 the
valadictorian of her class. Three years later Miss Wheaton
married Rev. A. Judson Lyon, a Baptist minister of Delaware, Ohio. She frequently wrote and published articles
in the Philadelphia Ledger and other journals. In 1897
there was published in the Independent an exquisite poem of
hers entitled "God Knoweth Best", the first line of which is
"The gates of life swing either way." The whole poem is
given in "Songs from the Hearts of Women" by Nicholas
Smith. Mrs. Lyon was one of those rare and beautiful souls
that are like the wood violet, too modest and sensitive to covet
the glare of the sun.

---

* This poem was sent to my mother by the aunt for whom I was
named, after the death of my sister, little Jennie.

Mrs. Frances L. Mace, née Laughton

1836-

"Only waiting till the shadows
Are a little longer grown."*

The incident which is the foundation of this valued hymn
was the reply of a very aged Christian in an almshouse who,
when asked what he was doing, replied, "Only waiting."

Mrs. C. D. Martin

1868-

"Be not dismayed whate'er betide,
God will take care of you."†

This hymn which was written on a sick bed at Leicester-
shire, N. Y., is by the wife of a Baptist preacher, W. Stillman
Martin, who works with his wife in the composition of gospel
hymns, Mrs. Martin usually composing the words and Mr.
Martin the music. Their songs have been published by the
"Hall Mack Co." of Philadelphia and by the "Standard
Publishing Co." of Cincinnati with which Mr. Martin is con-
nected. Mrs. Martin considers her "Sparrow Song" as the
best she has written. The music of this was written by
Mr. Charles Gabriel. It was sung in Albert Hall in the great
Torrey-Alexander revival. Mrs. Martin is a native of Can-
ada.

---

* "Only Waiting" was first published in the "Waterville, (Me.)
Mail" with the signature "Inez". It was written by the eighteen year
old daughter of a Bangor doctor. Frances was a silent dreamy girl
who had written verses from her childhood. She married at the age
of nineteen a lawyer of Bangor, and had eight children four of whom
died early. During these strenuous years of maternity and sorrow,
Frances dropped her writing, but returned to it after the removal of
the family to San José, Cal., when Frances was forty-nine. She subsequently published two books of poems, which brought her recognition.
She was a woman of commanding presence and of beauty and goodness.
For a time her claim to the authorship of "Only Waiting" was dis-
puted, but was eventually established.

† There is a story of a blind man who used to go over a dangerous
crossing singing "God will take care of you".

Mrs. Harriet Burn McKeever

1807-1887

"Jesus, high in glory",

This popular hymn for children was written by a Philadelphia teacher who was associated with St. Andrews Episcopal Church there. Her hymns were published under the title "Twilight Musings."

Margaret Mercer

1791-1846

"Not on a prayerless bed
Compose thy weary limbs to rest."

This hymn* was written by a noble lady of Annapolis, Md., the daughter of John Mercer, governor of Maryland. She reduced herself from affluence to poverty by giving freedom to her slaves. Thereafter she supported herself for twenty-five years by teaching school.

Emily Huntington Miller

1833-

"I love to hear the story
That angel voices tell."

The author of the above children's hymn was the daughter of Rev. Thomas Huntington of Brooklyn, Ct. The hymn was written in 1867 when Mrs. Miller was recovering from a severe illness. She was the joint editor of "The Little Corporal" published in Chicago and was expected each month to furnish a hymn to be set to music. Feeling troubled that her ill health had prevented her from writing anything, she took a pen and paper and began to write "I love to hear the story". The words were suggested rapidly as though dictated and the hymn was finished in fifteen minutes and sent away without any correction. Its subsequent popularity surprised the author. Mrs. Miller also wrote a child's hymn of great

---

* This hymn is found in "Evenings with the Sacred Poets", p. 431.

beauty which begins, "Father, while the shadows fall". It
contains these lines,

> "Like Thy patient love to me
> May my love to others be!
> All the wrong my hands have done
> Pardon, Lord, through Christ Thy Son."

Mrs. C. H. Morris

1862-

> "My stubborn will at last has yielded
> * * * * * * * * *
> Sweet will of God, still fold me closer."

This surpassingly beautiful hymn was written by a lady
whose education was obtained in the public schools of
McConnellsville, Ohio. She gave her heart to the Lord at
the age of ten and united with the Methodist church. In the
prime of womanhood she became totally blind but after a
time sight seemed to be gradually returning to her. Her
writing has been carried on by dictating to a daughter. She
has written about 900* hymns and composed the melodies as
well as the words. She has been her own cook and dish-
washer.

---

* Some of the familiar hymns she has written are these:
"Let Jesus come into your heart"
"Would you be free from your burden of sin?"
"The fight is on"
"Sweeter, as the years go by."
"Refining fire"
"Nearer, still nearer"

This last one is especially beautiful and tender. There is a picture
of Mrs. Morris on page 20 in Charles H. Gabriel's booklet entitled "The
Singers and their Songs".

EMILY SULLIVAN OAKEY

1829-1883

"Sowing the seed by the daylight fair

* * * * * * * *

What shall the harvest be?"

This hymn* which is sometimes erroneously attributed to P. P. Bliss, who wrote only the music for it, was written in 1850 by a frail woman who is said to have never had a well day in her life. Emily S. Oakey was born in Albany and became a teacher for many years in the Albany Female Academy from which she had graduated.

MRS. INA DULEY OGDEN

b. 1877 Hoopeston, Ill.

"Brighten the corner where you are"†

The writer of this hymn is an amiable lady who lives in Toledo, Ohio. Her girlhood was spent in the farming districts of the middle West. The winter of 1888 she was in So. Dakota at the time of the terrible blizzard when many lost their lives. She was a school teacher for many years before her marriage at the age of twenty-eight. Mrs. Ogden is much esteemed by a large circle of personal friends and her hymns are becoming national favorites.

---

* There is a story told by Sankey that this hymn was the means in 1876 of reclaiming a Chicago drunkard who had stumbled by mistake, half drunk, into one of Moody's meetings in which this hymn was sung. This stanza followed him,

   "Sowing the seed of a lingering pain;
   Sowing the seed of a maddened brain;
   Sowing the seed of eternal shame,
   What shall the harvest be?"

He was converted, sent for his wife and children, and became eventually a pastor of a church in Evanston, Ill. He wrote a hymn which begins, "Out of the darkness into the light."

† There are various stories told of the transformation this hymn has wrought in personal histories. One is about a wealthy man with a nationwide business, who had been unfeeling and unyielding with his employees. One night he was driving past the meeting of Wm. Sunday when he had to stop the car on account of a puncture. When his chauffeur had finished the repair he could not find his employer who had stepped into the meeting and heard, "Brighten the corner" with the result that he "hit the trail", and became the friend and adviser of his associates and employees.

Frances Sargeant Osgood

1812-1850

"To labor is to pray,

* * * * * * * *

Let thy great deed be thy prayer to thy God."

This hymn was written by a Boston girl named Frances Sargeant who married Samuel Osgood, a portrait painter, who took her to England where she published a book of poems entitled "A Wreath of Wild Flowers from New England." She returned to New York in 1840 and died at the age of thirty-nine.

Priscilla Jane Owens

1829-

"We have heard a joyful sound,

* * * * * * * *

Jesus saves."

This hymn was written by a public school teacher* of Baltimore. Miss Owens was of Scotch and Welsh descent. She was interested for fifty years in Sunday School work and wrote a number of hymns† for children's services.

Mrs. Phoebe Palmer

1807-1874

"O now I see the cleansing wave"

This much used hymn was written by an American Methodist who wrote several hymns. The one quoted above is the one of hers most used.

---

* At the age of sixty-seven she was still a teacher in Baltimore. I have not found the death date of this energetic lady.
† Another of her well-known hymns begins, "Will your anchor hold in the storms of life?" This is No. 564 in "Christ in Song".

Frances Coan Percy

1843-

"Lord, if one prayer alone"

This is the opening line of "A prayer of prayers" found
in "Songs from the hearts of women" by Nicholas Smith.
The author was the daughter of Richard D. Coan of Guilford,
Conn. She was an Episcopalian and taught the freedmen
in Norfolk, Va. Her school was under the supervision of
Mr. Henry Clay Percy whom Miss Coan married in 1866.
After her husband's death in 1898, Mrs. Percy lived in New
Haven, Conn., and afterward in New York City. She was
in later life an invalid and a great sufferer. "The Pilgrim
Hymnal" has two of her hymns of real merit. One begins,
"O Father, hear my morning prayer". The other begins,
"As swiftly, silently draws near the night." Her most im-
portant contribution to our literary heritage is her lovely
lyric "Rock me to sleep, mother".

Miss Emily S. Perkins

fl. 20th century

This New York lady is the founder of the Hymn Society
which is doing good service for hymnology by offering a
prize for the best hymn written on some specified topic such
as missions or world peace. Its chairman is Mr. Carl F.
Price, an authority and lecturer on hymnology.

Elizabeth Stuart Phelps

1844-

"It chanceth once to every soul"

This remarkable poem entitled "On the Bridge of Sighs"
which may properly be classed as a hymn* was written by

---

* Julian does not list her as a hymnist. The poem above quoted is
to be found, not in the hymn books but in Whittier's collection entitled
"Songs of Three Centuries" p. 306. It is very striking and solemn.

the daughter of Prof. Austin Phelps of Andover, Mass. Most of her literary work was in story writing and her most popular book, "The Gates Ajar", reached 20 editions in a year. Her writings are original and daring and are characterized by moral earnestness. Miss Phelps in 1888 was married to Rev. Herbert D. Ward, also a writer, and the two worked in collaboration.

JEAN SOPHIA PIGOTT

fl. 19th century

"Jesus, I am resting, resting"

This hymn which is No. 71 in "Hymns of the Gospel New and Old" became familiar to me in the devotional meetings of the South African General Mission in Johannesburg. I have no data about the author but place her among American hymnists.

JESSIE BROWN POUNDS

1861-

"I must needs go home by the way of the cross,
* * * * * * * *
The way of the cross leads home."

This popular gospel hymn was written by a native of Hiram, Ohio, a suburb of Cleveland. Jessie Brown, on account of ill health in childhood, was mostly educated at home. She began to write for newspapers at the age of fifteen. At the age of twenty-four she accepted an editorial position with the Standard Publishing Co., of Cincinnati. Eleven years later she married Rev. John E. Pounds, at that time a pastor in Indianapolis. He became later the college pastor at Hiram, Ohio. Mrs. Pounds has written a number of hymns one of which is called "The touch of His hand on mine". Her hymn "Anywhere with Jesus" was a comfort to two young murderers who were converted before their execution in Sing Sing prison, N. Y. Mrs. Pounds' obituary notice reads as follows:

"Writer of 600 hymns to be buried at Hiram, Ohio.

Mrs. Jessie Brown Pounds, a Christian Endeavor worker and hymn writer, who died Thursday, will be buried at Hiram, O., tomorrow. Of the 600 hymns she wrote, the best known is "Beautiful Isle of Somewhere." It was sung at President McKinley's funeral, it is said. It will be sung at her funeral services tomorrow."

ELIZABETH PAYSON PRENTISS

1818-1878

"More love to Thee, O Christ,"

This precious hymn* was written in 1856 at a time of great sorrow, and left incompleted. Mrs. Prentiss did not even show it to her husband until fourteen years later. She was the youngest daughter of the saintly and celebrated Edward Payson of Portland, Maine. She married at the age of twenty-seven George F. Prentiss, a Professor in Union Theological Seminary. She had been married nine years before her public career as a writer began. Her book, "Stepping Heavenward", was sold probably to the extent of 100,000 copies. She had delicate health, partly owing to her excessive literary labors. She died at the age of sixty.

NANCY PRIEST

1836-1870

"Over the river they beckon to me"

This beautiful hymn† was written by a factory girl of nineteen, at Hinsdale, N. H. Her birthplace was at Royalston, Vt. At the age of twenty-nine she married Lieut. A. C. Wakefield, an officer in a Vermont regiment during the Civil War and died five years later at the age of thirty-four.

---

* Sankey heard this hymn sung in Arabic at Cairo by a Syrian doctor who said it had been a great comfort to him on his hard marches. After Mrs. Prentiss's death some Chinese Christians sent a fan with the hymn written in Chinese characters upon it to Dr. Prentiss as an act of sympathy.

† This hymn was a great favorite in my childhood's home. We often used to sing it.

EDNA DEAN PROCTOR
1838-

"Through storm and sun the age draws on
When heaven and earth shall meet."

This hymn was written for the Women's Congress of Missions at the Columbian Exposition in 1893. The author was born at Herkimer, N. Y. She did not marry but devoted herself to literature. Pres. Harrison asked her to employ her poetic talent in the cause of protecting the forests of the White Mts. and she wrote a striking poem on "The Doom of the White Hills." Some of her poems are very beautiful.

MRS. MARY RUMSEY
fl. 1848

"Jesus when he left the sky"

This sweet children's hymn was written by the above named author. She is mentioned in Julian's appendix. The hymn is found in many collections, one of which is "Hymns of the Gospel New and Old". I do not know whether she is British or American.

MISS J. W. SAMPSON
fl. 1864

"Sweetly sing, sweetly sing
Praises to our heavenly King."

This Sunday School hymn was written by a lady who lived at Utica, New York. Some of her hymns appear in Bradbury's "Golden Chain" and in "Happy Voices," familiar collections in my childhood.

MARGARET ELIZABETH SANGSTER, NÉE MUNSON
1838-1912

"Thine is the power, Lord."

This hymn was written by a native of New Rochelle, N. Y.. who has been called "America's household friend" on account of her many helpful books for the young. Margaret E. Munson was married at the age of twenty to George Sangster of Williamburg, N. Y. She was intensely religious and a member of the Dutch Reformed Church. Her poems were largely composed when upon street cars in a subconscious mood. She was a voluminous writer for periodicals and greatly beloved.

ELIZA SCUDDER

1821-1896

"Thou Grace Divine, encircling all,
* * * * * * * * *
O love of God most free!"

This hymn of exceptional value was written in 1852 by a native of Barnstable, Mass., a niece of Edward Hamilton Sears. In early life she was associated with the Unitarians but later, it is thought through the influence of Phillips Brooks, she joined the Episcopalians and had sweet contentment in that church. She was an invalid, but a cheerful sufferer. The year she died there was a volume of her poems* published. She and her sister, Mrs. Andrews, died the same day in Weston, Mass. Eliza's death was without pain, a few hours later than that of her sister.

MARY S. B. SHINDLER
(See Mary S. B. Dana)

LYDIA HUNTLEY SIGOURNEY, NÉE HUNTLEY

1791-1865

"Laborers of Christ, arise!"

This inspiring hymn† was written by one of the most remarkable women of the nineteenth century. Mrs.

---

* One of her poems is pathetic and is entitled "An Epitaph for an Old Maid". She herself was never married. She wrote several hymns of merit.

† One of her popular hymns begins, "Blest Comforter divine". Another of great beauty and practical worth is given in full in "Songs from the hearts of women" by Nicholas Smith. It begins "Prayer is the dew of faith". She said her poems were "wild flowers which have sprung up in the dells or among the clefts of the rocks". The North American Review calls them "the favorites of the garden".

Sigourney was born in Norwich, Ct., and could read fluently at the age of three. She began to write verses when eight years old. During the fifty years of her literary career she wrote fifty-six books and two thousand contributions to periodicals. At the age of twenty-eight she married Charles Sigourney, a merchant of Hartford. In early womanhood she was a Congregationalist. After her marriage she united with the Episcopal church, of which she said the ritual touched the chords of her finer nature.

CAROLINE LOUISA SMITH, NÉE SPRAGUE

fl. 19th century

"Tarry with me, O my Savior"

This familiar hymn* was written by a native of Salem, Mass., after hearing Dr. H. M. Dexter preach a sermon on "The adaptedness of religion to the wants of the aged." In 1852 Miss Sprague married Rev. Charles Smith, a Congregational minister of Andover, who died in 1887, after which Mrs. Smith removed to New York City where her son, Prof. Charles Sprague Smith, had charge of the Cooper Institute.

LANTA WILSON SMITH

fl. 19th century

"Scatter sunshine all along your way."

This is the refrain of a gospel hymn written by the above author. It is No. 21 in "Jubilant Praise", published by E. O. Excell.

MARY LOUISE SMITH, NÉE RILEY

1842-

"Let us gather up the sunbeams"

This useful hymn was written in 1867 by the wife of Albert Smith. She is listed by Julian. She also wrote "Sometime when all life's lessons have been learned."

---

* This hymn was rejected by the paper to which it was first sent, but since then it has made its way into many hymnals and was translated into Syriac and became a favorite with Eastern converts. Mrs. Smith wrote many hymns for special occasions.

Louise M. R. Stead

fl. 19th century

" 'Tis so sweet to trust in Jesus"

This hymn and its author are not listed in Julian. It was set to music by W. J. Kirkpatrick and is found in "Christ in Song." No. 519.

Martha Matilda Stockton, née Brustar

1821-1885

"God loved a world of sinners lost"

This hymn was written in 1871 by the wife of Rev. W. C. Stockton of Ocean City, New Jersey. The hymn is found in the collection "Laudes Domini."

Harriet Beecher Stowe

1811-1896

"Still, still with Thee, when purple morning breaketh"

This exquisite hymn* was written by "the little woman who made a great war" by writing "Uncle Tom's Cabin" which made her name more familiar in all the civilized countries of the globe than that of any other woman of the time except Queen Victoria. "Uncle Tom's Cabin" came nearer to being a conflagration than a book. When she went to England the year after its publication a mob met her at the ship to see the most loved, most hated, and most talked-about woman in the world. Lord Shaftsbury presented her with a petition for the emancipation of the slaves signed by a million British women—this drab and weary little woman, "as thin and dry as a pinch of snuff", clothed in anything but cosmopolitan fashion.

---

* She also wrote "Knocking, knocking, who is there?" The Saturday Evening Post of Oct. 8, 1927 contains an attractive picture of Mrs. Stowe, with her hand on the shoulder of her brother, Henry Ward Beecher. She has a sweet appealing face.

Mrs. Stowe was born in Litchfield, Ct., the third daughter
of Lyman Beecher "the father of brains", whose seven sons
all became ministers, (one of them was Henry Ward
Beecher) and "who wished that Harriet had been a boy, she
would do more than any of them." (Did she not?) It was a
home of scanty means and about all the light reading Harriet
got in her childhood was "Pilgrim's Progress", "The Ara-
bian Nights" and Shakespeare. Lyman Beecher left Connecticut about 1834 and presided over Lane Seminary in
Ohio. Harriet married Calvin Stowe, one of the professors
there, a man of mystic turn who had mystic playmates in
childhood and who in manhood experienced the unknown.
The Stowes in 1864 moved to Hartford, Conn. Harriet
wrote many books. Her son published her life in 1889.

Anna Louise Strong

1885-

"The City of God"

This is the title of a hymn written by a notable promoter
of peace and international good understanding who was born
in Friend, Neb., the daughter of Dr. Sydney Strong, a Congregational minister, and a lady from Mansfield, Ohio, whose
maiden name was Ruth Maria Tracy. The ancestors of both
parents were old American families which came over in 1630
and settled in Connecticut.

Miss Strong is a graduate of Oberlin College and has been
a great traveler in many foreign lands in the capacity of
newspaper reporter, lecturer and writer. She made journeys
to China and Japan but her chief labor has been in Russia
where she went in 1921 to assist in famine relief under the
Friends. Later she began to write for the Russian peasants
and has organized a paper called "The Moscow News" for
which she is the managing editor with a staff of ten people.
This work keeps her up usually till after midnight. She considers it her job to promote friendly relations between the

United States and the U. S. S. R. She believes the two countries have much to learn from each other and each system must assimilate parts of the other. She wishes to help make this assimilation as peaceful and painless as possible.

NELLIE TALBOT

fl. 19th century

"Jesus wants me for a sunbeam"

This pretty children's hymn was written by an author of whom I have no data except that she wrote it for her grandson, Edwin O. Excell, Jr. It is copyrighted by E. O. Excell and the presumption is that Nellie Talbot was his mother-in-law, unless his mother had changed her name.

GEORGIANA M. TAYLOR

fl. 19th century

"O to be nothing, nothing!"

This hymn was set to music by P. P. Bliss. Sankey used it much as a solo in Great Britain.

CLARA TEARE

fl. 19th century

"All my life long I had panted"

This hymn which is found in "Hymns of the Gospel New and Old" became familiar to me in the meetings of the South African General Mission in Johannesburg. The author is not listed by Julian nor is the hymn.

Juliet Wilbur Tompkins

fl. 19th century

"I thank Thee, Lord, that I am straight and strong
    With wit to work and hope to keep me brave;
That two score years unfathomed still belong
    To the allotted life Thy bounty gave."

Other stanzas of this hymn* entitled "For all These" are
in a footnote. I consider it very beautiful, but have no data
about the author.

---

*"I thank Thee that the sight of sunlit lands,
    And dipping hills, the breath of evening grass,
That wet, dark rocks, and flowers in my hands
    Can give me daily pleasure as I pass.

I thank Thee that I love the things of earth,
    Ripe fruits, and laughter, lying down to sleep,
The shine of lighted towns, the graver worth
    Of beating human hearts that laugh and weep.

I thank Thee that as yet I need not know,
    Yet need not fear the mystery of end,
But more than all, and though all these should go,
    Dear Lord, I kneeling, thank Thee for my friend."

"Love, Love on earth appears, the wretched throng His way;
He healeth all their griefs and wipes their tears away.
        Soft and sweet the strain should be,
        Savior, when I sing of Thee.

Now in the grave he's laid in death's funereal gloom;
Stern watchmen in the shade, a seal upon the tomb.
        Hushed my heart, thy breathing be!
        Christ is sleeping there for thee!

He lives! Again He lives! The stone is rolled away!
The living dead is gone, and breaks eternal day.
        Joyful now the strain should be,
        Christ has conquered death for me!"

—Credit Lost

ANNA BARTLETT WARNER

1822-1915

"Jesus loves me, this I know,"

This sweetest of hymns for children was written by a Sunday School teacher at West Point, New York, for her tiniest pupils. She was accustomed to write a hymn each month for her scholars. This hymn is loved by children all over the world.* Anna B. Warner and her sister Sarah, who was the author of "Queechy", both wrote novels. Anna's pen name was Amy Lothrop. They lived on Constitution Island, not far from West Point. Anna is also the author of "One more day's work for Jesus"† and probably also of "We would see Jesus for the shadows lengthen", although this last is often attributed to Ellen Ellis, of whom nothing seems to be known. The novel "Dollars and Cents" published in London 1853, under the nom-de-plume Amy Lothrop, contained this hymn.

SUSAN WARNER

fl. 19th century

"Jesus bids us shine with a clear, pure light"

This valuable hymn for children which was found in a collection published by Mrs. Emily Huntington Miller and which has been usually attributed to Mrs. Miller's authorship, is said by Mrs. Miller herself to have been written by Susan Warner, of whom we know nothing. (See Julian's Dictionary· of Hymns, p. 1672).

---

* Dr. Jacob Chamberlain translated this hymn into Telagu. One day when riding on his pony he heard a little heathen boy singing it to a group of heathen. Dr. Chamberlain thereupon rode his pony away, well satisfied to have his little proxy preach the gospel for him.

† This hymn was set to music by Rev. Robert Lowry. A poor woman heard it sung when passing a mission chapel. The words followed her and brought about a change in her life. She began to wash clothes and do her house work for Jesus.

ELLEN H. WALLIS

fl. 19th century

"I left it all with Jesus
Long ago."

I have no data about the author of this familiar hymn.

FANNY J. WEBSTER

fl. 19th and 20th centuries

"Spirit of the coming year
Banish every anxious fear;
Bid dire strife and hatred cease,
Fill our hearts with joy and peace."

The lady who wrote the above lines as a New Year's greeting for friends, is a graduate of Oberlin College* who for many years taught in the schools of the A. M. A. at the South.

MRS. M. M. WEINLAND,

fl. 19th century

"O weary pilgrim, lift your head,
For joy cometh in the morning."

This hymn, which is found in "Hymns of the Gospel New and Old", was often sung in the South African General Mission in Johannesburg.

---

* I cannot omit here the recording of my gratitude to this beloved roommate of college days. My eyes gave out at the beginning of our senior year, and she read aloud to me daily our mutual lessons; without this help I could not have graduated.

ADELINE D. T. WHITNEY, NÉE TRAIN

"Among so many can he care?

*   *   *   *   *   *   *   *

I asked; my soul bethought of this,
In just that very place of His
Where He hath put and keepeth you,
God hath no other thing to do."

The above lines were written by a native of Boston who, at the age of thirty-three, married Seth D. Whitney of Milton, Mass. Mrs. Whitney contributed to several magazines and wrote popular stories.

ELLA WHEELER WILCOX

1855-1919

"The days grow shorter, the nights grow longer,
The headstones thicker along the way,
And life grows sadder, but love grows stronger,
For those who walk with us day by day."

This lovely poem,* almost a hymn, entitled "Growing Old", was written by a native of Johnstown Center, Wis. In 1884 she married Robert M. Wilcox of Meriden, Ct. a very happy marriage if we may judge by her song "Wander-lust". After her marriage she moved to New York and published many poems in periodicals. Literary critics refused to take her work seriously, but she found a large public for her writings. It is said she was an adherent of Christian Science in her religious belief.

---

* This poem was sent me by a lady friend with a warm letter. I love the poem very much.

EMMA C. WILLARD, NÉE HART

1787-1870

"Rocked in the cradle of the deep"

This immortal sailor's hymn was written by a teacher and educational writer born at Berlin, Ct., who lived for a time in Hartford. For many years she conducted a well-known school at Troy, N. Y. Her successful hymn, above quoted, is sometimes said to have been published in 1830, but this has not been verified. It is found in various hymnals, among them Beecher's Plymouth Collection.

FRANCES ELIZABETH WILLARD

1839-1898

"The hands are such dear hands"

This is the opening line of a sacred poem written by the distinguished founder of the World's Christian Temperance Union. Frances E. Willard was born at Churchill, N. Y., of intellectual Christian parents who removed to Oberlin, Ohio, to attend lectures. So five years of their daughter's childhood were spent at Oberlin, after which the family moved to Wisconsin. During her youth Frances was called Frank in the family circle. She graduated from the Northwestern College at Evanston in 1859 and became Dean of Women there in 1871, resigning three years later to become Secretary of the W. C. T. U. From this point she devoted herself mostly to temperance and woman's suffrage, winning the admiration and love of multitudes of people. She said, "Keep to your specialty, whether it is raising turnips or tunes". In 1892 she went to England and was associated with Lady Henry Somerset, addressing a huge audience in Exeter Hall. Willard Hall in Chicago is named for her. In front of it is a lovely drinking fountain: a child giving a cup of cold water.

HARRIET WINSLOW

1824-

"Why this longing, this forever sighing
For the far-off, unattained and dim,
While the beautiful all round thee lying
Offers up its low, perpetual hymn?"

This is the opening stanza of a fine hymn written by the above named American lady. It is found in the English collection "Hymns and Anthems" edited by W. J. Fox, the distinguished orator who carried on a chapel in London. The poem is also found on p. 252 of "Songs of Three Centuries." The name is there given as Sewall (her married name).

ANNE WITTEMEYER

fl. 19th century

"I have entered the valley of blessing so sweet."

This familiar hymn, which is found in "Christ in Song" No. 292, is not listed by Julian.

ALICE BOISE WOOD

fl. 19th and 20th centuries

"To the rock flies the coney,
The stork to her nest,
When tempests are gathering
And black is the west.
So swift, by life's trials
O'erwhelmed and oppressed,
I fly to my refuge,
Jehovah, my rest."

This beautiful hymn is found in "The Endeavor Hymnal" No. 104.

CHAPTER XI

ANONYMOUS* HYMNS AND ADDENDA

"It is only the burst of love, the joy and peace that voices the aspiration of the soul, which are deeper than our speculative opinions, that sing themselves into the immortal chants and anthems of history."

"What our mothers sang us when they put us to sleep is singing yet. There is a place in Switzerland where, if you distinctly utter your voice, there come back ten or fifteen echoes, and every song sung by a Christian mother in the ear of her child shall have ten thousand echoes coming back from the gates of heaven."

"When the voice of harmony thrills the bosom, let the critics go, but do you be true to yourselves and write, sing. We cannot tell beforehand the worth of your verses."

"Gloria in Excelsis"
This hymn is known as the Greater Doxology and is of unknown authorship and of great antiquity.

"Glory be to the Father and to the Son and to the
        Holy Ghost"
This is technically known as "The Gloria Patri", or "The Lesser Doxology". It is possibly, but not demonstrably of apostolic antiquity. It was in general use in the whole East, in Africa and Italy, in 529 A. D.

"Be Thou, O God, exalted high,
And as Thy glory fills the sky,
So let it be on earth displayed,
'Till Thou art here as there obeyed."

This old doxology which I heard sung regularly to the tune of Old Hundred at the opening of the morning service in the Congregational Church of my childhood, is mentioned without authorship by Julian. It is said to be a paraphase of the 57th psalm and is to be found in a Baptist hymnal published in Philadelphia in 1905.

---

* In characterizing the hymns mentioned in Chapter XI as anonymous, I mean that I have not been able to ascertain the authors of them.

"From all that dwell beneath the skies
Let the Creator's praise arise."
This doxology sung to the tune of Old Hundred is found
in "Songs of Zion enlarged".

"Fairest Lord Jesus"

The beautiful "Crusaders' Hymn", as it is called, is said
to have been sung by the German Pilgrims of the 12th
century on their way to Jerusalem. However, Julian says it
cannot be traced farther back than 1677 when it appeared
in the Munster collection. The melody of German origin
was arranged in 1850 by R. S. Willis, and now appears in
many standard hymnals of England and America. The
words are said to have been taken down from oral recitation
in the district of Glas, Germany, and to have been translated into English about 1815.

"Live out Thy life within me, O Jesus, King of Kings!
Be Thou Thyself the answer to all my questionings.
Live out Thy life within me; in all things have Thy way;
I, the transparent medium Thy glory to display.
The temple has been yielded, and purified from sin.
Let Thy Shekinah glory now flash forth from within,
And all the earth keep silence, the body henceforth be
Thy humble docile servant, moved only as by Thee.
Its members every moment held subject to Thy call.
Ready to have Thee use them or not be used at all.
Live out Thy life within me, O Jesus King of Kings!
Be Thou the glorious answer to all my questionings."

"Singing for Jesus! Singing for Jesus!
Trying to serve Him wherever I go;
Pointing the lost to the way of salvation,
This be my mission, a pilgrim below.
When in the strains of my country I mingle,
When to exalt her my voice I would raise,
'Tis for His glory whose arm is her refuge,
Him would I honor, His name would I praise."

This fragment from a simple song learned in childhood is unknown
to me as far as authorship and place of publication are concerned.
I commend it to such of my readers as have voices adapted to public
singing even in a moderate degree. I know of no higher aspiration or
ambition than to devote that supreme talent of a good voice to singing
the gospel message.

"As darker, darker fall around
The shadows of the night
* * * * * * * *
We pray Thee for all absent friends
* * * * * * * *
The sick, the poor, the tried, the fallen,
We pray Thee, God of love."

This lovely hymn for all conditions of men first appeared in Wm. Young's Catholic Chorolist in 1842. In 1864 S. Longfellow inserted it in the Unitarian "Hymns of the Spirit". Two of the stanzas as there given may be by S. Longellow, but the hymn as a whole seems to be anonymous. It is now found in various collections in Great Britain and America, as, for example, No. 638 in the Pilgrim Hymnal, the music by James Walsh, 1860.

"Praise the Lord, ye heavens adore Him."

This anonymous hymn is often ascribed to John Kempthorne, an English clergyman, 1775-1836, but was simply found in a collection of hymns he made for the use of his foundling hospital. There is no reason to believe that he wrote the hymn himself.

"I sat alone with my conscience
In a place where time had ceased,
And we talked of my former living
In the land where the years increased.
The ghosts of forgotten actions
Came floating before my sight,
And things that I thought were dead things
Were alive with a terrible might.
* * * * * * *
Then I woke from timely dreaming
And the vision that came to save,
And I pray I may not forget it
In this land before the grave,
And I know of the future judgment
How dreadful so e'er it be,
That to be alone with my conscience
Will be judgment enough for me."

The above lines are taken from an anonymous poem to be found in "Heart Throbs" No. 1 edited by J. M. Chapple and to be found in most libraries. It is also found in a slightly altered form and set to music in "The Air Pilot Hymnal, No. 267, but there a mistaken name has been put in as the author of the words.

"God is near thee, wherefore cheer thee,
        Sad soul."

This fine anonymous hymn was set to appropriate music
by L. Mason.   It is No. 146 in "Happy Voices", published
by the American Tract Society.   The third stanza particularly pleases me.   I insert it here.

"Mark the sea bird wildly wheeling
        Through the skies.
God defends him, God attends him,
        When he cries."

I wish I knew the author of this favorite hymn.

"I sought the Lord, and afterward I knew"
This beautiful anonymous hymn was published No. 38 in
the Pilgrim Hymnal in 1904.   It is a great favorite in our
family.

"I love Thee, I love Thee"

This anonymous hymn was set to music by Jeremiah Ingalls
and is found in "Christ in Song" No. 650.

"When shall we three meet again?
        *   *   *   *   *   *   *
Where immortal spirits reign,
There we three shall meet again."

These lines are taken from a hymn written by three Indians
who had been receiving Christian education at Dartmouth College.
They were parting at the close of their college course after planting a memorial pine tree.   They did meet once more on earth
at the same place and composed another hymn of which the closing lines are:

"Bound by love's unsevered chain
Here on earth we meet again."

I used in childhood to hear the first line quoted but did not know
until long years after, where the line came from.   This hymn is sometimes ascribed to Samson Occum, an Indian preacher.

"The Old Time Religion"

This is the title of a negro hymn set to a negro melody which came into hymn book circulation in the following way: Dr. Charlie D. Tillman, a hymn book publisher of Lyerly, Ga., somewhere about 1885 heard the negroes in South Carolina singing "The Old Time Religion" on Sunday afternoon. He took the negro leader for a walk in the woods, had him sit at his side and took down both words and tune in pencil from his singing. Mr. Tillman published it in his first hymnal. Since then it has been copied into hundreds of hymn books.

"Steal away to Jesus,
I aint got long to stay here."

"Swing low, sweet chariot,
Comin' for to carry me home."

The negro spirituals, specimens of which are given above, are thus commented upon by Joseph Wood Krutch, in the Nation of March 20, 1930. "The corpus of these spirituals constitute of course the finest expression of religious emotion achieved anywhere since the 17th century." These are strong words, but who that has listened to the songs of the Jubilee singers can doubt their truth, that is, if he had said the 18th century, which he doubtless meant.

"I have a Father in the promised land."

This anonymous hymn, so widely known that I heard it away among the Dutch farms of the Transvaal is found in "Happy Voices", page 205. It was a great favorite in my childhood.

"O do not be discouraged,
For Jesus is your friend."

This Sunday School hymn which was popular in the last half of the 19th century is found in "Happy Voices" No. 75.

"I'm glad salvation's free."

This is an anonymous chorus, No. 314 of the Service Hymnal. The music also has no author named but is exceedingly familiar. The sentiment is true, salvation is "free", but does it not take all we are, and have, to procure it?

"Meek and lowly, pure and holy,
Chief among the blessed three"
This fine hymn which is not listed by Julian is found in
"Christ in Song" No. 733. It is not set to music there but
there was a tune to which it was familiarly sung in my child-
hood days.

"Begone, vain world thou hast no charms for me."
This hymn is No. 220 in the Salvation Army Hymn Book
compiled by Gen. William Booth. I became familiar with
it in Lowell Mass., in the winter of 1925-6. It took hold of
me as a penetrating and forceful hymn.

"Our life is a dream, and time, like a stream,
Doth bear us away!
But the fugitive moment refuses to stay;
We aspire and yearn and in sorrow we learn,
But the fugitive moment will never return!"
This fragment of an old poem was preserved in the memory
of Caroline Lewis of Rochester, Mass., who used, in her child-
hood, to hear an old man named Charles Bonney repeat it regular-
ly in prayer meeting. She could not recollect the fourth line and
the old man was long dead and could not be asked to supply it.
Mrs. Lewis requested me to fill in the missing fourth line, to
which I shall have to plead guilty as it stands above. Another
version which I wrote for the fourth line is as follows:
"Its worth we may spurn, or its blessing may earn."

"Gone from my heart the world and all its charms"
This tender hymn (set to the tune of Foster's "Old Black
Joe") is found in "The Service Hymnal," No. 456. It first ap-
peared in "The London Hymn Book."

"I hear it singing, singing sweetly,
Softly, in an undertone,
Singing as if God had taught it,—
It is better farther on."
This hymn is from "The Chamber of Peace" and is signed
only with the initials. M.L.B.

"You're starting today on life's journey,
* * * * * * * *
Have courage, my boy, to say no."
This anonymous hymn which is found in "Heart Throbs"
No. 2, p. 210, is said to have been written by a devoted mother
and given to her son when he was entering business. My eldest
daughter when four years old, sang this often with her brother,
who was four years her senior.

"Fading, still fading, the last beam is shining,"

This lovely hymn is said to be of Roman Catholic origin. It was one of the Sunday night hymns in my childhood's home. I never heard it sung outside the family, and it seems strange to me that Julian does not list it. It was published in "Vestry Chimes" in 1864 by Asa Hull of Boston, also by Sheldon and Co. of New York and by Tomlinson Brothers of Chicago. I have not found it in any recent collections.

"Come from the loathsome way of sin.
Hide you in the blood of Jesus."

This anonymous hymn, which I have heard very effectively used in a pentecostal mission, was set to music by Mr. Thoro Harris of Chicago, a publisher of many gospel hymnals.

"Are you coming home, ye wanderers?"

This hymn which was set to music by James McGranahan, is in "Songs and Solos" which was published in 1881, attributed to "A. N." But in Sankey's "Reminiscences" published in 1906 it is attributed to "C. C.", a Scotch girl.

The following hymns are found without authorship in one of Bradbury's Sunday School Collections:

"Who shall sing if not the children?"
"Gather them into the Sunday School"
"Marching along, we are marching along"
"Come, come, sing to the Savior"
"There's a friend that's ever near"
"Shall we sing in heaven forever?"
"There is sweet rest in heaven"
"Whither, pilgrims, are you going?
Going to the better land."

"Where, O where, are the Hebrew children?
Safe now in the promised land.
By and by we'll go home to meet them."

This familiar religious ditty of childhood's days is not listed by Julian, and I have never, as far as I recollect, seen it in print. It would be interesting if its origin could be discovered. It is doubtless anonymous.

"Lord, for tomorrow and its needs
I do not pray."

This hymn was written in 1877 at Liverpool, England, by a lady who wished to be anonymous and witheld her name. She signed herself S. M T. In a collection of verses she published in 1903 she called herself "A sister of Notre Dame." This would seem to indicate that she was a Romanist.

" Trusting in the Lord thy God,
Onward go!"

This hymn is attributed to " E. B." in " Church Hymns and Gospel Songs" published by Bigelow and Main.

"A beautiful land by faith I see"

This old hymn which was set to music by Wm. B. Bradbury seems to be anonymous. It is found in " Songs of Zion enlarged." It was very familiar to me in childhood.

" We are joyously voyaging over the main,
Bound for the evergreen shore."

This anonymous hymn was set to music by Wm. B. Bradbury and is found in 'Christ in Song" No. 909.

" We're travelling home to heaven above.
Will you go?"

This anonymous hymn, popular in Sunday Schools in the last half of the nineteenth century in America, is No. 19 in " Happy Voices" published by the American Tract Society.

" My Savior's praises I will sing
* * * * * * * *
Every day will I bless Thee."

This paraphrase of psalm 145 is by an unknown author except that the initials T. E. O. are attached to it in Sankey's " Gospel Hymns No. 5." The fact that it is the opening hymn in that collection indicates that it was considered excellent by the compilers of that hymnal.

" Is not this the land of Beulah?"

This is the title and refrain of a hymn found in 'Hymns of the Gospel New and Old" that was often sung in the South Africa General Mission in Johannesburg. It is marked " Anon."

" Give me a heart like Thine."

This chorus-like anonymous hymn, familiarly used in after-meetings is found in Rodeheaver's " Songs of Service," where the tune is ascribed to Major James H. Cole, but no author is assigned to the words.

"Hark, the lilies whisper tenderly and low,
'In their quiet beauty see how fair we grow'.
Thus our heavenly Father careth for these,
The beautiful lilies of the field,
Our Father cares for these
And shall he not care for you?"

This is the opening stanza of a favorite Sunday School hymn of my childhood found in one of Bradbury's little books. I do not know the author.

"Build your hopes on things eternal,
Hold to God's unchanging hand."

This hymn, the authorship of which is unknown to me, became familiar in some meetings held in Milwaukee in 1913. One of those who attended the same meetings, quoted it lately in a letter as being a spiritual watchword to her. In truth it seems to me that these two lines embody the very crux of a Christian's practical working creed.

"The gospel ship along is sailing"

This anonymous hymn is much used in the Salvation Army. A different version, set to another tune, is found in one of Bradbury's little books. I do not know which version is the original one.

"A little talk with Jesus makes it right"

This is the chorus of an anonymous hymn which I used to hear frequently in the meetings of the South Africa General Mission in Johannesburg. It is a lively and arresting hymn, which doubtless all high-brow critics would turn down with great severity. I was pleased indeed to come across it like an old acquaintance in the "Air Pilot Hymnal" put out by Thoro Harris where it is No. 81.

"I entered once a home of care,
* * * * * * * *
Christ is all, all in all."

This anonymous hymn is No. 159 in Rodeheaver's "Songs for Service." The music there is ascribed to W. A. Williams of Philadelphia. I heard this sung in Africa many years ago to the same tune which Rodeheaver gives, therefore I believe that both words and music come from a rather far back source.

"We're bound for the land of the pure and the holy"

This anonymous hymn, much used by the Salvation Army, is found in Booth's collection, No. 83. It is also in Asa Hall's "Vestry Chimes", No. 96.

"Jesus hath died and hath risen again
* * * * * * * *
Jesus saves me now."

This hymn, which is No. 282 in "Hymns of the Gospel New and Old," is there ascribed to A. C. D. I have no other clue to the author. The hymn is not listed by Julian. I have heard it in gospel meetings.

"Hast thou within a care so deep
It chases from thine eyelids sleep?
To thy Redeemer take that care,
And change anxiety to prayer."

I do not know the author of this useful hymn which is called "A Baptist hymn". It has four stanzas and seems to be fairly familiar, but whether it is included in any hymnal I do not know. I have seen it only as a newspaper clipping.

"Come to Jesus just now."
This anonymous gospel hymn chorus is widely used. It was translated into Zulu and I heard it in the market square meetings in Johannesburg.

"A dear one has moved to the mansions above;
* * * * * * * * *
There's a light in the window for thee."
This comforting hymn for those who mourn departed friends, is found without authorship in one of Bradbury's little Sunday School books.

Two anonymous hymns of my childhood's period were these;
"How many sheep are straying?"
and
"Tis sweet to think when night draws on
Dark and drear,
* * * * * * * * *
There is a land where comes no night,"

"Come brethren, don't grow weary,
* * * * * * * * *
There is sweet rest in heaven."
This anonymous hymn which was set to music by Wm. B. Bradbury is found on p. 92 in "Vestry Chimes" published in 1864 by Asa Hull of Boston.

"There are angels hovering round
* * * * * * * * *
To carry the tidings home."
This useful revival hymn is found in "Vestry Chimes" p. 81 published by Asa Hull of Boston in 1864. The melody there is not the one I am familiar with.

"We are out on an ocean sailing
Millions now are safely landed."
This old hymn seems to be anonymous. It is found in "Songs of Zion Enlarged" and is there entitled "Golden Shore." The music is by Wm. B. Bradbury, who marks the hymn as from "Oriola."

"When I put out on the silver sea
May there be a blue night and a white moon
And the loneliness of God, and the low note
Of a lone bird, when I put out on the silver sea."

These lines, by an unknown author, on the Supreme Adventure of death, were published in "The Friends Intelligencer" of March 10, 1928. Most of us would rather that out of the dusk of death, friendly faces of those we have loved, and who have preceded us, should shine. Jesus said of Lazarus that he was carried by angels to Abraham's bosom. This implies that death will not be a lonely experience.

"No never alone."

This hymn much used by the Salvation Army, and attributed to A. F. O. was set to music by L. O. Brown. I believe this Brown was one of a pair of brothers prominent in the Holiness movement when I was a student in Oberlin, Ohio, 1873-1877. He is mentioned on p. 302 of this book.

"Nothing between, Lord, nothing between."

I have no light on the authorship of this hymn. I used to hear it sung in the Holiness meetings held by the South Africa General Mission in the eighteen hundred and nineties. It was in a book compiled by Mr. Frank Huskison, one of the leaders of that deeply spiritual mission in South Africa. The two following hymns also were in that book.

"Sitting at the feet of Jesus"

This useful and tender little hymn became familiar to me in South Africa. There is no author given where I saw it, but there is this clue, that "words by J. H." accompany the hymn. These words in the second stanza have been precious to me.

"Sitting at the feet of Jesus
I would look upon the past."

I cannot see where else we can bear to remember our past failings. Christ alone enables us to forgive ourselves.

"O for a life to please my God"

I regard this hymn as a fine one. It was in the collection made by Frank Huskison for the use of the South African General Mission.

" So we'll never mind the scoffs or the frowns of the world,
    For we all have a cross to bear.
It will only make the crown all the brighter to shine
    When we have a crown to wear."

—Anon

" God's anger now is turned away,
    My sins are under the blood."
This hymn which is not listed by Julian has been used effectively in gospel meetings.

" I can hear my Savior calling
    * * * * * * * *
    I'll go with Him all the way."
This anonymous hymn is familiarly sung in consecration meetings. It is used to fill in the gaps and pauses, and usually sung without recourse to books. It is No. 77 in " Familiar Songs of the Gospel."

" To love the work that is yours to do
    Will lead to the work that is joy to you."

" O that will be joyful
    When we meet to part no more"
This is a chorus familiarly sung in my childhood.

" Lord, I believe.
    Savior, raise my faith in Thee
    Till it can move a mountain."
The chorus frequently sung in gospel meetings is found on p. 17 in " Jubilee Songs" published by Thoro Harris. It is there attributed to " F.M.G." and " A.F.I." I have no data about these persons.

" Singing I go along life's road
    Praising the Lord."
Who that has heard " Black Susan" sing the above lines as her testimony, her dusky face illumined with the inner light, can ever forget it.

JAMES DAVIS KNOWLES—1798-1838 (American Baptist)
    " O God through countless worlds of light"

FREDERICK WHITFIELD—1829-1904 (English)
    " I need Thee precious Jesus"
He also wrote " There is a name I love to hear"

SEWELL SYLVESTER CUTTING—(American Baptist)
    1813-1882
    " O Savior I am blind, lead Thou my way"

" O God Eternal Right command us now."
                                    —Mrs. M. P. Boynton.
    This hymn on disarmament by a Chicago minister's wife is No. 31 in " Melodies of the People".

Mrs. Sarah McClain Greene
fl. 19th or early 20th centuries
"De Massa ob de sheepfol',
Dat guard de sheepfol' bin
Look out on de gloomerin' meadows,
Whar de long night rain begin—"

This tender hymn, written in negro dialect, is doubtless by an American lady. It is given entire in the Christian Century Pulpit of June 1931.

Robert Boswell
1746-1804
"Behold what love, what boundless love
The Father hath bestowed."*

These are the opening lines of an altered version of a beautiful hymn originally written by a Scotch minister, who left the regular ministry to become a ruling elder in the churches established by John Glas, who had been deposed on account of the Sandemanean views. Boswell died suddenly while preaching in London. He was a fine Hebrew scholar. His grandson, named for him, also connected with hymnody, was a missionary in Calcutta.

"Servant of God, well done!"—Montgomery, J.

"Lord of the grass and hill
* * * * * * * *
I shall put off this girth,
Go forth so glad and free,
Earth to my mother earth,
Spirit to Thee.   —*Bliss Carman*

"Brief life is here our portion"
—Bernard of Cluny

TO RHYMERS
Be sure your song is from the heart,
Not every theme is worth your art!
Seems then your subject worthy still?
Then give it naught but finest skill!
—*C. H. Crandall*

---

* I remember the singing of this hymn one Sunday evening about 1885. The missionaries of Adams mission in Natal, four families of us, were gathered in Mrs. Robbins' pretty parlor, for singing, which was led by our visiting missionaries, the Wilders. Most of that company have now joined the choirs above.

UNPROFITABLE SERVANTS

As doth the weary hind at close of day,
    Think not at once to seek his ease or bed
Till first he doth his master's table lay,
    And sees his lord refreshed and served and fed.

Thus when the love of ease assails the mind,
    Let us remember we are servants too,
And gird ourselves for service as the hind,
    Till that is done which is our task to do.

With stern rebuke the slothful spirit slay,
    Till better motives shall resume control,
And love, the baser mood shall chase away
    Which as an hireling would its duties dole.

Give us to say when every task is done,
    "Unprofitable servants" to the end,
While that reward awaits each faithful one,
    I call Thee not a servant, but a friend.
                                    —Caroline L. Goodenough

The hymns below were all written by Caroline L. Goodenough.

Had I the pinions of a dove—Ps. 55—from "Gospel Psalter"
Forsake me not O Lord my God—Ps. 71—from "Gospel Psalter"
Jerusalem is laid in heaps—Ps. 79—from "Gospel Psalter"
In Thy multitude of tender mercies—Ps. 51—from "Gospel Psalter"
When Israel went from Egypt—Ps. 114—from "Gospel Psalter"
I now resign before I sleep—from "Melody unto the Lord"
One song and then to sleep—from "Melody unto the Lord"
Teach us, O Lord to pray—from "Melody unto the Lord"
In time of our extremity—from "Melody unto the Lord"
Rest me Savior, I am weary—from "Melody unto the Lord"
Back to Thy bosom, everlasting God—from "Melody unto the Lord"
Rich is the man, though poor—from "Melody unto the Lord"
God only is my need—from "Melody unto the Lord"
Take not Thy presence from me—from "Melody unto the Lord"
Nothing shall daunt me—from "Melody unto the Lord"
From out my chastened heart—from "Palms of Elim"
How sweet is the sound of the bird's song—from "Palms of Elim"
There is a little low place of rest—from "Palms of Elim"
He hath borne our sorrows—from "Palms of Elim"
A stranger in a foreign land—from "Palms of Elim"
Thank God for clouds—from "Palms of Elim"
O how sweet my precious Savior—from "The Little Harp"
Night and storm were upon my heart—from "The Little Harp"
Let there be glory, round my dying bed—from "The Little Harp"
God be praised for nights and Sundays—from "The Little Harp"
I must have the smile of Jesus—from "The Little Harp"
Savior to Thee I bring—from "The Little Harp"
God of the social vision—from "Melodies of Life and Love"
As they come marching, marching—from "Melodies of Transition"
Stand we for peace, though war is rife—from "Melodies of Dawn"
Get bitterness out of the soul—from "The Same Old Gospel"
Canst Thou look in love upon me—from "The Same Old Gospel"

A PRAYER FOR SLEEP
Lord, thou hast promised to supply my need,
    Thy faithful promise is my only plea;
Do I not need a night of quiet sleep?
    Look on my weariness, my God, and see.

Thou seest how I toss and toss about,
    Too far fatigued, too overwrought, for rest;
Lord, as we mothers lull our restless babes,
    Gather me now upon Thy tender breast.

As the musician oft doth try the strings,
    Tuning their jangling notes to sweet accord,
So Thou, who knowest the harp-strings of the soul,
    Tune me to harmony within, O Lord.

Gently, as falls the mantle of the snow,
    Feather on feather piling soft and light,
So let the benediction of Thy slumber fall;
    For Jesus' sake, Lord, give me sleep 'tonight.
                —C. L. Goodenough

    The above hymn was composed mentally when lying wakeful
in an ox wagon in Africa during a trek. It was not written down
until the next day. It is to be found set to music on p. 22 of a
pamphlet called "The Little Harp."

BED ROCK
Scarcely I catch the words of God's revealing,
Hardly I hear Him, dimly understand;
Only the power that is within me pealing,
Lives on my lips and beckons to my hand.

Whoso has felt the Spirit of the Highest
Cannot confound or doubt Him or deny;
Yea, with one voice, O world, though thou deniest,
Stand thou on that side, for on this am I.

Rather the earth shall doubt, when her retrieving
Pours in the rain and rushes from the sod,
Rather than he for whom the great conceiving
Stirs in his soul, to quicken into God.
                    —F. Myers
    I have heard this poem quoted with great effect in a sermon
on the reality of God-consciousness.

    "Tears are the lenses which break up white light into all the
colors of the spectrum. The risen life takes the sigh, and out of it
builds the song. There is no great song that does not hold a sigh
imprisoned."

    "We must sing again. In joy we must build again.
    Religion is nothing if not a choir of angels."
                    John Ray Ewers.
From the Christian Century Pulpit March 1931.

    "HE HATH SET ETERNITY IN THEIR HEART."
                  Eccl. 3:11 Revised Version.
            FINIS

INDEX OF AUTHORS.

INDEX OF FIRST LINES

(Or titles or refrains)